The Imitative Mind

Recent scientific breakthroughs in the study of imitation at multiple levels from cell to behavior have deep implications for cognitive science, neuroscience, and evolutionary and developmental psychology. This volume provides a state-of-the-art summary of the research on imitation in both Europe and America, including work on infants, adults, and nonhuman primates, with speculations about robotics. A special feature of this book is that it provides a concrete instance of the burgeoning link between developmental psychology, neuroscience, and cognitive science. The book showcases how an in-depth, interdisciplinary approach to imitation can illuminate long-standing problems in the brain sciences, including consciousness, self, perception-action coding, theory of mind, and intersubjectivity. The book addresses what it means to be human and how we get that way.

Andrew N. Meltzoff is Professor of Psychology and Co-Director of the Center for Mind, Brain and Learning at the University of Washington. He is co-author of *Words, Thoughts, and Theories* (1997) and *The Scientist in the Crib: What Early Learning Tells Us About The Mind* (1999).

Wolfgang Prinz is Director at the Max Planck Institute for Psychological Research, Munich. He has published experimental, theoretical, and historical work on perception, action, attention and consciousness.

Cambridge Studies in Cognitive Perceptual Development

Series Editors
Kurt W. Fischer, Harvard University, USA
Giyoo Hatano, Keio University, Tokyo, Japan

Advisory Board
Gavin Bremner, Lancaster University, UK
Patricia M. Greenfield, University of California, Los Angeles, USA
Paul Harris, Harvard University, USA.
Daniel Stern, University of Geneva, Switzerland
Esther Thelen, Indiana University, USA

The aim of this series is to provide a scholarly forum for current theoretical and empirical issues in cognitive and perceptual development. As the new century begins, the field is no longer dominated by monolithic theories. Contemporary explanations build on the combined influences of biological, cultural, contextual and ecological factors in well-defined research domains. In the field of cognitive development, cultural and situational factors are widely recognized as influencing the emergence and forms of reasoning in children. In perceptual development, the field has moved beyond the opposition of "innate" and "acquired" to suggest a continuous role for perception in the acquisition of knowledge. These approaches and issues will all be reflected in the series which will also address such important research themes as the indissociable link between perception and action in the developing motor system, the relationship between perceptual and cognitive development to modern ideas on the development of the brain, the significance of developmental processes themselves, dynamic systems theory and contemporary work in the psychodynamic tradition, especially as it relates to the foundations of self-knowledge.

Published titles include

Jacqueline Nadel and George Butterworth (eds.)
Imitation in Infancy

Margaret Harris and Giyoo Hatano (eds.)
Learning to Read and Write: a cross-linguistic perspective

Michael Siegal and Candida C. Peterson (eds.)
Children's Understanding of Biology and Health

Paul Light and Karen Littleton
Social Processes in Children's Learning

Nira Granott and Jim Parziale (eds.)
Microdevelopment: Transition Processes in Development and Learning

Heidi Keller, Ype H. Poorhinga and Alex Schölmerich (eds.)
Between Biology and Culture: Perspectives on Ontogenetic Development

The Imitative Mind

Development, Evolution, and Brain Bases

edited by

Andrew N. Meltzoff and Wolfgang Prinz

CAMBRIDGE
UNIVERSITY PRESS

CAMBRIDGE UNIVERSITY PRESS
Cambridge, New York, Melbourne, Madrid, Cape Town, Singapore, São Paulo

Cambridge University Press
The Edinburgh Building, Cambridge CB2 2RU, UK

Published in the United States of America by Cambridge University Press, New York

www.cambridge.org
Information on this title: www.cambridge.org/9780521806855

First published 2002
Reprinted 2003

A catalogue record for this publication is available from the British Library

Library of Congress Cataloguing in Publication data
The imitative mind: development, evolution, and brain bases / edited
by A. N. Meltzoff and W. Prinz.
    p.   cm.
Includes bibliographical references and index.
ISBN 0 521 80685 2 (hardcover)
1. Imitation.   2. Imitation in children.   3. Psychology, Comparative.
I. Meltzoff, Andrew N.   II. Prinz, Wolfgang.
BF357 .I48   2002
156′.3 – dc21   2001037642

ISBN-13 978-0-521-80685-5 hardback
ISBN-10 0-521-80685-2 hardback

Transferred to digital printing 2005

Contents

Contributors

JENS B. ASENDORPF, Humboldt-Universität zu Berlin, Berlin, Germany, Institut für Psychologie

C. I. BAKER, Carnegie Mellon University, Center for The Neural Basis of Cognition, Pittsburgh, PA, USA

HAROLD BEKKERING, University of Groningen, The Netherlands, Experimental & Work Psychology

RICHARD W. BYRNE, University of St. Andrews, Fife, Scotland, School of Psychology

JEAN DECETY, Inserm unit 280, Lyon, France and University of Washington, Seattle, WA, USA, the Center for Mind, Brain and Learning

LUCIANO FADIGA, Istituto di Fisiologia Umana, University of Parma, Parma, Italy

LEONARDO FOGASSI, Istituto di Fisiologia Umana, University of Parma, Parma, Italy

VITTORIO GALLESE, Istituto di Fisiologia Umana, University of Parma, Parma, Italy

MERIDETH GATTIS, University of Sheffield, Sheffield, England, Department of Psychology

GEORG GOLDENBERG, Krankenhaus München-Bogenhausen, Munich, Germany, Neuropsychologische Abteilung

MIKAEL HEIMANN, University of Bergen, Norway, Regional Competence Center for Child and Adolescent

JOACHIM HERMSDÖRFER, Krankenhaus München-Bogenhausen, Munich, Germany, Neuropsychologische Abteilung

TJEERD JELLEMA, Utrecht University, The Netherlands, Helmholtz Research Institute

MARCEL KINSBOURNE, New School University, New York, USA

ANDREW N. MELTZOFF, University of Washington, Seattle, WA, USA, Center for Mind, Brain and Learning

JULIE BAUER MORRISON, Stanford University, Stanford, CA, USA, Department of Psychology

JACQUELINE NADEL, Unit CNRS Cognition and Communication, Paris, France, Laboratoire de Psychologie du Développement

MICHAEL W. ORAM, University of St. Andrews, Fife, Scotland, School of Psychology

DAVID I. PERRETT, University of St. Andrews, Fife, Scotland, School of Psychology

WOLFGANG PRINZ, Max Planck Institute for Psychological Research, Munich, Germany

CATHERINE L. REED, University of Denver, Denver, CO, USA, Department of Psychology

GIACOMO RIZZOLATTI, Istituto di Fisiologia Umana, University of Parma, Parma, Italy

PHILIPPE ROCHAT, Emory University, Atlanta, GA, Department of Psychology

BARBARA TVERSKY, Stanford University, Stanford, CA, USA, Department of Psychology

STEFAN VOGT, Lancaster University, Lancaster, UK, Department of Psychology

ANDREW WHITEN, University of St. Andrews, Fife, Scotland, School of Psychology

ANDREAS WOHLSCHLÄGER, Max Planck Institute for Psychological Research, Munich, Germany

JEFF ZACKS, Washington University, St. Louis, MO, USA, Department of Psychology

Acknowledgments

We thank Dr. Sabine Maasen for her assistance in organizing the conference that launched this volume. The conference was convened by the Max Planck Institute for Psychological Research, directed by Wolfgang Prinz, and funded by the Max Planck Society. It was held at the beautiful Kloster Seeon in Bavaria in March 1999. It is difficult to imagine a more peaceful setting; the collaborations and friendships that emerged from these magical few days will have an impact far into the future. We wish to thank Dr. Harold Bekkering for his insights in setting the agenda for the conference and Heidi John for her faithful secretarial assistance. The final stages of book preparation were supported by the Center for Mind, Brain, and Learning through funding by the Talaris Research Institute. We thank Craig Harris for help with assembling and submitting the manuscript. We are deeply indebted to our editors at Cambridge University Press, particularly Sarah Caro, Gillian Dadd, Sophie Read, and Ann Lewis. Finally, we wish to acknowledge the help of Dr. George Butterworth in fostering this project before his untimely death in February 2000. George was an internationally renowned scientist and an enthusiastic member of our conference. His unquenchable intellectual curiosity led him to promote international and interdisciplinary research. We dedicate this volume to him.

An introduction to the imitative mind and brain

Wolfgang Prinz and Andrew N. Meltzoff

Introduction

Imitation guides the behavior of a range of species. Advances in the study of imitation, from brain to behavior, have profound implications for a variety of topics including consciousness, the neural underpinnings of perception-action coding, and the origins of theory of mind. Human beings are the most imitative creatures on the planet. We create but we also imitate, and this combination provides us with a special (though perhaps not unique) cognitive-social profile. This book provides insights into the imitative mind and brain, its evolution, development, and place in adult psychology. In so doing, it addresses a longstanding puzzle about how "self" and "other" are coded within our brains.

Scope

Imitation has a long and rich history. From a historical perspective, the interest in imitation is much broader than the more focused treatment we give it in the present book. For example, in the past, the term imitation has been used in a number of different ways in domains as diverse as theory of art, theology, ethology, cultural anthropology, and psychology. Platonic and Aristotelian theories, drama, the visual arts, and music were conceived as using the imitation of nature (*imitatio naturae*) as a principle of aesthetic performance. In medieval theology, the notion of *imitatio christi* stood for the way man could regain resemblance with God (lost through the Fall of Man), by leading a life in humility, hardship, and poverty. In anthropology there has long been a focus on cultural variations caused by imitation-based practices of transferring customs and technologies across generations.

In this book, we do not use imitation in these broad senses, but rather in a narrower psychological sense. Our focus is not on imitative practices in art, religion, or technology, but rather on manifestations of imitation in individual behaviors. We realize, of course, that there is not really a

1

sharp demarcation between cultural and psychological uses of the term or between the respective areas of study. Still, science needs to be selective, and depends on focusing on certain things at the expense of neglecting some others. Accordingly, our emphasis is on imitation studied in the context of individual behavior, rather than the context of the spread of cultural practices across generations.

Further, within the broad field of imitation at the behavioral level, our focus will be on imitation performance, not on imitation learning. By this we mean that we will concentrate on the analysis of imitative acts referring to (relatively short-lived) body movements, instrumental, or communicative actions – and not to the role of imitation in the gradual build-up of (relatively long-lived) dispositions, like traits, attitudes, habits, or skills. The reason for selecting this particular focus is that we believe that much progress has been made in understanding the mechanisms underlying imitation of acts in recent years. And we believe that future breakthroughs in both cognitive science and neuroscience will continue to come in this area.

Imitation of behavioral acts is studied in many fields of inquiry, including developmental psychology, evolutionary biology, neuroscience, and experimental psychology. Often a major concern of research in these areas is identifying what species imitate, at what age imitation occurs, and what behaviors can be imitated. This style of research may be coined *What-research*. It is mainly interested in the conditions under which imitation occurs. Another major concern of research on imitation is to understand the functional architecture of the underlying mechanisms. This style of research may be coined *How-research*.

Again we realize that the dividing line is not really sharp. For example, in examining the imitation of facial gestures in human neonates, answers to the *What* also impose constraints on possible theories on the *How* of these imitative acts (Meltzoff, this volume). The same applies to the analysis of imitation in great apes (see Byrne, this volume; Whiten, this volume). Nevertheless the authors in this book emphasize *How*-questions over *What*-questions, and consider *What*-issues mainly in the service of helping to solve *How*-issues. Our focus will be on understanding mechanisms of imitation (*How*), not on studying the conditions under which people and animals make use of it.

In sum, this volume is deliberately selective in three major respects: we focus on imitation at the level of individual behavior, emphasize short-lived imitative acts, and are mainly interested in the functional architecture of how imitation is accomplished at the psychological and neurophysiological levels.

Contexts

The past twenty years have seen a renewed interest in imitation in at least four independent lines of inquiry.

One important contribution to reanimating scientific interest in the old theme of imitation came from developmental psychology. Meltzoff and Moore's (1977) paper on imitation of facial gestures in neonates opened up a new line of research and a discussion about the possibility of an innately shared code for perception and action. Initially, the debate focused on deconstructing Piaget's theory; but research on infant imitation quickly became a tradition in its own right, leading scientists to use imitation as a means of investigating the development of theory of mind, intentionality, memory, and clinical difficulties in atypical populations (e.g., Meltzoff, 1999; Meltzoff & Moore, 1997, 1998; Nadel & Butterworth, 1999).

A second line of rediscovery of the topic came from experimental studies in adult social cognition. Though the term imitation is often not used in that research, related concepts are often employed to account for findings in priming studies. The logic of these studies is surprisingly simple and straightforward. Participants who observe other people doing certain things or acting in particular ways tend to do similar things after the observation period (e.g., Bargh, 1997; Bargh & Barndollar, 1996; Dijksterhuis & van Knippenberg, 1998; Wegner & Bargh, 1998). These findings are usually interpreted as indicating automatic control of behavior and attributed to unconscious priming mechanisms. Priming is, of course, a candidate mechanism which may account for various other forms of imitation as well. But, we also must consider the possibility that what has become relatively automatic in adults may have developmental origins that once required more intentional control before becoming so "automatized."

A further new line of research came from the experimental analyses of human performance. In these experiments, people are required to do two things at the same time: perform certain actions by themselves and watch certain other actions being performed by somebody else (e.g., Stürmer, Aschersleben, & Prinz, 2000; Brass, Bekkering, & Prinz, 2001). These studies aim at specifying the interactions between action perception and action production – one of the crucial issues for understanding imitation.

Last, an important new context for studying and understanding imitation has emerged from neurophysiology and neuropsychology. Single-cell studies demonstrate that the brain has a number of sites where cells appear to be tuned to the perception of certain movements and/or interactions with objects. Interestingly, some of these cells also have motor properties, that is, they are also involved in the production of the very same actions the animal performs itself (Gallese, Fadiga, Fogassi, & Rizzolatti, 1996; Rizzolatti, Fadiga, Fogassi, & Gallese, this volume; Rizzolatti & Fadiga, 1998; Rizzolatti, Fadiga, Gallese, & Fogassi, 1996). Likewise, brain-imaging studies have recently corroborated the evidence for common brain bases for action perception and action production (Decety, this volume; Decety *et al.*, 1997; Grèzes & Decety, 2001; Iacoboni *et al.*, 1999).

Given these independent contexts for a revival of interest in imitation, it is perhaps not surprising that most recently imitation has emerged as a new topic for those studying artificial intelligence. We believe that at the present juncture Nature's solution to the imitation problem is doing more to inform imitation by machines than the other way around. However, we agree that this may change in the not-too-far future, and indeed one of the hopes of this volume is that it will inspire more work in the artificial intelligence community on robotic learning by watching or imitation.

Issues

What do we need to understand when we want to understand imitation? What questions must theories of imitation address? Two basic issues need to be addressed by any theory of imitation performance. We need to understand how actions are perceived and we need to know how similarity can be effective between perception and action. We do not claim that the two issues are independent. In fact, whether or not they are viewed as independent is itself dependent on the answers given to the more fundamental questions.

How are actions perceived?

Understanding action perception entails (at least) three interrelated issues.

First, how is the stream of *ongoing* behavior parsed, that is, what information is used for segmenting the pattern of stimulation arising from watching other people's actions? At this level, action perception may not be any different from the perception of non-action events: perceptual systems have evolved for individuating objects (extended in space) and events (extended in time), and for subjecting these spatiotemporal "units" to further analysis (Tversky, Morrison, & Zacks, this volume). A debate is whether parsing the actions of our conspecifics is achieved through specialized neural machinery or more general visual analyses.

Second, once parsed, what determines the *level of granularity* at which actions are coded and identified? For instance, is the grasping of an object represented in terms of the abstract type "grasping an object of category X", or is it represented in terms of the concrete token, the specific kinematic pattern by which the arm moves in the act of grasping? To paraphrase an example from Wegner and Vallacher (1986): what is one actually doing while brushing one's teeth? Is one preventing cavities? Is one moving one's hand in a particular way, or is one just brushing one's teeth? Obviously, the level at which an action is identified has important implications for the imitation of that action: type imitation will be fundamentally different from token imitation, and imitation of the act of preventing cavities will differ from imitation of the act of moving one's hands in a particular way.

Third, once an action is parsed and identified, how far and in which ways does the perception of that action *go beyond the information given* in the stimulus? Taken literally, the stimulus information is just a complex pattern of visual information on the imitator's retina. Still, as we know from numerous studies, perceptual systems have evolved to go beyond the information given in various ways (e.g., Bruner, 1973). Therefore, perception is not just a matter of the proximal stimulus but also a matter of the information extracted and inferred from the stimulus. This is of particular importance for action perception. The information given (in the visual field) is a more or less complex kinematic pattern. However, the information perceived (in the imitator's visual world) is much richer. For example, as has been shown in a seminal study by Runeson and Frykholm (1983), it may include the dynamics behind the kinematics (i.e., the force applied in lifting a heavy object), or certain dynamically relevant properties of the objects with which the movement is interacting (like the weight of the lifted object).

Importantly, though dynamics are extracted from kinematics, we do not feel as though they are being derived or inferred from them. Rather, the information extracted from the stimulus pattern attains the same perceptual status as the information given in that pattern. Further, perceiving actions may even include the invisible goals the visible movements are striving for, as well as mental states like intentions or desires underlying those goals. All of these invisible things are readily extracted, as it were, from the visible stimulus. What, then, forms the basis of the imitator's imitation? Do people copy the kinematics or the dynamics of an action they see? Do they copy the movements they see or the goals/intentions "behind" those movements? When do people do one thing, and when the other?

How can similarity be effective between perception and action?

This is a fundamental problem of all brands of theories about imitation. Actually, it addresses a classical topic of psychology, which goes back to Aristotle's discussion of association principles. Aristotle distinguished between four such principles: succession, coexistence, contrast, and similarity. According to the principles of succession and coexistence, ideas get associated with each other when they repeatedly occur in close temporal or spatial contiguity. According to the principles of contrast and similarity, the same may occur with ideas that resemble each other (hot–warm) or oppose each other (hot–cold). In modern cognitive theories, a role for similarity is usually acknowledged in domains like reasoning or judgment (e.g., Hahn & Chater, 1998; Sloman & Rips, 1998).

However, similarity at first appears to be an inappropriate construct for conceptualizing relationships between perception and action. This is because when it comes to understanding relationships between afferent input and efferent output, the classical approach is that they are coded in different ways. Historically, this has led theorists to resort to rule-based rather than similarity-based operations, as described next.

Approaches

A brief look at classical approaches to perception-action relationships may help us understand why they had no room for similarity within their framework (sensorimotor views). It can also help us discern what requirements new approaches need to meet (cognitive views).

Sensorimotor views

Since the times of Descartes, sensorimotor views have been prevalent in philosophical, psychological, and physiological theories about how we know about the world and act on it (Descartes, 1664; cf. Prinz, 1997; Hommel, Müsseler, Aschersleben, & Prinz, in press). Until recently, sensorimotor views have been the gold standard in the brain and behavioral sciences. Following Descartes, these views postulated two incommensurate systems, one for the afferent processing of stimuli and another one for the efferent generation of movements. Accordingly, research on sensation and perception for the past several decades, if not centuries, has been neatly kept separate from research on movement and action.

On the afferent side, it has generally been believed that external objects and events lead to internal patterns of stimulation in sense organs, which, in turn, lead to sensory codes in the brain. On the efferent side, the story goes the other way round. It starts with motor codes in the brain, which lead to patterns of excitation in effector organs, which, in turn, lead to movements. According to the logic of this scheme, sensory codes and motor codes have no way of talking to each other directly. Sensory codes and motor codes are incommensurate in terms of their contents. Sensory codes stand for patterns of stimulation in sense organs, while motor codes stand for patterns of excitation in muscles. Since they cannot talk to each other directly, some rule-based translation between the two is required. Rule-based translation serves to create mappings between stimuli and responses – be they innate (e.g., based on reflex arcs or instincts) or acquired (based on learned associations and their underlying neural networks).

Accordingly, in the experimental analysis of human performance, the metaphor of "translation" has become one of the most prominent theoretical notions to account for the operations underlying the mapping of responses to stimuli (Welford, 1968; Massaro, 1990). This metaphor stresses the incommensurability between sensory codes and motor codes, implying that both belong to separate representational domains and can, hence, only be linked to each other by way of creating arbitrary mappings.

An approach like this has no way to account for imitation in a functional sense, that is, based on similarity. If one believes that stimuli and responses are represented through sensory and motor features, respectively, the two sets of features are incommensurate – there is no way similarity, or overlap, could play a role in the mechanisms linking perception and action. (Still, since the incidence of imitation is too obvious to overlook, strict proponents of sensorimotor views have sometimes claimed that, though similarity cannot be functional between the imitator's perception and action, it can be functional in an observer's perception, who watches both the imitatee's and the imitator's action.)

A prominent example is provided by Gewirtz and Stingle's analysis of imitation learning (Gewirtz & Stingle, 1968; cf. Prinz, 1987). This account proposes that infants learn imitative responses in the same way as all other behaviors, that is, without any functional support by similarity between stimuli and responses. Instead, imitative responses initially occur by chance. They immediately get reinforced by observers (e.g., parents), who are capable of noticing their imitative character. Therefore, functionally speaking, the infant does not copy the parent, and certainly does not intend to copy, but rather the parent reinforces the infant on occasions when s/he happens to behave like him/herself (or some other model). According to this view, similarity is recognized by the observer who watches an imitator performing the same action as somebody else – but it does not play a functional role between the imitator's perception (of somebody else's action) and control of his or her own action. Accordingly, the true story for the imitator is a story about rule-based mappings – under conditions where the rules teach the imitator to act in a way that, from an observer's point of view, looks like the way the model acted immediately beforehand. Obviously, an account like this, though it may possibly account for certain learned imitative responses, cannot explain the occurrence of newborn imitation or the imitation of novel behaviors by adults.

Cognitive views

Recent cognitive views of relationships between perception and action have developed a way to overcome the limitations of the classical Cartesian view of separate and incommensurate systems. Cognitive views provide room for both rule-based translation and similarity-based induction. On the one hand, they acknowledge a strong role for rule-based mapping in order to account for many forms of learning. However, they also acknowledge a role for similarity-based matching that may operate in parallel to rule-based mapping.

Similarity-based matching takes care of two things at once: (a) extracting, from the perception of the model's ongoing action, certain features that go beyond the sensory information given and (b) using this extract for planning and controlling the imitator's own actions. Cognitive approaches invoke a common representational domain for perception and action – that is, for representing the model's actions and planning the imitator's own actions. Obviously, in order to be functional, common representations need to refer not only to body movements proper but also to the representation of other bodies and one's own body and the way the perception and control of one's own bodily activities are related to each other. Further, common representations may even refer to invisible physical and mental entities "behind" visible bodies and their movements, like forces or intentions. Within the common representational domain, perception and action can talk to each other directly in the same representational language, and there is no need for translation anymore. One can induce the other by virtue of similarity. Meltzoff's AIM mechanism (Meltzoff, this volume) or Gattis, Bekkering, and Wohlschläger's goal-directed theory (this volume) provide two examples of models of imitation in which this basic logic is embodied (see also Prinz, this volume).

Over the past ten years, the view that perception and action share certain representational resources has gained strong support from neurophysiology and brain imaging (see Rizzolatti, this volume; Decety, this volume). We can no longer rigidly maintain the neat separation of the domains of perception and action, on which we have lived so comfortably since the times of Descartes. This may be bad news for the Cartesian doctrine, but it is good news for the study of imitation. It is fitting that interest in imitation is waxing when the authority of Descartes' doctrine of incommensurability is waning.

The time for studies of imitation has arrived. Imitation is readily studied at multiple levels by interdisciplinary research teams. It informs us about perception, motor control, the mechanisms underlying perception-action coupling and self–other relations. Over the next decade it promises to become a prototypical case of interdisciplinary research on brain-behavior relations and to shed light on both cognitive questions and those aimed at understanding intersubjectivity.

Overview of the volume

This volume is divided into three parts. Part I concerns developmental and evolutionary approaches to imitation. It focuses on theories about the origins of the imitative mind as well as empirical findings from typically developing human infants, children with autism, and great apes. Part II presents cognitive approaches to imitation using adult subjects. It highlights what imitation tells us about perception-action coding and the body scheme. Part III analyzes the neural underpinnings of imitation. Exciting new work on "mirror neurons" and shared cortical regions for the observation and execution of action are presented. Taken together, the chapters provide a comprehensive analysis of the burgeoning multi-disciplinary field of research on imitation.

In Chapter 1 Meltzoff describes his work on imitation in human infants. In order to account for imitation by infants, he postulates a "common metric" between the observation and execution of acts. The importance of his studies on newborns is that they document a basic link between perception and production that is not forged through postnatal experience. This fits together well with the reports of "mirror neurons" and adult neuroimaging studies discussed in Part III of this book. Meltzoff also discusses child development after the newborn period. He proposes that infant imitation is a precursor to developing empathy toward others and a theory of mind. The chapter outlines a psychological mechanism for this important developmental transition.

Nadel examines the functional uses of imitation in typically developing children and children with autism. She presents data and theory that the preverbal child uses imitation to initiate social exchanges and to respond to other's initiations. Nadel reports fascinating data about the imitative deficits in children with autism and provides an analysis of how imitation may serve as a foundation for language and communication.

Asendorpf examines the relation between early imitation and self-awareness in the second year of life. His provocative studies indicate links between the development of self recognition (e.g., mirror recognition studies) and imitation. His emphasis on the communicative aspects of imitation complements those of Nadel.

Heimann summarizes research carried out in Sweden over the last fifteen years showing that newborns imitate a range of gestures, and also showing individual differences in imitative reactivity in infancy. Heimann was the first to document such early-emerging individual differences, and he describes interesting correlations between early imitation scores and subsequent functioning at older ages. This chapter foreshadows Part III of the book, which discusses the profound deficits in imitation manifest in certain adult syndromes (e.g., apraxia).

Rochat sets his sights on the development of the notion of "self" in infancy and believes that imitation is a tool for expanding the notion of self both for the adult scientist and the child. The crux of his chapter is that contemplation of the self as object (self-objectification) is a process emerging from young infants' propensity to reproduce their own actions and engage in self-imitation. From the repetition of one's own actions, the self becomes objectified, becoming both an embodied experience and a potential object of thought (i.e., self-reflection). Rochat, like Meltzoff and Nadel, emphasizes how imitation is used by the child to prompt development, going beyond the initial state.

Whiten reports his pioneering work on imitation in chimpanzees. The rationale for the experimental design is essentially ethological, with the tasks designed as analogues of foraging problems in the wild. Whiten constructs "artificial fruits" that duplicate features of real fruits by requiring the animal to perform a sequence of manipulations to successfully obtain the food reward. His experiments suggest that chimpanzees and young children can imitate both the shape and sequential structure of the model they witness, with children generating higher fidelity copies than chimpanzees. His chapter also includes comparative analyses of imitation in typically developing children and children with autism.

Byrne reports empirical and theoretical work based on many years of studying gorillas in the wild. He is concerned with the animals' ability to discern the principles and organization of observed behavior and thereby to selectively copy novel behavioral structure. Byrne explores the cognitive underpinnings that are necessary for what he has dubbed "program-level" imitation. The possibility of imitation by great apes has stirred a great deal of debate and discussion; Whiten and Byrne are among those who have done the most careful studies to date on this important topic.

In Part II the authors focus on imitation in human adults. Imitation is used as a tool to investigate classic topics in cognitive psychology. Prinz discusses experimental approaches to imitation and their background in ideomotor theory. Ideomotor theory bridges the gap between the perception of actions (in others) and the production of action (by oneself) by invoking a common representational basis for perception and production. As is shown in a number of experimental demonstrations, action perception and action production interfere with each other, depending on the similarity between the action perceived and the action to be produced.

Bekkering describes a variety of behavioral tests of an observation/ execution matching system using the stimulus-response compatibility paradigm from experimental psychology. He presents neuroimaging (fMRI) work providing evidence that common neurocognitive mechanisms underlie perception and action in imitation.

Gattis, Bekkering, and Wohlschläger review studies on imitative behavior in adults and school-aged children. Their main thesis is that observers do not imitate isolated body movements, but rather actively process the goals of an observed act. By taking into account goals it is possible to explain otherwise peculiar errors in imitative performances. This connection between imitation and goal-directed action in adults and older children fits hand-in-glove with the developmental work in Part I showing that toddlers are beginning to attend to and imitate the goals and intentions of adults at a very early age.

Vogt introduces a conceptual distinction between imitative parameter selection (where imitators focus on certain execution details of a given action) and imitative action selection (where imitators choose between different kinds of actions). His novel experiments provide empirical support for this differentiation and establish that, at least for imitative parameter selection, there exist very fast and automatic visuomotor couplings and the possible operation of a number of such couplings in parallel. Vogt's contribution is an empirically grounded attempt to analyze the microarchitecture of imitative actions while making cogent links to the chapters by Prinz, Bekkering, and Gattis *et al.*

Tversky, Morrison, and Zacks note that when human bodies interact with other objects, they compose a complex visual event, and an important question concerns how perceivers parse that event. They argue that events, such as making a bed, can be regarded as temporal analogs of spatial objects. Events are parsed into segments by objects; each successive segment typically involves a new object as well as new actions on the object. The authors' concern with the human body relates to work on the development of the notion of "self" in infancy (Part I), to the neural basis of body perception (see Part III), and fits nicely with the subsequent chapter by Reed.

Reed points out that the term "body schema" refers to both general body knowledge and immediate body perception. These two concepts are typically confounded in the literature, leading to confusion over the nature of the body schema. Reed uses the term "body schema" to refer to a particular class of long-term representations and includes the invariant properties of the human body. In contrast, the "body percept" refers to the instance of immediate body perception (cf., Gallagher, 1995). The distinction between these two concepts serves to clarify current uncertainty regarding the neural substrates of body representation and sets the stage for Part III of the book.

Part III opens with a chapter by Rizzolatti, Fadiga, Fogassi, and Gallese, the Italian team that is internationally renowned for their discovery of "mirror neurons" in the premotor cortex of monkeys. These neurons discharge both when the monkey performs an action and when it observes another individual making a similar action. The authors suggest that mirror neurons are part of an evolutionary ancient mechanism they call the "resonance" mechanism. A discussion is provided of the possible role of mirror neurons in imitation. This material relates to those chapters exploring the developmental and evolutionary aspects of imitation (Part I) and also ties to work on monkeys described in the subsequent chapter.

Jellema, Baker, Oram, and Perrett point out that the imitation of actions requires a visual representation of those actions. Their chapter shows how visually responsive neurons in the temporal cortex achieve a visual representation of actions such as walking, reaching, and redirecting attention. The representations are built in such a way as to allow the observer to generalize across different perspectives in which an agent may be seen performing an action, and to register the continuity in behavior of others despite their temporary occlusion from sight.

Decety focuses on human cognitive neuroscience. He reviews a series of groundbreaking studies in adults showing that common neural regions are activated by: (a) producing actions oneself, (b) perceiving actions produced by others, and even (c) thinking about actions through mental simulation. These regions potentially provide the neural substrate for the imitation found in human infants, children, and adults. A question that arises from this anatomical organization is why normal adults are not compelled to imitate, and Decety goes on to explore the basis for inhibiting imitation. The chapter also discusses the neural underpinnings of differentiating self- versus externally produced actions. This distinction is vital for how the brain keeps track of whether the subject is imitating another person or the other person is imitating oneself (thus linking back to the developmental work by Nadel and Asendorpf on mutual imitation by children during communicative episodes).

Kinsbourne discusses the role of imitation in bodily awareness and social interaction. He shows that both neuropsychological and neurodevelopmental literature suggest that percepts are encoded enactively, thus connecting to ideomotor theory discussed by Prinz. On the one hand, enactive encoding supports the ability to attend to specified body parts. On the other hand, it supports the ability to link one's own actions to other people's actions. Kinsbourne argues that enactive encoding and imitation provide a common root for both bodily awareness and social interaction, a position that fits well with the developmental theories described in Part I.

Goldenberg and Hermsdörfer discuss the psychological and neural bases for the disorders in imitation found in apraxic patients. Theories of apraxia have typically considered imitation deficits as based on faulty motor execution. This chapter provides several lines of evidence against this notion: (a) patients who fail on imitation of meaningless gesture, can perform gestures of similar complexity evoked from long-term memory; (b) patients who err in imitating meaningless gestures also err when manipulating an inanimate manikin to reproduce desired body configurations, and (c) these same patients also commit errors when they attempt to select a photograph that matches a target gesture. The authors propose that imitation requires conceptual knowledge about the human body and that access to this knowledge requires the integrity of the left hemisphere. This chapter weaves together strands from Parts I, II, and III of the book by showing the tragic consequences of patients who do not share the imitative mind and brain of the typical human adult.

References

Bargh, J. A. (1997). The automaticity of every-day life. In R. S. Wyer (Ed.), *The automaticity of everyday life: Advances in social cognition* (Vol. 10, pp. 1–61). Mahwah, NJ: Erlbaum.

Bargh, J. A., & Barndollar, K. (1996). Automaticity in action: The unconscious as a repository of chronic goals and motives. In P. M. Gollwitzer & J. A. Bargh (Eds.), *The psychology of action* (pp. 457–481). New York: Guilford.

Brass, M., Bekkering, H., & Prinz, W. (2001). Movement observation affects movement execution: Evidence from a simple response-task paradigm. *Acta Psychologica, 106,* 3–22.

Bruner, J. S. (1973). *Beyond the information given: Studies in the psychology of knowing.* New York: W. W. Norton.

Decety, J., Grèzes, J., Costes, N., Perani, D., Jeannerod, M., Procyk, E., Grassi, F., & Fazio, F. (1997). Brain activity during observation of actions: Influence of action content and subject's strategy. *Brain, 120,* 1763–1777.

Descartes, R. (1664). *Traitée de l'Homme.* Paris: Girard.

Dijksterhuis, A., & van Knippenberg, A. (1998). The relation between perception and behavior, or how to win a game of Trivial Pursuit. *Journal of Personality and Social Psychology, 74*, 865–877.

Gallagher, S. (1995). Body schema and intentionality. In J. Bermúdez, A. J. Marcel & N. Eilan (Eds.), *Body and the self* (pp. 225–244). Cambridge, MA: MIT Press.

Gallese, V., Fadiga, L., Fogassi, L., & Rizzolatti, G. (1996). Action recognition in the premotor cortex. *Brain, 119*, 593–609.

Gewirtz, J. L., & Stingle, K. G. (1968). Learning of generalized imitation as the basis for identification. *Psychological Review, 75*, 374–397.

Grèzes, J., & Decety, J. (2001). Functional anatomy of execution, mental simulation, observation, and verb generation of actions: A meta-analysis. *Human Brain Mapping, 12*, 1–19.

Hahn, U., & Chater, N. (1998). Similarity and rules: Distinct? Exhaustive? Empirically distinguishable? *Cognition, 65*, 197–230.

Hommel, B., Müsseler, J., Aschersleben, G., & Prinz, W. (in press). The theory of event coding (TEC): A framework for perception and action planning. *Behavioral and Brain Sciences.*

Iacoboni, M., Woods, R. P., Brass, M., Bekkering, H., Mazziotta, J. C., & Rizzolatti, G. (1999). Cortical mechanisms of human imitation. *Science, 286*, 2526–2528.

Massaro, D. W. (1990). An information-processing analysis of perception and action. In O. Neumann & W. Prinz (Eds.), *Relationships between perception and action: Current approaches* (pp. 133–166). Berlin: Springer-Verlag.

Meltzoff, A. N. (1999). Origins of theory of mind, cognition, and communication. *Journal of Communicative Disorders, 32*, 251–269.

Meltzoff, A. N., & Moore, M. K. (1977). Imitation of facial and manual gestures by human neonates. *Science, 198*, 75–78.

   (1997). Explaining facial imitation: A theoretical model. *Early Development and Parenting, 6*, 179–192.

   (1998). Object representation, identity, and the paradox of early permanence: Steps toward a new framework. *Infant Behavior and Development, 21*, 201–235.

Nadel, J., & Butterworth, G. (1999). *Imitation in infancy.* Cambridge: Cambridge University Press.

Prinz, W. (1987). Ideomotor action. In H. Heuer & A. F. Sanders (Eds.), *Perspectives on perception and action* (pp. 47–76). Hillsdale, NJ: Erlbaum.

   (1997). Perception and action planning. *European Journal of Cognitive Psychology, 9*, 129–154.

Rizzolatti, G., & Fadiga, L. (1998). Grasping objects and grasping action meanings: The dual role of monkey rostroventral premotor cortex (area F5). In G. Bock & J. A. Goode (Eds.), *Sensory guidance of movement* (pp. 81–103). Novartis Foundation Symposium 218. Chichester: Wiley & Sons.

Rizzolatti, G., Fadiga, L., Gallese, V., & Fogassi, L. (1996). Premotor cortex and the recognition of motor actions. *Cognitive Brain Research, 3*, 131–141.

Runeson, S., & Frykholm, G. (1983). Kinematic specification of dynamics as in informational basis for person-and-action perception: Expectation, gender recognition, and deceptive intention. *Journal of Experimental Psychology: General, 112*, 585–615.

Sloman, S., & Rips, L. J. (1998). Similarity as an explanatory construct. *Cognition, 65*, 87–101.

Stürmer, B., Aschersleben, G., & Prinz, W. (2000). Correspondence effects with manual gestures and postures: A study of imitation. *Journal of Experimental Psychology: Human Perception & Performance, 26*, 1746–1759.

Wegner, D. M., & Bargh, J. A. (1998). Control and automaticity in social life. In D. T. Gilbert, S. T. Fiske, & G. Lindzey (Eds.), *The handbook of social psychology* (pp. 446–496). Boston: McGraw-Hill.

Wegner, D. M., & Vallacher, R. (1986). Action identification. In R. M. Sorrentino & E. Tory Higgins (Eds.), *Handbook of motivation and cognition: Foundations of social behavior* (pp. 550–582). Chichester: Wiley & Sons.

Welford, A. T. (1968). *Fundamentals of skill.* London: Methuen.

Part I

Developmental and evolutionary approaches to imitation

1 Elements of a developmental theory of imitation

Andrew N. Meltzoff

Imitation promises to be a hot research topic in the coming decade. Interest in imitation spread from a small band of aficionados to the broader community of cognitive scientists, evolutionary biologists, neuroscientists, philosophers, and developmental scientists. What is sparking such widespread growth in this topic?

First, discoveries in developmental psychology have altered theories about the origins of imitation and its place in human nature. We used to think that humans gradually learned to imitate over the first several years of life. We now know that newborns can imitate body movements at birth. Such imitation reveals an innate link between observed and executed acts, with implications for brain science, and also reveals a primordial connection between the infant and caretaker, with implications for emotional development and intersubjectivity.

Second, there has been a change in the perceived value of developmental research. In classical psychological theories the child's mind was regarded as the antithesis of the adult mind. Adults were viewed as rational, planful, and operating with coherent perceptions; whereas infants were portrayed as slaves of the here-and-now, devoid of reason, and experiencing James' "blooming, buzzing, confusion." Scientists often assumed greater similarities between college students and rats than between college students and infants. This impeded scientists from using infants as informants about adult cognition. As experimental techniques improved, infants became good sources of information about fundamental principles of human thought. The increased value of developmental research brought studies of infant imitation to the foreground.

Third, evolutionary biologists have devised ways of comparing imitation in humans and nonhuman animals, and imitation has become a tool for examining continuities/discontinuities in the evolution of mind and intersubjectivity (Byrne, this volume; Tomasello & Call, 1997; Whiten, this volume). Darwin inquired about imitation in nonhuman animals, but in the last ten years, there has been a greater number of controlled studies of imitation in monkeys and great apes than there had been in the previous hundred years. The results indicate that monkey imitation is hard to come by in controlled experiments, belying the common wisdom of "monkey see monkey do." Nonhuman primates and other animals (e.g., songbirds) imitate, but their imitative prowess is more restricted than that of humans. The evolutionary basis of imitation will continue to be informative as direct cross-species comparisons are made.

Fourth, neuroscientists and experimental psychologists have discovered imitation. They are focused on the brain and psychological mechanisms connecting the observation and execution of actions, including the exploration of "mirror neurons" (e.g., Decety, this volume; Prinz, this volume; Rizzolatti, Fadiga, Fogassi, & Gallese, this volume).

Finally, the artificial intelligence community is beginning to create androids that can learn by registering the user's movements, rather than by line-by-line programming. This new endeavor is called "learning by example" (Berthouze & Kuniyoshi, 1998; Billard & Dautenhahn, 2000; Billard, Dautenhahn, & Hayes, 1998; Dautenhahn & Nehaniv, in press; Mataric & Pomplun, 1998). Learning by imitation is prompting an increased cross-fertilization between the fields of robotics and human psychology (Demiris *et al.*, 1997; Hayes & Demiris, 1994; Schaal, 1999).

Information in an imitative act

From a neuroscience and cognitive science perspective, the fundamental question posed by imitation concerns the mechanism that underlies it – the *How*-question. Consider what is involved in an act of imitation. The observer perceives the demonstrator's acts, uses visual perception as the basis for an action plan, and executes the motor output. This involves vision, cross-modal coordination, and motor control. If imitation takes place after a significant delay, memory and the representation of action come into play. For brain scientists, this is obviously a highly informative vein to mine in both verbal and nonverbal subjects.

Imitation also allows investigation of fundamental social processes. Cultures differ in customs, rituals, and technologies. Imitation provides a mechanism for a kind of Lamarckian evolutionary change in human societies by which adults pass on "acquired characteristics" to their young. Imitation also provides an avenue of nonverbal communication through the language of gestures. For example, new research indicates that young children use imitation as a way of determining a person's identity. If children are unsure about whether they have seen you before, they will reintroduce a game – often an imitative game – they had played with you to probe whether you are "the same individual again" (Meltzoff & Moore, 1994, 1998).

This chapter analyzes both the cognitive and the social aspects of imitation from a developmental approach. Special consideration will be given to the mechanism linking the perception and production of acts. I will propose that human infants code human acts within a "supramodal" framework that unites the observation and execution of motor acts and that this observation/execution system is innate. However, it is equally important that infants are not compelled to go immediately from perception to motor performance. Young children can observe a novel behavior on one day and imitate the next day. They also imitate in a selective and interpretive fashion (Meltzoff & Moore, 1997). The implications for memory and representation will be examined.

I will also examine the connection between infant imitation and childhood theory of mind. A developmental model is proposed: my thesis is that motor imitation is a foundation for the later development of empathy and a theory of mind. According to this view, empathy, role-taking, and theory of mind depend on the fundamental self-other equivalence first realized in infant imitation. Infants first grasp that others are "like me" in action; from this they develop the more mature notion that others are "like me" in abstract ways – having desires, emotions, intentions, and other internal states just like mine. The mechanisms of development are examined.

Mirror neurons and development

"Mirror neurons" in the premotor cortex of the monkey brain discharge both when an action is observed and when it is executed (e.g., Gallese, Fadiga, Fogassi, & Rizzolatti, 1996; Rizzolatti, Fadiga, Fogassi, & Gallese, this volume; Rizzolatti, Fadiga, Gallese, & Fogassi, 1996). Related findings in humans using PET and fMRI reveal common brain regions subserving both the perception and production of actions (e.g., Decety *et al.*, 1994, 1997; Decety & Grèzes, 1999; Fadiga, Fogassi, Pavesi, & Rizzolatti, 1995; Grèzes & Decety, 2001; Iacoboni *et al.*, 1999).

These are dramatic discoveries, but research from a developmental perspective would be valuable. Consider the case of a mirror neuron that discharges to "grasping-with-the-hand." This same cell fires regardless of whether that act is performed by the monkey or observed in another actor. A cell that discharges in both cases could mean that "grasping" is an innate act, and that prior to experience the cell is tuned to this category of action whether performed by the self or the other. Alternatively, it could mean the monkey has seen himself perform this action many times. If the monkey has watched himself perform grasping motions, there would have been repeated experience of linking the motor execution with the perception of the act. Observation and execution occur in synchrony whenever the monkey watches himself grasping with his hand. After such experience, the visual perception of "grasping" by another animal could activate neurons based on a *visual* "equivalence class" between the sight of one's own and another's hand.

If this analysis is correct, mirror neurons could result from learning and visual generalization. It is now critical for theories to investigate the ontogeny of mirror neurons. One needs to determine whether: (a) an animal is born with mirror neurons, (b) these neurons activate the first time the animal sees an act executed, or (c) the mirror neuron is activated only after an observation/execution association is built up over time. Developmental work with infant monkeys would help to clarify the origins of mirror neurons.

Imitation and experience

I have been using the word "imitation" broadly, but not all imitation is of the same type. Certain types of imitation are even more informative for brain and cognitive theories than others. From a developmental perspective, there are distinctions, for example, between imitation of hand movements and imitation of facial movements.

Human children can imitate hand movements in the first six months of life (Meltzoff & Moore, 1977, 1997; Piaget, 1962; Vinter, 1986). One possible mechanism would be for the infant to look at his or her own hand and use visual guidance as a way of achieving a match between self and other. The manual movements of self and other can both be seen. Visual pattern matching would specify when the target was achieved.

Such visual guidance is not trivial (see Goldenberg & Hermsdörfer, this volume). Infants must compare another's behavior to their own, despite differences in body size and perspective. Nevertheless, the visual system provides "form constancy" that would allow infants to extract equivalences across changes of size, visual orientation of the hand, and color. Also, young infants engage in hand-regard during the early months, so they have experience in watching their own hands move and transform. In principle, then, they have learning experiences in linking the observation and execution of manual acts.

Facial imitation presents a deeper puzzle. Newborn infants can see another's face, but they have never seen their own faces. There are no mirrors in the womb. Newborns can feel their own face move but have no access to the feeling-of-movement in others. There seems to be a gulf between self and other. It is no wonder that psychological theories from Freud to Piaget considered the imitation of facial actions as a milestone developmental achievement. The age at which infants were thought to imitate facial gestures was about one year old. Facial imitation at younger ages was theorized to be impossible – infants were supposed to lack the connection between observation and execution prior to associative experiences and reinforcement training.

Facial imitation: innate observation-execution links

Infant facial imitation is a behavior that assesses the link between observation and execution of motor actions. The empirical findings at first surprised psychologists. They showed that infants could imitate prior to the learning experiences, indicating an innate mapping between observation and execution.

In an early study, imitation of facial gestures was documented in two- to three-week-old infants (Meltzoff & Moore, 1977). A first question was whether infants would confuse all "protrusion" movements with one another. The results showed they did not inasmuch as they distinguished lip protrusion from tongue protrusion. A related question was whether infants could differentiate two movements using the same body part. The results showed they distinguished lip opening versus lip protrusion. Thus, the infants' responses were not global reactions to the sight of a face in general, not an arousal reaction, but were based on specific mappings.

This work implies that there is an intrinsic connection between perception and production. However, if we take the developmental viewpoint seriously, the subjects are not young enough. They were two weeks old and perhaps could have learned the relevant associations during early mother–child play. The definitive test requires newborns.

The relevant study involved 40 newborn infants with a mean age of 32 hours old. The oldest child in the study was 72 hours old, and the youngest was just 42 minutes old at the time of test. The results showed that human newborns imitate facial acts (Meltzoff & Moore, 1983, 1989). Newborn imitation provides an "existence proof" for a neural mapping between observed and executed movements in human infants.

Early imitation is not restricted to one or two oral movements. Imitative effects have been reported for a range of facial and manual movements (see Meltzoff & Moore, 1997, for a review). A sample of the acts that can be imitated include: tongue protrusion, lip protrusion, mouth-opening, hand gestures, head movements, cheek and brow motions, eye blinking, and components of emotional expressions (Abravanel & DeYong, 1991; Abravanel & Sigafoos, 1984; Field, Goldstein, Vaga-Lahr, & Porter, 1986; Field et al., 1983; Field, Woodson, Greenberg, & Cohen, 1982; Fontaine, 1984; Heimann, 1989; Heimann, Nelson, & Schaller, 1989;

Heimann & Schaller, 1985; Jacobson, 1979; Kaitz, Meschulach-Sarfaty, Auerbach, & Eidelman, 1988; Kugiumutzakis, 1985; Legerstee, 1991; Maratos, 1982; Meltzoff & Moore, 1977, 1983, 1989, 1992, 1994; Reissland, 1988; Vinter, 1986).

Infants in the first months of life are not limited to imitating while the target is in the perceptual field. In one study a pacifier was put in the child's mouth during the time that the adult demonstrated the target. The adult then terminated the display, assumed a neutral facial expression, and only then removed the pacifier. The results showed that infants can initiate perceptually absent models from memory (Meltzoff & Moore, 1977). In a further study, the delay between observation and production was increased to 24 hours. Infants watched gestures on one day and then returned to the laboratory to see the same person with a neutral face on the next day. Infants imitated after this lengthy delay (Meltzoff & Moore, 1994). Evidently, infants can store a representation of what they see another person do and imitate on the basis of that stored representation.

Other evidence also fits the idea that infant imitation is mediated by a stored representation. Imitative responses do not "pop out" fully formed. Infants correct their efforts. For example, when infants are shown a novel act such as tongue-protrusion-to-the-side, they begin by activating the correct body part, the tongue, and making small movements. They gradually modify this behavior so that it more and more accurately matches the gesture they see. This modification occurs with no feedback from the adult, who is either absent or sits with a neutral face (Meltzoff & Moore, 1994, 1997).

AIM mechanism

Meltzoff and Moore (1997) provided a detailed model of the mechanism underlying infant facial imitation. We hypothesized that infant imitation involves "active intermodal mapping" (AIM). Figure 1.1 provides a conceptual schematic. The crux of the AIM hypothesis is that infant imitation involves a goal-directed matching process. The goal or behavioral target is specified visually. Infants' self-produced movements provide proprioceptive feedback that can be compared to the representation of the observed act. AIM proposes that such comparison is possible because the observation and execution of human acts are coded within a common framework. We call it a "supramodal act space." AIM does not rule out direct imitation of certain elementary acts on "first try" without any need for feedback, but it allows for such proprioceptive feedback and correction of responses. Metaphorically, we can say that exteroception (perception of others) and proprioception (perception of self) speak the

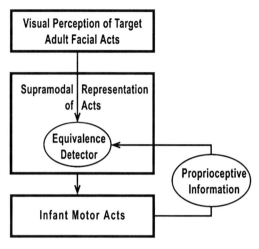

Figure 1.1. The AIM hypothesis for how infants perform facial imitation. (From Meltzoff & Moore, 1997.)

same language; there is no need for associating the two through prolonged learning because they are intimately bound at birth. Meltzoff and Moore (1995, 1997) provide further analysis of the common metric of equivalence between observed and executed acts as it subserves imitation in human newborns.

This idea of a supramodal coding of human acts that emerged from developmental psychology is highly compatible with Prinz' theory of common coding, which derived from cognitive experiments with adults (Prinz, 1990, 1992, this volume). It also dovetails well with the neuroscience discoveries about the brain bases for coupling observed and executed acts (Decety, this volume; Decety, Chaminade, & Meltzoff, in press; Iacoboni et al., 2001; Rizzolatti, Fadiga, Fogassi, & Gallese, this volume). An interesting challenge will be to determine the extent to which these mechanisms for linking perception and production are phylogenetically and ontogenetically related.

Imitation and identity: the uses of infant imitation

How do infants use imitation in their social interaction with people, and what good does it do them?

An interesting idea is that infants may use imitation to probe the identity of people. Adults keep track of individuals as they move and change in the visual field (Kahneman, Treisman, & Gibbs, 1992). Developmental studies indicate that infants are also concerned with keeping track of individuals (e.g., Meltzoff & Moore, 1998; Leslie, Xu, Tremoulet, & Scholl, 1998; Wilcox & Baillargeon, 1998; Xu & Carey, 1996). Of course, infants use facial features to help them identify people (they can recognize their mother's face), but there is growing evidence that they do not wholly rely on visual features. Infants also use a person's actions to determine who the person is.

In one study we presented six-week-old infants with people who were coming and going in front of them, as would happen in real-world interaction. The mother appeared and showed one gesture (say, mouth opening). Then she exited and was replaced by a stranger who showed a different gesture (say, tongue protrusion). The experiment required that infants keep track of the two different people and their gestures (Meltzoff & Moore, 1992).

When infants visually tracked the entrances and exits they imitated each person without difficulty. But we also uncovered an interesting error. If the mother and stranger surreptitiously changed places, infants became confused: is it the same person with a different appearance, or a new person in the old place? The visual features were suggesting one thing (new person) but the spatial cues were suggesting another (same old person). Infants used imitation as a means of settling this conflict. Infants stared at the new person, stopped behaving, and then intently produced the *previous* person's gesture.

Meltzoff and Moore hypothesized that when infants are confused about the identity of a person, they are motivated to test how the person will respond to actions. It is their way of asking: "Are you the one who does *x*?" Of course, adults use language to determine identity. We can ask: "Can you repeat the secret password?" Infants use an imitation game to check whether the adult responds with the "secret password in action." A series of further studies on imitation and identity reinforce this point (Meltzoff & Moore, 1994, 1995, 1998).

The discovery, then, is that human infants use imitative games to check the identity of the person in front of them. If infants see a person of unknown identity sitting in front of them with a neutral face, infants will often "imitate" an action that person has done in the past. This is a social-cognitive use of early imitation before verbal language is possible. It is a way of probing "Who are you?" or "Didn't we play this game before?" Infants probe whether the person acts correctly, because actions and expressive behaviors of people are identifiers of who the person is. It is not just what a person looks like (visual cues), or the spatial context of the encounter (spatial cues), but also a person's actions that determine their identity for infants.

Speech perception and production

Facial imitation involves the cross-modal processing of facial movements. There are other phenomena involving cross-modal knowledge of
faces. One such domain is speech. Empirical work reveals perception-
production links in speech that closely parallel the perception-production
links shown in motor imitation.

Mapping sound to sight

Work with adults shows that the speech code is not exclusively auditory
or motor, but is fundamentally multimodal in nature. A striking example
is the illusion that occurs when an auditory soundtrack of /b/ is combined
with a visual film of a person articulating the consonant /g/. Subjects report perceiving the consonant /d/ despite the fact that this consonant was
not delivered to either sense modality (McGurk & MacDonald, 1976).
The illusory percept is a "blend" or "intermodal best fit" that takes into
account both the auditory and the visual-motor information.

Speech information is even blended when the auditory and visual information come from a special tape of two talkers of different genders. In an
experiment involving college students, a male football player's face (a face
with whiskers, a large neck, and thick jaw bone) was paired with a high-
pitched female voice (Green, Kuhl, Meltzoff, & Stevens, 1991). Viewers
accurately reported seeing a male face and hearing a female voice, without
any perceptual blends or illusions regarding gender. These same subjects,
however, automatically blended the speech information and perceived the
illusory /d/.

At what age does cross-modal speech perception develop? In one study
four-month-old infants were presented with a baby-sized auditory-visual
lip-reading problem. They viewed two faces, side by side, one pronouncing the vowel /a/ (as in "pop") and the vowel /i/ (as in "peep"). While
viewing the two faces, infants heard one of the vowels (either /a/ or /i/)
played from a loudspeaker located midway between the two faces. The
film was arranged so the mouths on both faces opened and closed in
perfect synchrony.

The results showed that infants who heard the vowel /a/ looked longer
at the face pronouncing /a/, and the infants who heard the vowel /i/ looked
longer at the vowel /i/ (Kuhl & Meltzoff, 1982, 1984; Kuhl, Williams, &
Meltzoff, 1991). There were no temporal clues or spatial clues, because the sound came from midline and was synchronized with both
faces. The only way infants could solve this problem is by recognizing cross-modal correspondence between the auditory and visual speech

information, recognizing that a mouth shape of a certain kind goes with a speech unit of a certain form. Work in other laboratories has replicated and extended this work (MacKain, Studdert-Kennedy, Spieker, & Stern, 1983; Walton & Bower, 1993).

Mapping sound to production: vocal imitation

The previous experiment involved the matching of seen and heard speech. What about motor production? Can infants imitate the sounds they hear, producing the correct articulatory movements on the basis of auditory input? This was examined in a study of infant vocal imitation at three ages: twelve, sixteen, and twenty weeks of age (Kuhl & Meltzoff, 1996). Each infant listened to one of three vowels, /a/, /i/, or /u/ for fifteen minutes (five minutes for each of three days). Infants' vocalizations were recorded and analyzed perceptually by having them phonetically transcribed and analyzed via computerized spectrographic techniques.

The results demonstrated vocal imitation. Infants produced significantly more /a/-like utterances when exposed to /a/ than when exposed to /i/ or /u/ and so on for each of the vowels. There was a developmental progression such that the twenty-week-olds were better imitators than the younger infants, but infants imitated at all three ages.

If fifteen minutes of laboratory exposure to a vowel is sufficient to influence infants' vocalizations, then infants bathed in the ambient language of the culture could be affected (Kuhl, Tsao, Lui, Zhang, & de Boer, 2001). In fact, one can see the effects of such vocal imitation in cross-cultural work. By one year of age infants from different cultures babble differently. French infants babble with French speech units, Russian infants with Russian, and Japanese with Japanese (de Boysson-Bardies, Sagart, & Durand, 1984; de Boysson-Bardies, Halle, Sagart, & Durand, 1989; Gopnik, Meltzoff, & Kuhl, 1999).

Speech as a supramodal representation

Evidently, human speech, just like human body acts, is represented in a way that is not strictly unimodal. The auditory signal influences behavior in two other domains. The auditory signal influences where infants *look*. The auditory signal also influences the *motor* system. We hypothesize that both these phenomena, lip reading and vocal imitation, are underwritten by an infant speech code that is supramodal in nature and related to the common action code that subserves facial imitation (Kuhl, 2000; Kuhl & Meltzoff, 1982, 1984).

Object imitation and memory

Adults do not simply vocalize and move their bodies. Adults also act on the world of objects. We act on hammers, levers, wheels, and keyboards. If imitation is to fulfill its value in the transmission of culture and the use of artifacts, young children will need to be able to imitate the use of tools and other objects.

The data indicate that as soon as infants become capable of handling objects, imitation of object-directed acts begins to preoccupy them. One field observation from Western households will suffice. At about one to two years old, the baby's favorite plaything is a toy telephone. There is nothing "natural" about holding objects to our ear while we speak to invisible people. Why do infants do it? Although such behavior seems to have the hallmarks of imitation (it is not culturally universal, caretakers do not explicitly train it), developmentalists have conducted controlled laboratory studies to test this. These experiments also use imitation to investigate memory.

Memory without language

Imitation from memory goes beyond the direct coupling of an observation/execution system. It introduces memory and the representation of action. Cognitive psychologists have established that not all memory is the same (Schacter, 1996; Squire, Knowlton, & Musen, 1993; Wheeler, Stuss, & Tulving, 1997). For example, there is a distinction between retaining a familiar action or habit (habit memory) versus remembering information from one brief observation, without previous experience with the actions or objects (nonhabit or declarative memory).

Keeping the different types of memory in mind, laboratory experiments have investigated whether human infants must imitate the target act immediately in order to retain it in memory. In these studies, the children watched adults manipulate objects, but the children were not allowed to touch the objects. A delay was imposed, and then children were given the objects. Using this so-called "observation-only" design (Meltzoff & Moore, 1998), deferred imitation has been documented in infants as young as six to nine months of age (Barr, Dowden, & Hayne, 1996; Heimann & Meltzoff, 1996; Meltzoff, 1988b).

There is also evidence that a brief exposure to a novel act is enough to sear it into the memory of a toddler. In one study, infants witnessed a bizarre act, an adult who leaned forward and pressed a panel with his forehead. The infants were not allowed to handle the panel during the display. When they were given the panel one week later, 67 per cent of the infants duplicated the novel head-touch behavior. Such a novel use of the forehead was exhibited by 0 per cent of the controls, thus the object's properties alone did not call out the response à la an "affordance" (Meltzoff, 1988a). This research documents deferred imitation of a novel act after a brief exposure.

Deferred imitation has been used to explore the duration of preverbal memory. The results show that six- to nine-month-olds can imitate after a 24-hour delay (Barr, Dowden, & Hayne, 1996; Meltzoff, 1988b); twelve-month-olds after a four-week delay (Klein & Meltzoff, 1999); and infants in the second year after delays of four months or longer (e.g., Bauer & Wewerka, 1995; Meltzoff, 1995b). Evidently, preverbal infants can learn from watching and need not perform the target act immediately – observation and execution can be broken apart in time.

If children are to use deferred imitation in everyday life, it requires not only memory but also a certain freedom from context specificity. An adult can watch someone use a tool in one setting and recall that behavior in a new setting. Such "decontextualization" is important for language acquisition (Hockett, 1960); words are not just used in a single context but must be used flexibly in new settings.

In one study investigating context specificity, twelve-month-olds were shown target acts at home and one week later given their recall test in the laboratory. The results showed successful imitation (Klein & Meltzoff, 1999). In another study, toddlers in a day-care center watched "expert children" who were trained to use objects in peculiar ways. Two days later the observer children were tested at home. The results showed that the toddlers took their school lessons home with them and imitated after the two-day delay and contextual change (Hanna & Meltzoff, 1993). Finally, a study showed that fourteen-month-olds generalized their imitation across changes in the size and color of the test object (Barnat, Klein, & Meltzoff, 1996).

The findings support several inferences about the representation of human actions on objects: (a) these representations can be formed from observation alone; (b) they persist over lengthy delays and changes of context; (c) these representations are a sufficient basis on which to organize action. Human toddlers imitate, but they have loosened the shackles between observation and execution; they can tolerate long delays and radical shifts in context. (Interestingly, children with autism have difficulties with such memory-based imitation, Dawson, Meltzoff, Osterling, & Rinaldi, 1998.)

Roots of theory of mind and intersubjectivity

People are more than dynamic bags of skin that move, manipulate objects, and vocalize. Persons also have beliefs, desires, and intentions that underlie and cause the surface actions. One cannot directly see the underlying mental states, but it is an essential part of our adult understanding of people that others have them. "Theory of mind" research investigates the development of this understanding of other minds (Flavell & Miller, 1998; Perner, 1991; Taylor, 1996; Wellman, 1990).

Where does this tendency to treat others as sentient beings come from? Are we born with a theory of mind, naturally attributing mental states to others? Do we learn it in school?

Goals and intentions

A nonverbal procedure, called the "behavioral re-enactment technique," was devised to investigate the roots of theory of mind (Meltzoff, 1995a). The procedure capitalizes on imitation, but uses this proclivity in a new, more abstract way. It investigates children's ability to read below the visible surface behavior to the underlying goals and intentions of the actor.

One study involved showing eighteen-month-old children an unsuccessful act, a failed effort. For example, the adult "accidentally" under- or overshot his target, or he tried to perform a behavior but his hand slipped several times. Thus the goal-state was not achieved. To an adult, it was easy to read the actor's intentions although he did not fulfill them. The experimental question was whether children also read through the literal body movements to the underlying goal of the act. The measure of how they interpreted the event was what they chose to re-enact. In this case the "correct answer" was not to copy the literal movement that was actually seen, but the actor's goal, which remained unfulfilled.

The study compared infants' tendency to perform the target act in several situations: (a) after they saw the full target act demonstrated, (b) after they saw the unsuccessful attempt to perform the act, and (c) after it was neither shown nor attempted. The results showed that

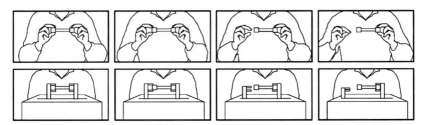

Figure 1.2. Human demonstrator (top panel) and inanimate device mimicking these movements (bottom panel). Infants attributed goals and intentions to the person but not to the inanimate device. (From Meltzoff, 1995a.)

eighteen-month-olds can understand the goals implied by unsuccess-ful attempts. Children who saw the unsuccessful attempt and infants who saw the full target act both produced target acts at a significantly higher rate than controls (Meltzoff, 1995a). Evidently, young toddlers can understand our goals even if we fail to fulfill them.

A recent experiment extended this work. In this study, eighteen-month-olds were shown the standard failed attempt display, but they were handed a trick toy. The toy had been surreptitiously glued shut before the study began (Meltzoff, 1996). When children picked it up and attempted to pull it apart, their hands slipped off the ends of the cubes. This matched the surface behavior of the adult. The question was whether this duplica-tion of the adults' behavior satisfied the children. Was it their goal? The results suggested it was not. They repeatedly grabbed the toy, yanked on it in different ways, and appealed to their mothers and the adult. Fully, 90 per cent of the children immediately looked up at the adult after failing to pull apart the trick toy (mean latency less than two seconds), and they vocalized while staring at the adult. They had matched the adult's surface behavior, but evidently they were striving toward something else. This work reinforces the idea that the toddlers are beginning to focus on the adult's goals, not simply their surface actions. It provides developmental roots for the importance of goals in organizing imitation in older children and adults (Chaminade, Meltzoff, & Decety, in press; Gattis, Bekkering, & Wohlschläger, this volume; Gleissner, Meltzoff, & Bekkering, 2000; and Bekkering, Wohlschläger, & Gattis, 2000).

If children are attending to the goal of the actor they should be able to achieve the target using a variety of means. This was tested in a study of eighteen-month-olds using a dumbbell-shaped object that was too big for the infants' hands. The adult grasped the ends of the large dumbbell and attempted to yank it apart, but his hands slid off so he was unsuccessful in carrying out his intentions. The dumbbell was then presented to the child. Interestingly, the infants did not attempt to imitate the surface behavior of the adult. They used different means from the adult, but toward the same end. For example, they put one end of the dumbbell between their knees and used both hands to pull it upwards, or put their hands on inside faces of the cubes and pushed outwards, and so on. This again supports the hypothesis that young children are sensitive to adult goals and are not confined to imitating surface behavior.

People versus things

In the adult psychological framework, human acts are goal-directed but the motions of inanimate objects are not (Heider, 1958). When do children begin to make this distinction between the acts of people and the motions of inanimates?

A study investigated how eighteen-month-olds respond to an inanimate device that mimicked the movements of the actor. An inanimate device was constructed that had poles for arms and mechanical pincers for hands. It did not look human, but it traced the same spatiotemporal path and manipulated the dumbbell-shaped object very similarly to the human (Fig. 1.2, bottom panel).

The results showed that the children did not attribute a goal or intention to the movements of the inanimate device when its pincers slipped off the ends of the dumbbell. Although the children were not frightened by the device and looked at it as long as at the human display, they simply did not see the sequence of movements as implying a goal. Children were no more likely to pull apart the toy after seeing the failed attempt of the inanimate device than they did in baseline levels (Meltzoff, 1995a). However, when the inanimate device successfully pulled the dumbbell apart, the children did successfully do so. This shows that children can pick up certain information from the inanimate device, but not other information (concerning intentions and goals).

Grounding a theory of mind

The raw fact that infants can make sense of a person's failed attempt indicates that they have begun to distinguish surface behavior (what people actually do) from another deeper level. They now imitate what the adult *meant to do* versus what he actually did do.

This differentiation is fundamental to our theory of mind and underwrites some of our most cherished human traits. Such a distinction is necessary for fluid linguistic communication, which requires distinguishing what was said from what was intended (Bruner, 1999; Grice, 1969). It is the basis for our judgments of morality, responsibility, and culpability, which require distinguishing intentions from actual outcomes. In civil human society it is not solely, or even primarily, the actual behavior of our social partners that carries weight, but their underlying intentions. The research indicates that eighteen-month-olds have begun to understand the acts of other humans in terms of a psychology involving goals, aims, and intentions, not solely the physics of the motions in space. In this sense they have adopted a primitive building block for a theory of mind. Recent advances in cognitive neuroscience complement this developmental work by suggesting there may be shared cortical regions for coding action, understanding goals/intentions, and processing theory-of-mind problems (e.g., Blakemore & Decety, 2001; Frith & Frith, 1999).

Concluding remarks on the importance of imitation in human development

The modern empirical findings establish a rich, innate foundation for human development. Infants are not blank slates waiting to be written on. They are born with predispositions, perceptual biases, and representational capacities. The research on infant imitation reveals three important aspects of the preverbal mind: cross-modal coordination, memory, and intersubjectivity.

Imitation and cross-modal coordination

Classical developmental theory held that the sense modalities were uncoordinated at birth (Piaget, 1952, 1954). The work on imitation discussed in this chapter suggests that infants use a "supramodal" code that unites input from different sensory modalities into one common representational framework. This provides a bridge between perception and production. From a developmental viewpoint it is interesting to consider that infants bring this multimodal processing of information to the task of language acquisition. It serves them well, because language can be seen as well as heard (lip reading), can be picked up through touching the lips (Tadoma method), and refers to multimodal events in the world. If the sense modalities were as separate as classical developmental theory supposed, imitation would be impossible and language learning would be delayed (Gopnik & Meltzoff, 1997).

Imitation and memory

Research on infant imitation has contributed to theories of memory development. The research shows that infants are not confined purely to recognition memory. Deferred imitation establishes that infants can *recall* absent information without language. Moreover, infant deferred imitation provides a developmental perspective on cognitive science and neuroscience discussions about multiple memory systems. The results suggest that preverbal humans are not limited solely to habit/procedural memory. Infants can remember novel acts without having performed the act themselves at the time of observation (i.e., without having developed a "habit"). These results suggest that both habit and declarative memory systems are functional in early infancy, rather than an initial habit memory system giving rise to a later-maturing nonhabit memory system (Howe & Courage, 1993; Meltzoff, 1995b; Meltzoff & Moore, 1998; Barr & Hayne, 2000).

Imitation as a precursor to theory of mind

Philosophers have long wondered how we come to ascribe beliefs, desires, and intentions to others – in short where our "theory of mind" comes from. New research shows that eighteen-month-olds have already adopted an essential aspect of the adult theory of mind, namely that people (and not things) act in purposeful, intentional ways. However, this framework does not come out of nowhere. It has developmental roots.

My thesis is that imitation provides a foundation for developing a theory of mind. Below is a sketch of a three-step developmental process. It shows how an organism with the imitative capacities of human infants could gain some purchase on other minds.

(1) *Innate equivalence between self and other.* Infants can imitate and recognize equivalences between observed and executed acts. This is a "starting state," as documented by motor imitation in newborns. This innate mapping between self and other provides a jump-start for theory of mind.

(2) *Self learning.* As infants perform particular bodily acts they have certain mental experiences. Behaviors are regularly related to mental states. For example, when infants produce certain emotional expressions and bodily activities, such as smiling or struggling to obtain a toy, they also experience their own mental states. Infants register this systematic relation between their own behaviors and underlying mental states.

(3) *Others in analogy to the self.* When infants see others acting similarly to them, they project that people are having the same mental experience as they themselves have when performing those acts. They use the behavior-mental state mappings registered through their own experience to make inferences about the internal states of others. In short, given the innate state (step #1 above) and the knowledge that behavior X maps to mental state X' in their own experience (step #2), infants have relevant data to make inferences about relations between the seen behavior of others and the underlying mental state (step #3). Other research demonstrates that such an inferential process is well within the capacity of human infants (Gopnik *et al.*, 1999; Gopnik & Meltzoff, 1997; Meltzoff, Gopnik, & Repacholi, 1999).

Recast in a different way: infants gain an understanding of others by analogy with the self. They use knowledge of how they feel when they produce an expression to infer how another feels. Infants imbue the acts of others with "felt meaning," because they are able to recognize the similarities between their own acts and those of others. Their experience of what it feels like to perform acts provides a privileged access to people not afforded by things. It prompts infants to make special attributions to people not made to inanimate things that do not look or act like them.[1]

Innate structure combined with developmental change

The crux of the developmental theory offered here is that imitation sets children on a trajectory for learning about the other's mind. The "like-me-ness" of others, first manifest in imitation, is a foundation for more mature forms of social cognition that depend on the felt equivalence between self and other. The Golden Rule, "Treat thy neighbor as thy self" at first occurs in action, through imitation. Without an imitative mind, we might not develop this moral mind. Imitation is the bud, and empathy and moral sentiments are the ripened fruit – born from years of interaction with other people already recognized to be "like me." To the human infant, another person is not an alien, but a kindred spirit – not an "It" but an embryonic "Thou."

Acknowledgements

Work on this chapter was supported by the National Institute of Health (HD-22514), the Center for Mind, Brain, and Learning, and the Talaris Research Institute. I am grateful for the advice of Keith Moore, Alison Gopnik, Pat Kuhl, Wolfgang Prinz, and Harold Bekkering. I also thank Craig Harris and Calle Fisher for their assistance in assembling this chapter.

Note

1 In real-world social interaction, learning is bidirectional. Infants learn about others by analogy to the self, but they also learn about themselves, their powers, and potential, through interaction with others. Parents and peers lead children to perform novel acts and gain self understanding that is not possible through independent discovery in social isolation (Meltzoff *et al.*, 1999).

References

Abravanel, E., & DeYong, N. G. (1991). Does object modeling elicit imitative-like gestures from young infants? *Journal of Experimental Child Psychology, 52*, 22–40.

Abravanel, E., & Sigafoos, A. D. (1984). Exploring the presence of imitation during early infancy. *Child Development, 55*, 381–392.

Barnat, S. B., Klein, P. J., & Meltzoff, A. N. (1996). Deferred imitation across changes in context and object: Memory and generalization in 14-month-old infants. *Infant Behavior and Development, 19*, 241–251.

Barr, R., Dowden, A., & Hayne, H. (1996). Developmental changes in deferred imitation by 6- to 24-month-old infants. *Infant Behavior and Development, 19*, 159–170.

Barr, R., & Hayne, H. (2000). Age-related changes in imitation: Implications for memory development. In C. Rovee-Collier, L. P. Lipsitt, & H. Hayne (Eds.), *Progress in infancy research* (Vol. 1, pp. 21–67). Mahwah, NJ: Ablex.

Bauer, P. J., & Wewerka, S. S. (1995). One- to two-year-olds' recall of events: The more expressed, the more impressed. *Journal of Experimental Child Psychology, 59*, 475–496.

Bekkering, H., Wohlschläger, A., & Gattis, M. (2000). Imitation of gestures in children is goal-directed. *Quarterly Journal of Experimental Psychology, 53A*, 153–164.

Berthouze, L., & Kuniyoshi, Y. (1998). Emergence and categorization of coordinated visual behavior through embodied interaction. *Machine Learning, 31*, 187–200.

Billard, A., & Dautenhahn, K. (2000). Experiments in social robotics–Grounding and use of communication in robotic agents. *Adaptive Behavior, 7*, 3–4.

Billard, A., Dautenhahn, K., & Hayes, G. (1998). *Experiments on human-robot communication with Roberta, an imitative learning and communicating doll robot.* Proceedings of "Socially Situated Intelligence" as part of Fifth International Conference of the Society for Adaptive Behavior '98, Zurich, Switzerland.

Blakemore, S.-J., & Decety, J. (2001). From the perception of action to the understanding of intention. *Nature Reviews Neuroscience, 2*, 561–567.

Bruner, J. S. (1999). The intentionality of referring. In P. D. Zelazo, J. W. Astington, & D. Olson (Eds.), *Development of intention and intentional understanding in infancy and early childhood* (pp. 329–339). Mahwah, NJ: Erlbaum.

Chaminade, T., Meltzoff, A. N., & Decety, J. (In press). Does the end justify the means? A PET exploration of the mechanisms involved in human imitation. *NeuroImage.*

Dautenhahn, K., & Nehaniv, C. (In press). *Imitation in animals and artifacts.* Cambridge, MA: MIT Press.

Dawson, G., Meltzoff, A. N., Osterling, J., & Rinaldi, J. (1998). Neuropsychological correlates of early symptoms of autism. *Child Development, 69*, 1276–1285.

de Boysson-Bardies, B., Halle, P., Sagart, L., & Durand, C. (1989). A crosslinguistic investigation of vowel formants in babbling. *Journal of Child Language, 16*, 1–17.

de Boysson-Bardies, B., Sagart, L., & Durand, C. (1984). Discernible differences in the babbling of infants according to target language. *Journal of Child Language, 11*, 1–15.

Decety, J., Chaminade, T., Grèzes, J., & Meltzoff, A. N. (In press). A PET exploration of the neural mechanisms involved in imitation. *NeuroImage.*

Decety, J., & Grèzes, J. (1999). Neural mechanisms subserving the perception of human actions. *Trends in Cognitive Sciences, 3*, 172–178.

Decety, J., Grèzes, J., Costes, N., Perani, D., Jeannerod, M., Procyk, E., Grassi, F., & Fazio, F. (1997). Brain activity during observation of actions: Influence of action content and subject's strategy. *Brain, 120*, 1763–1777.

Decety, J., Perani, D., Jeannerod, M., Bettinardi, V., Tadary, B., Woods, R., Mazziotta, J. C., & Fazio, F. (1994). Mapping motor representations with positron emission tomography. *Nature, 371*, 600–602.

Demiris, J., Rougeaux, S., Hayes, G. M., Berthouze, L., & Kuniyoshi, Y. (1997). Deferred imitation of human head movements by an active stereo vision head. *Proceedings of the 6th IEEE International Workshop on Robot and Human Communication* (Sept. 29–Oct. 1, Sendai, Japan).

Fadiga, L., Fogassi, L., Pavesi, G., & Rizzolatti, G. (1995). Motor facilitation during action observation: A magnetic stimulation study. *Journal of Neurophysiology, 73,* 2608–2611.

Field, T., Goldstein, S., Vaga-Lahr, N., & Porter, K. (1986). Changes in imitative behavior during early infancy. *Infant Behavior and Development, 9,* 415–421.

Field, T. M., Woodson, R., Cohen, D., Greenberg, R., Garcia, R., & Collins, E. (1983). Discrimination and imitation of facial expressions by term and preterm neonates. *Infant Behavior and Development, 6,* 485–489.

Field, T. M., Woodson, R., Greenberg, R., & Cohen, D. (1982). Discrimination and imitation of facial expressions by neonates. *Science, 218,* 179–181.

Flavell, J. H., & Miller, P. H. (1998). Social cognition. In W. Damon (Series Ed.), D. Kuhn & R. Siegler (Eds.), *Handbook of child psychology: Vol. 2. Cognition, perception, and language* (pp. 851–898). New York: John Wiley.

Fontaine, R. (1984). Imitative skills between birth and six months. *Infant Behavior and Development, 7,* 323–333.

Frith, C. D., & Frith, U. (1999). Interacting minds: A biological basis. *Science, 286,* 1692–1695.

Gallese, V., Fadiga, L., Fogassi, L., & Rizzolatti, G. (1996). Action recognition in the premotor cortex. *Brain, 119,* 593–609.

Gleissner, B., Meltzoff, A. N., & Bekkering, H. (2000). Children's coding of human action: Cognitive factors influencing imitation in 3-year-olds. *Developmental Science, 3,* 405–414.

Gopnik, A., & Meltzoff, A. N. (1997). *Words, thoughts, and theories.* Cambridge, MA: MIT Press.

Gopnik, A., Meltzoff, A. N., & Kuhl, P. K. (1999). *The scientist in the crib: Minds, brains, and how children learn.* New York: Morrow Press.

Green, K. P., Kuhl, P. K., Meltzoff, A. N., & Stevens, E. B. (1991). Integrating speech information across talkers, gender, and sensory modality: Female faces and male voices in the McGurk effect. *Perception and Psychophysics, 50,* 524–536.

Grèzes, J., & Decety, J. (2001). Functional anatomy of execution, mental simulation, observation, and verb generation of actions: A meta-analysis. *Human Brain Mapping, 12,* 1–19.

Grice, H. P. (1969). Utterer's meaning and intentions. *Philosophical Review, 78,* 147–177.

Hanna, E., & Meltzoff, A. N. (1993). Peer imitation by toddlers in laboratory, home, and day-care contexts: Implications for social learning and memory. *Developmental Psychology, 29,* 701–710.

Hayes, G., & Demiris, J. (1994). A robot controller using learning by imitation. Symposium conducted at the International Symposium on Intelligent Robotic Systems, Grenoble, France.

Heider, F. (1958). *The psychology of interpersonal relations.* New York: Wiley.

Heimann, M. (1989). Neonatal imitation, gaze aversion, and mother–infant interaction. *Infant Behavior and Development, 12,* 495–505.

Heimann, M., & Meltzoff, A. N. (1996). Deferred imitation in 9- and 14-month-old infants: A longitudinal study of a Swedish sample. *British Journal of Developmental Psychology, 14,* 55–64.

Heimann, M., Nelson, K. E., & Schaller, J. (1989). Neonatal imitation of tongue protrusion and mouth opening: Methodological aspects and evidence of early individual differences. *Scandinavian Journal of Psychology, 30*, 90–101.

Heimann, M., & Schaller, J. (1985). Imitative reactions among 14–21 day old infants. *Infant Mental Health Journal, 6*, 31–39.

Hockett, C. F. (1960). Logical considerations in the study of animal communication. In W. E. Lanyon & W. N. Tavolga (Eds.), *Animal sounds and communication* (pp. 392–430). Washington, DC: American Institute of Biological Sciences.

Howe, M. L., & Courage, M. L. (1993). On resolving the enigma of infantile amnesia. *Psychological Bulletin, 113*, 305–326.

Iacoboni, M., Woods, R. P., Brass, M., Bekkering, H., Mazziotta, J. C., & Rizzolatti, G. (1999). Cortical mechanisms of human imitation. *Science, 286*, 2526–2528.

Jacobson, S. W. (1979). Matching behavior in the young infant. *Child Development, 50*, 425–430.

Kahneman, D., Treisman, A., & Gibbs, B. J. (1992). The reviewing of object files: Object-specific integration of information. *Cognitive Psychology, 24*, 175–219.

Kaitz, M., Meschulach-Sarfaty, O., Auerbach, J., & Eidelman, A. (1988). A reexamination of newborn's ability to imitate facial expressions. *Developmental Psychology, 24*, 3–7.

Klein, P. J., & Meltzoff, A. N. (1999). Long-term memory, forgetting, and deferred imitation in 12-month-old infants. *Developmental Science, 2*, 102–113.

Kugiumutzakis, J. (1985). *Development of imitation during the first six months of life* (Uppsala Psychological Reports No. 377). Uppsala, Sweden: Uppsala University.

Kuhl, P. K. (2000). A new view of language acquisition. *Proceedings of the National Academy of Sciences, 97*, 11850–11857.

Kuhl, P. K., & Meltzoff, A. N. (1982). The bimodal perception of speech in infancy. *Science, 218*, 1138–1141.

(1984). The intermodal representation of speech in infants. *Infant Behavior and Development, 7*, 361–381.

(1996). Infant vocalizations in response to speech: Vocal imitation and developmental change. *Journal of the Acoustical Society of America, 100*, 2425–2438.

Kuhl, P. K., Tsao, F. M., Liu, H. M., Zhang, Y., & de Boer, B. (2001). Language/culture/mind/brain: Progress at the margins between disciplines. In A. R. Damasio *et al.* (Eds.), *Unity of knowledge: The convergence of natural and human science* (pp. 136–174). New York: The New York Academy of Sciences.

Kuhl, P. K., Williams, K. A., & Meltzoff, A. N. (1991). Cross-modal speech perception in adults and infants using nonspeech auditory stimuli. *Journal of Experimental Psychology: Human Perception and Performance, 17*, 829–840.

Legerstee, M. (1991). The role of person and object in eliciting early imitation. *Journal of Experimental Child Psychology, 51*, 423–433.

Leslie, A. M., Xu, F., Tremoulet, P. D., & Scholl, B. J. (1998). Indexing and the object concept: Developing "what" and "where" systems. *Trends in Cognitive Sciences, 2*, 10–18.

MacKain, K., Studdert-Kennedy, M., Spieker, S., & Stern, D. (1983). Infant intermodal speech perception is a left-hemisphere function. *Science, 219,* 1347–1349.

Maratos, O. (1982). Trends in the development of imitation in early infancy. In T. G. Bever (Ed.), *Regressions in mental development: Basic phenomena and theories* (pp. 81–101). Hillsdale, NJ: Erlbaum.

Mataric, M. J., & Pomplun, M. (1998). Fixation behavior in observation and imitation of human movement. *Cognitive Brain Research, 7,* 191–202.

McGurk, H., & MacDonald, J. (1976). Hearing lips and seeing voices. *Nature, 264,* 746–748.

Meltzoff, A. N. (1988a). Infant imitation after a 1-week delay: Long-term memory for novel acts and multiple stimuli. *Developmental Psychology, 24,* 470–476.

(1988b). Infant imitation and memory: Nine-month-olds in immediate and deferred tests. *Child Development, 59,* 217–225.

(1995a). Understanding the intentions of others: Re-enactment of intended acts by 18-month-old children. *Developmental Psychology, 31,* 838–850.

(1995b). What infant memory tells us about infantile amnesia: Long-term recall and deferred imitation. *Journal of Experimental Child Psychology, 59,* 497–515.

(1996). *Understanding intentions in infancy.* Paper delivered as part of an invited symposium entitled Children's theory of mind (A. Leslie, Chair), XXVI International Congress of Psychology, Montreal, Canada.

Meltzoff, A. N., Gopnik, A., & Repacholi, B. M. (1999). Toddlers' understanding of intentions, desires, and emotions: Explorations of the dark ages. In P. D. Zelazo, J. W. Astington, & D. R. Olson (Eds.), *Developing theories of intention: Social understanding and self control* (pp. 17–41). Mahwah, NJ: Erlbaum.

Meltzoff, A. N., & Moore, M. K. (1977). Imitation of facial and manual gestures by human neonates. *Science, 198,* 75–78.

(1983). Newborn infants imitate adult facial gestures. *Child Development, 54,* 702–709.

(1989). Imitation in newborn infants: Exploring the range of gestures imitated and the underlying mechanisms. *Developmental Psychology, 25,* 954–962.

(1992). Early imitation within a functional framework: The importance of person identity, movement, and development. *Infant Behavior and Development, 15,* 479–505.

(1994). Imitation, memory, and the representation of persons. *Infant Behavior and Development, 17,* 83–99.

(1995). Infants' understanding of people and things: From body imitation to folk psychology. In J. Bermúdez, A. J. Marcel, & N. Eilan (Eds.), *Body and the self* (pp. 43–69). Cambridge, MA: MIT Press.

(1997). Explaining facial imitation: A theoretical model. *Early Development and Parenting, 6,* 179–192.

(1998). Object representation, identity, and the paradox of early permanence: Steps toward a new framework. *Infant Behavior and Development, 21,* 201–235.

Perner, J. (1991). *Understanding the representational mind.* Cambridge, MA: MIT Press.

Piaget, J. (1952). *The origins of intelligence in children.* New York: International Universities Press.

(1954). *The construction of reality in the child.* New York: Basic Books.

(1962). *Play, dreams and imitation in childhood.* New York: Norton.

Prinz, W. (1990). A common coding approach to perception and action. In O. Neumann & W. Prinz (Eds.), *Relationships between perception and action* (pp. 167–201). Berlin: Springer-Verlag.

(1992). Why don't we perceive our brain states? *European Journal of Cognitive Psychology, 4,* 1–20.

Reissland, N. (1988). Neonatal imitation in the first hour of life: Observations in rural Nepal. *Developmental Psychology, 24,* 464–469.

Rizzolatti, G., Fadiga, L., Gallese, V., & Fogassi, L. (1996). Premotor cortex and the recognition of motor actions. *Cognitive Brain Research, 3,* 131–141.

Schaal, S. (1999). Is imitation learning the route to humanoid robots? *Trends on Cognitive Sciences, 3,* 233–242.

Schacter, D. L. (1996). *Searching for memory: The brain, the mind, and the past.* New York: Basic Books.

Squire, L. R., Knowlton, B., & Musen, G. (1993). The structure and organization of memory. *Annual Review of Psychology, 44,* 453–495.

Taylor, M. (1996). A theory of mind perspective on social cognitive development. In E. C. Carterette & M. P. Friedman (Series Eds.), R. Gelman & T. Au (Eds.), *Handbook of perception and cognition: Vol. 13. Perceptual and cognitive development* (pp. 283–329). New York: Academic Press.

Tomasello, M., & Call, J. (1997). *Primate cognition.* New York: Oxford University Press.

Vinter, A. (1986). The role of movement in eliciting early imitations. *Child Development, 57,* 66–71.

Walton, G. E., & Bower, T. G. R. (1993). Amodal representations of speech in infants. *Infant Behavior and Development, 16,* 233–243.

Wellman, H. M. (1990). *The child's theory of mind.* Cambridge, MA: MIT Press.

Wheeler, M. A., Stuss, D. T., & Tulving, E. (1997). Toward a theory of episodic memory: The frontal lobes and autonoetic consciousness. *Psychological Bulletin, 121,* 331–354.

Wilcox, T., & Baillargeon, R. (1998). Object individuation in infancy: The use of featural information in reasoning about occlusion events. *Cognitive Psychology, 37,* 97–155.

Xu, F., & Carey, S. (1996). Infants' metaphysics: The case of numerical identity. *Cognitive Psychology, 30,* 111–153.

2 Imitation and imitation recognition: Functional use in preverbal infants and nonverbal children with autism

Jacqueline Nadel

Introduction

Two options in developmental studies: search for precursors or search for adaptive behaviors

Early imitation is currently a major topic for developmentalists. They investigate its developmental role and elaborate models concerning the processes through which imitation may serve as a determinant building block for later cognitive and social development. Piaget (1945) consecrated this tradition, focusing on deferred imitation as a predictor of representational capacities. Recently, Meltzoff and Gopnik (1993) proposed the fascinating hypothesis that early imitation provides the means to elaborate human properties which will lead to a theory of the human mind. They see imitation as a machine to extract similarities, a *like-me mechanism* through which a neonate is supposed to draw equivalences between what she sees and what she does and vice versa, thus forming the concept of *like-me entities.*

While the predictive power of emerging imitative capacities is emphasized, and the cascading effect of their development is modeled, little attention is given to the functional use of these capacities by the developing child, in her everyday life. This information is crucial because the functional use of a behavior informs us about main developmental pathways, and especially about how the infant builds herself. Moreover, changes in functional use and transitory functional use of behaviors stress the nonlinear aspect of epigenesis, the flexibility of brain development and may be of help to understand the link between early behaviors of modern infants and ancestral behaviors of the human species in an evolutionary perspective.

My first aim in this chapter will be to highlight why a functionalist perspective is crucial for the study of imitation. I will show that the preverbal child uses imitation to initiate social exchanges and to respond to others' initiations, in short to communicate. In the second section of the chapter, I will analyze what notion of imitation and imitation detection is needed to account for the use of imitation as nonverbal language, and how far this "language" implies intentionality in self and other. Detection and monitoring of intentionality may be out of reach for the very young infant and also for some low-functioning children with autism. Finally, I will emphasize the developmental role of imitation as a semantic foundation for language development.

Imitation and the developing child

Preverbal children use imitation to communicate

In a series of experiments, we explored when and how children use imitation. To this aim, our studies were conducted in an interactive context without having an adult present. Dyads or triads of acquainted peer infants (who were not close friends) met in a setting furnished with two or three identical sets of ten attractive objects. The children were free to use the objects for solitary play, or in social games involving identical or different objects for cooperative or imitative purpose. Having filmed more than 150 children of different ages, we clearly found a predominant use of imitation during social exchanges after eighteen months with a peak of use around thirty months (Nadel, 1986). These imitations presented several characteristic features: they followed conventional rules, they were reciprocal, and they involved referential use of objects. Let us detail how.

In all triads and dyads, two "routines" invariably preceded the start of an imitative episode. One routine was for an infant to offer (or show) to another infant an object similar to the one s/he held. The partner most often took the object and imitated its use. Sometimes however s/he refused the initiator's suggestion. In these cases the initiator left the object s/he held and turned to imitate the partner's ongoing activity. An alternative routine was for an infant to directly start imitating another infant, using an identical object in the same way, without any request of the imitatee. The imitatee soon noticed being imitated and further proposed new instrumental activities to the imitator. From this we can conclude that primary conventional rules monitor and control imitative social exchanges, and regulate turn-taking and role-switching. Such a regulation is very efficient, even in triadic meetings where there are only two roles for three persons: in these cases indeed the number of times children imitated and the number of times they were imitated remained highly and positively correlated (Nadel-Brulfert & Baudonnière, 1982). Obviously the children found it as interesting to be an imitator as to be a model. Further studies with repeated meetings of the same partners led us to understand that imitations act like primary scripts: they convey

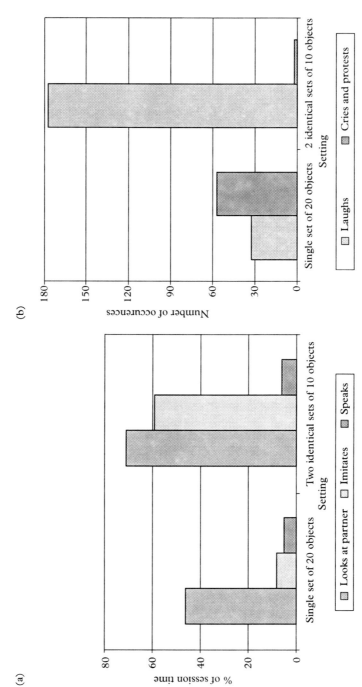

Figure 2.1. (a) Attention according to instrumental imitation availability (b) Emotions according to instrumental imitation availability

shared attention to the same topic through a similar use of similar objects as co-referents (Nadel, Guérini, Pezé, & Rivet, 1999).

In sum, we found that when children use imitation in their social exchanges, they can take turns, switch roles, share topics and apply conventional rules, thus, they can communicate. Later observations in naturalistic settings like preschool playgrounds persuaded us that our results reflect an effective everyday use of imitation as a way to communicate. Eckerman's data in naturalistic settings (Eckerman, 1993) corroborated these informal observations.

Our next finding was that the communicative function of imitation is transitory and disappears when language is mastered. This was demonstrated in an experiment in which dyads of two-year-olds and dyads of three-year-olds met either in a setting with two identical sets of ten objects or in a setting with a single set of twenty objects. Results did not show any setting effect for the three-year-olds who, regardless of setting, identical or single objects for cooperative but not imitative purposes (Nadel & Fontaine, 1989). By contrast, there was a strong setting effect for the two-year-olds, who significantly gazed less at their partners, engaged less frequently and for shorter durations in interactive episodes and laughed far less when they met in a setting with single objects rather than in a setting with identical objects (see Fig. 2.1). Interestingly, the preverbal children did not imitate their partners during the meeting with single objects. Indeed in this setting they could not synchronize their instrumental activity with the imitatee's, since there was only one object of each kind for two children. Of course the children had the opportunity to imitate body movements which do not involve objects, but we did not observe such imitations. It was as if two similar objects were needed to *afford* imitation, just as specific objects *afford* specific actions. This is not to say that all the actions imitated were already part of the imitator's repertoire.

The analysis of hundreds of imitations resulted in the distinction of two categories of matching: matching of familiar instrumental activities such as <put the sunglasses on nose>, and matching of a new procedural use of a familiar object, such as <put the sunglasses around the ears like earrings>, or <use the umbrella as a stick to conduct a concert>, or <walk with an upside-down chair above head> etc. (see Fig. 2.2). Strikingly, preverbal infants imitated novel actions as quickly and easily as familiar ones, and achieved an almost perfect temporal synchronism if an imperfect morphological matching. The temporal synchronism, I should add, was also monitored by the imitatee, who often slowed down the ongoing instrumental activity and waited for the imitator, when necessary.

Now the question is to know which are the prerequisites for this amazing ballet between two or three children who alternate roles, take turns,

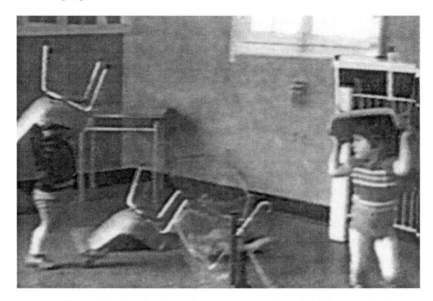

Figure 2.2. During imitative exchanges, infants inhibit learned schemes and imitate unexpected use of objects

coordinate their activities in time and in topic and follow conventional rules (see Fig. 2.3 for a summary). Is this ballet the sophisticated achievement of early developing socio-cognitive capacities? Is it the origin of more sophisticated communicative capacities?

The imitative language and the developing mind

The imitative language: a functional achievement of the "like-me mechanism"?

Maybe the more striking aspect of the imitative language is the communicative value of similarity (you do like me and I do like you). Obviously it shares common features with the innate *like-me mechanism* hypothesized by Meltzoff and Gopnik (1993) as mapping out (cross-modal) equivalences between *"movements-as-felt and the movements* [··] *performed by others"* (1993: 336) from birth on. Persons are *like-me entities* in so far as they can do like me (when they imitate me) and I can do like them (when I imitate them).

Similarly, in our description of the imitative system, imitator and imitatee have interchangeable roles acting out the same intention: being alike

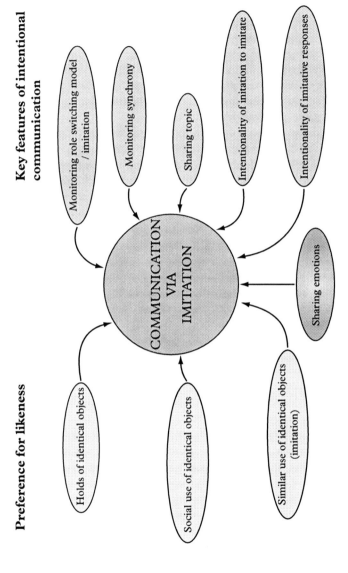

Preference for likeness

Key features of intentional communication

Monitoring role switching model / imitation

Monitoring synchrony

Sharing topic

Intentionality of imitation to imitate

Intentionality of imitative responses

COMMUNICATION VIA IMITATION

Sharing emotions

Holds of identical objects

Social use of identical objects

Similar use of identical objects (imitation)

Figure 2.3. The imitative language

(Nadel, 1986). Given this, it is very tempting to propose that the imitative system of communication is the functional achievement of the *like-me mechanism*. As a starting-point stage, and before the effective use of the imitative system, the *like-me mechanism* would generate implicit awareness of being imitated and unintentional imitation. Indeed, in the description of the *like-me mechanism*, imitation and imitation recognition are tightly linked as two facets of the same innate capacity to test structural similarities between self and other persons. Neonates are thus supposed to be not only imitators but also imitation recognizers. To date, however, if neonatal imitation is well documented, it is more difficult to assume that neonates have an implicit awareness of being imitated. Let us consider these elements more precisely.

It is now well established that neonates are imitators. The pioneer work by Maratos (1973) and the seminal studies published by Meltzoff and Moore (1977, 1983) opened new avenues which led to a spurt of exciting and converging researches in the field (Heimann, this volume; Fontaine, 1984; Kugiumutzakis, 1993). Newborns are not only able to imitate facial movements such as tongue protrusion, or mouth opening, they also imitate facial expressions (Field, Woodson, Greenberg, & Cohen, 1982), eye blinking, and vocal sounds (Kugiumutzakis, 1993, 1999). Whenever newborns produce imitation, they produce social contingency. The enthusiastic reaction of parents when they see their infant imitating a tongue protrusion or an eye blinking is a very convincing index of the fact that imitation is probably the unique signal of social contingency available for parents at birth.

Since newborns are imitators, we could intuitively reason that they are also imitation recognizers. This intuitive reasoning is based on the postulate that the detection of matched behavior (detection of an equivalence between what we do and what we see) requires the same capacity that the production of matched behavior (production of an equivalence between what we see and what we do). There is a large body of psychological and neuroimaging experiments that have demonstrated that perception of action shares some common neural and cognitive mechanisms with action generation, action simulation, action recognition and, to some extent, action imitation (Decety, this volume; for a review, see Decety & Grèzes, 1999). On the basis of these data, neuroscientists have proposed the concept of shared motor representations (Georgieff & Jeannerod, 1998). How this concept relates to neonatal imitation is of major interest. Indeed, primary imitations may be viewed as wired perceptual-motor coupling (Decety & Ingvar, 1990; Jeannerod, 1997), resulting from the activation of neural centers controlling movements, which Rizzolatti and colleagues metaphorically name a low-level resonance mechanism (Rizzolatti, Fadiga, Fogassi, & Gallese, this volume). Maybe such a simple mechanism can also explain early recognition of being imitated (or at least early detection of redundant information between what is done and what is seen). However there is an important difference in the social consequences of the two phenomena: early imitation can unintentionally convey a message of social contingency (*I act like you*), while imitation recognition will deliver a message of social contingency if and only if the infant *signals* that she has recognized being imitated and thus that she has attributed intentional imitation to the imitator (*I notice that you act like me*). This would lead me to predict later empirical evidence of imitation recognition than of imitation. And as a matter of fact, we have no demonstration that neonates detect imitation. The imitative newborn, however, is sensitive to temporal contingency between events (Blass, Ganchrow & Steiner, 1984), and after a few weeks, infants can form expectancies for social contingency.

Early detection of nonimitative and imitative contingency

Six-week-old infants react negatively to an experimental violation of social responsiveness by the mother posing a still face during a live interaction (Murray & Trevarthen, 1985; Tronick et al., 1978), or in a televised face-to-face interaction (Gusella, Muir, & Tronick, 1988; see Muir & Nadel, 1998 for a review). Similarly they withdraw when they are presented with a smiling and communicative but noncontingent mother (Murray & Trevarthen, 1985; Nadel et al., 1999).[1] Since mere temporal contingency is detected so early, structural similarities plus temporal contingency should be detected even more easily.

Of course, it is possible, as suggested by Meltzoff and Moore (1999), that there is a precocious implicit awareness of being imitated although there is no clear evidence of early specific responses to imitation. Implicit awareness is supposed to be captured by the increase of attention to the imitator. Stern (1977) and also Trevarthen and Hubley (1978) pointed to the early use of imitation by mothers as a strategy to attract and maintain their infants' attention. With older infants, Field (1977) found more gaze to mother when the mother imitated her 32-week-old than when she interacted in another way. Does this reflect imitation recognition? Specific social responses to maternal imitation would be more convincing indices than gaze.

To explore this question, we used a televised face-to-face design with mothers and their two-month-olds. Mothers were asked to get in touch and keep contact with their infants via a TV closed-circuit device. The face-to-face interaction lasted two minutes. Our first results with thirteen dyads show that ten of the thirteen infants imitated their mother's facial expressions, head postures, and hand movements. Eleven mothers imitated their infant, some of them very frequently, others scarcely. All eleven infants who were imitated reacted at some of the maternal imitations: we gathered 35 responses for 76 imitations. 40 per cent of the responses were focal looks at the mother. Only three infants used uniquely these very basic and nonspecific responses. The other 60 per cent of responses were social signals associating look at the mother with smile ($n = 18$) and/or tonguing or vocalizing ($n = 18$). Six of the eleven infants displayed such social signals whenever their mother imitated them. These results suggest that two-month-olds perceive their being imitated as a contingent social behavior to which they give a social answer (Nadel, 2000). Whether they detect a difference between imitative behaviors and other social behaviors of their mother deserves further examination, but it is a likely assumption if we follow Rochat and Striano (1999) who report that two-month-olds are sensitive to the form of their own action.

With three-month-olds, Uzgiris, Vase, and Benson (1984) found maternal imitation in 20 per cent of free interactive episodes, which is less than what we found with younger infants. It is reasonable to assume that the televised device that we used is a strong elicitor of eye-to-eye contact and is thus particularly propitious to imitative episodes. Uzgiris *et al.* report 12 per cent of two-round episodes where either the infant or the mother imitated in return. These data suggest that imitating in return is possibly the first specific response to imitation, which can be found at three months and even earlier (one of our two-month-olds showed imitations in return). This suggestion is strengthened by recent findings demonstrating that infants after three months are capable of differentiating between a live video feed-back of their movements and a delayed feed-back of their own moving legs. The three-month-olds preferred the on-line feed-back while the five-month-olds were more interested in the deferred feed-back (Bahrick & Watson, 1985; Rochat and Morgan, 1995; Schmuckler, 1996). This interesting finding suggests that five-month-olds have already formed primary representation of the bodily self and orient preferentially their attention toward external stimuli rather than toward overlapping self-produced ones (see Rochat, this volume). This may encourage one to predict that signaling imitation recognition would start being effective in young infants around five months as a phenomenon that Trevarthen *et al.* beautifully name "a translation between the affordances of proprioception and *alteroception*" (Trevarthen, Kokkinaki, and Fiamenghi, 1999: 136).

Specific responses signaling imitation recognition

To date, there is no valid demonstration of imitation awareness before fourteen months. Indeed, using a cross-target method, Meltzoff (1990) demonstrated that fourteen-month-olds prefer an imitative adult to a nonimitative adult, even when both behave contingently. The contingent imitator received more gaze and smile, and more testing behaviors aimed at checking whether the adult was intentionally imitating them. In more naturalistic conditions, Asendorpf, Werkentin, and Baudonnière (1996) showed that most but not all eighteen-month-olds reciprocate imitation, which may account for an explicit signal of imitation recognition. Similarly Eckerman (1993) demonstrated that being imitated prompts further imitation of the peer imitator in eighteen- to 24-month-olds.

In sum, we have drawn the picture of a very young infant who is able not only to detect noncontingency but also to expect contingent behavior from close partners and who is able to produce imitations long before she demonstrates explicit imitation recognition. Even if she has an implicit awareness of being imitated, she does not signal it and this awareness cannot be taken into account by others. She is thus able to take turns via imitation but not to turn roles. Some low-functioning children with autism appear to present the same pattern.

Imitation in low-functioning children with autism

When we read the literature concerning autism, it seems to be already established that children with autism have imitative impairments. Clinical researchers however mostly use imitation in their everyday practice to get in touch and maintain contact with those children, and they report that many of them are frequent imitators and/or appreciate being imitated. As a matter of fact, whether or not autistic children have specific imitative impairments is currently a controversial topic among psychopathologists.

The three main models aimed at accounting for the core developmental symptoms of autism are in striking disagreement on this matter. In Hobson's (1986) emotional theory of autism, imitative impairments are a secondary consequence of primary emotional disabilities. Baron-Cohen, Leslie, and Frith (1985) propose a simulation of autism in which pragmatic capacities related to the construction of a theory of mind are deficient, but primary social capacities (including immediate imitation) are intact, given the cognitive developmental level of the child. In contrast, Rogers and Pennington (1991) provide a model of the potential cascade effects on social development of a primary deficit in motor imitation from the beginnings of life. Rogers recently wrote that "studies published since

1991 have not disconfirmed Rogers and Pennington's hypothesis" (1999: 278). Rogers' argument relies on the fact that several studies have theorized (Donald, 1991) or documented (Dawson & Adams, 1984; Nadel & Pezé, 1993, Tiegerman & Primavera, 1984) a linkage between imitation and other social skills. However this does not validate the hypothesis of a primary and specific impairment of imitative capacities. Studies comparing autistic children and mentally deficient children matched on mental age give contradictory findings: some report significantly lower performances of children with autism, while others cannot differentiate autistic performances from MA matched ones (Charman & Baron-Cohen, 1994; Whiten & Brown, 1999). Other authors found imitation impairments in some autistic subgroups but not in all (Adrien *et al.*, 1987).

An interesting new perspective is to focus the concern on the description of imitative abilities and disabilities in autism rather than on the demonstration of the specificity and primacy of possible imitative impairments. In fact, several authors have found imitative deficits in different developmental disorders, including Down's Syndrome and other forms of mental retardation. If we follow Smith and Bryson (1994), imitation may be diagnostic of basic problems in the domain of action development rather than a basic impairment *per se*. In addition, we do not know enough about motor productions in children with autism, except that they are poor and infrequent, as poor and infrequent as imitations are. For instance, in three follow-ups, we found that imitative performance was at a higher level than spontaneous motor production (Nadel & Pezé, 1992).

Contradictory results also reflect the heterogeneity of the procedures used (clinical evaluations of imitative level, imitative scores in neuropsychological tasks, experimental designs, interactive designs) and the absence of a clear definition of the type of imitation explored: symbolic versus concrete, immediate versus deferred, simple versus complex, to which we can add imitation of action versus imitation of goal (Byrne & Russon, 1998), and spontaneous versus induced imitation. Studies generally focus on induced imitation rather than on spontaneous imitations which take place in a social context and may have a communicative meaning. It follows that careful investigations of the use of imitation by children with autism are very infrequent. For instance, there is only a handful of studies using an interactive design to investigate imitation, although most researchers in the field now consider imitation as a main component of social cognition (cf. Rogers, 1999; Rogers, Bennetto, McEvoy, & Pennington, 1996; Dawson, Meltzoff, Osterling, & Rinaldi, 1998; Meltzoff & Moore, 1999).

Our experiments, all conducted in a context of free social interaction, have shown that nonverbal children with autism – even very low-functioning children – mostly produce spontaneous imitations when meeting a nonautistic child (Nadel & Pezé, 1993) or a playful adult (Escalona, Nadel, Field, & Lundy, in press). The imitations produced concern either familiar or novel gestures, they are simple gestural matching or imitations of goal-directed actions involving objects. They are a good predictor of social capacities (Nadel & Pezé, 1993). Do all these imitative children also recognize being imitated?

Implicit and explicit recognition of being imitated in low-functioning children with autism

Children with autism are said to be impaired in imitation but able to recognize being imitated. This classical claim, however, is difficult to validate in the absence of a clear definition of what is called imitation recognition. Dawson and Adams (1984), and Tiegerman and Primavera (1981, 1984) found an increase of positive attention to the experimenter and an increase of object manipulation when the experimenter imitates the autistic child's procedural use of a similar object. Does this account for imitation recognition? Even if the children improved their social behavior, they did not address any explicit signal of imitation recognition to their partners, nor did they show any specific response to imitation compared to other social behaviors. We face the same kind of problem with our two-month-olds who look and smile to their imitative mother just the way they smile and look to their nonimitative mother.

In search of a reliable index of imitation recognition, we conducted a study where 25 low-functioning children with autism, all occasional or frequent imitators, met an unfamiliar adult who imitated systematically during three minutes any of their instrumental and stereotypic gestures as well as their meaningless or meaningful postures. To explore their capacity to recognize that they are imitated, we measured their gaze behavior during the experimenter's imitation. Alternations of gaze to their own object and gaze to the experimenter's activity with the identical object were considered as an index of imitation recognition (see Fig. 2.4). We found that only twelve out of the 25 children used such gaze strategies. Some of the others sometimes looked briefly at the adult as by chance, others did not seem to notice the experimenter's activity (Nadel & Bottai, 1999). These findings are in agreement with developmental data: like very young infants, some low-functioning children with autism are able to imitate (at least very simple gestures), but they do not show specific signals of imitation recognition. It remains of course to precisely define which kind of imitation and which kind of imitation recognition were assessed.

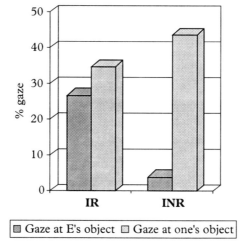

Figure 2.4. Gaze behaviors of children with autism facing an imitative adult. *IR* = children classified, as imitation recognizers. *INR* = children classified as non-recognizers.

Let us try to distinguish several levels of imitation and imitation recognition. At a low level of functioning, children with autism, like newborns, may produce perception-action coupling and imitate movements that they see without an explicit intention to do so. Furthermore, intentional imitation may involve no awareness that the imitated behavior is itself intentional. In contrast, at a higher level, imitative behavior is informed by the intention to do as the others intend to do. An even higher level is distinguished by Roessler (1999), when imitation is informed by the intention to do as the others intend for me to do (communicative imitation).

Imitation recognition also deserves several levels. A very simple level of imitation recognition does not imply attribution to the imitator an intention to imitate. Higher levels of recognition imply such an attribution and require understanding the imitator as an intentional agent planning to imitate your behavior. Hence the behavioral strategies to test the imitator (Meltzoff, 1995). Finally, we might talk of recognition of communicative imitation when the model understands the partner's imitation as caused by the intention to conform to what the model intends him/her to do. We found this kind of imitation recognition around 24 months.

In a recent study (Nadel, Field, & Potier, 2000), we explored other behaviors which may account for active testing strategies. 27 children with autism aged three to seven, with different cognitive levels, were shown a large variety of movements and actions which they were either requested to imitate or not. Alternately some of their movements and actions were emphatically imitated. All the children with autism were able to imitate something. For imitation recognition, we coded six possible responses: *shows no reaction; looks at the experimenter; looks at the experimenter plus gives a social signal* (smile, touch, offering); *alternates looks to the experimenter's object and looks to his/her object; tests the experimenter's intention to imitate* (changes action and/or object while looking at the experimenter); *tests the experimenter's intention to imitate what the child wants her to imitate* (proposes weird uses of objects, makes faces while performing, etc.). We found that only five children were able to recognize intentional communicative imitation, while the majority of children showed social signals which may account for imitation recognition without an understanding of the imitator's intention to imitate.

The imitative language: intentional primitives

Imitation recognition is a necessary condition for the infant to understand the other's imitation as intentional, but it is not sufficient to form expectancies for intentional imitation as a general feature of human beings (i.e. *here is somebody like me*, in Meltzoff and Gopnik's (1993) terms). Comparing the contingency preference of two-year-old infants and of MA matched children with autism, Gergely and Watson (1999) recently reported an interesting finding: the two-year-olds preferred an imitative contingency of their hand movements to a perfect computer-generated contingency, while children with autism preferred the perfect contingency.

My contention is that healthy infants were more interested in imperfect contingency because it met their expectancies for agency. They had already formed generalized expectancies for human social behaviors which include an awareness of the fact that social contingency is never perfect (Bigelow, 1999). What is important in the contingent imitation is not the quality of imitation but the human intentionality that imitation conveys. A computer-generated perfect contingency does not meet expectancies for human intentional contingency. Therefore, only children who cannot form this kind of expectancies will prefer the more perfect matching. Although they can perceive and expect social contingency after prior exposure, I shall argue, children with autism cannot expect contingency as a general property of human behavior.

One test of this claim is the reaction of low-functioning and nonverbal children with autism to a modified version of the Still Face paradigm

(Nadel *et al.* 2000). In this pilot study, each child met a stranger during a nine-minute session composed of 3 three-minute episodes including a first Still Face episode (SF1) followed by an Imitative Interaction, followed by a second Still Face episode (SF2), acted by a stranger. The eight children ignored the stranger and did not show much (or even not any) concern about her still behavior during Still Face 1. Six minutes later, however, during Still Face 2, the children showed contingency awareness and reacted to the violation of contingency. Indeed, the strong differences in autistic social behaviors that were found between the two Still Face conditions suggest that the adult had to prove to be a human being before some social expectancies can take place.

This contrasts strongly with the reactions of three-year-olds who refused from the start to stay alone in the room with the still stranger. Even five- to six-month-old babies are able to form a generalized expectancy that strangers will initially engage them in reciprocal interactions. When the stranger failed to do so in a noncontingent episode, visual attention and positive facial expression decreased (Hains & Muir, 1996). Similarly, Reyes, Striano, and Rochat (1998) showed that six-month-olds explored the still stranger more compared to a lively stranger. This result accounts for precocious expectancies about human behavior: infants as young as six months expect that human beings – even strangers – will behave in a particular way. Our results suggest that low-functioning children with autism do not form these generalized expectancies, even if they can expect imitative contingency after prior exposure to an imitative partner.

Some consequences follow. Indeed, if a child is able to develop expectancies for imitation, s/he is also able to monitor her/his being imitated by others. S/he is not only capable of recognizing when s/he is imitated and indicating that s/he understands imitation as a social signal, but s/he also can plan being imitated and signal to the partner her/his intention/desire to be imitated. S/he thus knows that the partner is able to understand an incitation to imitate. The socio-cognitive revolution of the nine-month-old, as Tomasello (1999) calls the remarkable social changes which occur when children start interacting about objects and understanding persons as agents, provides the means of an intentional use of imitation, of an explicit awareness of being imitated, and of generalized expectancies for intentional imitation. Why does the imitative system appear so late in the course of the second year? Maybe now it is time to analyze further the capacities required to take part as an imitator in the imitative system of communication.

The observation of a partner performing a familiar action with the appropriate object requires one to code the actions performed and plan complex imitations. However, as said earlier (see pp. 45–6 and Fig. 2.2), when they communicate via imitation, the infants imitated not only familiar actions but also a novel, unconventional and often funny use of familiar objects. They were thus able to inhibit the activation of learned actions and automatic schemes afforded by the familiar objects, and, following step by step the new motor procedure they saw, perform a novel action without an understanding of the imitatee's goal. Note that this looks exactly opposite to the results reported by Meltzoff (1995) at about the same age. In Meltzoff's experiment, eighteen-month-olds violated literal imitation when the modeling procedure failed to attend the end. I do not think, however, that these two reports are contradictory. In Meltzoff's study, the infants were able to activate a learned scheme at a program level and inhibit motor imitation at the action level (Byrne & Russon, 1998). In our studies, infants could inhibit the expected goal so as to perform literal imitation of weird actions, against cultural learning. In both cases the infants had to understand the model's intention and to use imitation accordingly: in Meltzoff's experiment, the adult intended to achieve a given action, in our experiments the peer partner intended to monitor the infant's activity in an unexpected way.

To use intentional imitation efficiently in social exchanges, the imitator has another intentional task to fulfill: s/he has to coordinate turn-taking and role-switching with the partner, sometimes agreeing with the role of imitator that the partner assigns to her/him, and sometimes refusing the role and suggesting to the model, through the routine of offering an identical object, to imitate her/him in return.

Final comments

Imitation as a language: a developmental role for a transitory function?

Imitation, imitation monitoring and public recognition of being imitated allow preverbal children to communicate with preverbal children during long-lasting episodes – a performance that they cannot achieve with other communicative means. The imitative language however, as a late achievement of the *like-me mechanism*, needs some cognitive and meta-cognitive ingredients such as the capacities to attribute intentions to the imitator, to plan and induce imitative behaviors, to understand incitation to imitate, to negotiate turn-taking and role-switching. These capacities are not to be found before eighteen months, and some low-functioning children with autism do not seem to benefit from (or at least to exploit) such capacities. If we add that the use of the imitative language is restricted to preverbal children addressing preverbal children and that it is a transitory system that vanishes when verbal language is mastered, we could then question whether or not this language has a developmental role.

Via imitation, infants can sustain long social exchanges and share intentions that can be fulfilled here and now. It is a powerful language which begins when the infant is around eighteen months, evolves in complex and coded combinations of imitating and being imitated throughout the two following years, and disappears when verbal language is mastered. Such a developmental curve suggests that imitative language prepares verbal language. Via imitation and recognition/monitoring of being imitated, young imitative minds can have common topics based on similar actions with similar objects, and they can take conversational turns. Via imitation and recognition/monitoring of being imitated, older imitative minds can share pretend play and memories of pretend events (Nadel *et al.*, 1999) and they can see themselves as part of a shared project.

Infants can do all this without words, on the basis of their felt likeliness, especially when they perform similar actions with similar objects. Turn-taking, topic-sharing, understanding the other's intentions, negotiating shared goals through codes and routines, all these features of verbal language are prepared by the use of the imitative system. The imitative language can therefore be seen as a semantic foundation for verbal language, in the way in which Donald (1991) describes the mimetic stage of humankind, compared to the stage of spoken language. Like the mimetic stage, the imitative stage of communication adds a representational dimension to imitation. It allows children to represent events, roles, and pretend goals and actions. And overall, it is a way to give an effective meaning to self and others' intentionality in motor actions. It is a self-sufficient, sophisticated tool for thought without verbal language. Most fascinating is that it is a transitory communicative system. Soon after the mastery of words, children will start avoiding imitation as mockery, thus indicating that imitation no longer sub-serves communication nor does it scaffold the understanding of intentionality.

Note

1 Rochat, Neisser, and Marian (1998) did not replicate Murray and Trevarthen's results. However they studied older infants and overall they compared the infants' responses to two different episodes of maternal communication, while Murray and Trevarthen, and Nadel *et al.* compared the same maternal episode, once on line and the second deferred.

References

Adrien, J.-L., Ornitz, E., Barthélémy, C., Sauvage, D., & Lelord, G. (1987). The presence or absence of certain behaviors associated with infantile autism in severely retarded autistic and non-autistic retarded children and very young children. *Journal of Autism and Developmental Disorders, 17 (3)*, 407–416.

American Psychiatric Association (1996). *Diagnostic criteria from DSM-IV.* Washington, DC: APA.

Asendorpf, J. B., Werkentin, V., & Baudonnière, P. M. (1996). Self-Awareness and other-awareness II: Mirror self-recognition, social contingency awareness, and synchronic imitation. *Developmental Psychology, 32 (2)*, 313–321.

Baron-Cohen, S., Leslie, A., & Frith, U. (1985). Does the autistic child have a "theory of mind"? *Cognition, 21*, 37–46.

Bahrick, L. S., & Watson, J. S. (1985). Detection of intermodal proprioceptive-visual contingency as a potential basis of self-perception in infancy. *Developmental Psychology, 21*, 963–973.

Bigelow, A. (1999). Infant's sensitivity to imperfect contingency in social interaction. In P. Rochat (Ed.), *Early social cognition* (pp. 137–154). Hillsdale, NJ: Erlbaum.

Blass, E. M., Ganchrow, J. R., & Steiner, J. E. (1984). Classical conditioning in newborn humans 2–48 hours of age. *Infant Behavior and Development, 7 (2)*, 223–235.

Byrne, R. W., & Russon, A. E. (1998). Learning by imitation: A hierarchical approach. *Behavioral and Brain Sciences, 21*, 667–721.

Charman, T., & Baron-Cohen, S. (1994). Another look at imitation in autism. *Development and Psychopathology, 6*, 404–413.

Dawson, G., & Adams, A. (1984). Imitation and social responsiveness in autistic children. *Journal of Abnormal Child Psychology, 12*, 209–226.

Dawson, G., Meltzoff, A. N., Osterling, J., & Rinaldi, J. (1998). Neuropsychological correlates of early symptoms of autism. *Child Development, 69*, 1276–1285.

Decety, J. (1996). Do imagined and executed actions share the same neural substrate? *Cognitive Brain Research, 3*, 87–93.

Decety, J., & Ingvar, D. H. (1990). Brain structures participating in mental simulation of motor behavior: A neuropsychological interpretation. *Acta Psychologica, 73*, 13–34.

Decety, J., & Grèzes, J. (1999). Neural mechanisms sub serving the perception of human actions. *Trends in Cognitive Sciences, 3*, 172–178.

Donald, M. (1991). *Origins of the modern mind.* Cambridge, MA: Harvard University Press.

Eckerman, C. (1993). Imitation and toddlers' achievement of co-ordinated action with others. In J. Nadel & L. Camaioni (Eds.), *New perspectives in early communicative development* (pp. 116–138). London: Routledge.

Escalona, A., Nadel, J., Field, F., & Lundy, B. (in press). Imitation effects on children with autism. *Journal of Autism and Developmental Disorders.*

Field, T. M. (1977). Effects of early separation, interactive deficits, and experimental manipulations on infant-mother face-to-face interaction. *Child Development, 48*, 763–771.

Field, T. M., Woodson, R. W., Greenberg, R., & Cohen, C. (1982). Discrimination and imitation of facial expressions by neonates. *Science, 218*, 179–181.

Fontaine, R. (1984). Imitative skills between birth and six months. *Infant Behavior and Development, 7,* 323–333.

Georgieff, N., & Jeannerod, M. (1998). Beyond consciousness of external reality: A who system for consciousness of action and self-consciousness. *Consciousness and Cognition, 7,* 465–477.

Gergely, G., & Watson, J. S. (1999). Infant's sensitivity to imperfect contingency in social interaction. In P. Rochat (Ed.), *Early social cognition* (pp. 101–136). Hillsdale, NJ: Erlbaum.

Gusella, J., Muir, D., & Tronick, E. (1988). The effect of manipulating maternal behavior during an interaction on three- and six-month-olds' affect and attention. *Child Development, 4,* 1111–1124.

Hains, S., & Muir, D. (1996). Effects of stimulus contingency in infant–adult interactions. *Infant Behavior and Development, 19,* 49–61.

Hobson, R. P. (1986). The autistic child's appraisal of expressions of emotions: A further study. *Journal of Child Psychology and Psychiatry, 27,* 321–342.

Jeannerod, M. (1997). *The cognitive neuroscience of action.* Oxford: Blackwell.

Kanner, L. (1943). Autistic disturbances of affective contact. *Nervous Child, 2,* 217–250.

Kugiumutzakis, G. (1993). Intersubjective vocal imitation in early mother–infant interaction. In J. Nadel & L. Camaioni (Eds.), *New perspectives in early communicative development* (pp. 23–47). London: Routledge.

(1999). Genesis and development of early infant mimesis to facial and vocal models. In J. Nadel & G. Butterworth (Eds.), *Imitation in infancy* (pp. 36–59). Cambridge: Cambridge University Press.

Maratos, O. (1973). *The origin and development of imitation in the first six months of the life.* Paper presented at the British Psychological Society Annual Meeting, Liverpool.

Meltzoff, A. N. (1990). Foundations for developing a concept of self: The role of imitation in relating self to other and the value of social mirroring, social modelling, and self-practice in infancy. In D. Cicchetti & M. Beeghly (Eds.), *The self in transition* (pp. 139–164). Chicago: University of Chicago Press.

(1995). Understanding the intentions in others: Re-enactment of intended acts by 18-month-old children. *Developmental Psychology, 31,* 838–850.

Meltzoff, A. N., & Gopnik, A. (1993). The role of imitation in understanding persons and developing a theory of mind. In S. Baron-Cohen, H. Flusberg & D. Cohen (Eds.), *Understanding other minds* (pp. 335–366). Oxford: Oxford University Press.

Meltzoff, A. N., & Moore, M. K. (1977). Imitation of facial and manual gestures by human neonates. *Science, 198,* 75–78.

(1983). Newborn infants imitate adult facial gestures. *Child Development, 54,* 702–709.

(1999). Persons and representation: Why infant imitation is important for theories of human development. In J. Nadel & G. Butterworth (Eds.), *Imitation in infancy* (pp. 9–35). Cambridge: Cambridge University Press.

Muir, D. W., & Nadel, J. (1998). Infant social perception. In A. Slater (Ed.), *Perceptual development: Visual, auditory, and speech perception in infancy* (pp. 247–285). Hove, UK: Psychology Press Ltd, Publishers.

Murray, L., & Trevarthen, C. (1985). Emotional regulation of interaction between two-month-olds and their mothers. In T. M. Field & N. A. Fox (Eds.), *Social perception in infants* (pp. 177–197). Norwood, NJ: Ablex.

Nadel, J. (1986). *Imitation et communication entre jeunes enfants.* Paris: PUF.

(2000). *Very young infants detection of imitation.* Paper presented at the ICIS 2000, Brighton.

Nadel-Brulfert, J., & Baudonnière, P. M. (1982). The social function of reciprocal imitation in 2-year-old peers. *International Journal of Behavioral Development, 5*, 95–109.

Nadel, J., & Bottai, B. (1999). *Imitation and touch in communication with autistic children.* Paper presented at The Annual Touch Research Symposium, SRCD, Albuquerque.

Nadel, J., Carchon, I., Kervella, C., Marcelli, D., & Réserbat-Plantey, D. (1999). Expectancies for social contingency in 2-month-olds. *Developmental Science, 2*, 164–174.

Nadel, J., Croué, S., Mattlinger, M.-J., Canet, P., Hudelot, C., Lécuyer, C., & Martini, M. (2000). Do autistic children have expectancies about the social behaviour of unfamiliar people?: A pilot study with the still face paradigm. *Autism, 2*, 133–145.

Nadel, J., Field, T., & Potier, C. (2000). *Imitation recognition as a communicative skill in low-functioning children with autism.* Paper presented at the ICIS 2000, Brighton.

Nadel, J., & Fontaine, A.-M. (1989). Communicating by imitation: A developmental and comparative approach to transitory social competence. In B. H. Schneider, G. Attili, J. Nadel, & R. P. Weissberg (Eds.), *Social competence in developmental perspective* (pp. 131–144). Dordrecht, Boston, London: Kluwer Academic Publishers.

Nadel, J., Guérini, C., Pezé, A., & Rivet, C. (1999). The evolving nature of imitation as a transitory means of communication. In J. Nadel & G. Butterworth (Eds.), *Imitation in infancy* (pp. 209–234). Cambridge: Cambridge University Press.

Nadel, J., & Pezé, A. (1992). Communication productive et communication en écho: un an d'évolution chez un enfant autiste. *Neuropsychiatrie de l'Enfance et de l'Adolescence, 40 (10)*, 553–558.

(1993). What makes immediate imitation communicative in toddlers and autistic children? In J. Nadel & L. Camaioni (Eds.), *New perspectives in early communicative development* (pp. 139–156). London, New York: Routledge.

Piaget, J. (1945). *La formation du symbole chez l'enfant.* Neuchâtel/Paris: Delachaux et Niestlé.

Reyes, L., Striano, T., & Rochat, P. (1998). *Determinants of the still-face phenomenon by 2 to 6-month-old infants.* Poster presented at the XIth Biennial International Conference on Infant Studies, Atlanta, Georgia, April 2–5.

Rochat, P., & Morgan, R. (1995). Spatial determinants in the perception of self-produced leg movements in 3- to 5-month-old infants. *Developmental Psychology, 31*, 626–636.

Rochat, P., Neisser, U., & Marian, V. (1998). Are young children sensitive to interpersonal contingency? *Infant Behaviour and Development, 21 (2)*, 355–366.

Rochat, P., & Striano, T. (1999). Emerging self-exploration by 2-month-olds. *Developmental Science, 2*, 206–218.

Roessler, J. (1999). *Imitation and simulation.* Workshop CREA "Simulation and the understanding of action." Paris.

Rogers, S. J. (1999). An examination of the imitation deficit in autism. In J. Nadel & G. Butterworth (Eds.), *Imitation in Infancy* (pp. 254–283). Cambridge: Cambridge University Press.

Rogers, S. J., Bennetto, L., McEvoy, R., & Pennington, B. F. (1996). Imitation and pantomime in high-functioning adolescents with autism spectrum disorders. *Child Development, 67*, 2060–2073.

Rogers, S. J., & Pennington, B. F. (1991). A theoretical approach to the deficits in infantile autism. *Development and Psychopathology, 3*, 137–162.

Schmuckler, M. A. (1996). Visual-proprioceptive intermodal perception in infancy. *Infant Behaviour and Development, 19*, 221–232.

Smith, I., & Bryson, S. (1994). Imitation and action in autism: A critical review. *Psychological Bulletin, 116*, 259–273.

Stern, D. (1977). *Mère et enfant, les premières relations.* Brussels: Mardaga.

Tiegerman, E., & Primavera, L. (1981). Object manipulation: An interactional strategy with autistic children. *Journal of Autism and Developmental Disorders, 11*, 427–438.

(1984). Imitating the autistic child: Facilitating communicative gaze behavior. *Journal of Autism and Developmental Disorders, 14*, 27–38.

Tomasello, M. (1999). Social cognition before the revolution. In P. Rochat (Ed.), *Early social cognition.* Mahwah, NJ: Lawrence Erlbaum Ass.

Trevarthen, C., & Hubley, P. (1978). Secondary intersubjectivity: Confiding and acts of meaning in the first year. In A. Lock (Ed.), *Action, gesture and symbol* (pp. 183–229). London: Academic Press.

Trevarthen, C., Kokkinaki, T., & Fiamenghi, G. A. (1999). What infants' imitation communicates. In J. Nadel & G. Butterworth (Eds.), *Imitation in infancy* (pp. 127–185). Cambridge: Cambridge University Press.

Tronick, E., Als, H., Adamson, L., Wise, S., & Brazelton, T. (1978). The infant's response to entrapment between contradictory messages in face-to-face interaction. *Journal of American Academy of Child Psychiatry, 17*, 1–13.

Uzgiris, I., Vase, M., & Benson, J. (1984). A longitudinal study of matching activity in mother–infant interaction. *Infant Behavior and Development*, Special Issue, *7*, 371.

Whiten, A., & Brown, J. (1999). Imitation and the reading of other minds: Perspectives from the study of autism, normal children and non-human primates. In S. Bräten (Ed.), *Intersubjective communication and emotion in ontogeny: A sourcebook* (pp. 260–280). Cambridge: Cambridge University Press.

3　Self-awareness, other-awareness, and secondary representation

Jens B. Asendorpf

In this chapter I summarize studies on the relation between early imitation and self-awareness that I conducted in collaboration with Pierre-Marie Baudonnière (Asendorpf & Baudonnière, 1993; Asendorpf, Warkentin & Baudonnière, 1996), and relate them to more recent work. Our studies emerged from French studies of early social cognition and peer communication (Baudonnière, 1988; Nadel, 1986; Nadel-Brulfert & Baudonnière, 1982). We added the hypothesis that the development of self-awareness and certain forms of social imitation may be closely linked because both the ability for self-awareness and the ability for sustained immediate imitation as a form of early nonverbal communication depend on a common cognitive capacity, the capacity for secondary representation. This hypothesis linked the French tradition with theories on the development of children's theory of mind, particularly Perner's (1991) work.

Synchronic imitation and secondary representation

During the second year of life, children become increasingly able to communicate with others through *synchronic imitation,* which quickly becomes the most important preverbal form of communication among peers (Baudonnière, 1988; Nadel-Brulfert & Baudonnière, 1982). In synchronic imitation, two children simultaneously play with the same type of objects in a similar, though not always identical, way. They regularly look at the partner and seem to realize and enjoy the reciprocity inherent in their joint play, as indicated by a positive mood, and they often begin and end the object use at the same time or shift to a different activity almost synchronically.

Synchronic communication is different from ritualized forms of dyadic play such as peek-a-boo that appear much earlier in infant–adult communication and require only the acquisition of simple stimulus–response rules, such as turn alternation (see Bruner, 1983). What appears to emerge during the second year is the more advanced ability to co-ordinate one's behavior with the nonritualized behavior of an adult (e.g., Eckerman & Didow, 1989) or a peer (Eckerman, Davis, & Didow, 1989). Ritualized behavior can be excluded best by observing unfamiliar dyads in unfamiliar settings that involve unfamiliar objects.

Synchronic imitation is also different from mere attraction to the same type of objects. The main distinctive feature is the continuous visual regard of the *partner* during synchronic imitation (visual regard of the partner's objects is not sufficient). Finally, synchronic imitation is different from mere parallel play because it is real communication as indicated by the usage of a common code (the shared activities) and the reciprocity of the behavior. Thus, it is important to include criteria of visual regard of the partner and contingent object use in operationalizations of synchronic imitation.

The idea that the crucial cognitive ability underlying synchronic imitation is the capacity for secondary representation was suggested to us by the emerging theories on the origins of children's theory of mind (e.g., Leslie, 1987), particularly by Perner's approach (Perner, 1991). According to both Leslie and Perner, infants can form primary representations that are more or less accurate reflections of one's perception of the current situation. What seems to emerge during the second year of life is the ability to coordinate primary representations with secondary representations (Perner, 1991), cognitions that represent past, future, pretended, or purely hypothetical situations in propositional form. Thus, they represent situations that are detached from one's immediate perceptual reality.

A secondary representation that is important for social interaction is one's view of one's partner's perception of the current situation. It is a mental image of the partner's view, not a simple perception of the situation, and hence not a primary representation. Instead, it is a hypothetical situation and thus a secondary representation. Our central assumption was that it is necessary to be able to take the perspective of the interaction partner in order to coordinate one's behavior with the nonritualized behavior of the partner during synchronic imitation for a longer period of time and in order to develop the feeling of "Thou" (Buber, 1970), i.e., the intuitive understanding that I share common intentions or plans for action with my interaction partner. This "Thou feeling" was in our view the primary motivating force that keeps synchronic imitation going for prolonged periods of time, accompanied by positive affect.

The capacity for synchronic imitation requires multiple specific abilities that develop earlier. A first requirement is that children must be able to look where adults are looking (joint attention). First forms of joint attention emerge around nine months of age (Carpenter, Nagell, & Tomasello, 1998). A second requirement is that children must be able to imitate the unfamiliar activity of a stranger. This ability develops between nine and fourteen months of age (Hanna & Meltzoff, 1993) but does not require secondary representation because it can be accomplished on the basis of primary representations.

A third requirement is that children must be able to recognize the contingency between their own behavior and that of their partner. Meltzoff (1990) had an unfamiliar adult imitating activities of fourteen-month-old children and compared this imitation condition with a control condition in which another adult performed an activity that was unrelated to the child's behavior. The children in the imitative condition showed more "testing behavior" according to the subjective judgment of observers. Meltzoff (1990) described this testing behavior as a systematic variation of activity while closely watching the adult partner. Although this ability already comes close to the capacity for synchronic imitation, it is not sufficient because contingency awareness does not require an understanding that the adult partner acts according to intentions.

A fourth requirement is that children can distinguish between accidental and intentional actions by others. This ability develops between fourteen and eighteen months (Carpenter, Akhtar, & Tomasello, 1998). However, the "Thou feeling" during synchronic communication is based on an understanding that I share the intentions of my interaction partner, which may be more difficult than to merely recognize that others have intentions of their own.

Clear indications that children are able to understand others' intentions and act accordingly are not observed before approximately eighteen months of age. For example, when eighteen-month-olds see how an adult tries but fails to perform certain acts, they are able to re-enact the complete acts (Meltzoff, 1995), and many eighteen-month-olds offer help to someone in distress (Bischof-Köhler, 1991).

It is important to note that this assumed form of spontaneous perspective taking in the second year of life is different from the much later appearing ability to take the perspective of others deliberately. Deliberate perspective-taking or role-taking is typically studied in situations when children are verbally instructed to take the view of others, for example, by asking them to choose a birthday present for a friend that the friend would like (e.g., Flavell et al. 1968). In contrast, we were influenced by the position developed by Norbert and Doris Bischof that two-year-olds "find themselves in the perspective of others" by a *spontaneous* act of empathic identification (Bischof-Köhler, 1991).

Thus, in a nutshell, our hypothesis is that synchronic imitation requires the capacity for spontaneous perspective-taking which is an instance of forming secondary representations.

Mirror self-recognition and secondary representation

Different sequences have been proposed for the development of the self during the first two years of life. Despite some differences in their definitions of the developmental levels, these authors agree that a critical step is reached when children become able to represent themselves as an object of knowledge and imagination (the representational self, Emde, 1983; the categorical self, Lewis, 1986; and the verbal self, Stern, 1985). This capacity for self-awareness sets the stage for self-conscious social emotions such as embarrassment, pride and shame, which are triggered by self-evaluation in the presence of others (Lewis, Sullivan, Stanger, & Weiss, 1989). Self-awareness is also a prerequisite for self-presentation in social interaction (e.g., deception: Lewis, Stanger, & Sullivan, 1989).

Research on self-development in the second year of life has found that many children show indications of self-awareness before using verbal labels for themselves (Lewis & Brooks-Gunn, 1979). According to this research, the best empirical indicator of self-awareness is the mirror self-recognition test that was independently developed by Gallup (1970) for chimpanzees, and Amsterdam (1972; study conducted in 1969) for children. Children are unobtrusively marked with a spot of rouge on their face. Mark-directed behavior (instead of mirror-directed behavior or no reaction) is interpreted as evidence that the children infer from the mirror-image that they themselves have a mark.

Mirror self-recognition requires coordinating a mirror-image (primary representation) with one's representation of oneself (the "Me"; James, 1890). This latter representation is a secondary representation because it is not a perceptual reality. Instead, it is a constructed mental image of oneself that can be manipulated in fantasy. Thus, self-awareness requires the capacity for secondary representation.

Additional requirements for mirror self-recognition develop earlier. Most important is the ability to recognize the contingency between one's own behavior and the movement of the mirror-image. Lewis and Brooks-Gunn (1979) found that a majority of twelve-month-olds engaged in contingent play in front of a mirror ("movement testing" by repeating particular actions under close visual control). This movement testing seems to be analogous to the "testing behavior" observed by Meltzoff (1990). As Lewis (1986) and others have noted, the perceived contingency between one's behavior and the movement of the mirror-image may assist the young child in determining the source of the image in the mirror. However, without the ability to represent this source of movement as oneself (secondary representation), contingency awareness alone would not enable children to pass the mirror rouge test.

The main hypothesis

The main hypothesis that guided our work was, therefore, that mirror self-recognition and synchronic imitation develop in close synchrony during the second year of life because they require the same crucial cognitive ability: the capacity for secondary representation. Because mirror self-recognition is often interpreted as indexing a capacity for self-awareness, we introduced the parallel term other-awareness for the capacity to spontaneously take the perspective of others (see Fig. 3.1).

Because of a lack of accepted empirical indicators for the capacity for secondary representation, the testable hypothesis was weaker than the guiding hypothesis: self-awareness and other-awareness develop in close synchrony during the second year of life.

Evidence for the hypothesis in the literature

A few empirical studies on the relationship between self- and other-awareness exist, and their results were consistent with our synchrony hypothesis. Zahn-Waxler, Radke-Yarrow, and King (1979) found that children began to react with empathic behavior to victims of distress around the age of eighteen months – behavior that could not be explained by emotional contagion. In a later study (Zahn-Waxler, Radke-Yarrow, Wagner, & Chapman, 1992), self-recognition as assessed by the visual self-recognition test of Bertenthal and Fischer (1978) showed modest relations with prosocial and empathic behaviors directed to victims of distress at twenty-four months but not at eighteen months. Because mirror self-recognition was only one of five components of the measure of visual self-recognition, these results are only tangential to our synchrony hypothesis. Direct support came from two studies with sixteen- to

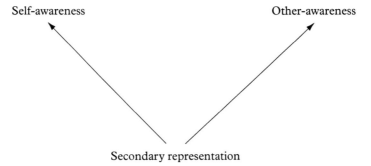

Figure 3.1. Main guiding hypothesis.

twenty-four-month-old children by Bischof-Köhler (1991), who found a strong correlation between mirror self-recognition and empathic responses to a victim of distress, even after partialing out chronological age.

Two empirical tests of the synchrony hypothesis

In order to test the synchrony hypothesis, we conducted two cross-sectional studies. We also took a longitudinal study into consideration but refrained from implementing it, mainly because we expected problems with repeating the mirror rouge test. We feared that children who were frequently exposed to a marked face in the mirror would ignore the mark in later testing sessions because they remembered the mark being part of the "story."

In Study 1 (Asendorpf & Baudonnière, 1993), we related mirror self-recognition and synchronic imitation in 56 dyads of unfamiliar nineteen-month-old children who were systematically paired according to self-awareness. The critical analyses for the present research questions referred to a comparison of nine nonrecognizer dyads (both children of the dyad did not pass the mirror rouge test and could be observed for a sufficiently long time) and twelve recognizer dyads (both children of the dyad passed the mirror rouge test and could be observed for a sufficiently long time); see Asendorpf and Baudonnière (1993) for details.

In Study 2 (Asendorpf, Warkentin, & Baudonnière, 1996), we confronted 109 eighteen-month-old children with an unfamiliar experimenter who either invited them to synchronically imitate her behavior or who synchronically imitated their behavior for quite some time. Thus, we studied both children's spontaneous imitation of peers and their reaction to adults who scaffolded their imitative tendencies. Also, we could test in Study 2 whether children who did not recognize themselves in a mirror were able to realize that they were imitated by someone else (social contingency awareness).

In this second study, half of the sample was tested with a revised mirror rouge test in an attempt to increase the validity of the recognizer–nonrecognizer distinction. In the classic rouge test, many children closely inspect their mirror-image for a long time but neither react to their face nor to the mirror. When these children are classified as nonrecognizers, the test may produce false negatives. In our alternative procedure the children are shown a doll with a spot of rouge on the face and are asked to clean the doll's face with a tissue. Later, the classic test is applied. If the children do not show mark-directed behavior, they are offered a tissue and are asked to "clean the face." If they now show mark-directed behavior, while observing themselves in the mirror, they are classified as recognizers. We (Asendorpf, Warkentin, & Baudonnière, 1996) found that the rate of ambiguous cases could be strongly reduced through this procedure.

In both studies, *sustained* synchronic imitation (synchronic imitation exceeding ten seconds) was strongly associated with the result of the mirror rouge test. In Study 1, only one of the nine nonrecognizer dyads showed sustained imitation, compared with ten of the twelve recognizer dyads. In Study 2, only one nonrecognizer showed sustained imitation at all compared with 33 per cent of the recognizers. Thus, children's mirror status produced the expected effect although only a minority of the recognizers engaged in sustained imitation. Perhaps the experimenter did not show the activity sufficiently long enough to engage most children in sustained imitation. Despite this problem, our hypothesis that both recognizers and nonrecognizers are able to imitate the unfamiliar activity of an unfamiliar adult but that only recognizers are capable of sustained synchronic imitation was fully confirmed in both studies.

When the experimenter imitated the child's activity, posture, and vocalizations for five minutes in Study 2, a majority of *both* recognizers and nonrecognizers engaged in at least one testing sequence, and mirror status was unrelated to the number and the mean length of these sequences. Only one mirror effect was found: recognizers varied their activity significantly more during the first testing sequence than nonrecognizers. This result suggests that recognizers tested the experimenter more intensely than did nonrecognizers, but that both recognizers and nonrecognizers became aware of and tested the social contingency in this situation.

We interpreted these results as a close synchrony in the development of self- and other-awareness due to the emergence of a capacity for secondary representation. Mirror self-recognition marks this capacity because children must be able to represent themselves as an object of their imagination in order to react appropriately to a mirror-image showing a child with a mark. Sustained synchronic imitation may also reveal this capacity because sustained synchronic imitation as a form of preverbal communication requires that the child intuitively (not deliberately!) takes the perspective of the interaction partner, in order to coordinate his or her behavior with the nonritualized behavior of the partner for a longer period of time, and in order to develop an intuitive understanding of sharing common intentions or plans for action. This "Thou feeling" may be the primary motivating force that keeps synchronic imitation going for prolonged periods of time, accompanied by positive affect.

Recent related studies

Recently, Povinelli, Landau and Perilloux (1996) showed convincingly in a series of three experiments that mirror self-recognition is not sufficient for a cognitive representation of a *continuous* self. Only three-to four-year-old children showed self-directed behavior when they were shown a videotape or a photograph of their own behavior recorded a few minutes earlier, not two-year-olds. Povinelli, Landau and Perilloux' interpretation of these findings is that two-year-olds who recognize themselves in a mirror may not understand that past events in which they participated (and which they easily remember) happened to *them*: they lack a sense of self that extends back to the past (and possibly also a sense of self that extends to the future).

In light of this refinement of the self-concept in the second year, it is important to note that we did not assume in our work on self- and other-awareness that the secondary representations of self in the mirror test or of self and other during synchronic imitation extend to the past. It is fully sufficient to assume that children relate the mirror-image of their face to a representation of their "current self" and that they take the "current perspective" of the other during imitation. Current self and current perspective of the other are secondary representations not because they refer to entities that are continuous in time but because they are detached from the immediate perceptual reality. A capability for secondary representation is a necessary but not a sufficient condition for a continuous concept of self and other. The implicit continuity assumption in the concept of self and other that seems so natural to us adults develops later than the concept of a current self and a current other.

Two other recent studies found that infants as young as three or five months of age discriminated between silent video recordings of their own past face (offline recording) and a peer's face by looking longer to the peer's face (Bahrick, Moss, & Fadil, 1996; Legerstee, Anderson, & Schaffer, 1998). The authors interpreted these results within the novelty preference paradigm: the infants looked longer to the peer's image because they recognized their own face as a familiar stimulus. Thus, young infants may recognize their own face as a familiar stimulus long before they are able to pass the mirror rouge test at approximately eighteen months of age.

The recognition of one's face as familiar does not necessarily imply *self-awareness*, however. Infants may form memory traces about faces, including their own mirror-image, long before they are able to relate these memories to a concept of their self (the critical cognitive capacity for self-awareness). Therefore, these findings on early facial recognition seem to be only marginally related to our research on self- and other-awareness.

Conclusion

More studies are surely needed on the behavioral subtleties, the cognitive underpinnings and the emotional concomitants of sustained synchronic imitation, this early form of peer communication. It may be particularly useful to assess the capacity for secondary representation in nonsocial situations and to relate it to mirror self-recognition and synchronic imitation because it cannot be excluded that the link between these two developmental phenomena is based on early personality differences. For example, more sociable children who are more interested in people than in nonsocial objects (a) may be more attracted to mirror-images of human faces and therefore learn to recognize themselves in mirrors earlier, and (b) may be more interested in peers and adults and therefore show more synchronic imitation behavior. To exclude such an alternative interpretation, one possibility would be to use the spontaneous generation of pretend play with an imaginary object in nonsocial settings as an indication of the capacity for secondary representation. Demonstrating a correlational link between such a pure cognitive assessment and both self- and other-awareness would support our main hypothesis more strongly than our own studies.

References

Amsterdam, B. K. (1972). Mirror self-image reactions before age two. *Developmental Psychobiology, 5,* 297–305.

Asendorpf, J. B., & Baudonnière, P.-M. (1993). Self-awareness and other-awareness: Mirror self-recognition and synchronic imitation among unfamiliar peers. *Developmental Psychology, 29,* 88–95.

Asendorpf, J. B., Warkentin, V., & Baudonnière, P.-M. (1996). Self-awareness and other-awareness II: Mirror self-recognition, social contingency awareness, and synchronic imitation. *Developmental Psychology, 32,* 313–321.

Bahrick, L. E., Moss, L., & Fadil, C. (1996). Development of visual self-recognition in infancy. *Ecological Psychology, 8,* 189–208.

Baudonnière, P. M. (1988). *L'évolution des compétences à communiquer chez l'enfant de 2 à 4 ans* [Development of communicative competences between 2 and 4 years of age]. Paris: PUF.

Baudonnière, P. M., Werebe, M. J. G., Michel, J., & Liégeois, J. (1988). Development of communicative competences in early childhood: A model and results. In B. H. Schneider, G. Attili, J. Nadel, & R. P. Weisberg (Eds.), *Social competence in developmental perspective* (pp. 175–193). Boston: Kluwer Academic.

Bertenthal, B. I., & Fischer, K. W. (1978). Development of self-recognition in the infant. *Developmental Psychology, 14,* 44–50.

Bischof-Köhler, D. (1991). The development of empathy in infants. In M. E. Lamb & H. Keller (Eds.), *Infant development: Perspectives from German-speaking countries* (pp. 1–33). Hillsdale, NJ: Erlbaum.

Bruner, J. (1983). *Child's talk.* New York: Norton.

Buber, M. (1970). *I and You.* New York: Charles Scriber's Sons.

Carpenter, M., Akhtar, N., & Tomasello, M. (1998). Fourteen- through eighteen-month-old infants differentially imitate intentional and accidental actions. *Infant Behavior and Development, 21,* 315–330.

Carpenter, M., Nagell, K., & Tomasello, M. (1998). Social cognition, joint attention, and communicative competence from 9 to 15 months of age. *Monographs of the Society for Research in Child Development, 63* (4, Serial No. 255).

Eckerman, C. O., & Didow, S. M. (1989). Toddlers' social coordinations: Changing responses to another's invitation to play. *Developmental Psychology, 25,* 794–804.

Eckerman, C. O., Davis, C. C., & Didow, S. M. (1989). Toddlers' emerging ways of achieving social coordinations with a peer. *Child Development, 60,* 440–453.

Emde, R. N. (1983). The prerepresentational self and its affective core. *The Psychoanalytic Study of the Child, 38,* 165–192.

Flavell, J. H., Botkin, P. T., Fry, C. L., Wright, J. W., & Jarvis, P. E. (1968). *The development of role-taking and communication skills in children.* New York: Wiley.

Gallup, G. G., Jr. (1970). Chimpanzees: Self-recognition. *Science, 167,* 86–87.

Hanna, E., & Meltzoff, A. N. (1993). Peer imitation by toddlers in laboratory, home, and day-care contexts: Implications for social learning and memory. *Developmental Psychology, 29,* 701–710.

James, W. (1890). *The principles of Psychology* (Vol. 1). New York: Holt.

Legerstee, M., Anderson, D., & Schaffer, A. (1998). Five- and eight-month-old infants recognize their faces and voices as familiar and social stimuli. *Child Development, 69,* 37–50.

Leslie, A. M. (1987). Pretense and representation: The origins of "Theory of mind." *Psychological Review, 94,* 412–426.

Lewis, M. (1986). Origins of self-knowledge and individual differences in early self-recognition. In A. G. Greenwald & J. Suls (Eds.), *Psychological perspectives on the self* (Vol. 3, pp. 55–78). Hillsdale, NJ: Erlbaum.

Lewis, M., & Brooks-Gunn, J. (1979). *Social cognition and the acquisition of self.* New York: Plenum Press.

Lewis, M., Stanger, C., & Sullivan, M. W. (1989). Deception in 3-year-olds. *Developmental Psychology, 25,* 439–443.

Lewis, M., Sullivan, M. W., Stanger, C., & Weiss, M. (1989). Self-development and self-conscious emotions. *Child Development, 60,* 146–156.

Meltzoff, A. N. (1990). Foundations for developing a concept of self: The role of imitation in relating self to other and the value of social mirroring, social modeling, and self practice in infancy. In D. Cicchetti & M. Beeghly (Eds.), *The self in transition: Infancy to childhood* (pp. 139–164). Chicago: University of Chicago Press.

(1995). Understanding the intentions of others: Re-enactment of intended acts by 18-month-old children. *Developmental Psychology, 31,* 838–850.

Nadel, J. (1986). *Imitation et communication entre jeunes enfants* [Imitation and communication among young children]. Paris: PUF.

Nadel-Brulfert, J., & Baudonnière, P. M. (1982). The social function of reciprocal imitation in 2-year-old peers. *International Journal of Behavioral Development,* 5, 95–109.

Perner, J. (1991). *Understanding the representational mind.* Cambridge, MA: MIT Press.

Povinelli, D. J., Landau, K. R., & Perilloux, H. K. (1996). Self-recognition in young children using delayed versus live feedback: Evidence of a developmental asynchrony. *Child Development,* 67, 1540–1554.

Stern, D. N. (1985). *The interpersonal world of the infant.* New York: Basic Books.

Zahn-Waxler, C., Radke-Yarrow, M., & King, R. A. (1979). Child-rearing and children's prosocial initiations toward victims of distress. *Child Development,* 50, 319–330.

Zahn-Waxler, C., Radke-Yarrow, M., Wagner, E., & Chapman, M. (1992). Development of concern for others. *Developmental Psychology,* 28, 126–136.

4 Notes on individual differences and the assumed elusiveness of neonatal imitation

Mikael Heimann

This chapter summarizes research on early imitation carried out in Sweden over the last fifteen years. Research showing that imitation observed in the newborn period can be demonstrated, but also that the processes behind imitation in the neonate are both complex and fragile. One example of such processes is the large variability in imitative responses observed by many investigators studying imitation in the newborn period. This variability has been specifically studied in the Swedish cohorts, and it seems as if real individual differences are at play from the very beginning.

Where to start

The basic procedure used by almost all studies to date has been to compare the frequency of a target behavior after modeling (e.g., tongue protrusion) with the observed frequency of that behavior in a control situation (e.g., after modeling of mouth opening). Thus, neonatal imitation can be described as a behavioral phenomenon based on statistical comparisons between target and nontarget frequencies. Viewed in this way, there is no doubt that neonatal imitation is a real phenomenon. It does exist and it can be demonstrated as has been shown by numerous research groups (for list of studies see Heimann, 1991, 1998a; Kugiumutzakis, 1999; Meltzoff & Moore, 1994, 1998a), exemplified here by the results from three Swedish studies:

(1) Our first study (Heimann & Schaller, 1985) revealed support for imitation of both tongue protrusion and mouth opening among eleven participating children (mean age: seventeen days). It is one of the few studies that have used the mother as a model and also one of the first to seriously suggest that individual differences might explain the wide variation in reported results between studies.

(2) Our second attempt used a more strict experimental design (e.g., an experimenter was used as a model instead of the mother) with the aim to study the development of imitation over the first three months of life (Heimann, 1991; Heimann, Nelson, & Schaller, 1989). About

two-thirds of the children imitated tongue protrusion and approximately half the group imitated mouth opening at both three days and three weeks. The number of children imitating tongue protrusion decreased over age (only one-third imitated at three months) while the number of children imitating mouth opening stayed almost constant (approximately 50 per cent).

(3) The findings from our second study have recently been corroborated in our third study (Heimann, 2001b). Imitation of both tongue protrusion and mouth opening was once again found among 31 children at two days of age. It is thus obvious from the Swedish studies, as well as from all other studies having been carried out over the last two decades, that we can conclude beyond doubt that imitation is a capacity which the newborn child can use immediately after birth. In addition, imitation has also been observed among newborn infants with Down's Syndrome (Heimann, Ullstadius, & Swerlander, 1998).

Function

Although the evidence is based on a strict behavioral definition, the meaning of this fascinating capacity most probably has to be sought within the social domain. To view neonatal imitation only as a spurious capacity of the child's brain is probably not a fruitful stance. Instead, I propose that this early imitative ability is exerting its main influence within the continuous dyadic interaction that takes place between parent and child from birth. The child's imitation serves a purpose within the relationship and will have an impact upon the caregiver; the child's imitation affects the parents' behavior and their responses. Thus, neonatal imitation plays a role in the early dialogue between the infant and his or her parents (cf. Bråten, 1988, 1998; Fogel, 1993; Meltzoff & Moore, 1994; Trevarthen, Kokkinaki, & Fiamenghi, 1998). Another way to phrase this is to say that the newborn human child has an inborn capacity to repeat what others do. To repeat or to imitate are basic communicative acts, especially when used selectively. The story behind neonatal imitation might thus be rephrased as if the child is communicating that: "I am here," or "I am with you" or "I would like you to continue." This is the *social function* of neonatal imitation: the child is biologically motivated to imitate in order to promote closeness to an important other. Maybe one could say that the child tries, in his immature way, to establish a first link, to start the process that will later lead to both forming of an attachment as well as companionships.

An alternative motivation behind imitation is to increase our knowledge about the world. This is the *cognitive explanation*, often referred to as imitative learning (Tomasello, Kruger, & Ratner, 1993) and the development of deferred imitation is especially relevant to this function. These two functions (the social and the cognitive) must be studied and analyzed separately (as suggested by Uzgiris already in 1981; see also Rochat & Striano, 1999). They might be linked with one another but are probably governed by separate processes. Moreover, they also follow different timetables in development. The cognitive function in its pure sense is probably at a very low level at birth (OFF or almost OFF) while the social function of imitation is already at work (ON although not yet fully developed).

Remaining issue: Individual differences

In spite of the fact that many studies have been able to document the phenomenon, neonatal imitation is still in some way an elusive phenomenon. There are still some "pockets of resistance," some skeptics (e.g., Anisfeld, 1996; Anisfeld *et al.*, 2001). The reason for this, as I see it, is mainly an underestimation of early individual differences between children at birth or shortly thereafter. The following section provides a brief summary of observations relevant to this issue based upon findings from our Swedish studies (see also Heimann, 1998a, 2001a):

The huge variation across individuals in observed imitative responses was initially viewed as error variance if at all commented upon. However, some early investigators (e.g., Hayes & Watson, 1981; Heimann & Schaller, 1985; Kugiumutzakis, 1985) stressed that the observed variation might reflect real individual differences observable very early in life. Thus, we have to consider the possibility that infants differ in their proneness to imitate immediately after birth. An idea explicitly suggested by Field already in 1982 and supported by the following observations:

Short-term stability

Heimann, Nelson, and Schaller (1989) reported that imitation displayed during the first two days of life was significantly related to imitation three weeks later. Relatively strong relationships were noted for imitation of both mouth opening ($r = .68$) and tongue protrusion ($r = .49$) between observations made at the ages of three days and three weeks. In fact, 72 per cent of the children received an identical classification as either imitating or not imitating mouth opening at both ages.

More surprisingly, a separate analysis revealed a link between children judged as high imitators at day three and at three months (see Heimann, 1998a, 2001a). Children displaying very low imitation levels shortly after birth were significantly more often judged as low on imitation at three months as well. These results are at odds with what is generally believed to be true of early behavioral observations. Due to the rapid growth of the CNS during the early months it is commonly assumed that behavioral stability is unlikely to be observed (cf. Bronson, 1982; Johnson, 1998) and thus in great need of support from replication studies. They do, however, raise the possibility that stability within groups of high and low imitators *might* exist as early in life as from birth to three months of age.

Long-term stability

A follow-up found no direct relationship between imitation observed during the newborn period (at three days or at three weeks) and imitation observed at twelve months (Heimann, 1998a). However, the study did reveal some interesting evidence of a possible relationship between early imitation (at three months) and imitation observed later. Children imitating tongue protrusion at three months (which only one-third of the participants did) displayed more vocal imitation nine months later ($r = .42$, $p < .05$) while imitation of mouth opening was related to the child's tendency to imitate action on objects at twelve months ($r = 38$, $p < .05$). These observations, although fragile and preliminary, do suggest that early imitation (but *not* neonatal imitation) is in some way linked to imitative responses observed nine months later.

Imitation and temperament

How a child reacts to an invitation to imitate might in part be explained by temperamental factors as explicitly suggested by Field (1982). She hypothesized – based on her own studies on early facial imitation – that young babies are either "internalizers" or "externalizers." This idea motivated us (see Heimann, Nelson, & Schaller, 1989; Heimann, 1998a, 2001b) to add temperament measures to our Swedish studies (the Baby Behavior Questionnaire, BBQ; Hagekull, 1985; Hagekull, Lindhagen, & Bohlin, 1980). Overall, we have found some support for Field's idea that temperament might play a role for imitation observed this early in life although we have not specifically studied if the children can be grouped into the categories used by Field (that is, being either "internalizers" or "externalizers"). What we have demonstrated in two separate studies is that the child's activity level, as measured by BBQ at three months, is significantly correlated with imitation at three weeks and at three months (range of $r = .33$ to $.41$). Moreover, our second study also indicated a significant relationship between imitation and the subscale measuring "Attentiveness" (r = .52). Recently, we have failed to find strong support for relationships between imitation at later ages and temperament although "Attentiveness" at nine months correlated significantly with deferred imitation observed at the same age (r = .42; Swerlander, 2001).

These findings do suggest that a link exists between early imitative tendencies and emerging personality characteristics of the child. Field (1982) might very well be right when she suggested that more expressive infants (as indicated by their activity level) are to be expected among infants displaying high levels of imitation although a word of caution must be added here: no significant relationship was detected between temperament measures and imitation observed *before* three weeks of age. Moreover, even if taken as hard facts, the obtained correlations only explain between 9 and 25 per cent of the variance. Thus, temperament might tell us an important part of the story, but far from the whole story.

Imitation and the early relationship

Heimann (1989) reported that the proneness to imitate in the neonatal period co-varied with how the children responded while in face-to-face interaction with their mother. Brief episodes of gaze aversion were negatively correlated with imitation of facial gestures at three days, three weeks and three months. Thus, imitation might facilitate each participant's sensitivity to subtle social cues embedded in the rich interactive flow between the mother and her infant (Heimann, 1998a).

Deferred imitation

Heimann and Meltzoff (1996), studying deferred imitation among nine- and fourteen-month-old children, also noted possible indices of individual differences: seventeen out of 26 children were judged as high imitators at both ages, while four children remained low at both ages or, in other words, over 80 per cent of the infants (21 of 26) did not change their overall imitative performance.

Putting it all together

There is no doubt in my mind that the evidence favors the conclusion that neonatal imitation is a real phenomenon (Heimann, 1998b). It does exist and it can be demonstrated, but not always easily. The infant must be alert, attentive, and motivated to engage with another person. Factors like noise, light, hunger, and how the baby is being handled also affect the possibility of eliciting an imitative response from a newborn baby. Thus, for a parent imitation might still seem to be an elusive phenomenon in spite of all the positive reports. Reports also suggest that neonatal imitation might be easier to elicit directly after birth when the infant often is in a state of elevated attentiveness due to the high levels of catecholamines that are common as a result of the birth process.

In other words, imitative reactions by newborn babies might be viewed as a by-product of the infant's readiness to explore the social world already from birth. Neonatal imitation is an early indicator of this early ability, but it is also in some way a mistake. Parents do not spend much of their time trying to engage their newborn child in imitative games (at least not before this knowledge became popularized). Instead, I believe that mothers and fathers are unaware of neonatal imitation in their daily interactions with their child. They experience it as a global social effect, noting that their child "is there" or that "she is with me."

This capacity to react, to imitate, to create a sense of togetherness, is most likely a result of our evolutionary history. It has served our species and helped newborns to be taken care of by their parents. The chance for an infant to survive increases rapidly if the child is able to engage the caretaker in social situations that also evoke strong emotional responses in the adult. This is, I believe, the main reason for why the capacity to imitate has become an integrated part of the newborn child's social and cognitive competence. A similar assumption has been made by Fridlund (1997) who writes, "the primary selection pressures on children are to capture and hold the attention of caretakers" (p. 110). In Fridlund's words, neonatal imitation might be viewed as one of the important "attention grabbers" that evolution has produced.

However, it is also a fact that to talk about an imitative capacity in early infancy has irritated some people within the field of developmental and cognitive psychology. Many have viewed imitation as an "advanced cognitive capacity" that cannot be operating early on in life. The problem is that observation after observation and study after study seem to come up with this finding that infants do imitate a large range of facial, hand, and head gestures. Or, in other words, at a behavioral level: they repeat what others do. If you stick out your tongue, open your mouth or pout your lips, they tend to do it! Maybe not instantaneously and maybe not always. But in the end, they will match the gesture just presented. These observations need to be explained and related to the social *and* cognitive development during the first year and also to what has been called "imitative learning".

To imitate is a difficult task for the newborn child. Observations have shown that it might take between 30 and 60 seconds before clear imitation is displayed (Heimann, 1991, 1998a; Holmlund, 1995; Kugiumutzakis, 1993; Meltzoff & Moore, 1994). It is also a task carried out by a nervous system that has yet to develop most of its detailed architecture. Thus, a newborn child achieving reasonable matching does so in spite of the fact that many systems are immature. This is something we still have to find an explanation for. The facts we have today suggest to me that the ability to imitate is dependent on:

(1) Currently unknown subcortical and cortical processes (Stein & Meredith, 1993; Dawson & Fischer, 1994) based on mirror neurons similar to the ones found in the rostral part of the ventral premotor area (Rizzolatti & Arbib, 1998). The process will probably also include some frontal lobe activity. Recent observations have taught us that the frontal lobes become functional already *before* birth (Bates, Thal, Finley, & Clancy, in press).
(2) The child's ability to represent both perception and production within a single amodal or supramodal neural net (Meltzoff & Moore, 1997).
(3) The child's ability to detect facial configurations (eyes and mouth) and moving stimuli (Johnson & Morton, 1991, Blass, 1999).
(4) Motivational processes that direct the child's attention to the relevant aspects of the environment (Trevarthen, Kokkinaki, & Fiamenghi, 1998).
(5) Transactional interactions with the environment (Fogel, 1993; Thelen & Smith, 1994).

The capacity to imitate belongs to the biological set-up of our central nervous system. Neonatal imitation is not a direct response, not even certain response, but a response that emerges from the interplay between what the child sees (e.g., tongue movements), what the child wants (motivational state, alertness, and attention) and what the child selects to do (motor output). This is a "softwired" system (as opposed to hard-wired) that develops over time through maturation and transactional interactions with the environment. To me, the concept "fuzzy dynamical processes" (FDP) is a good way to conceptualize both the ability of the nervous system to process and respond to complex social situations already at birth and the problem the young infant has in responding to complex social situations. The system is not specific to imitation but, rather, an effect of the initial settings (the initial weights and existing connections before any clear visual input has acted upon the child's brain) and constraints governing the immature nervous system. It is an imperfect system and the child does not succeed in imitating all of the time.

Thus, it is possible to understand why children respond slowly and why some children are more prone to respond than others. This last fact can also be conceptualized in connectionist terminology (McLeod, Plunkett, & Rolls, 1998; Rolls and Treves, 1998): we have to envision an imperfect network at the outset – maybe lesioned (not all connections have developed yet), maybe with too many hidden nodes (cell death is still taking place) and maybe with leaking attractor basins (in order to explain why children have to work themselves up to an imitative response and why they make more mistakes than later in life).

A newborn child achieving reasonable matching does so in spite of the fact that many systems are immature. This raises problems for any modeling approach (see also Meltzoff & Moore, 1997). If there are several ways within an FDP framework to reach an acceptable match then this might help to explain how early individual differences develop. It is probable to assume that networks capable of representing patterned stimuli build up over time, starting already before birth as the fetus moves around in the uterus. Furthermore, it is also probable that newborn children differ in how these patterned movement representations actually are constructed. If indeed comparative processes between own movements and other movements are involved in neonatal imitation, and if prenatal differences in patterned movements exist, then this comparison must lead to different outcomes between children. Differences that are relatively stable characteristics of the network architecture and thus the first early signs of individual differences.

Acknowledgements

This chapter is partly based upon research supported by grants to Mikael Heimann from the Bank of Sweden Tercentenary Foundation (# 89/313), Stockholm, the Swedish Council for Research in the Humanities and the Social Sciences (HSFR F 709/94 and F193/95), and the Swedish First of May Flower Foundation, Göteborg, Sweden. I also wish to express my thanks to Keith E. Nelson for stimulating discussions, important criticism, and invaluable input. Special thanks are also due to all participating children and their families.

References

Anisfeld, M. (1996). Only tongue protrusion modeling is matched by neonates. *Developmental Review, 16*, 149–161.

Anisfeld, M., Turkewitz, G., Rose, S. A., Rosenberg, F. R., Sheiber, F. J., Couturier-Fagan, D. A., Ger, J. S. & Sommer, I. (2001). No compelling evidence that newborns imitate oral gestures. *Infancy, 2* (1), 111–122.

Bates, E., Thal, D., Finlay, B., & Clancy, B. (in press). Early language development and its neural correlates. In I. Rapin & S. Segalowitz (Eds.), *Handbook
of neuropsychology, Vol. 7: Child neurology* (2nd ed.). Amsterdam: Elsevier.

Blass, E. M. (1999). The ontogeny of human infant face recognition: Orogusta-
tory, visual, and social influences. In P. Rochat (Ed.), *Early social cognition:
Understanding others in the first months of life* (pp. 35–65). Mahwah, NJ:
Erlbaum.

Bråten, S. (1988). Dialogic mind: The infant and the adult in protoconversa-
tion. In M. E. Carvallo (Ed.), *Nature, cognition, and system I* (pp. 187–205).
Dordrecht: Klüwer Academic Publishers.

   (1998). Infant learning by altercentric participation: The reverse of egocentric observation in autism. In S. Bråten (Ed.), *Intersubjective communication
and emotion in early ontogeny* (pp. 105–126). Cambridge: Cambridge University Press.

Bronson, G. W. (1982). Structure, status, and characteristics of the nervous
system at birth. In P. Stratton (Ed.), *Psychobiology of the human newborn*
(pp. 99–118). New York: Wiley.

Dawson, G., & Fischer, K. W. (Eds.) (1994). *Human behavior and the developing
brain*. New York: Guilford Press.

Field, T. M. (1982). Individual differences in the expressivity of neonates and
young infants. In R. S. Feldman (Ed.), *Development of nonverbal behavior in
children* (pp. 279–298). New York: Springer-Verlag.

Fogel, A. (1993). *Developing through relationships*. Chicago: University of Chicago
Press.

Fridlund, A. J. (1997). The new ethology of human facial expression. In J. A.
Russell & J. M. Fernández-Dols (Eds.), *The psychology of facial expression*
(pp. 103–127). Cambridge: Cambridge University Press.

Hagekull, B. (1985). Individual stability in dimensions of infant behavior. *Infant
Behavior and Development, 4*, 97–108.

Hagekull, B., Lindhagen, K., & Bohlin, G. (1980). Behavioral dimensions in
one-year-olds and dimensional stability in infancy. *International Journal
of Behavioral Development, 3*, 351–364.

Hayes, L. A., & Watson, J. S. (1981). Neonatal imitation: Fact or artifact? *Developmental Psychology, 17*, 655–660.

Heimann, M. (1989). Neonatal imitation, gaze aversion, and mother–infant interaction. *Infant Behavior and Development, 12*, 495–505.

   (1991). Neonatal imitation: A social and biological phenomenon. In T. Archer
& S. Hansen (Eds.), *Behavioral biology: The neuroendocrine axis* (pp. 173–
186). Hillsdale, NJ: Erlbaum.

   (1998a). Imitation in neonates, in older infants and in children with autism:
Feedback to theory. In S. Bråten (Ed.), *Intersubjective communication and
emotion in early ontogeny* (pp. 89–104). Cambridge: Cambridge University
Press.

   (1998b). When is imitation imitation and who has the right to imitate? [com-
mentary to Byrne & Russon]. *Behavioral and Brain Sciences, 21 (5)*, 693.

   (2001a). Imitation – a "fuzzy" phenomenon? In F. Lacerda, C. v. Hofsten, &
M. Heimann (Eds.), *Emerging cognitive abilities in early infancy* (pp. 231–246).
Mahwah, NJ: Erlbaum.

(2001b). Neonatal imitation – A new piece for the puzzling imitation puzzle. Manuscript submitted for publication.

Heimann, M., Nelson, K. E., & Schaller, J. (1989). Neonatal imitation of tongue protrusion and mouth opening: Methodological aspects and evidence of early individual differences. *Scandinavian Journal of Psychology, 90,* 90–101.

Heimann, M., & Meltzoff, A. N. (1996). Deferred imitation in 9- and 14-months old infants: A longitudinal study of a Swedish sample. *British Journal of Developmental Psychology, 14,* 55–64.

Heimann, M., & Schaller, J. (1985). Imitative reactions among 14–21 days old infants. *Infant Mental Health Journal, 6,* 31–39.

Heimann, M., Ullstadius, E., & Swerlander, A. (1998). Imitation in eight young infants with Down's syndrome. *Pediatric Research, 44 (5),* 780–784.

Holmlund, C. (1995). Development of turntakings as a sensorimotor process in the first 3 months: A sequential analysis. In K. E. Nelson & Z. Réger (Eds.), *Children's language Volume 8* (pp. 41–64). Hillsdale, NJ: Erlbaum.

Johnson, M. H. (1998). Developing an attentive brain. In R. Parasuraman (Ed.), *The attentive brain* (pp. 427–443). Cambridge, MA: MIT Press.

Johnson, M. H., & Morton, J. (1991). *Biology and cognitive development: The case of face recognition.* Oxford: Basil Blackwell.

Kugiumutzakis, J. (1985). *The origin, development and function of early infant imitation, Doctoral dissertation.* Department of Psychology, University of Uppsala, Sweden.

(1993). Intersubjective vocal imitation in early mother–infant interaction. In J. Nadel & L. Camioni (Eds.), *New perspectives in early communication development* (pp. 23–47). London: Routledge.

(1999). Genesis and development of early infant mimesis to facial and vocal models. In J. Nadel & G. Butterworth (Eds.), *Imitation in infancy* (pp. 63–88). Cambridge: Cambridge University Press.

McLeod, P., Plunkett, K., & Rolls, E. T. (1998). *Introduction to connectionist modelling of cognitive processes.* Oxford: Oxford University Press.

Meltzoff, A. N., & Moore, M. K. (1994). Imitation, memory, and the representation of persons. *Infant Behavior and Development, 17,* 83–99.

(1997). Explaining facial imitation: A theoretical model. *Early Development and Parenting, 6,* 179–192.

(1998a). Object representation, identity, and the paradox of early permanence: Steps toward a new framework. *Infant Behavior and Development, 21 (2),* 201–235.

(1998b). Infant intersubjectivity: Broadening the dialogue to include imitation, identity and intention. In S. Bråten (Ed.), *Intersubjective communication and emotion in early ontogeny* (pp. 47–62). Cambridge: Cambridge University Press.

Rizzolatti, G., & Arbib, M. A. (1998). Language within our grasp. *Trends in Neuroscience, 21 (5),* 188–194.

Rochat, P., & Striano, T. (1999). Social-cognitive development in the first year. In P. Rochat (Ed.), *Early social cognition: Understanding others in the first months of life* (pp. 3–34). Mahwah, NJ: Erlbaum.

Rolls, E. T., & Treves, A. (1998). *Neural networks and brain function.* Oxford: Oxford University Press.

Stein, B. E., & Meredith, M. A. (1993). *The merging of the senses.* Cambridge, MA: MIT Press.

Swerlander, A. (2001). Imitation in early childhood. Doctoral dissertation. Department of Psychology, Göteborg University, Sweden.

Thelen, E., & Smith, L. B. (1994). *A dynamic systems approach to the development of cognition and action.* Cambridge, MA: MIT Press.

Tomasello, M., Kruger, A. C., & Ratner, H. H. (1993). Cultural learning. *Behavioral and Brain Sciences, 16,* 495–552.

Trevarthen, C., Kokkinaki, T., & Fiamenghi, G. A. Jr. (1998). What infants' imitations communicate: With mothers, with fathers and with peers. In J. Nadel and G. Butterworth (Eds.), *Imitation in infancy: Progress and prospects of current research* (pp. 127–185).Cambridge: Cambridge University Press.

Uzgiris, I. C. (1981). Two functions of imitation during infancy. *International Journal of Behavioral Development, 4,* 1–12.

5   Ego function of early imitation

Philippe Rochat

Early imitation is typically associated with cognitive and social-communicative functions (Uzgiris 1981, 1999; see also Nadel & Butterworth, 1999). The cognitive function of infant imitation is put forth in theories such as Piaget's (1962) who considers imitation as a central process by which infants develop an ability to function symbolically, performing actions (signifier) as standing for the action of someone else (signified). The cognitive aspect of early imitation is also emphasized in current research and theories suggesting that via imitation, infants pick up information about the identity of others and might express a sense of others as equivalent to themselves. Accordingly, from an early age infants take a "like-me stance" (Meltzoff & Moore, 1994, 1999; Gopnik & Meltzoff, 1997).

Early imitation is also discussed in relation to its potential social-communicative function, a way by which infants maintain contact and social-proximity with others (Uzgiris, 1981, 1999). The early propensity to imitate would not only be the expression of cognitive capacities, but also a means for infants to create interpersonal contacts and establish grounds for shared experiences, hence to develop intersubjectivity. In support of this contention, infants are shown for example to repeat an imitative act in the presence of the experimenter who modeled the action, for no other apparent reason than the maintenance of dialogic interaction (Killen & Uzgiris, 1981).

In this chapter, I argue that aside from a cognitive and social-communicative function, early imitation serves an *ego function*. Aside from the willful (i.e., nonautomatic) attempt to reproduce more or less accurately the behavior of others, imitation is viewed here as part of the general propensity of young organisms to *repeat* their own actions and engage in what has been described for a long time by pioneer infancy students as "circular reactions" (Baldwin, 1925; Piaget, 1952). In general, early imitation is considered here as a basic mechanism contributing to the emergence of self-objectification in early ontogeny.

At the crux of my argument is the idea that self-reflection or contemplation of the self as object (self-objectification) is a process emerging from
young infants' propensity to reproduce their own actions and engage in
self-imitation. From the repetition of own actions, the self becomes objectified, becoming both an embodied experience and a potential object of
thoughts (i.e., self-reflection).

The chapter is organized as follows. First, I use the example of mirrors
as perfect imitators of the self to introduce the idea that self-objectification
emerges from the process of self-imitation. I show that the process underlying mirror self-recognition is self-imitation or the reproduction of own
action. Then, I link own action reproduction by young infants to self-
exploration and the intermodal calibration of the own body. The body
is considered here as a primary object of exploration in infancy. Next, I
try to articulate the process of self-objectification putatively attached to
action reproduction in early infancy. For that purpose, four determinants
of self-objectification in early development are proposed. Together, these
determinants would account for the emergence of a *contemplative stance*
taken by infants at around two months of age. This stance is viewed as
the first developmental sign of a self-reflective process.

In general, what is proposed here is that the systematic repetition of
self-produced action (i.e., self-imitation) is a mechanism contributing to
the emergence of a contemplative stance in infant psychological development. Again, aside from a cognitive and social-communicative function,
there is a primary *ego* function attached to early imitation when considering young infants' playful and gratuitous propensity to reproduce their
own action.

Imitation is a primary source of knowledge about the self and a basic
process by which infants gain self-reflective abilities. Such abilities are
arguably a trademark of human cognition and the question of their origins
is among the most challenging empirical issues in both the perspective of
primate evolution and child development.

Mirrors as perfect imitators

In its simplest acceptation, imitation is the process by which one behavior
is mapped onto another. In relation to this definition, the specular images or image of the self reflected by mirrors provide a perfect, absolute
version of this process. What a mirror projects back to actors, assuming
that their surface is well polished and flat, is a perfect visual reproduction
of self-produced action, an absolute visual analog of what is felt proprioceptively by the actor behaving in front of the mirror. The visual analog
of the specular image is absolute both in terms of its perfect temporal

contingency and relative spatial congruence. Spatially, although the specular image is inverted along its vertical axis in relation to the actor standing in front of the mirror, it provides absolute spatial congruence in terms of the form and amount of self-generated movements.

Fundamental to the issue of imitation is the issue of the differentiation between imitator and imitated. When standing in front of a mirror, one might ask who is imitating whom. Is it me or my reflection? Of course, this question is absurd if we take for granted that what is seen in the mirror is the specular image of the embodied self. There is no imitator nor any imitated, but one self. This realization can occur only when the inclination to dissociate the embodied self from its specular image is overcome. This realization is not a simple feat. This is particularly evident in the temporary puzzlement adults typically experience while trying to make sense of the left–right reversal of mirrors: that when lifting my left arm the specular image of myself is actually lifting its right arm. The rationality of light bouncing from the self onto the flat surface of the mirror alleviates such apparent dissociation.

Interestingly, the question of who is imitating whom in front of mirrors, hence specular dissociation, becomes eventually obsolete only after some major evolutionary and developmental changes. For example, regardless of age, a dog facing its specular image will smell it, growl, or engage in playful engagement while maintaining eye contacts, as if encountering another dog (Zazzo, 1979). Aggressive responses are found in fish (Tinbergen, 1951) and birds (Smythe, 1962) encountering their own reflection on a polished surface. Children up to about three years will sometimes search behind the mirror to find the other child they confound with the specular image of themselves (Zazzo, 1981).

It might be argued that these kinds of behavior are unusual and due essentially to the peculiar optical affordances of mirrors which make them unique among other objects in the environment (Loveland, 1986). However, beyond the perceptual learning attached to mirrors and their unique properties, behavioral changes in front of them index unmistakable, interesting, and reliable cognitive changes in the perspective of both phylogeny and ontogeny (Gallup, 1970; Lewis & Brooks-Gunn, 1979; Zazzo, 1981).

From a comparative perspective, only a few of our close primate relatives demonstrate clear evidence of mirror self-recognition in the context of the "rouge task" (i.e., orangutans and chimpanzees, see the thorough review by Tomasello & Call, 1997). On the other hand, from a developmental perspective, it is only by the middle of the second year that children pass the rouge task, touching with embarrassment the rouge spot put surreptitiously on their face and that they detect in the specular image (Amsterdam, 1972; Lewis, Sullivan, Stanger, & Weiss, 1989). This novel reaction to mirrors indexes unambiguously a concept of self as "me and only me" in the mirror, not another individual facing and imitating me. From then on, the question of "who is imitating whom?" does indeed become absurd.

So how do children develop an ability to recognize that it is themselves in mirrors, not someone else reproducing their acts perfectly? I will submit that it is by developing a sense of self-agency via repetition of self-produced action, namely *self-imitation* construed as the systematic attempt to *reproduce* and *match* previous patterns of self-generated action. To illustrate this process, I will use a simple example that I suppose we all can relate to. Suppose that you enter a video store full of TV monitors all projecting an online "security" view, from different angles, of the crowd in the store. Suppose now that you wonder whether it is actually an on-line view of the store. The way you will untangle this question is by trying to recognize yourself on the TV monitors. You would scan the screens until you recognize yourself. But that would not give you any certitude as to whether the image of the store is actually online. The faster and more accurate way to address this question would be to move in an identifiable fashion and explore the perfect temporal contingency and spatial form between felt and seen movements on the screens. This is what you would do also if different cameras were filming you simultaneously, providing different views of yourself and you wanted to figure where the cameras are actually located in the store. You would move around and compare the proprioceptive sense of your own body in space and its various visual projections on the screens.

In these examples, the untangling of the question of what view is projected on the screens, and whether it includes oneself, entail the systematic comparison between self-produced action and its online visual consequences. From this intermodal comparison, one can overcome the dissociation between the embodied self and its specular image (or TV's images in the above examples). What is important here is the systematicity aspect of this comparison which makes it deliberate and intentional, in the sense that it is based on repeated actions as part of a plan (e.g., figuring the cameras' locations in the store). Such comparisons express a sense of *self-agency* on the part of the perceiver/actor.

I propose here that such a process of intentional comparison and, in general, the sense of self-agency originates in early development from the propensity of young infants to repeat actions that are self-produced. Self-imitation is presented as a primary mechanism for the calibration of the self as both embodied and reflected back by objects such as mirrors, shadows, videos, calm liquid surfaces, acoustical echoes, as well as the social mirroring provided by others.

Action repetition and self-exploration

First signs that infants contemplate their own body as an object to be explored arise by the second month when they start to bring, for example, their own hands in the field of view and move their own limbs for long bouts of visual exploration (Piaget, 1952). There is a mutual, synchronous feedback from vision and proprioception, infants experiencing with apparent pleasure this intermodal correspondence. But what makes it so compelling for the infant? From a cognitive and epistemological standpoint, Piaget (1952, 1954) proposed that infants when first engaging in repeated visual tracking of their own hand, do so because they visually perceive a dynamic, nonself object. This object is not yet perceived as part of their own body or moving as a function of their own agency. For Piaget, it is as compelling to the young infant as any other dynamic objects in the environment would be, whether their movements are self-produced or not. Accordingly, early on infants would not perceive the intermodal correspondence between what they feel proprioceptively and what they see. We know now that this interpretation is probably wrong. Since Piaget, multiple pieces of evidence have been reported demonstrating that from a very early age, and even from birth, infants are capable of matching visual, haptic, proprioceptive, and auditory percepts (Clifton, Morrongiello, Kulig, & Dowd, 1981; Gibson & Walker, 1984; Jouen, 1984; Meltzoff & Borton, 1979). It is thus probable that when young infants start moving their hand systematically in their field of view, they perform this action repeatedly as part of self-exploration, and not as random visual tracking. Such repeated multimodal activity enables them to discover their own body configuration and its degrees of behavioral freedom.

Via self-exploration, young infants develop an intermodal sense of their own body which is a primary object of exploration. Systematic reproduction of self-produced actions allows them to calibrate synchronous information from various perceptual systems. It is probably based on this intermodal calibration that infants develop the perception of their own body as a differentiated entity among other entities in the environment (Rochat, 1995, 1997, 1998). In this calibration process, self-imitation or the propensity to reproduce own actions is a central mechanism.

From birth, infants kick their legs repeatedly (Thelen & Fisher, 1983) or wave their arms (Van der Meer & Van der Weel, 1995), and tend to bring their hands to the mouth (Rochat, Blass, & Hoffmeyer, 1988; Rochat, 1993). Self-imitation as the process by which actions are systematically reproduced is arguably the most pervasive behavioral propensity expressed from birth, even prior to birth (Hopkins & Prechtl, 1984). It is certainly the most readily observable behavioral trait of young infants and I propose that it is also an important mechanism by which infants come to *objectify* themselves and eventually become self-reflective. But how might such a mechanism of self-objectification via repeated self-produced actions work?

Putative determinants of early self-objectification

There might be only a few basic determinants accounting for the mechanism by which infants may start to show first signs of self-reflection, beginning to contemplate themselves as agent and differentiated entity among other entities in the environment. I identify four putative determinants of early self-objectification: (1) the functional pleasure attached to the production of bodily movements expressed by infants from birth; (2) the unique perceptual experience of the self attached to bodily movements; (3) the canalization towards repeated actions due to the prolonged postural immaturity of early infancy; and (4) the contemplative stance arising from patterns of action that are repeated in a process of self-imitation. I describe each of these determinants next.

Functional pleasure of self-produced action

From birth, infants are compelled to move for the apparent sake of moving. They express functional pleasure in setting their own body in motion (Baldwin, 1925; Piaget, 1952; Wallon, 1942/1970). Infant behavior from birth is in great proportion gratuitous, namely without any apparent functional reason attached to it, except for putative "pleasure." Aside from sucking, crying, or breathing, which have clear adaptive and survival functions, young infants' wakeful behavior is characterized by many bodily movements that appear to be performed for the sake of exhausting possibilities for action and exploring behavioral degrees of freedom. This apparent functional pleasure goes beyond the expression of fixed-action patterns or automatic reflexes triggered by nonspecific external stimulation. It is the sensorimotor expression of an early propensity to play. It is worth noting that the propensity to play is not unique to human infancy, it being observed in other young animals. However, the tendency to play is a particular trademark of human infancy, inseparable from its prolonged immaturity in comparison to other primate species (Bruner, 1972; Rochat, 2001).

For example, it is now well established that infants from birth demonstrate hand–mouth coordination, compelled to repeatedly transporting their hand(s) to the perioral region. This action is systematically reproduced, under the control of mechanisms that are not rigidly tight, to afferent–efferent loops or reflex arcs. It entails some form of sensori-motor anticipation, the mouth typically opening in anticipation of manual contact (Blass *et al.*, 1989; Butterworth & Hopkins, 1988; Rochat, Blass, & Hoffmeyer, 1988; Rochat, 1993).

Hand–mouth coordination, leg kicking, head turning, mouth opening and closing, arm waving, grasping movements, all these actions form complex yet clearly differentiated behavioral patterns displayed by healthy newborns. These behavioral patterns are typically repeated by the infant, in protracted bouts while awake and active (Hopkins & Prechtl, 1984; Wolff, 1987). Aside from an outlet of energy expenditure, the repetition of such action patterns is the source of perceptual experiences that uniquely specify the self. As I will suggest next, it is indeed a primary source of self-knowledge at the origin of self-objectification.

Unique perceptual experience gained from self-produced action

When moving their limbs, touching their own body, or hearing their own voice in crying or cooing bouts, infants make the unique experience of themselves as differentiated entities in the environment. This unique perceptual experience is intermodal, involving proprioception plus other modalities (e.g., touch, vision, or audition).

Proprioception is indeed the sensory modality of the self "par excel-lence." When uttering sounds, they make the unique experience of propri-oceptive feedback accompanying sound production and its actual audi-tion. When bringing their hand(s) to the mouth or field of view, they make the unique experience of joint haptic- or visual-proprioceptive feedback. In addition, in the case of hand-to-mouth contacts, infants experience a "double touch" that is uniquely specifying the self (hand touching the mouth and mouth touching the hand, von Glasersfeld, 1988; Rochat, 1995, 1998).

From moving their limbs, vocalizing and touching themselves, infants have the opportunity to specify perceptually (i.e., intermodally) their own body as differentiated from other entities in the environment. This is ob-viously the most basic requirement of self-objectification. We recently collected data suggesting that from birth infants do pick up the inter-modal information accompanying self-produced movements and spec-ifying themselves as differentiated entities. Analyzing neonates' rooting response (head turn and mouth opening) towards a perioral tactile stimu-lation, we found that this response varies systematically whether the stim-ulation is caused by the experimenter's finger or the infant's own hand touching the face (Rochat & Hespos, 1997). In particular, we found that healthy newborns aged less than eighteen hours tended to display signif-icantly more rooting responses (i.e., head turn towards the stimulation with mouth open and tonguing) following external compared to self-stimulation. In the context of our research, such differential responding is possible only to the extent that newborns pick up on the specificity of double touch and the presence or absence of proprioceptive feedback accompanying the touch stimulation that specifies either self or nonself experience.

Postural immaturity as a constraint toward action repetition

The prolonged postural immaturity characterizing human infancy does not only determine powerlessness and vulnerability due to a lack of mobility, hence lack of self-reliance in escaping from most adverse environmental circumstances. It also canalizes infants' bodily movements toward the repetition of identifiable, hence explorable, action patterns. Aside from reflexes and pre-adapted action systems such as sucking or tracking moving targets with the eyes, infants' propensity to move their body for the apparent sake of moving, is highly constrained by the limitation in degrees of behavioral freedom. So for example, when lying supine in their crib, the possible repertoire of limb and head movements is greatly limited and relatively sluggish for at least the first eight weeks of life. Head rotation, hand transport to face and mouth, rhythmical flexion and extension of the limbs are the main features of this early "play" repertoire. This, I propose, has great functional significance and probably contributes to the development of self-objectification as it promotes self-imitation.

Moving for the sake of moving is highly constrained early in development due to postural immaturity that reduces the degrees of movement freedom. In dynamic systems terminology, free play in early development has few stable attractors (Thelen & Smith, 1994). This means that in moving for the sake of moving, young infants are limited to a very small range of possible bodily movements. This state of affairs constrains them toward repetition. This is one way to account for the cardinal rhythmicity of bodily movements early in development. My contention is that the lack of postural control of young infants has as a consequence *scaffolding self-imitation*, namely the basic propensity to reproduce systematically the same (possible) self-generated action pattern, and engaging in so-called "circular reactions" (Baldwin, 1925; Piaget, 1952).

Contemplative stance arising from repeated actions

The fourth putative determinant of self-objectification rests on an important developmental transition observable by the second month of life. This transition marks the passage from actions repeated by the infant for the sake of repetition, to actions that are reproduced in order to explore systematically the range of their perceptual effects or consequences. This transition characterizes the adoption by the infant of a contemplative stance (Rochat & Striano, 1999a; see also Werner & Kaplan, 1963).

As an illustration, we captured such transition in a recent study in which we compared newborns' and two-month-old infants' sucking behavior on a dummy pacifier, experimental situations where each suck was accompanied by a contingent sound (Rochat & Striano, 1999b). The sound consisted of a sequence of discrete tones that varied in pitch. Infants were tested in two experimental conditions. In one condition, each time they sucked on the pacifier above a minimum pressure threshold, they heard a contingent sound with a pitch variation that was commensurate to the pressure variation they applied on the pacifier. In other words, in this condition, infants were presented with a continuous auditory *analog* of the pressure they exerted on the pacifier: the more they pressed on it, the higher the pitch, and inversely. In another experimental condition, each time they sucked above the minimum threshold, they heard a two-second series of discrete tones that varied randomly in pitch. The tone series were repeated in succession when the oral pressure on the pacifier was above threshold. In this situation, the infant heard a contingent but *nonanalog* auditory feedback. We found that two-month-olds sucked differentially (i.e., frequency of pressure just at threshold, average pressure amplitude on the pacifier, standard deviation of pressure amplitude) in the analog compared with the nonanalog condition, evidently attentive to the form of the auditory feedback that reflects or does not reflect what they do on the pacifier. They appeared to modulate their oral activity on the pacifier as a function of the relative audio-proprioceptive congruence. In contrast, newborns do not demonstrate any evidence of such discrimination, sucking in similar ways in both experimental situations (Rochat & Striano, 1999b).

Such findings indicate that by the second month infants appear to develop a sense of their own agency, controlling their own actions to contemplate their perceptual consequences. This indexes the emergence of a contemplative stance, itself the first manifestation of a self-reflection process. But how to account for such emergence in early development?

I propose that the emergence of the contemplative stance is tied to self-imitation. By virtue of their systematic reproduction, self-generated action patterns become objects of exploration. From the functional pleasure of being executed (e.g., sucking for sucking, kicking for kicking), actions and their intermodal consequences emerge as objects of contemplation for the infant. This cognitive breakthrough finds its roots in the propensity of infants to repeat highly constrained and uniquely self-specifying motor patterns. It is best described as a new cognitive form emerging from systematic self-imitation.

The actual mechanism of such emergence is speculative but it is easy to consider that being repeated, action patterns can be remembered and compared as they leave memory traces. By being reproduced these patterns become also highly automatized leaving much room for novel attentional focus by the infant: from a focus on the here and now of the action execution, to an anticipation and control of the perceptual consequences of such action (e.g., Rochat & Striano, 1999b). Once again, this contention is highly speculative and more research is needed to unveil the exact mechanism of this key developmental transition. Interestingly, Meltzoff & Moore (1997) recently proposed a theoretical model of facial imitation by young infants that also capitalizes on what they coin "body babbling" or movement practice gained through self-generated action. If body babbling is potentially an important mechanism for the early understanding of others, it is also potentially a primary mechanism for the understanding of the self, as proposed in this chapter.

Summary and conclusion

The argument proposed here is that first signs of self-reflection and in particular the emergence of a contemplative stance by which the self is perceived as agent in the environment are co-determined in part by (1) the functional pleasure attached to the repetition of action from birth and possibly prior to birth; (2) the unique perceptual experience of the self attached to bodily movements; and (3) the constraining effect of prolonged postural immaturity in early human infancy. Together, these three factors would co-determine the early manifestation of self-imitation from which the contemplative stance probably emerges as a new cognitive form by the second month of life.

By imitating their own action in patterns described by pioneer infancy researchers as "circular reactions," young infants gain a sense of themselves as differentiated agents in the environment. Self-imitation, or the propensity of infants from birth to repeat systematically highly constrained movement patterns, serves primarily an *ego* function: the function of giving infants an opportunity to specify themselves as differentiated and agent entities among other entities in the environment.

In conclusion, an important aspect of early imitation is self-imitation, the process by which infants develop knowledge about themselves and an ability to contemplate the perceptual consequences of their own actions. It serves primarily an *ego function*. The ego function of early imitation is too often overlooked by researchers and theorists (but see Meltzoff & Moore, 1995). It is of great interest, particularly when considering that self-imitation is probably at the origin of what is arguably one of the trademarks of human cognition: the capacity for self-reflection and the ability to generate thoughts that fold back upon themselves.

Acknowledgments

Thank you to Tricia Striano for her helpful comments on an earlier version of the manuscript. While writing this chapter, the author was supported by a grant No SBR-9507773 from the National Science Foundation. Request for reprints and correspondence should be addressed to Philippe Rochat, Department of Psychology, Emory University, Atlanta, GA 30322 (e-mail: PSYPR@EMORY.EDU).

References

Amsterdam, B. (1972). Mirror self-image reactions before age two. *Developmental Psychobiology, 5*, 297–305.

Baldwin, J. M. (1925). *Mental development in the child and the race.* New York: The Macmillan Company.

Blass, E. M., Fillion, T. J., Rochat, P., Hoffmeyer, L. B., & Metzger, M. A. (1989). Sensorimotor and motivational determinants of hand-mouth coordination in 1–3 day old human infants. *Developmental Psychology, 25*, 963–975.

Bruner, J. S. (1972). Nature and uses of immaturity. *American Psychologist, 27(8)*, 687–708.

Butterworth, G., & Hopkins, B. (1988). Hand–mouth coordination in the newborn baby. *British Journal of Developmental Psychology, 6*, 303–314.

Clifton, R. K., Morrongiello, B. A., Kulig, J. W., & Dowd, J. M. (1981). Newborns' orientation toward sound: Possible implications for cortical development. *Child Development, 52*, 833–838.

Gallup, G. G., Jr. (1970). Chimpanzees: Self-recognition. *Science, 167*, 86–87.

Gibson, E. J., & Walker, A. S. (1984). Development of knowledge of visual-tactual affordances of substance. *Child Development, 55*, 453–461.

Glasersfeld, E. von (1988). *The construction of knowledge: Contributions to conceptual semantics.* Salinas, CA: Intersystems Publications.

Gopnik, A., & Meltzoff, A. N. (1997). *Words, thoughts, and theories.* Cambridge, MA: MIT Press.

Hopkins, B., & Prechtl, H. F. R. (1984). A qualitative approach to the development of movements during early infancy. In H. F. R. Prechtl (Ed.), *Continuity of neural functions from prenatal to postnatal life* (pp. 179–197). Oxford: Blackwell.

Jouen, F. (1984). Visual-vestibular interactions in infancy. *Infant Behavior and Development, 7*, 135–145.

Killen, M., & Uzgiris, I. C. (1981). Imitation of actions with objects: The role of social meaning. *Journal of Genetic Psychology, 138*, 219–229.

Lewis, M., Sullivan, M., Stanger, C., & Weiss, M. (1989). Self-development and self-conscious emotions. *Child Development, 60*, 146–156.

Lewis, M., & Brooks-Gunn, J. (1979). *Social cognition and the acquisition of self.* New York: Plenum Press.

Loveland, K. A. (1986). Discovering the affordances of a reflecting surface. *Developmental Review, 6,* 1–24.

Meltzoff, A. N., and Borton, R. W. (1979). Intermodal matching in human neonates. *Nature, 282,* 403–404.

Meltzoff, A. N., and Moore, M. K. (1994). Imitation, memory, and the representation of persons. *Infant Behavior and Development, 17,* 83–99.

(1995). A theory of the role of imitation in the emergence of self. In P. Rochat (Ed.), *The self in infancy.* Advances in Psychology Book Series (pp. 73–94). Amsterdam: North Holland, Elsevier.

(1997). Explaining facial imitation: A theoretical model. *Early Development and Parenting, 6,* 179–192.

(1999). Persons as representation: Why infant imitation is important for theories of human development. In J. Nadel & G. Butterworth (Eds.), *Imitation in infancy* (pp. 9–35). Cambridge: Cambridge University Press.

Nadel, J., & Butterworth, G. (1999). Immediate imitation rehabilitated at last. In J. Nadel & G. Butterworth (Eds.), *Imitation in infancy* (pp. 1–5). Cambridge: Cambridge University Press.

Piaget, J. (1952). *The origin of intelligence in children.* New York: International Universities Press.

(1954). *The construction of reality in children.* New York: International Universities Press.

(1962). *Play, dreams, and imitation in childhood.* New York: Norton Press.

Rochat, P. (1993). Hand–mouth coordination in the Newborn: Morphology, determinants, and early development of a basic act. In G. Savelsbergh (Ed.), *The development of coordination in infancy.* Advances in Psychology Series (pp. 265–288). Amsterdam: Elsevier.

(1995). Early objectification of the self. In P. Rochat (Ed.), *The self in infancy.* Advances in Psychology Book Series (pp. 53–71). Amsterdam: North Holland, Elsevier.

(1997). Early Development of the Ecological Self. In C. Dent-Read & P. Zukow-Goldring (Eds.), *Evolving explanations of development* (pp. 91–122). Washington, DC: American Psychological Association.

(1998). Self-perception and action in infancy. *Experimental Brain Research, 123,* 102–109.

(2001). *The infant world: Self, objects, and people.* Cambridge, MA: Harvard University Press.

Rochat, P., Blass, E. M., & Hoffmeyer, L. B. (1988). Oropharyngeal control of hand-mouth coordination in newborn infants. *Developmental Psychology, 24,* 459–463.

Rochat, P., & Hespos, S. J. (1997). Differential rooting response by neonates: Evidence for an early sense of self. *Early Development & Parenting, 6(2),* 150.1–8.

Rochat, P., and Striano, T. (1999a). Social cognitive development in the first year. In P. Rochat (Ed.), *Early social cognition* (pp. 3–34). Hillsdale, NJ: Lawrence Erlbaum Associates.

(1999b). Emerging self-exploration by 2 month-olds. *Developmental Science, 2(2),* 206–218.

Smythe, R. H. (1962). *Animal habits: The things animals do.* Springfield, IL: Charles C. Thomas Publisher.

Thelen, E., & Fisher, D. M. (1983). The organization of spontaneous leg movements in newborn infants. *Journal of Motor Behavior, 15,* 353–377.

Thelen, E., & Smith, L. B. (1994). *A dynamic systems approach to the development of cognition and action.* Boston: MIT Press.

Tinbergen, N. (1951). *The study of instinct.* London: Oxford University Press.

Tomasello, M., & Call, J. (1997). *Primate cognition.* New York: Oxford University Press.

Uzgiris, I. (1981). Two functions of imitation during infancy. *International Journal of Behavioral Development, 4,* 1–12.

(1999). Imitation as activity: Its developmental aspects. In J. Nadel & G. Butterworth (Eds.), *Imitation in infancy* (pp. 186–206). Cambridge: Cambridge University Press.

Van der Meer, A. L. H., & Van der Weel, F. R. (1995). Move yourself, baby! Perceptuo-motor development from a continuous perspective. In P. Rochat (Ed.), *The self in infancy.* Advances in Psychology Book Series (pp. 257–277). Amsterdam: North Holland, Elsevier.

Wallon, H. (1942/1970). *De l'acte à la pensée: Essai de psychologie comparée.* Paris: Collection Champs, Flammarion.

(1981). Comment se développe chez l'enfant la notion du corps propre. *La reconnaissance de son image chez l'enfant et l'animal* (pp. 21–46). Collection Textes de Base en Psychologie (Ed. P. Mounoud & A. Vinter). Paris: Delachaux et Niestlé.

Werner, H., & Kaplan, B. (1963). *Symbol Formation.* New York: John Wiley & Sons.

Wolff, P. (1987). *The development of behavioral states and the expression of emotions in early infancy.* Chicago: University of Chicago Press.

Zazzo, R. (1979). Des enfants, des singes et des chiens devant le miroir. *Revue de Psychologie Appliquée, 2,* 235–246.

(1981). Miroir, images, espaces. *La reconnaissance de son image chez l'enfant et l'animal.* Collection Textes de Base en Psychologie (Ed. P. Mounoud & A. Vinter) (pp. 77–110). Paris: Delachaux et Niestlé.

6   The imitator's representation of the imitated: Ape and child

Andrew Whiten

I had the good fortune to have an interest in the origins of mind kindled in the heady atmosphere of Jerry Bruner's group at Oxford – alongside A. Meltzoff, as it happens – so it is apt to begin this chapter with the conception of imitation that Bruner offered in his insightful analysis of "The nature and uses of immaturity" (Bruner, 1972).

Bruner highlighted two sophisticated cognitive aspects of imitation. First, it involves the imitator in a complex "deictic" mental transformation, translating from an act originally done from the perspective of the model (yet perceived from the perspective of the imitator) to what is involved in doing a matching act from the imitator's own perspective. Second, Bruner suggested imitation may involve "the construction of an action pattern by the appropriate sequencing of a set of constituent subroutines to match the model." Here, Bruner is suggesting that imitation of a complex behavioral structure might be built by the orchestration of existing action-components.

Each of these two "sophisticated abilities" are subjects of this chapter. That concerning the translation from model's to self's actions I address later in the chapter, considering whether apes evidence perception-action mappings akin to those of humans analyzed elsewhere in this volume. I will address the second ability Bruner highlighted by describing experiments on imitation of the sequential and hierarchical structure of actions by chimpanzees and children.

The over-arching question that unites these issues is: *what is the imitator's mental representation of what is being imitated?* We have tackled this question through experiments dissecting just what an imitator selectively acquires (and what they neglect) given all the potential information available in a model. Some readers may wonder if that can do the trick. Are we just describing the imitation the subject does, rather than discriminating between alternative hypotheses about possible underlying cognitive processes? Our answer is simply that in appropriately designed experiments, subjects make transparent to us what they are and are not representing in the imitative translation process. Kinsbourne argues elsewhere in this volume that imitation is effectively a "read-out" of how the imitator represents the actions of others. Readers will judge for themselves how well we are beginning to succeed by adopting this perspective.

The imitation we are studying

Imitation is defined in somewhat different ways by different authors. Here I follow the relatively simple definition of Whiten and Ham (1992:247), that individual B imitates individual A when "B learns from A some part of the form of a behavior." Note this sets a very basic requirement, that there must be *some* minimally recognizable match between what A and B do, rather than that B's behavior is exactly like A's.

The methodological approach: Ethology and experimentation

My approach to the study of imitation is fundamentally ethological, following the strategy of pioneers like Niko Tinbergen (1951). One begins by observing and documenting the phenomena of interest under natural conditions. This is a good way not only to generate hypotheses that can be rigorously framed and tested by further systematic observations or by experimentation in field and laboratory, but to get to those hypotheses that are most worthwhile in the first place. This is because they are likely to *make functional sense*, being founded on an adequate grasp of the subject species' natural history.

In my case, the first 'natural history' phase involved, for human infants, extensive observations of everyday social behavior and play in homes and other natural settings, both in the UK and in Africa (e.g. Whiten & Milner, 1984). For nonhuman primates the naturalistic foundations range from observations of infant baboons developing their foraging abilities on the African savannah, to variation in chimpanzee behavior profiles between the long-term African study-sites (e.g. Whiten, 1989; Whiten et al., 1999). In humans, apes, and monkeys, one will see infants closely observe what their mothers or others are doing; for example, peeling a tricky food item in a particular way. Later, one will see the infant perform similar behavior. Did they acquire the behavior by copying it? Naturalistic observations of spontaneous behavior are crucial in framing such questions, but they are severely limited in supplying clear answers. The main reason is simply that young primates typically take weeks or months becoming more and more proficient in processing difficult foodstuffs (and other tasks), eventually in the ways adults do. One cannot know how much of the match to adult behavior is based upon imitation, or on one of many other forms of social learning (Whiten & Ham, 1992), or on the juvenile discovering the optimal technique by its own efforts. King (1994), having attempted to observationally discriminate social learning in wild baboons, came to the same pessimistic conclusion.

This is the point at which ethologists like Tinbergen turn to experiments, ideally in field as well as captivity. Imitation is a very apt target for experimentation, which is powerful in testing causal hypotheses, like "The form of B's acts is shaped by its observation of A's." The job experiments do best is to test hypothesized causal processes like imitation. They should, however, be complemented by what the field observations do best: generating the causal hypotheses, establishing the functional context of the phenomenon of interest, and indicating valid naturalistic forms of experimental approach.

This rationale has been "fruitful" in a quite concrete way. It led my colleague Debbie Custance and I to create "artificial fruits," that can be opened ("shelled") by the kinds of actions primates use to deal with wild foods. These artificial foods have been designed so that each of a number of "shell components" can be dealt with through alternative actions. Different groups of experimental subjects then see only one set of these alternative techniques. Whether subjects later differ in corresponding ways in their own acts is a powerful way to test for imitation, controlling for simpler social learning like stimulus enhancement, because the alternative acts were performed on the same parts of the fruit.

This aspect of the fruits' design exemplifies what has come to be called "the two-action method" in animal studies, where it was first developed by Dawson and Foss (1965). In developmental psychology a logically similar rationale acquired a different label, the "cross-target method," developed in the study of infant imitation (Meltzoff & Moore, 1977; and see Meltzoff, this volume).

I want to make two claims for the power of this approach before presenting experimental findings. First, note that the underlying logic is not limited to paired alternative actions (so "cross-target" is perhaps better than "two-action"). Thus, the essential rationale of the method extends to the "Do-as-I-do" method, in which subjects are trained (or in the human case, sometimes just asked) to copy each of what may be a large battery of actions, when accompanied by a signal like "do this" (Hayes & Hayes, 1952). The power of this approach has enormous potential especially where available subjects are few (often the case with great apes, and patients with rare neurological deficits), because with a large array of modeled actions, an ability to match several different target acts can be shown clearly to exceed chance levels of probability (Custance, Whiten, & Bard, 1995).

My second and more important claim is that the basic logic of the cross-target approach can be used to establish which of the many different structural aspects of an action pattern that might be imitated, are in fact represented and copied. In this chapter, I shall illustrate this in experiments that contrast not only two different action-shapes, but also different sequential and hierarchical patterns of action. To these we now turn.

Imitating the shape and sequencing of actions

Using artificial fruits like that shown in Figure 6.1, we have investigated imitation in various groups of children, chimpanzees, and other species (Caldwell & Whiten, 1999; Custance, Whiten, & Fredman, 1999; Custance, Whiten, Sambrook, & Galdikas, in press; Whiten *et al.*, 1996; Whiten & Brown, 1999). The "fruit" I describe here (our "pin-apple") was constructed to present a controlled analog of natural foods requiring

Figure 6.1. An "artificial fruit." The pin is being spun using an index finger. Above the pin is the "handle" component that is freed by removing the pin. Two embedded "bolts" can also be seen at the top. Once all defenses are removed or disabled, the lid-top can be opened to gain the edible part inside. See Whiten (1998a) and Custance, Whiten, & Fredman (1999) for more detailed illustrations of fruit components and opening actions.

manipulation. It was designed so it can be opened using not only different sequences of steps to remove the fruit's "defenses" (pin, handle, two bolts and a lid), but differently "shaped" alternative techniques can also be used at each step, like poking the bolts through, versus pulling and twisting them out. This means that many different patterns of behavior can be modeled and in a recent experiment four were generated, each one being observed by a different chimpanzee (Whiten, 1998a). Two chimps saw one sequential pattern (outer bolt, inner bolt, pin, handle, lid), two another (pin, handle, outer bolt, inner bolt, lid). Each of the pair witnessing one of these sequence patterns also saw different techniques used within the sequence (e.g., poke bolts versus twist-and-pull bolts).

These chimpanzees showed copying of both the action-shapes and sequences they had witnessed, although individuals varied much in the fidelity of the match they produced. Interestingly, it was in the third and final trial that imitation of sequential structure emerged, after subjects had several times seen the fruit opened and manipulated and opened it themselves. The sequential match was statistically significant; indeed, it was exact for three of the four subjects and close in the fourth. It is worth noting that traditionally it has been assumed that the first trial is particularly critical for detecting true imitation, but this result highlights the fact that the cross-action method has the power to detect imitation effects that may require significant periods to appear. This perhaps parallels findings from human infancy studies, where matching has been shown to achieve a progressive convergence (Meltzoff & Moore, 1994).

By contrast, signs of copying the shape of the actions used were apparent in the first trial. For example, one subject persisted in spinning the pin with his index finger 54 times in his first trial, despite the fact that the pin does not need to be spun to remove it – we spin it specifically to see if chimpanzees copy this physically unnecessary act. However, as in all experiments we have conducted with the fruit, the main locus of imitation was the bolts, where the alternative acts of pulling and twisting versus poking through were the best matched. Figure 6.2 shows coders' estimates of overall matching to these alternatives in subjects' actions on the bolts, obtained in the experiment described here and in a previous study comparing both chimpanzees and human children (Whiten *et al.*, 1996). Similar levels of matching were found for the chimpanzees in both studies. This is interesting because in the earlier study we tested subjects on a fruit with just the bolts-defense in place, and separately on one with just the pin-handle complex in place. Being faced with a more complex task that led subjects to copy sequential structure did not appear to reduce the extent of copying such details of technique in the second study. Note, however, that in all these studies there were many details the chimpanzees did not copy, such as the method used to disable the

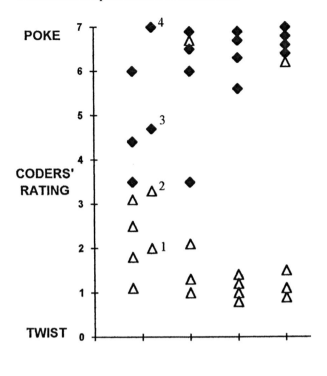

CHIMPS   2-YR   3-YR   4-YR

Figure 6.2. Judgments of matching to either the "poke" or "twist" technique by coders blind to what each subject had seen, for each subject that had witnessed either "poke" (dark symbols) or "twist" (clear symbols). 7 = judged most similar to poke; 1 = judged most similar to twist. Chimps = chimpanzees dealing with only bolts (on left) or with whole fruit (Ss numbered 1–4); 2-yr, 3-yr, 4-yr = two-, three-, and four-year-old children respectively. After Whiten *et al.*, 1996, with the addition of subjects 1–4 from Whiten 1998a).

handle component. Each sample of chimpanzees and children varied in the degree of fidelity their imitation expressed, with the older children tending towards the greater fidelity.

The finding of sequential copying in this chimpanzee study appears to be the first demonstration of this aspect of imitation in animals (Whiten, 1998a). Despite Bruner's theoretical treatment of the topic as long ago as 1972, as cited at the outset of this chapter, demonstrating imitation of sequential structure by children has also been achieved only recently (Brown, 1996; Call & Tomasello, 1995; Bauer, Hertsgaard, Dropnik, & Daly, 1998).

Imitation of hierarchical structure

Byrne (1994) & Byrne and Russon (1998) (see also Byrne, this volume) have made the interesting suggestion that some animals might copy not only sequential structure, but also the hierarchical structure of complex actions (see Fig. 6.3). Byrne and Russon went on to offer hypothesized instances of this in the foraging behavior of wild gorillas and the ways in which orangutans copy human habits at a rehabilitation camp. For the

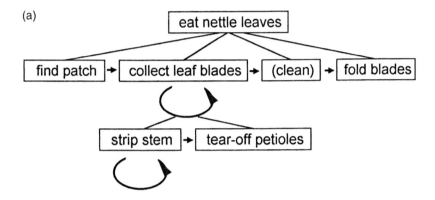

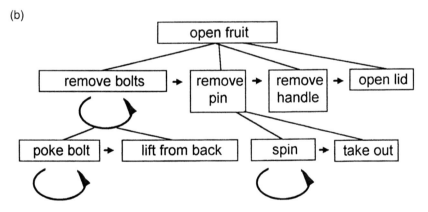

Figure 6.3. Potentially imitatable hierarchical structure in (a) gorilla feeding on nettles (after Byrne & Russon, 1998, Fig. 2); (b) opening of the artificial fruit (after Whiten, 1998b, Fig. 1). Curved arrows represent cycles repeated to a criterion before proceeding to the next component to the right.

reasons discussed earlier, the observations Byrne and Russon report may not yet demonstrate imitation of this kind – the peer commentary attached to the 1998 article judges not – but the idea is surely an interesting one, addressing an important aspect of the way in which imitators represent the actions of the imitated.

One reason for this is that possibly all skilled actions are hierarchically organized. Indeed, hierarchical organization pervades animal behavior (Dawkins, 1976). However, the criteria needed to show that a hierarchical organization is *imitated* are quite different to those required to demonstrate hierarchical organization itself, such as Byrne describes in gorilla foraging skills. Finding recognizable matching of hierarchical structure in the behavior of two individuals, such as a juvenile and an adult in the same group, we must discriminate between several alternative hypotheses for how the matching came about. One hypothesis will be that the hierarchical structure is itself imitated. Another is that, in facing similar environmental contingencies, the two individuals come up with the same behavioral solution without any observational learning at all (this is the conclusion favored by Tomasello and Call (1997), for example, in evaluating the gorilla foraging data against other evidence for imitation in apes). A third hypothesis is that one individual copied various elements of the behavior from the other, but structured them hierarchically itself ("hierarchized" them: Russon, 1999) to meet the task demands. In a highly intelligent species such processes might operate quite rapidly, making it difficult to discriminate this possibility from that in which the individual is instead actually *getting* the hierarchical structure through imitation.

Want and Harris (1998) suggested several ways by which we might hope to identify imitation of hierarchical structure. First, they dismiss three "weak indices." One is that the imitation is done in outline only, omitting details of the original model. This in itself is inadequate as a criterion for imitating hierarchical structure, for it applies to all imitations that are merely vague or even poor (indeed it applies to all imitation, as defined by Whiten and Ham (1992); all imitation, by its nature, involves some degree of infidelity to the original). A second index would be copying just the outcome of the act; but as Want and Harris recognize, this need not entail encoding the hierarchical structure of acts needed to achieve the final outcome. The third weak index is copying of sequential order, but that might be achieved by copying just a chain of actions, rather than recognizing any underlying hierarchical structure.

Want and Harris then offer a stronger index. They suggest that an imitation that can overlook temporary interruptions in the model's program of behavior shows that the imitator recognizes subgoals that hierarchically structure the overall action. As an example, they cite their finding that young children may learn from, but neglect to actually copy, an inappropriate act emitted before the correct solution to a task is performed. I think that Want and Harris are correct to conclude that this interesting finding means the child is parsing what it sees in such a way as to copy the action sequence leading to the desired outcome and ignore the causally irrelevant one. However, this does not amount to *hierarchical structure being copied*. I offer instead the experimental design below as a direct test of imitating hierarchical structure.

Identifying imitation of hierarchical structure: Experimental rationale

Recall that imitation of *sequential* structure was tested by presenting different sequences constructed from the same elements (e.g., A, B). The minimum experimental design thus offers sequence A–B versus sequence B–A, as the contrasting models. Extending this logic to the copying of *hierarchically* structured actions requires a minimum of four action-elements; A1, A2, B1, and B2. The two alternative hierarchical patterns can be thought of as branching trees (see Fig. 6.4); they are the "row-wise" approach "do A(A1, then A2); then do B(B1, then B2)" versus the "column-wise" alternative "do 1(A1, then B1); then do 2(2A, then 2B)." In our experiment this minimal 2×2 design was expanded to a bigger array of four columns and four rows. Each subject sees just one of the two patterns that can be followed – "row-wise" or "column-wise," after which we can measure the extent to which the approach witnessed is copied.

Note that this design requires an artificial fruit different to the pin-apple. To be sure, opening the pin-apple involves a hierarchy of actions, shown in Figure 6.4 alongside the kind of gorilla foraging patterns portrayed by Byrne and Russon (1998). However, these do not have the necessary scope for alternative hierarchical arrangement of constituent elements required for experimental testing. Accordingly, a further "artificial fruit" has been designed for the purpose (Whiten, 1999, 2000).

The Study

The "key-way fruit" (Fig. 6.5), like the pin-apple, is built around a perspex box containing edible treats. The lid is not hinged but overlaps the top of the box (like a shoe-box) and is held in place by skewers running through lid and box. Each skewer is normally flush with the back of the lid, protruding a little into a shaped recess at the front such that it cannot

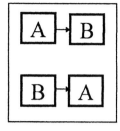
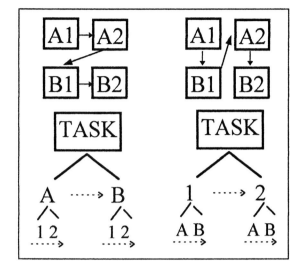

Figure 6.4. Experimental designs for identifying imitation of sequential and hierarchical structure of actions. Left box, models for testing imitation of sequence: A-then-B (upper sequence) versus B-then-A (lower sequence). Right box, models for testing imitation of hierarchical structure; "row-wise" hierarchy (on left) versus "column-wise" hierarchy (on right). In each case the hierarchical tree structure is shown below, and the corresponding sequence of action above. See text for further explanation.

be reached with fingers. The skewers must somehow be got out before the lid can be raised.

In the "column" method of opening the key-way, one of the four sticks is taken from the central well and stabbed into a hole in the left-most tablet that is resting in an appropriately shaped recess at the back of the lid. This picks up the tablet, making a "key" that can be poked into the corresponding (left-most) recess in the front of the lid. This forces the skewer out at the back, to be grasped and pulled out. Then the "key" is taken out of the recess and discarded. The four steps (stab, poke, pull, take) are then repeated on the other rows in turn, each of which incorporates a differently shaped and colored tablet. Finally, the lid can be removed and the food procured.

In the alternative demonstration (the "row" approach), the sticks are stabbed in all the tablets before any tablets get moved out of their recesses. Then, all these tools are poked in turn into the recesses in the lid, after which all the skewers can be removed in a row, as, finally, can the keys. Thus each "row" is completed before proceeding to the next. In

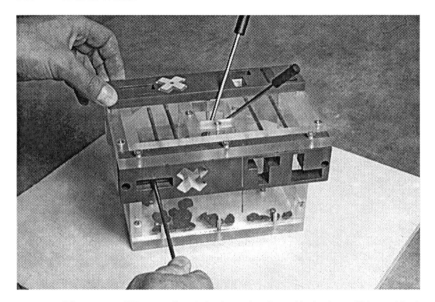

Figure 6.5. "Key-way" task for investigation of imitation of hierarchical structure. The first tablet has been stabbed with a stick, creating a key that in the second step of this "column-wise" approach is being poked into the corresponding recess on the lid front, pushing through one of the skewers holding the lid in place.

the column approach, it is instead each column that is completed before proceeding to the next column. Each child watched one of these two approaches modeled by an adult twice, before being offered their own turn. There was no invitation to imitate – only to try to get the reward out. This seems an appropriately pitched task for three-year-old children (and so, we anticipate, for chimpanzees also), because most, yet not all, subjects (18/22) managed to open the box after watching the demonstration.

However, we anticipated a residual problem in the design. If subjects copied perfectly what they saw, we would not be sure they were copying hierarchical structure; they might instead be imitating the linearly encoded sequence of sixteen acts seen. To test for hierarchy-copying in such an eventuality, the first observation and test session were performed with the third (blue) tablet and skewer missing; a further demonstration was then given and the task presented to the child but now with all tablets and skewers in place. We reasoned that if the child was simply copying the sequence witnessed, they should stall on reaching the new tablet or omit it; conversely if they were truly imitating the tree structure they had witnessed they might incorporate the blue tablet into it.

The principal results were clear. Counting the row-wise and column-wise transitions made by each child as they worked through the task, irrespective of whether they followed the same *direction* as had the model within the rows and columns, then there was a striking difference in the proportions of row versus column steps, depending on which model the subject had seen; there was thus a strong tendency to match the type of hierarchical tree structure subjects had witnessed beforehand (Fig. 6.6). Readers will note the match was not perfect; it was possible, because of the design of the test, to perform the task using either of the two tree structures – or a mixture of both – and some children explored these alternatives.

Results for the critical test, in which the missing blue tablet and skewer were added, are shown within Figure 6.6. As can readily be seen, the additional tablet and skewer were incorporated into the adoption of the row-wise or column-wise approach witnessed. Thus, there is no doubt these children were showing a tendency to imitate the hierarchical structure they had seen.

When we turn to the sequential structure of the acts we find a different story. Half the children saw transitions modeled left-to-right, half the opposite. So first, we can ask if the row-wise group tended to follow the within-row sequence (direction) they had seen; likewise, whether column-wise children followed the within-column sequence (leaving aside the first transition, that in the key-way cannot physically follow the reverse order). In both cases the answer is negative. The median number of row-wise transitions in the modeled direction was similar to that in the opposite direction in both phases of the experiment (tablet-missing and tablet-added). For column-wise transitions there were small but equally insignificant differences. Transitions in the opposite direction to that modeled are indicated by pale arrows in Figure 6.6 (which for illustrative purposes treats the modeled direction as always left-to-right).

Accordingly, as a group, the children can be said to have copied the basic hierarchical tree structure (i.e., they copied whichever of the two alternative tree structures they witnessed), but without apparently encoding sequential structure at either level of the hierarchy; they followed the sequential order they witnessed only when it was a physical necessity (as in the need to stab before poke).

There were some individual children who *did* enact modeled sequential structures and so they may have been imitating the model in these respects. If that were true, what they *imitated* would be correctly expressed by diagrams including horizontal sequence-arrows of the kind shown in Figure 6.4. However, that some individuals truly imitated with sequence fidelity must remain only a hypothesis given that other children performed so many transitions in the opposite direction.

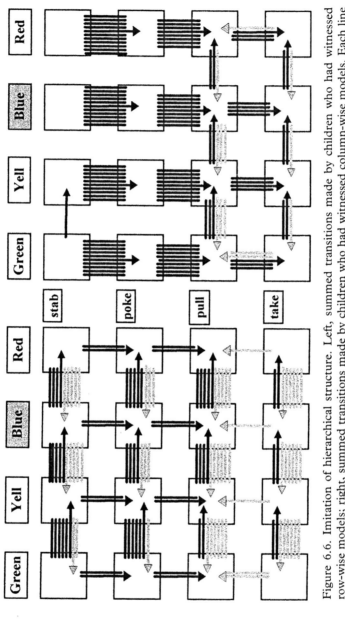

Figure 6.6. Imitation of hierarchical structure. Left, summed transitions made by children who had witnessed row-wise models; right, summed transitions made by children who had witnessed column-wise models. Each line represents one move by one child. Black lines, transitions in direction child had witnessed; grey lines, transitions in opposite direction to that witnessed.

The finding that in this key-way study, hierarchical structure was clearly copied, but sequential structure not, appears to be in conflict with the earlier results from the pin-apple studies, showing copying of sequence. We shall review these results in the general discussion further below.

Imitation relative to self

From imitation of sequential and hierarchical structure, we turn finally to a rather different aspect of the imitator's representation of what he or she imitates. This concerns the imitator's representation of actions relative to the body. This has been of great interest in human studies, particularly in the case of infants' imitation of actions they cannot see themselves perform (Meltzoff & Moore, 1977, 1994; Meltzoff, this volume) or in patients with apraxias and other relevant kinds of neurological difficulties (Goldenberg, this volume). However, it has yet to receive significant analysis in animal studies. Here, I highlight two sets of results, one from our primate studies, another concerning imitation by autistic children.

Non-visual feedback: Chimpanzee Do-as-I-do ("DAID") experiments

As noted earlier, the basic logic of the two-action/cross-target method can be extended to large batteries of modeled actions. If a subject can be taught to attempt to imitate each new modeled action on some signal ("Do this!" in our experiments), this becomes a powerful way to explore just what subjects can and cannot copy (Call & Tomasello, 1995). Note, however, that in so doing we are asking an importantly different question from that which motivated the studies described above. In those, we presented a naturalistic model and then measured what, if anything, the observer subject extracted and copied. Subjects were not encouraged to imitate: we were asking "*do* these subjects spontaneously imitate, and if so, what do they acquire?" In the DAID approach we are asking instead "*can* these subjects imitate, and if so, what?" The two approaches thus investigate different but complementary issues.

Custance, Whiten, and Bard (1994, 1995) applied this method to two young chimpanzees, replicating and extending an earlier attempt (Hayes & Hayes, 1952) that had lacked various aspects of the rigor we nowadays demand. Custance showed that after months of training, these two chimpanzees had grasped what was required of them sufficiently well that they could match a significant number of the novel actions they were then presented with.

This is an important result for a number of reasons, perhaps the most basic of which is that it is a form of evidence that one of the severest skeptics of imitation in nonhuman primates finds the most compelling (Heyes, 1998)! However, there are more particular cognitive implications of these results. The fact that an animal can learn what is required of it in the DAID paradigm seems to show that in some sense it can mentally represent the phenomenon of imitation itself, a feat so far claimed for only apes and dolphins (Whiten, 2000a).

The key result I focus on here is that Custance, Whiten, and Bard (1994) showed that these young chimpanzees were as competent at imitating actions concerning body parts they could not see as those they could. Such acts included touching body parts out of sight, like the back of the head, and facial movements. This suggests that chimpanzees are equipped with the kind of extensive cross-modal body-mapping that Meltzoff and others have described in the case of human infants (see Meltzoff, this volume). Important qualifications to this, however, are that the fidelity of matching was often low. Overall, there were more failures to match than successes, the reverse of what we find with pre-school children.

Face-and-body-mapping was thus definitely present, yet crude and tentative by human standards. However, of special interest with respect to the representation of the imitated act is the way in which fidelity was shown to change during performance. Subjects were recorded as initially making crude matches, sometimes by performing one of the acts used in the initial DAID training, then overtly modifying this to provide a better match. Two aspects of this finding deserve emphasis. First, the act chosen was a relevant one from the available repertoire, even though not initially a close match; for example, choosing "touch chin" as the response to modeling of "touch nose." Second, subjects did not generalize from this action in trial-and-error fashion, but instead tended to track in the correct direction – thus, in the example above they would trace their finger upwards from the chin, towards the nose (Custance, Whiten, & Bard, 1994). These results suggest that the self-other body-mapping is sufficiently competent to launch a roughly appropriate response without benefit of body-surface feedback (although it may well require proprioceptive feedback; see Meltzoff, this volume for more discussion on related issues). However, once body-surface feedback becomes available, the chimp can use that to pursue an appropriate increase in fidelity. Note that both these steps are done in cases where the action on oneself cannot be based on visual guidance; they depend on cross-modal mapping, from visual information (observing the model) to two different kinds of matching bodily feedback (body-surface and non-body-surface).

Visual feedback: difficulties in autistic children

It strikes us as particularly "magical" when imitation occurs without the imitator being able to see their own actions. But this should not let us lose sight of the difficulty that still remains for imitations executed with visual guidance, because of the translation between perspectives required, as Bruner (1972) had emphasized.

Julie Brown has used the DAID procedure to assess the imitative abilities of autistic children, comparing their performance with control groups including young normal children and children with learning difficulties (Brown, 1996; Whiten & Brown, 1999). One reason such work is important is that imitation has been hypothesized to play a foundational role in the development of children's abilities to engage with the minds of others (Rogers & Pennington, 1991; Meltzoff & Gopnik, 1993). A large literature has developed on theory of mind deficits in autism (e.g., Happe, 1994, for a review), but a smaller one on deficits in imitation (Whiten & Brown, 1999). However, there are many puzzling contradictions in the latter corpus of studies, so research on imitation in autistic people is much needed.

Overall, the autistic individuals tested by Brown showed significantly better imitative abilities than was found by several older studies in the literature. However, they did have particular difficulty with certain actions. Of particular interest in the context of the present chapter is copying of an act called "grasp thumb," in which one hand is held palm out, and its thumb grasped with the other hand (Fig. 6.7). Several responses to this were clearly imitations, in which the two hands were held in approximately the correct shapes, but showed lack of fidelity in intriguing ways, including allowing the hand to face the wrong way and placing the second hand on the wrong side of the other (not grasping the thumb). What these kinds of errors imply is a particular difficulty in translating between the others' perspective to one's own. Such errors were most common amongst the autistic subjects but young normal children also often expressed them. Thus, this is a difficult act to imitate faithfully. Why might that be? Only further study will tell, but what appears to make this particularly complex is that it involves executing acts in which the hands are simultaneously oriented in a particular way with respect to the rest of the body and with respect to each other. By experimentally testing such hypotheses we are likely to achieve a clearer model

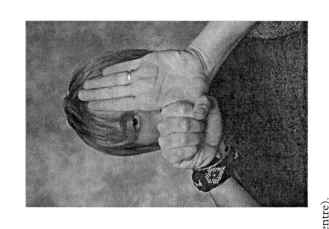

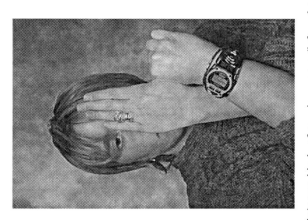

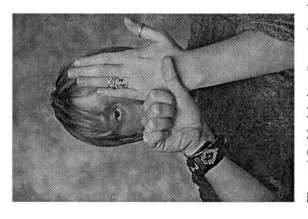

Figure 6.7. Modeled act "grasp thumb" (right); two kinds of copying errors (left and centre).

of how imitators with various levels of competence represent what they are imitating, around the borderline where the encoding partly succeeds and partly misfires.

General discussion

Types of Imitation

Despite a century's research, the study of imitation by animals (including human infants) is still seething with disputes about what phenomena have been properly established. In part this arises because of differences within the scientific community about the concepts and terms that we should be guided by. A pertinent illustration relevant to this chapter concerns contemporary concepts and terms relating to the "construction of an action pattern by the appropriate sequencing of a set of constituent action patterns to match a model" of which Bruner (1972) spoke. As we have seen, active research and thinking about this has only recently experienced a renaissance, and I claim results summarized in this chapter as the first to actually demonstrate imitation of sequential and hierarchical structure.

Should these, then, be classed as instances of what Byrne and Russon (1998:677) called program-level imitation (PLI), since they define this as "copying the structural organisation of a complex process (including the sequence of stages, subroutine structure, and bimanual coordination), by observation of the behavior of another individual, while furnishing the exact details of actions by individual learning?" Although at first sight this looks a promising fit, further thought leads to concern that confusion would follow.

The principal problem derives from the multicomponent definition given to PLI (above), different aspects of which tend to be appealed to in different contexts, when the existence of PLI is at stake. At one extreme, this has the potential to lead to PLI being very widely "identified" in animal imitation. This is so when PLI is described as "copying only the outline structure of a task" (Byrne, 1994), which appeals to the part of the fuller definition above specifying that details are learned not socially but by individual learning. Hosey, Jacques, and Pitts (1997), for example, take PLI to be "performing the overall structure of the behavior, without necessarily duplicating the detailed motor units which make up that structure" (p. 421). Accordingly they ascribe to PLI a case in which lemurs apparently showed observational learning of dipping their tails in water to get a drink, yet the dipping methods differed. This nicely illustrates the "schematic" aspect that Whiten and Ham's (1992) definition assumed would characterize imitation generally; but leaning on this component of their definition, as Byrne and Russon themselves do intermittently,[1] puts PLI in danger of too-easy identification.

This can only happen if the other parts of the definition of PLI are ignored. However, if they are instead insisted on, we swing to the other end of the scale and PLI becomes a very demanding phenomenon to identify, requiring an experiment as complex as that described earlier in this chapter; moreover, copying of hierarchical organization remains to be demonstrated in nonhuman species. This is a very different outcome to that resulting from leaning on the element of the definition discussed in the last paragraph and there is thus much scope for confusion in the research literature.

Whiten (1998b) thus advocated that the part of the definition concerned with copying details (or not) be set aside as a logically separate issue; also, that the "bimanual" criterion be dropped as well, as not necessary to the core interest of Byrne and Russon's project (much of the sequential and hierarchical imitation identified in this chapter was essentially done with one hand). This leaves the sequential and hierarchical ("subroutine structure") components of PLI. But again, there are good reasons why these should be kept conceptually separate, rather than rolled together with the other two criteria into PLI. In this chapter, we have seen cases where hierarchical structure is copied, yet not sequential structure. This suggests that avoiding the potentially misleading implications of a global "PLI" concept is to be preferred, in favor of focusing separately on each of the two most interesting possibilities, imitation of sequential and hierarchical structures.

Powerful methods

Equally important as thinking about the underlying concepts in imitation research are the methods at our disposal. I have tried to show that the basic logic of the "two-action" (or "cross-target") methodology has peculiarly appropriate power in the study of imitation. So far, in animal work it has been used to get to first base, establishing whether members of such-and-such a species imitate. However, the method also has much potential to tease out the underlying cognitive mechanisms, as in answering questions about what the imitator does and does not encode about the model's actions. I have illustrated this by extending the "two-action" logic to "two-sequences" and "two-hierarchies" experimental designs. The DAID experiments I described also embody the essential logic of this approach.

The imitator's representation of the imitated

I have described research on both chimpanzees and children, targeted at the issue of what is selectively imitated. The aim of our research program is to approach as closely as we can to valid comparisons between these species, as well as other primates, although at any one stage it may have been possible to pursue an experiment with one species and not yet achieve the comparable study with another. Such is currently the case with imitation of hierarchical structure, where young children have been the pioneer subjects. It will of course be important to establish if other species show the copying of hierarchical structure (and neglect of sequential order) that we found in children's approaches to the task.

With respect to studies where we *have* compared the two species, the overall conclusion is that what the chimpanzee and children represent in their imitations appears qualitatively quite similar. We find that children generally tend to achieve a match to what they see faster and with a higher degree of fidelity, but these are quantitative rather than qualitative differences, even if sometimes they are very large. Thus, both species can master the basic idea of the DAID game and attempt to copy relatively novel actions. Given the battery of actions used, chimpanzees fail in a majority, as noted above, whereas pre-school children succeed in copying virtually all of them (Brown, 1996). Even so, if the act is "hard" enough, children who have got the idea of DAID fail to copy well (there are probably dance steps for which the same is true for readers!). Both species appear to have extensive cross-modal body maps through which to execute imitation, although children appear to become much more proficient at using these to generate fast, high-fidelity matching. It may be that our chimpanzee subjects would have been more proficient if they had spent more of their day experiencing opportunities for copying that our child subjects have had.

When we turn to imitation of action-shape and sequential structures, we find the same story. We found that children and chimpanzees copy actions like poke-versus-twist selectively, with the children operating with higher fidelity overall. Likewise, as reported above, imitation of sequential structure emerged in chimpanzees after several tests; in children, Brown (1996) found high fidelity in the first imitation trial.

A pervading theme in these experiments, with respect to the issue of what both chimpanzees and children represent of what they see, is selective copying. This is true of both species, but the selectivity varies a lot between species and situations. This is an issue that deserves more attention and it is the final issue I discuss.

The integration of imitative and nonimitative information

Recall that in our experiments manipulating sequential patterning, both chimpanzees and children *copied* sequential structure, even when the sequence was in fact arbitrary. Yet, in imitation of hierarchical structure, children tended to *ignore* the sequencing they had observed. Why the difference? Note that in both studies, the sequential patterns under discussion were arbitrarily imposed, for experimental purposes, so they *could* have been ignored in all cases. This is a feature of all two-action alternatives – the chimps *could* just always pull the bolts out of the fruit, instead of copying the typically more laborious poking technique. In the case of the handle, they did appear to ignore the arbitrary alternatives demonstrated by the model. The question raised, then, is what exactly is happening when imitators' representations of what they imitate sometimes discounts certain information and sometimes incorporates it. What makes the difference?

I suggest that broadly, the answer may lie in the imitator's prior "world knowledge" (including self-knowledge); its procedural and perhaps declarative knowledge about what it is capable of doing and about how the world works. In the case of the "hierarchy" experiment, children may simply know enough about the relevant aspects of the world to be able to judge that it really does not matter in which sequence they proceed. In other contexts they may not know enough to judge this and so – more conservatively, as it were – they copy the sequence, with the implicit hypothesis that maybe the sequence is critical for success. The truth of this kind of interpretation rests upon the selectivity of such imitation being an adaptive part of the organism's design, but the extent to which this applies in each situation is an empirical question. It could be that instead, children failed to copy sequence while copying hierarchical structure because of information processing limits. Indeed, in DAID examples discussed earlier, chimpanzees appeared to be affected by their prior knowledge, when they responded with an earlier-trained action that loosely approximated the model; this was presumably not adaptive selectivity so much as initial inability to generate a more exact match.

Thus, an inexact match may be generated for two quite different reasons, each the product of the imitator's previous experience and current cognitive contents; it may either not know enough to copy better, or it may know enough to be able *to do better* than copy all it saw the model do. The latter may depend on capacities to analyze such things as which events in the world are causally related to others, which outcomes were goals of the model and which yet-unattained goals the model is pursuing. Systematic study of the cognitive bases for selectively discounting information in the model, and the way in which nonimitative information is integrated with that acquired by imitation, appears yet to be sparse (the earlier cited Want & Harris, 1998, offers but one illustration). It remains nonexistent in the animal literature. It is an exciting prospect now to move on from whether imitation actually exists to cognitive questions like these.

Note

1 For example, Byrne and Russon describe as a hypothetical example of PLI the copying of "repeatedly pick green strands of galium with one hand, then use the other to fold in loose strands etc.," whereas "action-level" imitation they distinguish as including additional details such as left-versus-right hand and use of a precision grip (p. 675, Table 1). This way of portraying PLI focuses on the criterion of "overall structure" (neglecting details), ignoring the other criteria, such as hierarchical organization, which are not referred to here.

Acknowledgements

I am grateful to Debbie Custance, Andy Meltzoff, and Ádam Miklósi for comments on earlier drafts of this chapter.

References

Bauer, P. J., Hertsgaard, L. A., Dropnik, P., & Daly, B. P. (1998). When even arbitrary order becomes important: Developments in reliable temporal sequencing of arbitrarily ordered events. *Memory, 6,* 165–198.

Brown, J. (1996). Imitation, play and theory of mind in autism: an observational and experimental study. Ph.D. thesis, University of St. Andrews.

Bruner, J. S. (1972). Nature and use of immaturity. *American Psychologist, 27,* 687–708.

Byrne, R. W. (1994). The evolution of intelligence. In P. J. B. Slater & T. R. Halliday (Eds.), *Behaviour and evolution.* Cambridge: Cambridge University Press.

Byrne, R. W., & Russon, A. E. (1998). Learning by imitation: A hierarchical approach. *Behavioral and Brain Sciences, 21,* 667–709.

Caldwell, C., & Whiten, A. (1999). Observational learning in the marmoset monkey, Callithrix jacchus. *Proceedings of the AISB Convention, Symposium on Imitation in Animals and Artifacts, Edinburgh* (pp. 27–31). The Society for the Study of Artificial Intelligence and simulation of Behaviour.

Call, J., & Tomasello, M. (1995). The use of social information in the problem-solving of orangutans (*Pongo pygmaeus*) and human children (*Homo sapiens*). *Journal of Comparative Psychology, 109,* 308–320.

Custance, D. M., Whiten, A., & Bard, K. A. (1994). The development of gestural imitation and self-recognition in chimpanzees (*Pan troglodytes*) and children. In J. J Roeder *et al.* (Eds.), *Current primatology Vol. 2* (pp. 381–387). Strasbourg: Université Louis Pasteur.

(1995). Can young chimpanzees imitate arbitrary actions? Hayes and Hayes (1952) revisited. *Behaviour, 132,* 839–858.

Custance, D. M., Whiten, A., & Fredman, T. (1999). Social learning of an artificial fruit task in capuchin monkeys (*Cebus apella*). *Journal of Comparative Psychology, 113*, 1–11.

Custance, D. M., Whiten, A., Sambrook, T., & Galdikas, B. (in press). Testing for social learning in the 'artificial fruit' processing of wildborn orangutans (*Pongo pygmaeus*), Tanjung Puting, Indonesia. *Animal Cognition*, in press.

Dawkins, R. (1976). Hierarchical organisation: A candidate principle for ethology. In P. P. G. Bateson & R. A. Hinde (Eds.), *Growing point in ethology* (pp. 7–54). Cambridge: Cambridge University Press.

Dawson, B. V., & Foss, B. M. (1965). Observational learning in budgerigars. *Animal Behaviour, 13*, 470–474.

Happe, F. (1994). *Autism*. London: LSE Press.

Hayes, K. J., & Hayes, C. (1952). Imitation in a home-reared chimpanzee. *Journal of Comparative Psychology, 45*, 450–459.

Heyes, C. M. (1998). Theory of mind in nonhuman primates. *Behavioral and Brain Sciences, 21*, 101–148.

Hosey, G. R., Jacques, M., & Pitts, A. (1997). Drinking from tails: Social learning of a novel behaviour in a group of Lemurs (*Lemur catta*). *Primates, 38*, 415–422.

King, B. J. (1994). *The information continuum*. Santa Fe, NM: SAR Press.

Meltzoff, A. N., & Gopnik, A. (1993). The role of imitation in understanding persons and developing a theory of mind. In S. Baron-Cohen, H. Tager-Flusberg, & J. D. Cohen (Eds.), *Understanding other minds: Perspectives from autism* (pp. 335–366). Oxford: Oxford University Press.

Meltzoff, A. N., & Moore, M. K. (1977). Imitation of facial and manual gestures by human neonates. *Science, 198*, 75–78.

   (1994). Imitation, memory and the representation of persons. *Infant Behavior and Development, 17*, 83–99.

Rogers, S. J., & Pennington, B. F. (1991). A theoretical approach to the deficits in infantile autism. *Development and Psychopathology, 3*, 137–162.

Russon, A. E. (1999). Orangutans' imitation of tool use: A cognitive interpretation. In S. T. Parker, H. L. Miles, & R. M. Mitchell (Eds.), *The mentalities of gorillas and orangutans* (pp. 117–146). Cambridge: Cambridge University Press.

Tinbergen, N. (1951). *The study of instinct*. Oxford: Clarendon Press.

Tomasello, M. (1990). Cultural transmission in the tool use and communicatory signalling of chimpanzees? In S. Parker & K. Gibson (Eds.), *Language and intelligence in monkeys and apes: Comparative developmental perspectives* (pp. 274–311). Cambridge: Cambridge University Press.

Tomasello, M., & Call, J. (1997). *Primate cognition*. Oxford: Oxford University Press.

Want, S. C., & Harris, P. L. (1998). Indices of program-level comprehension. *Behavioral and Brain Sciences, 21*, 706–707.

Whiten, A. (1989). Transmission processes in primate cultural evolution. *Trends in Ecology and Evolution, 4*, 61–62.

   (1998a). Imitation of the sequential structure of actions by chimpanzees (*Pan troglodytes*). *Journal of Comparative Psychology, 112*, 270–281.

(1998b). How imitators represent the imitated: the vital experiments. Commentary on Byrne & Russon: Learning by imitation: a hierarchical approach. *Behavioral and Brain Sciences*, *21*, 707–708.

(1999). Imitation of sequential and hierarchical structure in action: Experimental studies with children and chimpanzees. *Proceedings of the AISB Convention, Symposium on Imitation in Animals and Artifacts*, Edinburgh (pp. 38–46).

(2000a). Primate culture and social learning. *Cognitive Science, 24,* 477–508.

(2000b). Chimpanzee cognition and the question of mental re-representation. In D. Sperber (Ed.), *Metarepresentation.* (pp. 139–167). Oxford: Oxford University Press.

(2002). Imitation of sequential and hierarchical structure in action: experimental studies with children and chimpanzees. In K. Dautenhahn & C. L. Nehaniv (Eds.), *Imitation in Animals and Artifacts.* Cambridge, MA: MIT Press.

Whiten, A., & Brown, J. (1999). Imitation and the reading of other minds: Perspectives from the study of autism, normal children and non-human primates. In S. Bråten (Ed.), *Intersubjective communication and emotion in ontogeny: A sourcebook* (pp. 260–280). Cambridge: Cambridge University Press.

Whiten, A., Custance, D. M., Gomez, J.-C., Teixidor, P., & Bard, K. A. (1996). Imitative learning of artificial fruit processing in children (*Homo sapiens*) and chimpanzees (*Pan troglodytes*). *Journal of Comparative Psychology, 110,* 3–14.

Whiten, A., Goodall, J., McGrew, W. C., Nishida, T., Reynolds, V., Sugiyama, Y., Tutin, C. E. G., Wrangham, R. W., & Boesch, C. (1999). Cultures in chimpanzees. *Nature,* 399, 682–685.

Whiten, A., & Ham, R. (1992). On the nature and evolution of imitation in the animal kingdom: Reappraisal of a century of research. In P. J. B. Slater, J. S. Rosenblatt, C. Beer, & M. Milinski (Eds.), *Advances in the study of behavior* (pp. 239–283). San Diego: Academic Press.

Whiten, A., & Milner, P. (1984). The educational experiences of Nigerian infants. In H. V. Curran (Ed.), *Nigerian children: Developmental perspectives* (pp. 34–73). London: Routledge and Kegan Paul.

7   Seeing actions as hierarchically organized structures: Great ape manual skills

Richard W. Byrne

The word "imitation" has seen its meaning change many times over the years, a process that has narrowed down its scope onto an ever-decreasing range of referents. Most of these revisions have been driven by debate in the literature concerning nonhuman animals (hereafter, "animals"), but may have implications for those studying imitation in humans, especially at preverbal stages where many of the same issues occur. Before Thorndike's (1898) definition "learning to do an act from seeing it done," imitation seemed not even to require a causal role for observation – and this sense is preserved in everyday talk, when people say, for instance, "this is a case of nature imitating art." More recently, the notion of *stimulus enhancement* was introduced (Spence, 1937): seeing some act done in a particular place, or to some particular object, has the effect of increasing the observer's probability of going to that place or interacting with that object. This, as Spence noted, would make subsequent individual learning very much more efficient, and many behaviors that were formerly (and are still popularly) considered imitation were thereby explained away – as trial and error learning aided by social circumstances (Galef, 1988). Tomasello further drew attention to the possibility of learning about the physical situation as an indirect consequence of another's behavior, introducing the concept of *emulation* (Tomasello, 1990). This refers to the many things that may be learnt from what happens to objects in the environment as an indirect result of an individual's actions: strength, brittleness, weight, what an object is made of or contains, and so forth. According to Tomasello, in imitation, it is the actions themselves which are learnt; in emulation, an observer learns environmental properties disclosed by the actions. Thus, if an individual sees a coconut smashed against a rock, breaking to disclose edible flesh, then by stimulus enhancement she may focus her subsequent behavior in the region below the coconut tree and onto coconuts in particular, and by emulation she may now know that coconuts are breakable and edible – all without learning the behavior she saw, the particular method of breaking employed. The contrast with emulation thus serves to restrict imitation to cases where particular nuances or techniques of behavior are copied, not simply actions of equivalent ultimate effect on the environment. Yet even replicating the behavior that has been observed can be accounted for without invoking imitation, if the behavior is a familiar one in the observer's repertoire. In the same way that one stimulus may be enhanced over another, increasing the probability that the individual would interact with it, so one response (i.e., a behavior in an individual's existing repertoire) may be enhanced by seeing it done, causing a higher probability of that behavior occurring subsequently (Byrne, 1994). This *response facilitation* can only affect behavior already in the repertoire, it cannot on its own cause novel skills to be acquired; however, many cases that are called imitation in everyday, and all experimental tests of animal imitation that depend on the two-action, directional control methodology (Dawson & Foss, 1965; Heyes, 1993; Whiten *et al.*, 1996; and see Whiten, this volume) are vulnerable to reinterpretation in this way. In the light of response facilitation, to be sure of imitation in animal behavior it will be necessary to insist upon the criterion that novel behavioral techniques must be copied (Byrne, 1998b; Byrne & Tomasello, 1995). This is a purely pragmatic demand: from our own experience, we know that evoking pre-existing behavior, or applying a familiar behavior to a new circumstance, *may* be a consequence of imitation, but it would not be possible to reliably detect such imitation in animal behavior – nor in preverbal humans, with whom novelty has already been used to rule out priming effects (e.g. Meltzoff, 1988a).

What has been the point of narrowing the scope of "imitation" in these ways? At first sight, continual definitional change (often accompanied, as they have been, with claims that the new definition alone captures "true imitation") is unhelpful and confusing. There seem to be two potential benefits that these theoretical reworkings are grasping towards. In some cases, the alternatives are cognitively simpler to model (stimulus enhancement, response facilitation), and so an argument for parsimony can be made. It is not that behavior shown to result from the new concepts is uninteresting – indeed, these mechanisms may be biologically more important and evolutionarily prior to imitation. But the concepts are easier to understand. In the case of emulation, which is itself potentially complex in cognitive terms – it may involve representation of relationships among parts of objects, and of cause and effect linkages – the argument seems to be just that it is another, different process to imitation. While both depend on observation, imitation refers to behavior-copying, emulation means learning about the everyday physics of objects. To rule out all of these alternative mechanisms, what would be needed is evidence of an individual copying some behavior, where (1) the behavior is of sufficient *complexity* to trace its origin; (2) the copying *depends on observing* a model; (3) there is a lack of environmental constraints that could otherwise *reinforce or shape* the behavior; (4) the behavior acquired is *novel* to the imitator. This is quite a tall order, and by this criterion the set of behaviors that can unequivocally be ascribed to imitation is now very small in nonhuman animals. (Though note that in many of the excluded cases the possibility of imitation is not yet ruled out, it is only arguable that this would be a less parsimonious explanation.)

If the process of reinterpretation in terms of other mechanisms continues, the set of candidates for imitation may eventually become empty. Such an outcome might be no bad thing, provided that each of the proposed mechanisms is mechanical and open to empirical verification, rather than mysterious and unspecified: "imitation" would then be understood. (Though note that emulation does not meet this criterion of clarity, as far as it has been sketched so far: see Byrne, 1998a.) Furthermore, if *all* the possible mechanisms by which an animal could "learn to do an act from seeing it done" were properly understood, we could apply a more balanced, Bayesian approach to deciding in a given circumstance just which mechanism(s) had been important. This would enable researchers to get away from the current unfortunate necessity to argue in terms of which unsupported beliefs are most appropriate as null hypotheses, and which explanations are the most parsimonious.

This chapter will argue, firstly, that some natural behaviors of great apes are most easily understood as depending on imitation, in the narrow sense in which the term is currently used; secondly, that great ape imitation depends on interpreting observed behavior as hierarchical structures, it is imitation at "program-level"; and finally, that such a process of interpretation need not imply understanding the intentions and goals in the mind of the model whose behavior is copied, but that the imitation of complex behavior can in principle be a rather mechanical, statistical process.

Great ape manual skills

Among the four species of nonhuman great apes, only the (common) chimpanzee *Pan troglodytes* is renowned for its learnt manual skills, those that involve tool-use. Unlike any other nonhuman animal, chimpanzees use tools for a wide range of mechanical and social purposes (McGrew, 1992). Among this range are three particularly complex and elaborated skills: using plant probes to "fish" for termites (*Macrotermes* and *Pseudocanthotermes*) and *Campanotus* ants (Goodall, 1964; Nishida, 1973), using woody sticks to "dip" for *Dorylus* ants (McGrew, 1974), and using hammer and anvil stones to crack *Panda* and *Coula* nuts (Boesch & Boesch, 1983). In all three cases, an organized sequence of behavior is required, beginning from selection of the tool or the material from which it is made, and the choice of each act in the sequence is under-determined by the stimulus. This is most obvious in the case of tool making or tool selection in advance of arriving at the site of use. Un-like other chimpanzee manual action which is typically unlateralized (Marchant & McGrew, 1996), these tool-using tasks show strong be-havioral lateralization[1] (Boesch, 1991a; McGrew & Marchant, 1996; Sugiyama, Fushimi, Sakura, & Matsuzawa, 1993). Only for nut-cracking has active teaching been reported (Boesch, 1991b), but it is very rare, only two cases in eleven years, and evidently not the major means of ac-quisition. However, numerous inter-population differences in tool using and other behaviors have long implied that social learning was important in maintenance of these traditions, and the more complex of them were taken to rely on imitation (Nishida, 1986). Tomasello challenged this in-terpretation, suggesting emulation as sufficient explanation, arguing that the traditions did not show distinctive styles in different populations; thus, all that need be learnt by observation was physical properties of sticks, rocks, nuts, and insects (Tomasello, 1990). Subsequent compar-ative analyses have shown this to be incorrect, at least in the case of the fishing and dipping techniques which do show clear local styles unrelated to ecological constraints (McGrew, 1998). For instance, in different pop-ulations probing tools are resharpened by biting frayed tips, rotated to use the other end, or simply discarded (McGrew, Tutin, & Baldwin, 1979). Most tellingly, the same species of *Dorylus* ants are eaten with different techniques of dipping in different populations. In East Africa, the ants are allowed to swarm up a long wand which is then swept through a precision grip of the other hand to accumulate a handful of ants for rapid chewing (McGrew, 1974). In West Africa, a shorter stick is used, one-handed, and the ants are bitten off the end (Boesch & Boesch, 1990; Sugiyama, 1995; Sugiyama, Koman, & Bhoye Sow, 1988). This method is less efficient, yet the tradition is widespread and persistent.

A comparable level of manual skill has also been identified in the plant-processing techniques of mountain gorillas, in which tools are not used. Mountain gorillas *Gorilla g. beringei* in the Virunga mountains of cen-tral Africa live in areas where almost no fruit is available, by exploiting herbaceous vegetation (Watts, 1984). In these temperate and sub-Alpine zones the herbs largely lack toxic secondary compounds, and some are relatively rich sources of protein (Waterman, Choo, Vedder, & Watts, 1983). However, the commoner plants are defended physically, either by specific adaptations that reduce palatability (stings of *Laportea* nettles, spines covering *Carduus* thistle) or as a structural consequence of their growth form (tiny hooks allowing *Galium* to clamber, woody exterior of pithy stems of *Peucedanum*). The techniques gorillas use to circumvent the defenses of these important herb foods are complex in more than one sense (Byrne & Byrne, 1993). Each involves several discrete stages of processing, in which many manual actions are organized into mechanically efficient combinations, mostly involving bimanual coordination between the two hands used in complementary roles, and the overall organization is hierarchical, with subroutines used iteratively at some stages. As with chimpanzee tool use and most skilled human manual behavior, high degrees of behavioral lateralization are found (Byrne & Byrne, 1991). Each of the four plants requires a very different, but more or less equally complex, technique, yet all individuals have reached adult levels of proficiency by the age of weaning, as measured by the time to process the average handful (Byrne & Byrne, 1991). In this case, the evidence for transmission by imitation is more circumstantial: the wide geographical spread, that in common chimpanzees permitted inter-population differences in technique, is missing. There is no serious likelihood that the various different techniques are genetically transmitted, since each technique is only valuable for dealing with a particular species, and all these herbs are restricted to a limited altitudinal zone on a few mountains. Nevertheless, the overall organization of each technique is remarkably standardized across the study population, despite the fact that the choice of which general type of act to apply next is massively under-determined by the stimulus – indeed, completely alternative techniques are readily invented by human observers. This high consistency in technique, combined with the inherent improbability of arriving at these complex techniques by individual exploration, has been used to argue that some sort of imitation is involved (Byrne & Byrne, 1993; Byrne & Russon, 1998).

Less clear evidence exists for the other great ape species, but the recent discovery of tool-using and tool-making techniques in one population of orangutans (Fox, Sitompul, & Van Schaik, 1999) supports the belief, long held from captive studies (Wright, 1972), that orangutans *Pongo pygmaeus* are able to learn skills just as dexterous and elaborate as those of chimpanzees. Bonobos *Pan paniscus* show even greater manual skill and tool-making ability in captivity (Toth *et al.*, 1993); no data on bonobo food-preparation are yet available from the wild. On present evidence, the safest assumption would seem to be that the ability to acquire complex and highly organized manual programs, by a combination of individual experience and imitation, is shared by all great apes. It is important to stress that these manual programs are not simply "complicated," as a long but ordered string of elements would be, but "complex" in the sense of

(1) possessing *modular* structure, with some sections tightly organized and uninterruptible; (2) *hierarchically* organized, with some modules iterated to a criterion or used in more than one different program; (3) *coordinated*, with the two hands, and sometimes the mouth and feet, taking complementary roles in the service of a single subgoal (Byrne, 1999b; Byrne & Russon, 1998).

Program-level imitation

Imitation can in principle occur at different levels, from the meticulous copying of details right up to broad-brush copying of a general approach (Byrne, 1993; Byrne & Russon, 1998). Note that the *level* of imitative copying is conceptually quite independent of its *accuracy*. If a copy is simply inaccurate, those parts that are missing are random with respect to the structure of the original; to be able to copy specifically the higher organizational level of an action presupposes the ability to detect and react to that organizational structure.[2] (Similarly, in a broad-brush copy of a scene, an artist is selecting out those parts to be represented on the basis of an understanding of the objects and how they interact: broad-brush copying presupposes the ability to see what is going on and select out the important parts. In broad-brush copies of both scenes and actions, there may additionally be error, but what is systematically left out is a matter of organizational level.) To determine whether a given instance represents high-level rather than merely inaccurate copying, it is therefore essential to examine a substantial sample of behavior: a small fragment might be quite ambiguous of interpretation. The possibility of imitation at different levels is a consequence of the hierarchical organization of complex behavior (Dawkins, 1976; Lashley, 1951), and the freedom to do so necessitates an ability to perceive that organization in the behavior of others.

In practice, there are reasons to believe that imitation shown by non-human great apes in learning manual skills is usually towards the broad-brush end of the spectrum, although at times highly selective copying of more precise details may occur. The nature of the task of skill learning by imitation suggests that this should be so: attempting detail-by-detail duplication of precisely observed acts would seldom be a good way to acquire an efficient technique. The perspective transformations that would be needed for exact copying of finger movements mean that this would inevitably be a slow and difficult process. The alternative, of letting individual trial-and-error converge on the most convenient way of doing each part of the overall process, is a far more attractive one. In any case, the learner is often likely to be an infant, with hands very much smaller and weaker than those of the model. Different methods may therefore be needed to achieve the same result: too precise copying might even cause *dis*advantage. Empirical results also point in this direction. In the complex food-preparation techniques of mountain gorillas, where feeding techniques are so standardized across the population as to suggest they are imitated, the precise actions used to achieve each stage of processing, and the laterality of the whole bimanual program of actions, vary between animals and show no sign of running in families. Although this idiosyncratic variation in the precise actions gorillas use implies that details are generally learnt by individual experience, one observation suggests that imitation may occasionally play a part even at this level (Byrne, 1999a). A female, Picasso, born in a group living at lower altitudes than those at which *Laportea* nettles are a major food, immigrated into the study population. Yet five years later she could still not perform the folding of the prepared bundle of leaf-blades which minimizes contact of stings with lips; she ate rather few nettles, perhaps as a consequence. As an adult, Picasso would not have been permitted to feed near enough to other adults to see the fine detail of their food processing. Intriguingly, her juvenile also lacked this behavior, which was found in every one of the 36 other adults and juveniles. Similar cases of copying particular details have been noted in the imitation of orangutans (which, like that of gorillas, is largely at program-level: Byrne & Russon, 1998). For instance, in one case the precise angle at which a tin disc is held when it is being used to fan embers into life was copied (Russon & Galdikas, 1993). When specifically trained to do so, chimpanzees can certainly copy precise details of some novel actions, but they do not do so with high accuracy (Custance, Whiten, & Bard, 1995; Hayes & Hayes, 1952). Untrained great apes[3] do not show the great enthusiasm for imitating the actions of other individuals that is so striking in children's development, and a social function for this trait seems likely, rather than a role in skill-acquisition (Byrne & Russon, 1998; Meltzoff, 1988b; Meltzoff & Gopnik, 1993).

In order for imitation to occur at a broad-brush, outline level – and indeed for occasional important details to be extracted from a matrix of action which is not generally copied – it is necessary for the behavior which is observed to be understood, in the sense of *represented as a hierarchical organization* rather than a linear string of acts. That is what is implied by "program-level imitation" (Byrne & Russon, 1998), and it is this meaning of imitation that is claimed for great apes. There is no doubt that adult humans can do this routinely. Moreover, two-year-old children when describing events show an ability to select out the overall structure or gist, since they tend to leave out details which are unimportant for the logical sequence (Bauer & Mandler, 1989); this again implies program-level imitation. Delayed imitation of actions, some apparently novel for the children, has been shown as early as nine months (Meltzoff, 1988a, 1988c). The challenge now is to find out what is the cognitive basis for this ability: how can watching a fluid and linear stream of behavior result in an understanding that the behavior is *organized*, with an underlying structure of modules, hierarchical deployment of subroutines, and coordination of methods towards a final goal or result?

Understanding structure by watching fluid action

One view is that a crucial aspect of this process is intersubjectivity, an understanding of what the model is intending to achieve. To imitate, "the child must imaginatively place herself in the circumstances of the adult and determine what is the purpose of the behavior and how one goes about accomplishing that purpose" (Tomasello, Kruger, & Ratner, 1993, for whom it forms part of the definition of imitative learning). However, I will argue here that an understanding of the model's intentions is not essential for imitation. This is not to say that the two will not often occur simultaneously, or that one would not ramify and bolster the other: these are both possible, and perhaps common. Certainly, we feel that we understand another's behavior better and more properly if we can see to what goal it is aimed. But imitation, based on understanding the organizational structure, does not absolutely require understanding intentions; imitation by string-parsing (Byrne, 1999b) can side-step any need for prior understanding of intention.

The underlying structure of complex, hierarchically organized, goal-directed behavior leaves visible traces in observable behavior. These include:

1. *Interruptibility.* The elements within modules are tightly bound together, as a result of their practiced and frequent co-occurrence, whereas at a junction between modules the link is weaker (e.g., if letters are used to represent elemental units of action, A=B=C–D=E=F). Interruptions occurring at these points will permit smooth resumption once the distraction is past; in contrast, interruptions within a module will force the animal to "begin at the beginning again," either the beginning of the module or of the entire program.
2. *Omission.* In a flexible organization of behavior, unnecessary stages or modules can be omitted, on the basis of local circumstances. For instance, in the case of a gorilla eating nettles the penultimate stage in the process, opening the hand to enable removal of inedible debris, is only done if there is indeed such debris. Thus, in repeated strings

that are broadly similar, certain sections will occur in some strings but not others, signaling the underlying modular structure (e.g., observing numerous instances of both A,B,C,D,E,F and A,B,E,F signals A=B–C=D–E=F).

3. *Repetition*. Modules, used as subroutines in a hierarchical organization, may be employed iteratively until some criterion is reached (cf. the Test-Operate-Test-Exit unit of Miller, Galanter, & Pribram, 1960), and repeated "loops" around a subroutine give a distinctive sequence of sequential elements: a series of repeated short strings, embedded within the main sequence (e.g., A,B,C,B,C,B,C,D,E signals that B=C is an iterated subroutine). In the case of a gorilla eating nettles, the three successive stages (i) pulling a stem into reach; (ii) stripping the leaves from the stem; and (iii) detaching and discarding the leaf-stems, may be repeated several times in just this way before continuing with the main sequence.

4. *Natural end-points and starts*. In many cases, planned behavior leads to the achievement of a goal. Consummatory activity (e.g., eating a food item, such as a folded parcel of stemless whorls of nettle leaves), coming after a sequence of elements, indicates a proper end to that sequence. In some cases, the proper start to a sequence might also be visible in behavior, if no other activity occurred immediately beforehand; thus some "complete" strings of elements corresponding to goal-directed behavior can be identified. More generally, the appropriate phase, in which sequences need to be meshed to detect the recurring patterns, may be indicated in this way.

5. *Invariant elements*. In minor and trivial ways, every execution of a behavior is slightly different. The characteristics that always occur, in regular positions in every string of elements leading to the same outcome, must be the necessary ones, whereas those that do not are revealed as inessential. Thus, by comparing a series of strings that lead to the same outcome, the ordered sequence of necessary elements that leads to it can be identified. In the case of a gorilla eating nettles, these recurring stages include (i) holding a fistful of leaf-blades, with leaf-stems protruding at one side, (ii) holding the base of a handful of stemless leaf-blades, and (iii) a small parcel of leaf-blades, folded neatly and held between finger and thumb.

6. *Reuse of strings*. A subroutine may be used in more than one program, or one program may be used as a subroutine in another. Once some strings have been identified as forming discrete modules or more complex structures, then these patterns can be picked out in as-yet-unparsed strings of elements. For instance, in gorilla feeding the subprocess, consisting of partly opening the hand that contains part-processed leaf food and deftly removing inedible debris with a

precision-grip by fingers of the other hand, occurs in dealing with several species of plant.

And no doubt there are other clues that can be used reliably to extract underlying structure (see Tversky, this volume, for a parallel approach to a similar problem in human behavior). The point I wish to make is that all the details needed to fabricate a imitative copy of a novel organization of actions can be gained without any understanding of the overall purpose of the behavior. Such copying could, under some restrictions, be evolutionarily highly adaptive: for instance, there are many circumstances in which it would pay an infant mammal to have a generalized tendency to copy any complex behavior shown repeatedly by the mother, especially if the behavior was food-related. In some species, this tendency might go along with understanding the purpose of these actions, in others (unable to conceive of purpose) it would simply contribute to survival.

Two components are necessary for this hypothetical system to become practical. The first is some way of segmenting perceived action into units, a "vocabulary" of primary elements out of which more complex behavior can be built. These units must already be in the repertoire of the observer, to be of any use for imitation. What is needed then is a system for matching manual gestures in the observer's repertoire with those same actions in the observed behavior of another individual. Just such systems have already been identified in the pre-motor cortex (area F5) and other connected areas of monkey cortex (Gallese & Goldman, 1998; Perrett et al., 1989; Rizzolatti, 1981; Rizzolatti & Gentilucci, 1988). The critical cells are termed "mirror neurons" and they respond only to purposive actions in the animal's repertoire, such as a precision grasp of a small food item; however, each cell responds equally to its triggering stimulus whether the action is performed by the animal itself or another. In short, this system appears to be the neural mechanism of response facilitation, and its discovery supports the existence of this mechanism, originally proposed as a hypothesis to account for behavior in some "imitation" experiments (Byrne, 1994). Response facilitation by mirror neurons has just the properties needed to segment the fluid action of a conspecific into elemental units, and each will automatically be an action in the repertoire of the observer. (The level at which this segmentation can be done will depend, of course, on just what *is* in the observer's pre-existing repertoire. If large chunks of observed behavior can already be performed, the segmentation will be a simple one, whereas if the actions are unfamiliar segmentation will necessarily occur at a very detailed level, in extreme cases perhaps down to the level of individual motor actions. In this case, program-level and action-level descriptions would perforce converge.) Segmentation alone is not, however, sufficient to allow program-level imitation – and indeed, monkeys have in practice signally failed to show any such imitation (Whiten & Ham, 1992).

The other essential component is a *string-parsing* mechanism capable of extracting the statistical regularities that characterize organized manual action; some of the ways of extracting regularities have been described above. Segmentation by response-facilitation produces linear strings of elements, each of which is an action that the observer can perform; string-parsing imposes higher-order organization on this sequence, and if it is successful then this will mirror the original planning structure that produced the behavior. A mental apparatus to (in effect) cross-correlate among very large numbers of sequences is likely to be a specialized system, functioning automatically and efficiently without demands on central capacity. A possible candidate is the supplementary motor area in the medial frontal cortex, an area richly interconnected with pre-motor F5 in macaque monkeys, and in which single neurons have been shown to code for sequences of manual movements (Halsband, Matsuzaka, & Tanji, 1994; Tanji, 1996; Tanji & Shima, 1994). Whatever its neural instantiation, the string-parsing system will require *multiple* presentations of organized actions in order to have the raw material from which to extract regularities: experiments that present to-be-copied behavior only one or a few times are unlikely to detect the ability.

At present, there is no evidence to suggest that monkeys (rather than apes) are able to learn complex, novel organizations of behavior by observation alone. Given the inherent fragility of purely negative evidence, it may be unwise to conclude that under no circumstances can they do so, although their possession of mirror neurons points to any real difficulty lying in string-parsing – perhaps something as simple as having a working memory too small to allow much pattern detection in strings. However, another possibility is that the neural areas that subserve imitation by string-parsing evolved originally in response to quite different pressures, and have only been secondarily recruited for skill learning in the great apes. Indeed, Rizzolatti and his co-workers believe that the primary evolutionary function of mirror neurons is the interpretation of social behavior and dispositions (Gallese & Goldman, 1998). Thus it is possible that monkeys already possess all the component aptitudes, but not integrated into a process that allows program-level imitation.

Concluding thoughts

The debate on imitation in recent years has had its share of cross-purposes argument, not helped by the variation in usage of the term itself. Rather than hope that – for once – a set of novel proposals have total clarity, it is probably safer to anticipate the variety of unwanted ways in which they might be understood, and attempt to explain how the intended interpretation differs. Most pernicious would be any implication that what great apes do in learning their complex manual skills is "not really" imitation, unlike what humans do in acquiring theirs. Then, segmentation and string-parsing might be appropriate to describe animal imitation but irrelevant to imitation in humans. Logically possible, this is surely unlikely given the closeness of the biological relationship between humans and nonhuman great apes. Certainly my intention is that, if these proposals have merit, they should apply equally to imitation of complex, novel manual procedures in human and nonhuman great apes. Another response might be to assert that "real imitation" requires an understanding of cause-and-effect and the intentions of the observed model; then, any imitation that lacks these, whether by human or ape, is disqualified. This is of course just a matter of definition, but seems to stretch the normal understanding of imitation an unhelpful amount. True, in many cases, imitation may co-occur with an understanding of the cause-and-effect of the mechanical actions and the goals and intentions of the model, but these are surely not defining features of imitation *per se*, and it seems plain confusing to say they are necessarily part of the process. On the account offered here, it is an empirical question whether imitation in particular cases or particular species is characteristically associated with such extra understanding, or not. Another view might be that this theory merely resuscitates and redescribes a behaviorist account of imitation. True, association learning by classical conditioning is based on repeated exposure to chains of co-occurring events, but there the similarity ends, because behaviorist accounts reject the need for mental mechanisms and structured mental representations (see further discussion in Byrne, 1999b). The products of string-parsing are not linear strings of response habits, as in the case of classical conditioning, but hierarchical planning structures requiring a cognitive architecture to build. Even the preliminary process of response facilitation by mirror neurons may go beyond anything proposed by animal learning theory, if the neurons are sensitive to motor actions in another individual's behavior that have first to be learned by the observer. Equally, it is important not to take this account as claiming that mirror neurons alone are "how imitation works." Their properties make them a feasible and adequate instantiation of the first part of the two-stage process I propose, but on their own they could not produce imitation, and they likely evolved for a very different function in a wider range of species than those that can imitate. Finally, the string-parsing account might be construed as claiming that imitation does not exist at all; but this would be a mere naming game, not a dangerous misunderstanding. If it is helpful to change the meaning of imitation once again, this can do no harm as long as its new sense is made clear and overt. However, I suggest that it is more useful to retain the term for the ability to copy behavior by observation alone, *whether or not the imitator has an intentional/causal understanding of what it is copying.* (To be sure that the copying is really a matter of imitation, rather than some form of priming, it will often in practice be necessary to require the behavior to be novel and complex – although of course imitation may also be applied to familiar, simple actions.)

In order to detect whether an individual who imitates novel action is doing so *with* insight into the causal/intentional nature of the behavior, it is clear that an experimental test would be desirable. Meltzoff's (1995) elegant experiment appears suitable for this: a demonstrator tries – but in the end fails – at some everyday task. Eighteen-month-old children, seeing this performance, copy the apparently intended action, not the ineffectual struggles. However, if the observed struggles were not aimed at a novel task it might be objected that the child could have seen the (complete) behavioral sequence before, and a partial match prompted the complete action sequence. (And expecting young children to copy novel, complex actions which are not even completed would be asking too much.) Instead, a task devised by Want & Harris (1998) may be ideal. In this, children watched a model attempting to push a small reward from a horizontal, transparent tube with a stick. The problem is that the tube has a pitfall trap built into it, so that pushing the reward in one direction causes it to be lost, a modification invented by Visalberghi & Limongelli (1994). One group of children saw the model push the reward in the correct direction on every trial; the other saw the model move the stick to the wrong end of the tube, but retract it (apparently correcting a near-error) and then place it in the correct end to retrieve the reward. String-parsing would cause copying of the redundant near-error, because it was an invariant part of the sequence, but in fact there was no such tendency. However, both groups were aided in their learning of the successful method by seeing the demonstrations, and in fact those who saw the corrected errors learnt more quickly. This shows, in children, skill learning which is based on causal/intentional understanding rather than simply string-parsing; the task has yet to be presented to any nonhuman primate subjects, and at present we do not know if the imitative learning of children is qualitatively different to that of great apes.

The relationship between imitation and causal/intentional understanding is a fascinating one. It seems possible that, in the absence of instructional teaching by language, an organism could not in principle understand the purpose of another's behavior and how it physically achieved this purpose if it could not first parse the behavior into its appropriate components. From this hypothesis, several predictions follow. Firstly, it will not be possible to find organisms that can achieve a causal/intentional understanding of complex behavior but cannot imitate it. Second, imitation of behavior of any real complexity will generally require repeated exposure to the model behavior, in order for statistical parsing to extract the necessary regularities. One-shot imitation will be the exception, and it will be limited to copying of simple actions (and thus be vulnerable to explanation as response facilitation not imitation). In this context, it is of interest that in the only experimental demonstration of imitation of the sequential order of actions by chimpanzees, the subjects required several exposures to the demonstrations before their attempts reached a statistically significant match (Whiten, 1998). Under the environmental circumstances in which imitation by string-parsing presumably evolved, the manual skills involved in feeding present innumerable opportunities for watching repetitive sequences of complex action. Finally, once imitation is seen as something that can take place without *prior* causal/intentional understanding of what is imitated, then a prediction is that sometimes the process of imitation may be helpful for acquiring such understanding. That is, an organism may imitate a complex behavioral process without understanding it, and by doing so come to grasp better the cause-and-effect nature of the process and its purpose. Indeed, imitating behavior "mindlessly" may be one way of gaining a fuller understanding of its purpose (and this has been suggested as one reason that orangutans are motivated to imitate humans: Russon, 1997). The developmental sequence of imitation in human infants is also consistent with the possibility that imitating actions may be causal in developing an understanding of the intentions behind actions. Infants as young as fourteen months have been found capable of imitating novel actions (Meltzoff, 1988a), but the first signs of understanding the intentions of the adult demonstrator have come from eighteen-month-old infants, who copy the goals of acts even when the acts themselves are apparently thwarted and fail to reach any goal (Meltzoff, 1995). In this area of developmental psychology, just as in our attempts to understand the skill learning of nonhuman great apes, it has evidently been useful to consider imitation as independent from, and perhaps necessarily prior to, causal-intentional understanding of acts. The convergence of approach across disciplines perhaps suggests that this is the right track.

Notes

1 With the exception of ant-fishing for *Campanotus* ants, which shows little or no individual hand preference (Nishida & Hiraiwa, 1982).

2 In contrast, Whiten & Custance (1996:309) state that "any imitated act can be broken down into a number of sub-goals, the details of how each is achieved varying [from the original]." This seems to *assume* that the structure of subgoals can be detected simply by watching; on the analysis of the current chapter, doing just that is one of the fundamental problems of program-level imitation, and a major reason for being interested in it. If all imitation were necessarily program-level, then Whiten and Custance's statement would be unexceptionable; however this is surely too strong a claim.

3 But see Tanner (1998, Chapter 8) for an unusual case of a nursery-reared zoo gorilla that chose to imitate human gestures, including novel actions, without any history of reward.

Acknowledgements

I would like to thank several of the participants at the conference "The imitative mind: development, evolution and brain bases" (Kloster Seeon, March 18–21, 1999), organized by Wolfgang Prinz and Andy Meltzoff, for their valuable comments, in particular Giacomo Rizzolatti and David Perrett. Discussing these issues with Anne Russon, many times over several years, has always been helpful in clarifying my ideas. The help of Andy Meltzoff and two anonymous reviewers is gratefully acknowledged in improving the precision of the chapter and removing many errors and infelicities.

References

Bauer, P., & Mandler, J. (1989). One thing follows another: Effects of temporal structure on 1- and 2-year-olds' recall of events. *Developmental Psychology, 25,* 197–206.

Boesch, C. (1991a). Handedness in wild chimpanzees. *International Journal of Primatology, 12,* 541–558.

(1991b). Teaching among wild chimpanzees. *Animal Behaviour, 41,* 530–532.

Boesch, C., & Boesch, H. (1983). Optimisation of nut-cracking with natural hammers by wild chimpanzees. *Behaviour, 26,* 265–286.

(1990). Tool use and tool making in wild chimpanzees. *Folia Primatologica, 54,* 86–99.

Byrne, R. W. (1993). Hierarchical levels of imitation. Commentary on M. Tomasello, A. C. Kruger and H. H. Ratner "Cultural learning." *Behavioural and Brain Sciences, 16,* 516–517.

(1994). The evolution of intelligence. In P. J. B. Slater & T. R. Halliday (Eds.), *Behaviour and evolution* (pp. 223–265). Cambridge: Cambridge University Press.

(1998a). Comments on C. Boesch and M. Tomasello "Chimpanzee and human cultures." *Current Anthropology, 39,* 604–605.

(1998b). Imitation: The contributions of priming and program-level copying. In S. Braten (Ed.), *Intersubjective communication and emotion in early ontogeny* (pp. 228–244). Cambridge: Cambridge University Press.

(1999a). Complex object manipulation and skill organization in natural food preparation by mountain gorillas. In S. T. Parker, R. W. Mitchell, &

H. L. Miles (Eds.), *The mentality of gorillas and orangutans* (pp. 147–159). Cambridge: Cambridge University Press.

(1999b). Imitation without intentionality: Using string parsing to copy the organization of behavior. *Animal Cognition, 2,* 63–72.

Byrne, R. W., & Byrne, J. M. E. (1991). Hand preferences in the skilled gathering tasks of mountain gorillas (*Gorilla g. beringei*). *Cortex, 27,* 521–546.

(1993). Complex leaf-gathering skills of mountain gorillas (*Gorilla g. beringei*): Variability and standardization. *American Journal of Primatology, 31,* 241–261.

Byrne, R. W., & Russon, A. E. (1998). Learning by imitation: A hierarchical approach. *Behavioral and Brain Sciences, 21,* 667–721.

Byrne, R. W., & Tomasello, M. (1995). Do rats ape? *Animal Behaviour, 50,* 1417–1420.

Custance, D. M., Whiten, A., & Bard, K. A. (1995). Can young chimpanzees (*Pan troglodytes*) imitate arbitrary actions? Hayes & Hayes (1952) revisited. *Behaviour, 132,* 11–12.

Dawkins, R. (1976). Hierarchical organisation: A candidate principle for ethology. In P. P. G. Bateson & R. A. Hinde (Eds.), *Growing points in ethology* (pp. 7–54). Cambridge: Cambridge University Press.

Dawson, B. V., & Foss, B. M. (1965). Observational learning in budgerigars. *Animal Behaviour, 13,* 470–474.

Fox, E., Sitompul, A., & Van Schaik, C. P. (1999). Intelligent tool use in wild Sumatran orangutans. In S. T. Parker, H. L. Miles, & R. W. Mitchell (Eds.), *The mentality of gorillas and orangutans* (pp. 99–116). Cambridge: Cambridge University Press.

Galef, B. G. (1988). Imitation in animals: History, definitions, and interpretation of data from the psychological laboratory. In T. Zentall & B. G. Galef, Jr. (Eds.), *Social Learning: Psychological and biological perspectives* (pp. 3–28). Hillsdale, NJ: Erlbaum.

Gallese, V., & Goldman, A. (1998). Mirror neurons and simulation theory of mind-reading. *Trends in Cognitive Sciences, 2 (12),* 493–501.

Goodall, J. (1964). Tool-using and aimed throwing in a community of free-living chimpanzees. *Nature, 201,* 1264–1266.

Halsband, U., Matsuzaka, Y., & Tanji, J. (1994). Neuronal activity in the primate supplementary, pre-supplementary and pre-motor cortex during externally and internally instructed sequential movements. *Neuroscience Research, 20,* 149–155.

Hayes, K. J., & Hayes, C. (1952). Imitation in a home-raised chimpanzee. *Journal of Comparative and Physiological Psychology, 45,* 450–459.

Heyes, C. M. (1993). Imitation, culture, and cognition. *Animal Behaviour, 46,* 999–1010.

Lashley, K. S. (1951). The problem of serial order in behavior. In L. A. Jeffress (Ed.), *Cerebral mechanisms in behaviour: The Hixon symposium* (pp. 112–136). New York: Wiley.

Marchant, L. F., & McGrew, W. C. (1996). Laterality of limb function in wild chimpanzees of Gombe National Park: Comprehensive study of spontaneous activities. *Journal of Human Evolution, 30,* 427–443.

McGrew, W. C. (1974). Tool use by wild chimpanzees feeding on driver ants. *Journal of Human Evolution, 3,* 501–508.

(1992). *Chimpanzee material culture: Implications for human evolution.* Cambridge: Cambridge University Press.

(1998). Culture in nonhuman primates? *Annual Review of Anthropology, 27,* 301–328.

McGrew, W. C., & Marchant, L. F. (1996). On which side of the apes? Ethological study of laterality of hand use. In W. C. McGrew, L. F. Marchant, & T. Nishida (Eds.), *Great ape societies* (pp. 255–272). Cambridge: Cambridge University Press.

McGrew, W. C., Tutin, C. E. G., & Baldwin, P. J. (1979). Chimpanzees, tools, and termites: Cross cultural comparison of Senegal, Tanzania, and Rio Muni. *Man, 14,* 185–214.

Meltzoff, A. N. (1988a). Infant imitation after a one week delay: Long term memory for novel acts and multiple stimuli. *Developmental Psychology, 24,* 470–476.

(1988b). The human infant as *Homo imitans.* In T. Zentall & B. Galef (Eds.), *Social learning: Psychological and biological perspectives* (pp. 319–341). Hillsdale, NY: Erlbaum.

(1988c). Infant imitation and memory: nine-month-olds in immediate and deferred tests. *Child Development, 59,* 217–225.

(1995). Understanding the intentions of others: Re-enactment of intended acts by 18-month-old children. *Developmental Psychology, 31 (5),* 838–850.

Meltzoff, A. N., & Gopnik, A. (1993). The role of imitation in understanding persons and developing a theory of mind. In S. Baron-Cohen, H. Tager-Flusberg, & D. J. Cohen (Eds.), *Understanding other minds: Perspectives from autism* (pp. 335–366). Oxford: Oxford University Press.

Miller, G. A., Galanter, E., & Pribram, K. (1960). *Plans and the structure of behavior.* New York: Holt, Rinehart, and Winston.

Nishida, T. (1973). The ant-gathering behavior by the use of tools among wild chimpanzees of the Mahali Mountains. *Journal of Human Evolution, 2,* 357–370.

(1986). Local traditions and cultural transmission. In B. B. Smuts, D. L. Cheney, R. M. Seyfarth, R. W. Wrangham, & T. T. Struhsaker (Eds.), *Primate societies* (pp. 462–474). Chicago and London: University of Chicago Press.

Nishida, T., & Hiraiwa, M. (1982). Natural history of a tool-using behavior by wild chimpanzees in feeding on wood-boring ants. *Journal of Human Evolution, 11,* 73–99.

Perrett, D. I., Harries, M. H., Bevan, R., Thomas, S., Benson, P. J., Mistlin, A. J., Chitty, A. J., Hietanen, J. K., & Ortega, J. E. (1989). Frameworks of analysis for the neural representations of animate objects and actions. *Journal of Experimental Biology, 146,* 87–113.

Rizzolatti, G. (1981). Afferent properties of periarcuate neurons in macaque monkey. II. Visual responses. *Behavioural Brain Research, 2,* 147–163.

Rizzolatti, G., & Gentilucci, M. (1988). Motor and visual-motor functions of the premotor cortex. In P. Rakic & W. Singer (Eds.), *Neurobiology of neocortex* (pp. 269–284). New York: John Wiley & Sons.

Russon, A. E. (1997). Exploiting the expertise of others. In A. Whiten & R. W. Byrne (Eds.), *Machiavellian intelligence II: Extensions and evaluations* (pp. 174–206). Cambridge: Cambridge University Press.

Russon, A. E., & Galdikas, B. M. F. (1993). Imitation in free-ranging rehabilitant orangutans. *Journal of Comparative Psychology, 107*, 147–161.

Spence, K. W. (1937). Experimental studies of learning and higher mental processes in infra-human primates. *Psychological Bulletin, 34*, 806–850.

Sugiyama, Y. (1995). Tool-use for catching ants by chimpanzees at Bossou and Monts Nimba, West Africa. *Primates, 36 (2)*, 193–205.

Sugiyama, Y., Fushimi, T., Sakura, O., & Matsuzawa, T. (1993). Hand preference and tool use in wild chimpanzees. *Primates, 34*, 151–159.

Sugiyama, Y., Koman, J., & Bhoye Sow, M. (1988). Ant-catching wands of wild chimpanzees at Bossou, Guinea. *Folia Primatologica, 51*, 56–60.

Tanji, J. (1996). Involvement of motor areas in medial frontal cortex of primates in sequencing of multiple movements. In R. Caminiti, K.-P. Hoffman, F. Lacquaniti, & J. Altman (Eds.), *Vision and movement mechanisms in the cerebral cortex*. Strasbourg: HFSP.

Tanji, J., & Shima, K. (1994). Role of supplementary motor cells in planning several movements ahead. *Nature, 371*, 413–416.

Tanner, J. (1998). *Gestural communication in a group of zoo-living lowland gorillas.* Unpublished Ph.D., St Andrews University.

Thorndike, E. L. (1898). Animal intelligence: An experimental study of the associative process in animals. *Psychological Review and Monograph, 2 (8)*, 551–553.

Tomasello, M. (1990). Cultural transmission in the tool use and communicatory signaling of chimpanzees? In S. T. Parker & K. R. Gibson (Eds.), *"Language" and intelligence in monkeys and apes* (pp. 274–311). Cambridge: Cambridge University Press.

Tomasello, M., Kruger, A. C., & Ratner, H. H. (1993). Cultural learning. *Behavioral and Brain Sciences, 16*, 495–552.

Toth, N., Schick, K. D., Savage-Rumbaugh, E. S., Sevcik, R. A., & Rumbaugh, D. M. (1993). Pan the tool-maker: Investigations into the stone-tool-making and tool-using capabilities of a bonobo (Pan paniscus). *Journal of Archaeological Science, 20*, 81–91.

Visalberghi, E., & Limongelli, L. (1994). Lack of comprehension of cause–effect relationships in tool-using capuchin monkeys (*Cebus apella*). *Journal of Comparative Psychology, 103*, 15–20.

Want, S. C., & Harris, P. L. (1998). Indices of program-level comprehension. *Behavioral and Brain Sciences, 21*, 706–707.

Waterman, P. G., Choo, G. M., Vedder, A. L., & Watts, D. (1983). Digestibility, digestion-inhibitors and nutrients and herbaceous foliage and green stems from an African montane flora and comparison with other tropical flora. *Oecologia, 60*, 244–249.

Watts, D. P. (1984). Composition and variability of mountain gorilla diets in the central Virungas. *American Journal of Primatology, 7*, 323–356.

Whiten, A. (1998). Imitation of the sequential structure of actions by chimpanzees (*Pan troglodytes*). *Journal of Comparative Psychology, 112*, 270–281.

Whiten, A., & Custance, D. (1996). Studies of imitation in chimpanzees and children. In C. M. Heyes & B. G. Galef (Eds.), *Social learning in animals: The roots of culture* (pp. 291–318). San Diego: Academic Press.

Whiten, A., Custance, D. M., Gomez, J.-C., Teixidor, P., & Bard, K. A. (1996). Imitative learning of artificial fruit processing in children (*Homo sapiens*) and chimpanzees (*Pan troglodytes*). *Journal of Comparative Psychology, 110,* 3–14.

Whiten, A., & Ham, R. (1992). On the nature and evolution of imitation in the animal kingdom: Reappraisal of a century of research. In P. J. B. Slater, J. S. Rosenblatt, C. Beer, & M. Milinski (Eds.), *Advances in the study of behavior* (pp. 239–283). San Diego: Academic Press.

Wright, R. V. S. (1972). Imitative learning of a flaked-tool technology – The case of an orang-utan. *Mankind, 8,* 296–306.

Part II

Cognitive approaches to imitation, body scheme, and perception-action coding

8   Experimental approaches to imitation

Wolfgang Prinz

The title of this chapter can be read in two ways, referring to method and theory. As regards method I will discuss a number of experimental paradigms we have been developing in our lab over the past few years in order to elucidate the mechanisms underlying performance in imitation tasks. As regards theory I will elaborate on the broader theoretical framework that forms their background. In the first place, this framework provides us with principles to direct our research. At a later point it will, hopefully, also provide us with more detailed models and mechanisms to account for the basic findings. In this chapter I will first introduce the theoretical framework, then discuss pertinent experimental work from our lab, and finally draw some major general conclusions.

Framework

The study of imitation has two faces. On the one face, imitation and related phenomena have never been an object of systematical study in the experimental analysis of human performance in adults. In a way, imitational behavior appears to be too complex for experimental analysis. This is mainly because a number of things need to be studied at the same time. When A mimics B, we need to give an account of (1) the model's actions (as a stimulus for the imitator), (2) the imitator's perception of the model's action, and (3) the imitator's action itself. Obviously, this is quite a complex network of variables as compared to the standard type of situation normally captured in experiments on cognition and action.

However, on the other face, there is both a nineteenth-century theoretical tradition and a twentieth-century experimental tradition that lend themselves to application to imitative action. The theoretical tradition comes from theories of the functional anatomy of voluntary action. The experimental tradition refers to research on stimulus-response compatibility. In the following I will try to show how these two strands of thought can be brought to bear on imitation.

Nineteenth century: Lotze and James on ideomotor action

The ground for the ideomotor framework was laid by Lotze (1852) and James (1890) in their discussion of voluntary action. However, their ideas were by no means formed in an attempt to give an account of imitation. Though Lotze occasionally speaks of imitational movements (*Nachahmungsbewegungen*), it is clear from his examples that he is not referring to situations where a person acts in an attempt to act like another person. The same applies to James. In his famous chapter XXVI on the will, where the ideomotor framework is outlined, there is no mention of imitation at all.

Lotze's and James' accounts of voluntary action are virtually identical and James refers to Lotze's discussion several times. According to the Lotze–James account, two conditions must be fulfilled for voluntary action to occur: (1) an idea, or representation, of what is being willed or intended (Lotze: *Vorstellung des Gewollten*), and (2) a lack, or removal, of any conflicting ideas (Lotze: *Hinwegräumung aller Hemmungen*). The first condition refers to a state of cognition, the second to a state of volition. Whenever both conditions are fulfilled at the same time, then the cognitive representations of the intended goal states will produce the action directly, that is, without intervention of any additional volitional activity: "We think the act, and it is done" (James, 1890: vol. II, p. 522).

Accordingly, any cognitive state is "in its very nature impulsive" (p. 526). This is true of all cognitive states, but it is particularly true of cognitive representations that refer to movements and actions. To these representations the ideomotor principle of human action applies: "Every representation of a movement awakens in some degree the actual movement which is its object; and awakens it in a maximum degree whenever it is not kept from doing so by an antagonistic representation present simultaneously in the mind" (James, 1890: vol. II, p. 526).

Where does the impulsive nature of cognition come from? Lotze and James both argue that there is no mystery at all. Rather, the impulsiveness of cognition derives from previous learning. When a motor act is performed (for whatever cause or reason) it goes along with a number of perceivable effects. Some are close to the action in the sense of being accompaniments of the act's execution (kinesthetic sensations, etc.). Some others may be more remote, like the fact that a light goes on at a distance when one's fingers operate a light switch.

To the extent such regular connections exist between motor acts and perceivable bodily and environmental events, these regularities can be used and exploited in two ways. The first is *to expect certain events*, given certain acts, that is, to predict an ongoing action's perceivable consequences. The second way is *to select and initiate a certain act*, given an intention to achieve certain effects, that is, to derive a goal-directed action from a predefined goal.

This latter relationship – which leads from intended effects to acts – is considered the functional basis of the ideomotor principle. Any representation of an event of which we know from previous learning that it either accompanies, or follows from, a particular action will hereafter have the power to call forth the action that produces the event. This will, in the first place, apply to any idea that refers to bodily movements themselves (e.g., thinking of one's finger operating a light switch) but in the second place it will also apply to ideas that refer to more remote action effects (e.g., thinking of the light going on).

Lotze and James were both predominantly concerned with the issue of how action is guided by thoughts and ideas. They were less interested in how action is guided by perception. Obviously, though, if the mere thought of an act or its effect has the power to awaken it to some degree, this should likewise be true, or perhaps even more so, in the case of bluntly perceiving the act being performed by somebody else.

Twentieth century: Greenwald on ideomotor compatibility

Couldn't it be that, for example, my smiling can get awakened, or induced, by *seeing somebody else's smile* – in exactly the same way as by thinking of myself smiling? It took another 80 years after James' *Principles* until Greenwald suggested an interesting extension of James' principle of ideomotor action, which also included the case of action being induced by perception (Greenwald, 1970, 1972).

Greenwald's extended principle was meant to be a contribution to the then emerging literature on skilled performance, particularly on stimulus-response compatibility (Fitts & Deininger, 1954; Kornblum, Hasbroucq, & Osman, 1990; for an overview, see Hommel & Prinz, 1997). This literature was (and still is) concerned with the conditions and factors that affect the ease of establishing mapping relationships between stimuli and responses, or stimulus sets and response sets, respectively. Greenwald proposed the notion of ideomotor compatibility as a new explanatory concept to account for some recurrent observations in this literature. By this he referred to situations where responses are mapped to stimuli such that the stimuli which trigger them exhibit some resemblance, or feature overlap, with feedback that arises from their required responses. An example is a situation where a red stimulus light requires an arbitrary manual response that, in turn, triggers a red feedback flash – in which case the two stimuli involved (stimulus light and feed-back flash) share the same color. Obviously, in a situation like this, the red stimulus light takes exactly the role of the movement-awakening thought or idea in the Lotze–James approach. It should be particularly powerful in eliciting the response by virtue of its overlap with features of the response and/or its outcome.

Therefore, with this extension, the Lotze/James/Greenwald approach lends itself as a straightforward framework for action imitation. It relies on the extended ideomotor principle, that is, on the notion that *the perception of an event that shares features with an event that has been learnt to accompany, or follow from, one's own action, will tend to induce that action.* The strength of the induction will depend on the degree of feature overlap between the stimulus event and the action-related event. In other words, the perceptual system may induce, or seduce if you will, the action system to perform certain actions under certain perceptual conditions and it does so by virtue of similarity between the percept and the act.

Clearly, this view does not provide a functional model of imitation. It is rather meant to provide a framework that makes the elusive phenomena of imitation seem somewhat less mysterious. It may also help to direct our research in two ways. First, concerning heuristics, it may help us to ask new questions and develop new experimental paradigms. Second, concerning theory, it may help us with some answers and narrow down the space for more detailed functional models.

Experimental investigations

In the following I will go through some experimental paradigms we have developed to study some aspects of imitation behavior. I will discuss four classes of such paradigms, requiring *movement reproduction, movement selection, movement initiation,* and *movement production.*

The tasks to be discussed differ in the constraints imposed on the participants' actions. Reproduction and selection tasks are constrained in the sense that participants are required to reproduce, or select, certain actions in response to certain relevant stimuli while ignoring irrelevant stimuli that are presented as well. In these tasks we study how performance in response to the relevant information is modulated by the irrelevant information. The same problem is also studied in initiation tasks, where the requirement is to initiate a prespecified movement upon the presentation of relevant and irrelevant information. Finally, in unconstrained production tasks, we study the spontaneous occurrence of movements and try to disentangle to what extent they are guided by competing aspects inherent in the stimulus pattern.

Movement reproduction

In the first two paradigms the task requires to reproduce previously seen target movements. In both cases we study how reproduction performance is modulated by additional distractor movements that are either shown before or concurrent with the reproduction and tend to compete with the target movements. An important difference between the two paradigms is that in one of them distractors are closely linked to targets (in both temporal and causal terms), whereas in the other paradigm distractors and targets are completely unrelated.

Related movements. In the first task the target movements that need to be reproduced and the distractor movements that need to be ignored are closely linked to each other. Participants are required to first observe two consecutive object movements and then reproduce the first of them as precisely as possible while ignoring the second (for details, see Kerzel, Bekkering, Wohlschläger, & Prinz, 2000). When the two movements follow each other immediately and adjacently, the total sequence tends to be parsed into cause and effect, and a collision is perceived between the two.

In one way, our task studies nothing but the perception of physical events. However, as is well known since the pioneering work of Heider and Simmel (1944) and Michotte (1946/1963), there is often not much of a difference between event perception and action perception. Event configurations with implied causal linkages are often perceived as if intentional agents were involved – in which case the cause–effect sequence tends to be seen as an action–effect sequence. Therefore, our task, though it studies the perception of physical events in the first place, contributes at the same time to the study of the perception and reproduction of intentional events, or actions.

On each trial participants saw two disks, A and B, moving on a display, and the task required them to watch both A and B and then reproduce, in their own actions, the velocity of A. We assumed that the causal link perceived between them would create some functional integration between A and B, or their respective working memory codes, and that, due to this integration, the velocity of the reproduction would not only be affected by A (the relevant target) but by B as well (the irrelevant distractor). A typical trial is shown in Figure 8.1a. At the beginning, the two disks, A (yellow) and B (white), were stationary. Then A started traveling from left to right inside the frame, with traveling velocity manipulated in three steps. When A reached the inner right edge of the frame, B would start moving, giving the impression of a collision between A and B. B would then travel from left to right at one of the same three velocities

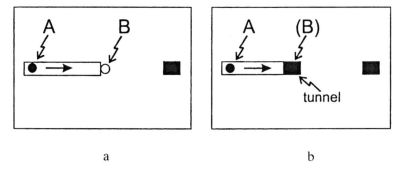

a   b

Figure 8.1. Stimulus display in the movement reproduction task designed by Kerzel, Bekkering, Wohlschläger, & Prinz (2000). (a) basic
experiment, (b) tunnel experiment (see text for details).

and eventually vanish in the rectangle shown on the right-hand side. Participants were instructed to reproduce A's movement and ignore B. Their
reproductions were recorded from stylus movements on a graphic tablet.

Results indicated that reproduction velocity was, of course, strongly
dependent on A's actual velocity. More interestingly, however, it was also
clearly affected by B's velocity: A's reproduction tended to be faster, the
faster B was. Obviously, then, a cause's, or action's, apparent effect (= B)
gets somehow assimilated to the cause, or the action itself (= A).

In a further experiment, we examined whether a more continuous appearance of the movement pattern would modulate the assimilative integration of the two segments (cf. Fig. 8.1b). In this experiment, A and B
traveled at the same velocities as before. There were, however, two slight
alterations. First, the two objects were now identical in color and, second,
the point of impact was concealed within a tunnel. These two measures
were meant to produce a tunnel effect: when one object disappears into
the tunnel and a similar object leaves the tunnel immediately afterwards,
people tend to see a single object disappear and reappear, and no causal
impact of one on the other object is seen (Michotte, 1946/1963; Burke,
1952). We reasoned that this manipulation would help to reveal what the
critical factor underlying the observed assimilative integration is. A natural view would be to believe that making the entire movement appear
more continuous would strengthen the assimilative impact of B on the reproduction of A. However, the reverse view is possible as well, that is, that
perceived continuity will weaken the assimilation because it is critically
dependent on a perceived cause–effect link between the two.

The results were in line with the second of these two views: the impact of B's velocity on A's reproductions had gone. Though this result

still needs further support and clarification, it is obvious that the tunnel manipulation, if any, did not strengthen assimilation but rather weakened it, suggesting that the assimilative integration of the two components is strongly dependent on a causal link perceived between them.

Unrelated movements. The second task also required to reproduce a previously seen target movement under distractor conditions (Schuboe, 1998; Schuboe, Aschersleben, & Prinz, 2001). However, it was different in some important details. First, and most importantly, distractor movements were unrelated to target movements in both temporal and causal terms. Second, distractor movements did not intervene between target movements and their reproductions, but were always presented simultaneously with the participant's reproductions. Third, though distractors were completely irrelevant for the ongoing reproductions, they could not be ignored because they were relevant for the subsequent reproduction.

The task was a serial response task with overlapping S-R assignments. On each particular trial (n) a stimulus (S_n) was presented and a response (R_n) was delivered, as is usually required in serial-response tasks. However, what was unusual was that the response (R_n) was assigned to the *previous* stimulus (S_{n-1}), whereas the stimulus (S_n) was to be responded to by the *subsequent* response (R_{n+1}). The task was therefore overlapping in the sense that two independent S-R assignments overlapped on each particular trial. Therefore, participants had to do two things simultaneously on any given trial (cf. Fig. 8.2): (1) watch a sinusoidal dot movement and keep it in memory for reproduction on the subsequent trial, and (2) copy the dot movement seen on the previous trial. Dot movements were presented on a computer screen and reproductions were again recorded with a stylus on a graphic tablet. Three different stimulus movements, differing in amplitude (large/medium/small) and, correlated with this, in tangential velocity (fast/medium/slow), were presented in randomized order over the sequence of trials. On each trial the stimulus movement presented and the stylus movement performed were strictly concurrent.

The critical question was whether and how stylus movements would be affected by concurrent distractor movements. On the one hand, the task imposes severe time constraints by requiring participants to reproduce the old movement and encode the new movement strictly concurrently – which might support, if not enforce, assimilation of the two. On the other hand, it also puts strong demands on keeping the two separate and apart. This is because the distractor is not just irrelevant, but needs to be encoded for future processing – which might counteract, if not impede, assimilation and even support contrast. This view is also supported by the

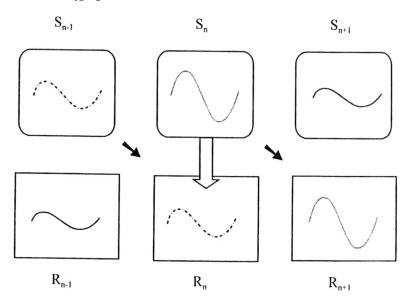

Figure 8.2. Trial sequence in the serial overlapping response task (SORT) used by Schuboe *et al.* (2001). On a given trial (n) the task requires participants both to encode stimulus movement S_n (for later reproduction) and to perform stylus movement R_n (in response to the previous stimulus movement).

fact that no perceived causality is involved: there is no reason to believe that two events, that are both functionally separate and causally unrelated, should become assimilated to each other.

Which one is true – assimilation or contrast? How do stylus movements depend on the size and velocity of concurrently presented stimulus movements? In a number of experiments results indicated an inverse similarity effect, suggesting contrast rather than assimilation. With large distractors, reproductions tended to be small whereas reproductions tended to be large with small distractors. This contrast pattern was observed in both amplitudes and velocities. Obviously, then, under the conditions of the overlapping response task, the perception of the stimulus movement and the production of the stylus movement were not integrated and assimilated with each other, but rather kept strictly separate and – metaphorically speaking – even pulled away from each other. This occurred despite the fact that the two processes were strictly concurrent.

These observations may be taken to suggest that movement perception and movement production draw on common representational resources – resources that cannot be used for both of these processes simultaneously (cf. Hommel, 1997; Müsseler, 1999; Hommel, Müsseler, Aschersleben, & Prinz, in press; Prinz, 1990, 1997a, b). In other words, two concurrent operations – encoding and reproduction for two independent S-R assignments – cannot address, and make use of, identical representational resources at the same time. With this view the critical differences between the two reproduction paradigms lie in two factors, namely, the relationship between the two events and the time constraints for reproduction. With concurrent encoding and reproduction of two unrelated events (as in Schuboe's, 1998, paradigm), competition for shared resources will arise, yielding contrast and separation. However, with reproduction following two related events (as in Kerzel, Bekkering, Wohlschläger, & Prinz's 2000, paradigm) there is no such competition, yielding assimilation and integration. It seems that the two paradigms mark the poles of a continuum of distractor-dependent reproduction tasks that needs further study and elaboration.

Movement selection

This section brings us somewhat closer to imitation proper. In the following experiments we consider tasks where body gestures were shown as stimuli and similar gestures were required in response. However, like in the Stroop task or the Simon task, these stimulus gestures provided both relevant information that needed to be translated into proper action, and irrelevant information that needed to be prevented from triggering inappropriate action.

Gesture selection. In the gesture selection task devised by Stuermer (1997; cf. Stuermer, Aschersleben, & Prinz, 2000), two hand movements were presented as stimulus gestures, either a hand spreading apart (with fingers extending) or a hand grasping (with fingers flexing). Both gestures would start from the same neutral initial posture. On each trial one of the two gestures was shown, and participants were required to perform one of the same two hand movements as a response gesture. However, the identity of the stimulus gesture presented was completely irrelevant for the selection of the response gesture to be performed. Instead, the color of the stimulus hand was the relevant cue for the gesture to be performed. If the stimulus hand was red, the participant had to spread his or her hand and if it was blue, he or she had to grasp (cf. Fig. 8.3).

Results from a number of experiments provided clear evidence that Stroop- or Simon-like compatibility effects can be observed with hand gestures as stimuli and responses as well. The speed with which a particular hand gesture can be selected as a response was substantially modulated

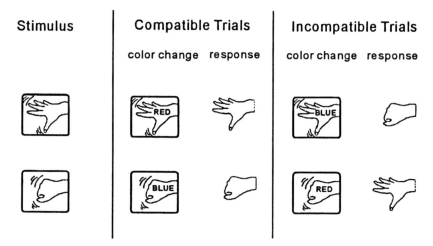

Stimulus	Compatible Trials		Incompatible Trials	
	color change	response	color change	response

Figure 8.3. Gesture selection task designed by Stuermer (1997). On each trial a manual gesture is shown and a color change is superimposed. Color is relevant and gesture identity is irrelevant for the specification of the response gesture (see text for further details).

by the (irrelevant) hand gesture on which the imperative stimulus (color change) was superimposed. Selection of response gestures was faster with correspondence between stimulus and response gestures as compared to trials with no such correspondence.

In one of her experiments, Stuermer manipulated the time of the color change relative to the onset of the gesture. What we initially expected with regard to this manipulation was a gradual build-up of the compatibility effect over time. This was based on the reasoning that capturing the dynamics of the stimulus gesture would require some time for the gesture to build up. What we observed, instead, was a pronounced compatibility effect which was there from the outset, that is, even in the condition in which color change would coincide with the onset of the gesture.

Therefore, in a further experiment, Stuermer presented stationary hand postures rather than dynamic gestures. Actually, she chose the two hand postures representing the final end states in the gestures of the spreading and grasping gestures (as shown in Fig. 8.3). Again, we expected weaker effects with postures than with gestures, mainly because we reasoned that static stimuli exhibit less overlap with dynamic responses than dynamic stimuli do. Once more, however, we observed substantial compatibility effects from the outset, if any, somewhat larger ones than in the gesture experiment. As was shown in a further experiment, the size of this effect depends on the unequivocality between stimulus postures and response gestures: postures reflecting intermediate states of gestures are less powerful in seducing the action system than the end state postures themselves.

In sum, we may now bear in mind two major points: (1) The gesture selection task yields pronounced compatibility effects, based on both stimulus gestures and stimulus postures; (2) postures reflecting end states of gestures may be at least as effective as gestures in inducing corresponding response gestures – perhaps even more effective. We believe that these findings suggest two major conclusions. One is that we take them as another piece of evidence supporting our basic claim that identical representational structures are involved in the perceiving and the performing of actions (cf. Prinz, 1990, 1992; Hommel, Müsseler, Aschersleben, & Prinz, in press). Without a common representational scheme underlying both it would not be easy to understand how the perception of a particular action can prime its execution. The second conclusion is that end-state postures appear to be particularly effective primes for triggering the gestures leading to them. This may be surprising in view of the fact that full-blown gestures provide both static and dynamic information, whereas in postures dynamic information is lacking by definition. This may suggest that end states, or action goals, play a particularly prominent role in the mechanism underlying the compatibility effect in our task (see Bekkering, this volume; Meltzoff & Moore, 1997; Gattis et al., this volume, for similar views on the functional role of goals in imitation).

Effector selection. In the effector selection paradigm devised by Brass (1999; Brass, Bekkering, Wohlschläger, & Prinz, 2000), the gesture to be performed was always fixed, but the choice was between two effectors that could be used to perform the gesture. The gesture was the lifting of a finger, and the choice was between the index and the middle finger of participants' right hands. The stimulus was provided by a hand on the screen which was the mirror-image of participant's right hand.

Brass used two instructions. One was iconic, or imitative, requiring the participant to lift the same finger as was being lifted by the hand on the display. The other instruction was symbolic, requiring the participant to lift the same finger as was marked by a cross on the display. With each of these two instructions, three classes of stimuli were presented: baseline, congruent, and incongruent. For baseline stimuli, only one of the two features was shown (under iconic instructions one finger was lifted and no cross was shown; under symbolic instructions one finger was marked by a cross, and no lifting was shown). For congruent stimuli, the same finger that was lifted was also marked by a cross, whereas for incongruent stimuli one finger was lifted and the other one was marked by a cross.

The major results from this experiment can be summarized as follows. First, when the finger to be lifted was cued by a stimulus finger doing the same (baseline/iconic), response times were much shorter than when it was cued by a cross on a stationary stimulus finger (baseline/symbolic). This seems to reflect a pronounced difference in the degree to which the selection of a given effector can be supported by iconic versus symbolic information. Second, there was strong iconic interference with symbolic instructions, and it was observed in both directions: iconic congruency helped and iconic incongruency hurt (relative to baseline). Third, there was also an (albeit weaker) symbolic interference effect with iconic instructions, this time only in the sense that symbolic incongruency hurt (relative to baseline). In sum, the results suggest that iconic cueing of response gestures is much more powerful than symbolic cueing.

In a further experiment Brass decided to weaken the iconic similarity between stimulus and response gestures, with everything else completely unchanged. In this experiment the same two instructions and the same three types of stimuli were combined, but a different response gesture was used throughout: instead of an upward lift, the task this time required a downward tap of the finger indicated by the stimulus. Under these conditions (1) the baseline difference virtually disappeared, (2) iconic incongruency was still effective under symbolic instructions, and (3) a slight effect of symbolic incongruency was still preserved under iconic instructions. In sum, though the strong advantage of iconic over symbolic response specification had now gone (no difference any more between the two instructions in the baseline conditions), a substantial impact of iconic incongruency was still preserved (as evidenced by iconic interference under symbolic instructions). These findings suggest that weakening gesture similarity also weakens the impact of iconic effector specification without, however, deleting it completely.

Movement initiation

In a further set of experiments we addressed the issue to which extent iconic cueing can even be effective under conditions of full response certainty, that is, when the response to be generated is kept constant over a number of trials (Brass, 1999; Brass, Bekkering, & Prinz, 2001; see also Bekkering, this volume). The issue of whether or not compatibility effects are obtained in simple reaction tasks is controversial in the literature. If any such effects are observed they tend to be weak and not very robust. This has often been taken to support the claim that stimulus-response compatibility effects arise at the processing stage of response selection – a stage that, by definition, is involved in choice tasks but not in simple tasks (see Hommel, 1996, for discussion and overview). There-fore, if one could demonstrate that substantial compatibility effects arise in a task involving no choices and, hence, no response selection at all, this would challenge the notion that this particular stage is the functional locus where compatibility effects emerge.

In the experiments participants were presented with a randomized se-quence of two stimulus gestures. One stimulus gesture showed an index finger that started from a fixed position and then moved upwards at an unpredictable point of time. The other stimulus gesture showed the same index finger starting from the same fixed position and then moved down-wards at an unpredictable point in time. The participants' task was to respond with one of the same two gestures with their own index finger. This time, however, response gestures were kept constant within blocks – to the effect that no selection of response gestures was required. There-fore, since stimulus gestures and stimulus onset times were randomized within blocks, the task exhibited (1) stimulus uncertainty, (2) temporal uncertainty, but at the same time (3) full response certainty.

Over a large series of experiments we observed huge compatibil-ity effects for both response gestures, somewhat more pronounced for downward than for upward movements. This pattern of results appears to rule out the classical view that compatibility effects arise in response selection. Instead, it supports the notion that iconic or imitative response specification is highly effective even under conditions in which the action to be performed is completely prespecified and predetermined.

Movement production

In the last paradigm I want to consider, participants were not required to perform any movements at all, nor did they need pay attention to cer-tain aspects of the stimulus situation and ignore certain others. What we studied instead was the spontaneous occurrence of movements and their relation to events going on in the actor's environment. Such move-ments have sometimes been called ideomotor movements or actions (cf. Prinz, 1987). The term of ideomotor action, as a descriptive category for certain actions, must not be confounded with theoretical concepts like ideomotor principle or ideomotor mechanism as discussed in the intro-ductory section (though there are, of course, close relationships between the descriptive and the theoretical notions).

Ideomotor movements may, under certain conditions, arise in a person, who is observing the course of certain events. Classical examples of ideo-motor action are body movements induced by watching other people's actions. For instance, while watching, in a slapstick movie, an actor who

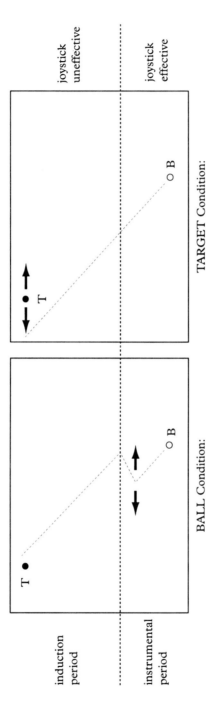

Figure 8.4. Movement production paradigm developed by Knuf *et al.* (2001). On each trial, the ball (B) travels from the starting position at the bottom to the target position at the top (T). Joystick movements act to displace the ball and the target (in the ball and the target condition, respectively).

walks along the edge of a plunging precipice, observers may often be unable to sit still and watch quietly. They will move their legs and their arms or displace their body weight to one side or the other. Ideomotor movements may also be induced by watching physical events resulting from actions. For instance, bowlers who push a ball and then follow its course can often hardly prevent themselves from moving their hands or twisting their bodies, as if to exert some magical impact on the ball. People are frequently unable to resist these movement tendencies. The involuntary, or even countervoluntary, nature of ideomotor actions has placed them among the curious phenomena of mental life. Moreover, the fact that they are instrumentally completely ineffective makes them even more mysterious (cf. Prinz, 1987).

How is the pattern of body movements, that is induced in the observer, related to the course of events that induce them? Basically, two answers to this question have been suggested. The classical answer believes in *perceptual induction*, that is, induction based on similarity between the events perceived and the movements induced. This answer was already inherent in James' aforementioned Ideomotor Principle, according to which the mental act of representing certain movements (like perceiving them) will always induce a tendency to perform the same or similar movements. Accordingly, perceptual induction invokes that the observer tends to repeat in her actions *what she sees happening* in the scene. It considers ideomotor actions a special class of imitative actions – special in the sense of lacking an underlying intention to imitate.

A competing answer is offered by *intentional induction*. This principle relies on intended rather than perceived events. It holds that the observer tends to perform actions that are suited to realize *what he wants to see happening*. In other words, he is believed to act in a way that would be suited to reach certain intended goals if his movements were effective. In a way, then, this principle considers ideomotor actions a special class of goal-directed, instrumental actions – special in the sense of being instrumentally ineffective.

We developed a paradigm that should allow us to study the relative contributions of perceptual and intentional induction (Knuf, 1998; Knuf, Aschersleben, & Prinz, 2001). The task was modeled after the logic of the bowling-ball example (cf. Fig. 8.4). On each trial, participants watched a ball moving toward a target on a screen, either hitting or missing it. At the beginning of a trial, the ball was shown at its starting position at the bottom, and the target position was shown at the top. Starting positions and target positions were always chosen such that the ball had either to travel in a north-eastern or north-western direction in order to hit the target. Participants triggered the ball's computer-controlled travel and observed its course.

The ball's travel was divided into two periods, instrumental and induction. During the instrumental period (which lasted about 1 sec) participants could manipulate either the ball's or the target's horizontal position by corresponding joystick movements. In the ball condition, horizontal joystick movements would act to shift the ball to the left or the right (after which it would continue traveling in the same direction as before). By this means participants could shift the ball's trajectory and get a chance of hitting the target. In the target condition, horizontal joystick movements would act to shift the target to the left or the right, in an attempt to give it a chance of getting hit. (Initial motion directions were chosen such that the ball would never hit the target without correction.)

We reasoned that this task should allow us to study ideomotor movements occurring during the induction period (which followed the instrumental period and lasted for about 2 sec). We examined how joystick movements occurring during this period (where they are no longer effective) were related to the happenings on the screen. Perceptual induction predicts the same pattern of joystick movements for both conditions: they should always point into the same direction as the ball motion (leftwards with the ball traveling north-east, rightwards with the ball traveling north-west). Intentional induction predicts a more complex pattern. First, it leads one to expect that systematical joystick movements should only occur on trials with upcoming misses but not with upcoming hits. On upcoming hits, participants should be able to see, or extrapolate, that the ball would eventually hit the target, so that no further instrumental activity was required to achieve the goal. On upcoming misses participants should likewise be able to extrapolate that the ball would eventually miss the target – which should then induce ideomotor movements performed in a (futile) attempt to affect the further course of events.

We reasoned that the details of these attempts should depend on two factors: the object under initial instrumental control (ball vs. target) and the side on which the ball is expected to miss the target (left vs. right misses). In the ball condition (where the ball is under initial control), joystick movements should act to push the ball toward the target (i.e., rightward in case of a left miss, and leftward in case of a right miss). In the target condition (where the target is under initial control), joystick movements should act to push the target toward the ball (leftward in case of a left miss and rightward in case of a right miss).

The results of our experiments lent strong support to intentional induction but not to perceptual induction. First, the direction of ball movement (north-west vs. north-east) did not appear to be a major determinant of the direction of induced movements. This rules out perceptual induction. Second, on trials with upcoming hits, induced movements were virtually absent. Third, on trials with upcoming misses, we observed pronounced induced movements, whose directions were dependent on both the object under initial control (ball vs. target) and the side of the upcoming target miss (left vs. right), exactly in line with the pattern predicted by intentional induction. These findings seem to suggest that, at least in our paradigm, ideomotor movements are much more strongly governed by representations of intended than of perceived events.

Further experiments have shown that perceptual induction may in some cases be effective, too. For instance, when one looks at ideomotor movements induced in effectors that are not instrumentally involved in joystick control (like head and foot movements), one sometimes sees perceptual induction, too, suggesting that noninstrumental effectors tend to follow the ball's traveling direction. Intentional induction was, however, also effective in head and foot movements. Accordingly, a more comprehensive view will need to encompass both (weak) perceptual induction and (strong) intentional induction.

What can we learn from ideomotor action about the mechanisms underlying imitation? Two major lessons appear to emerge. The first one, which adds to the main conclusion drawn from the earlier studies, is that watching actions or action effects may automatically induce the production of similar actions in observers. This corroborates James' ideomotor principle of human action once more. More crucial is the second lesson: when people watch actions or their effects they represent them not only in physical terms, that is, in terms of their spatiotemporal pattern, but in semantic terms as well, that is, their underlying goals and the extent to which the goals are being achieved.

On the basis of these observations we have every reason to believe that intentional induction is no less automatic than perceptual induction. This links our observations to two different literatures, one on the role of implied intentions in event perception and imitation in early infancy (Csibra et al., 1999; Rochat, 1995; Meltzoff, 1995; Gergely & Watson, 1999) and another one on the automaticity of perception and cognition in social interaction (Bargh, 1996, 1997). It seems that understanding actions and their consequences in terms of their underlying intentional semantics develops very early in life and then remains so deeply rooted in our cognitive machinery that we have no way to escape from it.

Conclusions

What do our experiments tell us about the mechanisms underlying imitation? Rather than summarizing the evidence I would like to submit three major conclusions that have emerged from our work so far:

- A number of experimental observations suggest a functional role for similarity in the mediation between perception and action. These observations suggest common representational resources for perception and action: perceptual cognition shares representational resources with action planning.
- Action imitation is therefore a natural by-product of action perception (and, hence, an important ingredient in many forms of social communication). In a way, then, the problem is not so much to account for the ubiquitous occurrence of imitation, but rather for its notorious nonoccurrence in many situations.
- Theories of imitation need to provide a special role for action effects, even more so for intended action effects or goals. Action goals seem to play a dominant role in the representational structures mediating between perception and action.

References

Bargh, J. A. (1996). Principles of automaticity. In E. T. Higgins & A. W. Kruglanski (Eds.), *Social psychology: Handbook of basic principles* (pp. 169–183). New York: Guilford Press.

(1997). The automaticity of everyday life. In R. S. Wyer Jr. (Ed.), *Advances in social cognition* (Vol.10, pp. 1–62). Mahwah, NJ: Erlbaum.

Brass, M. (1999). Imitation and ideomotor compatibility. Dissertation, University of Munich.

Brass, M., Bekkering, H., & Prinz, W. (2001). Movement observation affects movement execution in a simple response task. *Acta Psychologica, 106,* 3–22.

Brass, M., Bekkering, H., Wohlschläger, A., & Prinz, W. (2000). Compatibility between observed and executed finger movements: Comparing symbolic, spatial, and imitative cues. *Brain and Cognition, 44,* 124–143.

Burke, L. (1952). On the tunnel effect. *Quarterly Journal of Experimental Psychology, 4,* 121–138.

Csibra, G., Gergely, G., Biró, S., Koós, O., & Brockbanck, M. (1999). Goal attribution without agency cues: The perception of "pure reason" in infancy. *Cognition,72,* 237–267.

Fitts, P. M., & Deininger, M. I. (1954). S-R compatibility: Correspondence among paired elements within stimulus and response codes. *Journal of Experimental Psychology, 48,* 483–492.

Gergely, G., & Watson, J. S. (1999). Early social-emotional development: Contingency perception and the social-biofeedback model. In P. Rochat (Ed.), *Early social cognition* (pp. 101–136). Hillsdale, NJ: Erlbaum.

Greenwald, A. G. (1970). Sensory feedback mechanisms in performance control: With special reference to the ideo-motor mechanism. *Psychological Review, 77,* 73–99.

(1972). On doing two things at once: Time sharing as a function of ideomotor compatibility. *Journal of Experimental Psychology, 94,* 52–57.

Heider, F., & Simmel, M. (1944). An experimental study of apparent behavior. *American Journal of Psychology, 57,* 243–259.

James, W. (1890). *The principles of psychology* (2 vols.). New York: Holt.

Hommel, B. (1996). S-R compatibility effects without response uncertainty. *Quarterly Journal of Experimental Psychology, 49,* 546–571.

(1997). Towards an action-concept model of stimulus-response compatibility. In B. Hommel & W. Prinz (Eds.), *Theoretical issues in stimulus-response compatibility* (pp. 281–320). Amsterdam: North-Holland.

Hommel, B., Müsseler, J., Aschersleben, G., & Prinz, W. (in press). The theory of event coding (TEC): A framework for perception and action. *Behavioral and Brain Sciences.*

Hommel, B., & Prinz, W. (Eds.) (1997). *Theoretical issues in stimulus-response compatibility.* Amsterdam: North-Holland.

Kerzel, D., Bekkering, H., Wohlschläger, A., & Prinz, W. (2000). Launching the effect: Representations of causal movements are influenced by what they lead to. *Quarterly Journal of Experimental Psychology, 53* (4), 1163–1185.

Knuf, L. (1998). Ideomotorische Phänomene: Neue Fakten für ein altes Problem. Entwicklung eines Paradigmas zur kinematischen Analyse induzierter Mitbewegungen. [Ideomotor phenomena: New facts for an old problem. A paradigm for the kinematic analysis of induced ideomotor movements.] Dissertation, University of Munich. Aachen: Shaker.

Knuf, L., Aschersleben, G., & Prinz, W. (2001). An analysis of ideomotor action. *Journal of Experimental Psychology: General, 130,* 779–798.

Kornblum, S., Hasbroucq, T., & Osman, A. (1990). Dimensional overlap: Cognitive basis for S-R compatibility – a model and taxonomy. *Psychological Review, 97,* 253–270.

Lotze, H. (1852). *Medicinische Psychologie oder Physiologie der Seele.* Leipzig: Weidmannsche Buchandlung.

Meltzoff, A. N. (1995). Understanding the intentions of others: Re-enactment of intended acts by 18-month-old children. *Developmental Psychology, 31,* 838–850.

Meltzoff, A. N., & Moore, M. K. (1997). Explaining facial imitation: A theoretical model. *Early Development and Parenting, 6,* 179–192.

Michotte, A. (1946/1963). *La perception de la causalité.* Louvain: Publications Universitaires. [*The perception of causality.* London: Methuen, 1963.]

Müsseler, J. (1999). How independent from action control is perception? An event-coding account for more equally ranked crosstalks. In G. Aschersleben, T. Bachmann, & J. Müsseler (Eds.), *Cognitive contributions to the perception of spatial and temporal events (Advances in Psychology,* Vol. 129, pp. 121–147). Amsterdam: Elsevier.

Prinz, W. (1987). Ideomotor action. In H. Heuer & A. F. Sanders (Eds.), *Perspectives on perception and action* (pp. 47–76). Hillsdale, NJ: Erlbaum.

(1990). A common-coding approach to perception and action. In O. Neumann & W. Prinz (Eds.), *Relationships between perception and action: Current approaches* (pp. 167–203). Berlin: Springer-Verlag.

(1992). Why don't we perceive our brain states? *European Journal of Cognitive Psychology, 4,* 1–20.

(1997a). Perception and action planning. *European Journal of Cognitive Psychology, 9 (2),* 129–154.

Prinz, W. (1997b). Why Donders has led us astray. In B. Hommel & W. Prinz (Eds.), *Theoretical issues in stimulus–response compatibility* (pp. 247–267). Amsterdam: North-Holland.

Rochat, P. (1995). Early objectification of the self. In P. Rochat (Ed.), *The self in infancy. Theory and research* (pp. 53–72). Amsterdam: Elsevier.

Schuboe, A. (1998). Interferenz von Wahrnehmung und Handlungssteuerung. [Interference between perception and action control.] Dissertation, University of Munich. Aachen: Shaker.

Schuboe, A., Aschersleben, G., & Prinz, W. (2001). Interactions between perception and action in a reaction task with overlapping S-R assignments. *Psychological Research / Psychologische Forschung, 65(3),* 145–157.

Stuermer, B. (1997). Organisationsprinzipien an der Schnittstelle zwischen Wahrnehmung und Handlung: Kompatibilitätseffekte unter Verwendung dynamischer Reiz- und Reaktionseigenschaften. [Organizational principles at the interface of perception and action.] Dissertation, University of Munich. Aachen: Shaker.

Stuermer, B., Aschersleben, G., & Prinz, W. (2000). Correspondence effects with manual gestures and postures: A study on imitation. *Journal of Experimental Psychology: Human Perception & Performance, 26* (6), 1746–1759.

9 Imitation: Common mechanisms in the observation and execution of finger and mouth movements

Harold Bekkering

Introduction

Imitation, or performing an act after perceiving it, has attracted the attention of researchers from many different disciplines. The present chapter addresses possible common neurocognitive mechanisms underlying perception and action in imitation. First, the transformation problem between actions perceived and actions performed will be outlined. Then, it is proposed that the neurocognitive mechanisms underlying perception and action in imitation, to some extent, may be one and the same. Neurophysiological evidence for this view, mostly deriving from single-cell studies regarding hand and mouth movement observation and execution, will be described. Also, a link to general cognitive psychology theories about stimulus-response couplings will be made. In the third section, recent tests of an action observation/execution matching system in so-called stimulus-response compatibility paradigms will be discussed. A recent fMRI study employing one of these paradigms will provide further evidence for the assumption that common neurocognitive mechanisms are underlying perception and action in imitation. Finally, the chapter will consider the impact of a direct matching system on the topic of the transformation problem in imitation. However, it will also point out the limitations of a system that directly matches actions observed and actions-to-be-executed at the motor act level.

The transformation problem of imitation: How can we do what we see?

Although imitation is well documented in different species, one question unresolved yet, is how a motor act is constructed from a perceived action performed by a model. It becomes clear that the processes underlying such a sensory-motor transformation must be complex, when one thinks about a typical real-life example. For instance, a small child that attempts, despite the large differences in body size and available motor skills, to imitate an adult throwing a baseball.

163

At least two important theoretical problems are underlying this transformation problem: (1) how can we perceive the intent of somebody else's action, and (2) how can we initiate the execution of our own actions. Traditionally, these issues are distinguished in terms of perceptual versus motor processes, respectively. Research on imitation, however, indicates that the two may, in fact, show a common explanation. The present chapter is thus designed to address this possibility.

The first of these two problems is, "How can we perceive the intent of somebody else's action out of available sensory information?" In other words, how can we recognize the purpose of the action made by a model? That this is not a trivial question becomes clear when one contemplates the density of the sensory information an observer needs to deal with when watching a model's movement. The model might move different effectors, use different tools, and still, the observer is typically able to recognize the intent of the action, for instance, the grasping of a cup of tea.

The second old problem is, "How can we initiate the execution of our own actions?" As early as 1852, Lotze pointed out that while we as actors know much about what we intend, or are going to do in a particular situation, we do not have the slightest idea about the processes or mechanisms that underlie the execution of these intended acts. In other words, although we are able to give a number of reasons for why we want to undertake an upcoming action, or where our actions are aimed at, we are not able to describe consciously how we can realize the action in terms of the muscles we need for it, the forces necessary to initiate the muscles, or the co-ordination processes between the muscles and so forth (see for a recent elaboration of this view, Hommel, 1998). In imitation, these two problems assemble: sensoric input (afferent event) must be transformed in motor output (efferent event) (see also Prinz, 1987). Here, this is called the *transformation problem* in imitation.

When ordering on a continuum the present theories about the transformation mechanisms in imitation, it becomes evident that on one side there are theories assuming a direct route between the perception of an act and the production of an act. That is a perception-production transduction transfers directly the perceptual information into innervatory motor patterns (e.g., Butterworth, 1990; Gray, Neisser, Shapiro, & Kouns, 1991; Vogt, 1995, 1996).

On the other side of the continuum are theories which interpret imitation as a goal-directed behavior and postulate the presence of high-level information processing during imitation (e.g., Bekkering, Wohlschläger, & Gattis, 2000; Bekkering & Prinz, in press; Gleissner, Meltzoff, &

Bekkering, 2000). Within these poles are theories which negate a direct perceptuo-motor transduction but state that the perceptual system and the action system are commensurable because they share equivalences such as the spatio-temporal structure or the metric used to equate acts seen and acts done in commensurable terms (e.g., the active inter-modal mapping (AIM) theory of Meltzoff & Moore, 1977; Meltzoff, 1993). For instance, according to AIM, the observer codes the motor acts of another in terms of "organ relations," that is spatial arrangements between significant body parts, such as hands, head, tongue, lips, etc.

Where we have stressed the importance of action goals in imitation elsewhere (see also the Gattis, Bekkering, & Wohlschläger's chapter in this book), the present chapter concentrates on the tightness between action observation and action execution processes in imitation. Noticeably, the absence of such a tight link between perception and action would question the validity of the research field of imitation in general. That is, if imitation is not more than the sum of action (event) perception and action execution, one might doubt the significance of studying these two complex areas together.

Common neurocognitive mechanisms for perception and action

Support for the idea that the neurocognitive mechanisms underlying perception and action in imitation, to some extent, may be one and the same can be found in many different neurophysiological studies, using different techniques to measure brain activity during perception and action. Since a lot of this evidence will be presented in this book elsewhere, I will limit myself to the studies which have motivated the recently used paradigms, described below, in our group directly.

Some years ago, Rizzolatti and colleagues were able to observe single-cell activity in the rostral part of the inferior premotor cortex, area F5, of the monkey during goal-directed hand movements such as grasping, holding, and tearing, but also when the monkey only observed these actions performed by the experimenter (di Pellegrino, Fadiga, Fogassi, Gallese, & Rizzolatti, 1992). In most of these so-called mirror neurons, there needed to be a clear link between the effective observed movement and that executed by the monkey in order to find discharges in the same neuron (Gallese, Fadiga, Fogassi, & Rizzolatti, 1996) which led the authors to propose that these mirror neurons form a system for matching observation and execution of motor action (see Rizzolatti, this volume, for an overview).

A recent study by Fadiga, Fogassi, Pavesi, and Rizzolatti (1995) took this notion one step further. The results of their transcranial magnetic stimulation experiment showed that the excitability of the motor system increased when an observer watched grasping movements performed by a model. Furthermore, the pattern of muscle activation evoked by the transcranial magnetic stimulation during action observation was very similar to the pattern of muscle contraction present during the execution of a similar action.

Clearly, such mirror activity has the potential to shine some light on the two addressed translation problems in imitation. If a direct match takes place between actions observed and the actions represented in the observer's own action vocabulary, one might argue that we know the intention of the act seen by mapping it to the actions represented in our own brain. That is, a match takes place between the (premotor) activation caused by the action observed and that of an (imaginary) existing motor act (see the chapter by Byrne, this volume for more details about the notion of action vocabulary). Importantly, the experiments showed that the activity of the F5 neurons is correlated with specific *hand* and *mouth* motor acts and not with the contractions of individual muscle groups. That is, typically, the neurons are only active when a goal, an object, is present and they stay silent when the same movement is performed without this goal.

Ideally, the mirror system might also elucidate how we can initiate the execution of our own actions. When new motor skills are learned, one often spends the first training phase trying to replicate the movements of an observed instructor. In other words, according to the mirror system theory, it might be postulated that one learns how to initiate one's own actions by imitation. However, such a learning by imitation only theory fetches new problems into a more general understanding of action initiation. If one assumes that humans can only learn by experience (i.e., experientialism), this, of course, implies that we can only produce those actions that we have perceived before[1] (and see for conflicting evidence, for instance, the chapter by Meltzoff, this volume). In addition, Gallese and Goldman (1998) argue that it is more likely that instead of motor acts, the mirror neurons might be important in representing the specific mental states of others, for example their perceptions, goals, expectations, and the like. That normal humans develop the capacity to represent mental states in others, which is often referred to as folk psychology, seems to be widely accepted these days (e.g., Davies & Stone, 1995).

Also in cognitive psychology, a functional-related concept to link perception and action has been offered. Some time ago, James postulated the ideomotor principle, the idea that an anticipatory image of feedback from an action participates in the selection and initiation of that action. More recently, the ideomotor principle has received renewed attention. For instance, Greenwald (1970) elaborated the idea of ideomotor control in action by stating that (a) voluntary responses are represented centrally in the form of images of the sensory feedback they produce, and (b) such images play a controlling role in the performance of their corresponding actions. In other words, the ideomotor theory stresses the fact that action (anticipation of sensory consequences) and perception (perceiving the sensory consequences) are necessarily closely linked (see also Prinz, 1992, 1997 for a more general common coding theory of perception and action).

Recent experimental findings of common perception-action mechanisms in imitation

The notion that the same neurocognitive structures are involved in action observation as well as in action execution – particularly in finger and mouth motor acts – have inspired some experiments recently performed in our laboratories and some of the main findings will be discussed below in relation to the ideas as currently present in cognitive psychology.

Evidence from stimulus-response compatibility paradigms

One main line of research in cognitive psychology that investigates the relationship between stimulus and response is the field of stimulus-response compatibility (SRC). A classic finding in SRC research is that stimulus location strongly interacts with response location, which is called the Simon effect (i.e., Simon & Rudell, 1967). For instance, when a subject is instructed to press a left button after the presentation of a red circle on the screen and to press a right button after the presentation of a green circle, left responses are found to be much faster if the command signal (red circle) was presented to the left than to the right and vice versa (for an overview, see Lu & Proctor, 1995). Interestingly, most studies within the SRC field have used highly abstract relations between stimulus and response like tone pitch (Simon & Small, 1969) and visual color (Craft & Simon, 1970), showing that what matters is the relationship between stimulus location (being irrelevant for the task) and response location (being task relevant), and not that between the irrelevant (stimulus location) and relevant (stimulus meaning) stimulus dimensions.[2]

The recent findings of the above-described mirror neurons would suggest that stimulus-response translations should interact much more directly when one would use a (quasi-)imitative stimulus-response arrangement. Particularly, employing finger and mouth movement stimuli might activate directly the pre-motor areas necessary to initiate the correct responses. This is exactly what we investigated in the experiments described next.

Comparing symbolic, spatial, and imitative finger cues

A direct way to compare a (quasi-)imitative stimulus-response arrangement with traditional spatial compatibility would be to present the whole visual image of the movement to be executed, and compare such a situation with more abstract response cueing conditions. Typically, in SRC, an interference paradigm is used in which three different conditions are contrasted. A baseline condition establishes the standard reaction time (RT) for a specific S-R ensemble with a single, relevant, imperative stimulus. For instance in Kornblum and Lee (1995), the letter J appeared as the imperative stimulus in between the two hands (e.g., the "J" indicated a key press of the right-hand middle finger). In the congruent condition, the response is again indicated by the imperative stimulus (e.g., the letter "J") and this relevant stimulus dimension is shown in a congruent relation to the response irrelevant stimulus dimension (e.g., the "J" indicated a key press of the right-hand middle finger and appeared on the fingernail of the right-hand middle finger). In the incongruent condition, the imperative stimulus and the irrelevant stimulus indicated different responses (e.g., "J" appeared on the left-hand index finger). Introducing a baseline condition enables one to evaluate the functioning of irrelevant stimulus information in congruent trials, that is whether response initiation is facilitated, and the functioning of the irrelevant dimension in incongruent trials, that is whether response initiation is interfered by the irrelevant stimulus dimension.

Recently, Brass, Bekkering, Wohlschläger, and Prinz (2000) used an interference paradigm which was similar to the one described above. The question addressed was whether visual sensory feedback of a response (the visual impression of a similar finger movement) would lead to a higher degree of compatibility compared to a symbolic cue and compared to a spatial cue of the response position. Therefore, a movement observation-execution ensemble was compared with a symbolic S-R ensemble. In their first experiment, two types of stimuli were presented: observed finger movements (lifting movement of index or middle finger) and symbolic cues (the digit *1* and *2*). Participants had to execute a finger movement in response to either the symbolic cue (*1* – index finger movement or *2* – middle finger movement) or to imitate the observed movement. Like in a Simon task, a relevant and an irrelevant dimension were contrasted. Consistent with the ideas of a system that matches observation and execution of motor action, an RT advantage is expected if the observed finger movement is the relevant dimension compared to the symbolic cue. In addition, when the symbol is the relevant dimension, a facilitative influence is expected by the irrelevant congruent movement. That is, observing a congruent finger movement should activate the congruent response and, hence, should facilitate response initiation, and observing an incongruent irrelevant movement should activate the incorrect response and lead to interference effect. On the other hand imitating a movement is expected to be unaffected by the congruent or incongruent symbolic cue.

Indeed, a main effect was found for type of instruction indicated that responses were faster initiated in the imitative condition than in the symbolic instruction condition (see also Fig. 9.1). In addition, responses to the symbolic instructions were facilitated when the irrelevant finger

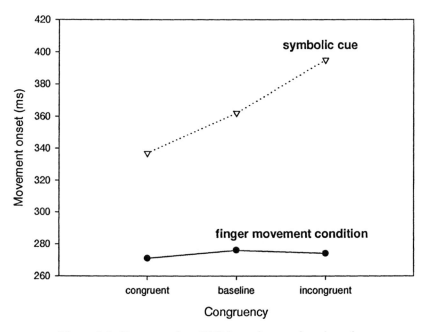

Figure 9.1. Response-time (RT) latencies as a function of congruency (congruent, baseline, and incongruent trials) and type of instruction (move the same finger – index or middle finger – as the observed finger movement, or move the finger identified by the symbol – index = 1, middle finger = 2).

movement was congruent and an interference effect was found when the irrelevant finger movement was incongruent. Both the facilitation and the interference effect described above provide evidence for an automatic influence of movement observation on movement execution. On the contrary, the presentation of the symbolic cue had no automatic influence on the response in the imitative instruction condition. Even if these results are quite consistent with our hypothesis, similar results have been found for comparisons between symbolic instructions and direct spatial cueing of the response position (e.g., Kornblum & Lee, 1995). The study of Brass *et al.* (2000), however, wanted to go one step further and show that presenting the whole visual image of the movement directly activates the motor preparation processes beyond spatial compatibility. A way to test this assumption was to compare the present movement observation-execution ensemble with spatial cueing of the response position, similar to the one used by Kornblum and Lee (1995).

Therefore, in their second experiment, the symbolic instruction was replaced by a spatial finger-cue condition (see also Fig. 9.2). The finger

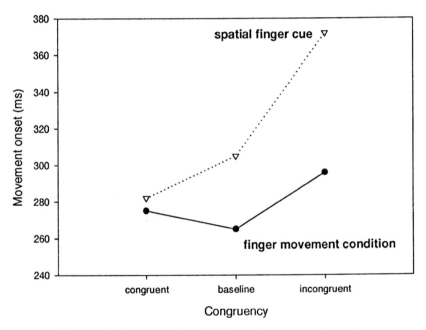

Figure 9.2. Response-time (RT) latencies as a function of congruency (congruent, baseline, incongruent) and type of instruction (move the same finger – index or middle finger – as the observed finger movement, move the finger identified by a cross on the fingernail – index or middle finger).

was cued by a cross which was drawn on the fingernail of either the index or middle finger. Again, both stimulus dimensions were contrasted in an interference paradigm in which each dimension was relevant in one block and irrelevant in the other block. From a traditional spatial compatibility perspective, the finger cue is as compatible to the response as the movement cue, that is, for both dimensions the finger is cued directly. From the perspective of a system that matches observation and execution of motor actions, however, the finger movement is more similar to the sensory feedback from its required response and hence is more ideomotor compatible than the spatial finger cue. Thus, if sensory feedback images play a controlling role in the performance of voluntary action, the finger-movement presentation is predicted to affect response initiation more than the spatial finger-cue presentation. As a consequence, faster responses are expected if the finger movement is the relevant dimension compared to the condition in which the finger cue is the relevant dimension. In addition, it is predicted that the irrelevant finger movement should affect the finger-cue trials. In other words, congruent finger movements should facilitate response initiation and incongruent finger movements are expected to slow down response initiation in the finger-cue condition.

The results of their Experiment 2 demonstrated that the observation-execution matching ensemble dominated the spatial finger-cue condition. Again, it was found that when finger movement was the relevant stimulus dimension, participants were faster compared to the case that the spatial finger cue was the relevant dimension. Responses to the spatial finger cue were facilitated when the irrelevant finger movement was congruent and an interference effect was found when the irrelevant finger movement was incongruent. Both the facilitation and the interference effect described above provided evidence for an influence of movement observation on movement execution that goes beyond cueing of the response position. Interestingly, spatial finger cueing as the irrelevant stimulus dimension produced an interference effect but no facilitation effect within the imitative response condition. That is, a congruent spatial cue provides no additional benefit for response initiation, but it seems to negatively influence response initiation processes when it is incongruent with the relevant finger-movement dimension. These results are consistent with the predictions deriving from the ideomotor theory, that a movement observation-execution condition leads to a higher degree of compatibility than a spatial finger cue.

However, before the findings of Experiment 2 can be attributed to the (quasi-)imitative stimulus-response arrangement, one needs to exclude one alternative explanation. That is, it can be argued that the finger movements are perceptually more salient than the spatial finger cues. In other words, the effects found so far are not necessarily related to a match between stimulus and response characteristics, but might be due to a difference at the perceptual side only. That is, the moving finger might be faster to encode than the spatial finger cue, and as a consequence the effects observed are related to perceptual processes only. The suggestion that interference effects are related to stimulus encoding was proposed by Hasbroucq and Guiard (1991) for the Simon effect and by Seymour (1977) for the Stroop effect. The action-perception matching hypothesis, however, would suggest that the higher similarity between the stimulus and the sensory feedback from the response was responsible for the influence of finger-movement observation on movement execution processes. A straightforward way to test this alternative explanation is to minimize the relationship between the response required and the stimulus observed, while keeping the stimulus display constant. Therefore, in contrast to Experiment 2, where participants needed to lift the index or middle finger, respectively, here participants needed to initiate a tapping movement with the index or middle finger. Since the display is identical to the one used in their Experiment 2, a perceptual account of the effects observed would predict a similar pattern of results.

However, the results of Experiment 3 showed that minimizing the relationship between the response required and the stimulus observed drastically influences the pattern of results. Importantly, in contrast to Experiment 2, responding to an observed finger movement was not any faster than responding to a spatial finger cue. This result indicated that at least a major part of the reaction time advantage for finger movement compared to spatial finger cueing was due to the imitative character of that action and not to the perceptual advantage of observing a finger movement compared to observing a spatial finger cue. Also, observing an irrelevant finger movement had no facilitative effect any longer in the finger-cueing condition. This demonstrated that the facilitation effect of Experiment 2 was due to the (quasi-)imitative stimulus-response arrangement and not to response activation of observing a finger movement *per se*. In addition, the interference effect of the incongruent finger movement was largely reduced. Even if the incongruent irrelevant finger movement still interfered with a response to a spatial finger cue, this interference effect decreased from 70 ms to 43 ms. In sum, the data of Experiment 3 showed that the perceptual saliency interpretation between the relevant and irrelevant stimulus dimensions cannot solely explain the effects observed previously. However, the results are consistent with an ideomotor compatibility interpretation in terms of a match between the action observed and the action to-be-executed.

So far, it has been argued that the cognitive psychological theory of ideomotor compatibility and the neurophysiological findings of mirror neurons might rely on the same mechanism, namely that of a match between the action observed and the action to-be-executed. A much more straightforward line of evidence for such a hypothesis would be to directly measure brain activity in the paradigm described above. The action observation and the action execution matching hypothesis predicts that the areas where matching occurs must contain neurons that discharge during action execution regardless of how action is elicited, and that at least a subset of them should receive an input that represents the action that is coded by them. Cortical areas endowed with a matching mechanism should therefore have motor properties and, more importantly, they should become more active when the action to be executed is elicited by the observation of that action.

To assess whether such a mechanism exists we used functional magnetic resonance imaging (fMRI, Iacoboni *et al.*, 1999), which allows the in-vivo study of human brain functions. The paradigm involved three observation conditions and three observation/execution conditions. In the observation/execution conditions, imitative and nonimitative behavior of simple finger movements was compared. In an imitative condition subjects had to execute the observed finger movement. In the two nonimitative conditions subjects had to execute the same movement in response to spatial or symbolic cues.

The imitation task produced reliably larger signals when contrasted to the other two observation/execution tasks, either individually or together, in three areas: the left frontal operculum, the right anterior parietal region, and the right parietal operculum. In the first two areas, activation was present also during all three observation tasks. In fact, during scanning the subjects knew that the task was either to move a finger or to refrain from moving it. Thus, the mental imagery of their finger (or of the finger movement) should have been present constantly. This background activity was potentiated when the stimulus to be imitated was presented. These findings indicate therefore that the left frontal operculum (Brodmann area 44) and the right anterior parietal cortex (PE/PC) have an imitation mechanism as postulated by the direct mapping hypothesis.

Above all, the additional activity for manual imitation found in Broca's area (Brodmann area 44), supports the idea that a match between the action observed and the action to-be-executed can explain the behavioral data of Brass, Bekkering, Wohlschläger, and Prinz (2000) as described above. Area 44 is one of the relatively few cortical areas where distal movements (the type of movements copied in the present experiments) are represented in humans (e.g., Krams *et al.*, 1998). Also, area 44 is considered the human homologue of monkey area F5 (e.g., Rizzolatti & Arbib, 1998). As mentioned earlier, an action observation/execution matching system exists in this area. Third, Broca's area is the motor area for speech and it is likely that learning by imitation plays a crucial role in language acquisition. Finally, as will be described in more detail below, and as persuasively argued previously, language perception should be based on a direct matching between linguistic material and the motor actions responsible for their production (e.g., Liberman & Mattingly, 1985). Broca's area is the most likely place where this matching mechanism may occur.

Matching observed and to-be-executed mouth movements

From the idea that Broca's area is the likely location where a matching between actions observed and actions to-be-executed takes place, it is only a small step to the hypothesis that such a matching should also occur when observing and executing mouth movements, that is in producing and perceiving (visible) speech.

The idea of a tight relation between sensory and motor processes in speech is not new. The revised version of the motor theory of speech perception (e.g., Liberman & Mattingly, 1985) claims that the objects of speech perception are the intended phonetic gestures of the speaker. Speech gestures are represented in the brain as invariant motor commands that do not have an equally invariant manifestation in the acoustic signal or in the observable articulatory movement. The motor commands of a gesture configure the articulators to produce traditional phonetic features such as "lip rounding" and "jaw raising." Thus, the same entities that are used in speech perception also command movements of the articulators in speech production. Liberman and Mattingly claim that speech perception and production are realized by a specialized module, a so-called innate vocal-tract synthesizer. After the listener has formed an initial hypothesis about what gestures may be contained in an acoustic speech signal, the module tests the hypothesis in a process of "analysis-by-synthesis." In this way, the speech module translates the acoustic signal into its invariant gestural representation. Because some form of synthesis requiring motor commands is necessary to decipher the speech signal, speech perception and speech production are intimately linked in the motor theory of speech perception.

One of the most compelling examples of the general principle of the motor theory of speech as described above is the McGurk effect (McGurk & MacDonald, 1976; MacDonald & McGurk, 1978) in which listeners are supposed to integrate visual and acoustic cues in a common phonetic percept. McGurk and MacDonald (1976) showed subjects a movie of a speaker's head in which repeated utterances of the syllables /bʌ/ or /gʌ/ had been dubbed onto lip movements for /bʌ/ or /gʌ/. When the lip movements did not correspond with the auditory syllable, the two sources of information were perceived into the auditory percept /dʌ/ for a visible /gʌ/ or /bgʌ/ for a visible /bʌ/. However, if presented only in the auditory modality, the syllables were unambiguously perceived as /bʌ/ or /gʌ/.

The McGurk effect exemplifies the general principle of the motor theory in which speech perception is seen to involve the extraction of information about a distal event, namely vocal-tract activity. According to this theory, the visual and acoustic sources of information converge on a common phonetic percept because the bimodal information provides information about one and the same distal event, the speech gesture. Importantly, visual information is able to access the speech module where phonetic information is stored in gestural format. The same analysis-by-synthesis process that is used in dealing with acoustic input should be active when visual information about articulatory activity is supplied. In other words, visual information about vocal-tract activity should lead to an activation of motor commands that are used in speech production – a view closely related to the concept of ideomotor compatibility as described previously.

Recently, Kerzel and Bekkering (2000) examined in more detail whether evidence for direct perception-action links can be obtained in a McGurk-like setup. The question they tried to answer was whether watching a speaker's mouth movements produces activity in response-related stages. The purpose of the first experiment was to establish a basic interference effect that may be localized at either a response-related or a perceptual processing stage. Participants were shown a speaker's mouth articulating either /bʌ/ or /dʌ/. While the mouth was moving, the written syllables "Ba" and "Da" were briefly presented on the mouth. Subjects were instructed to respond to the letters by producing either /bʌ/ or /dʌ/ and to ignore the lip movements of the mouth. If – as claimed by the motor theory – the perception of articulatory movements and the production of speech pass through a shared processing stage, then both response-related and stimulus-related interference is expected. In the motor theory, speech perception is motoric from the start such that conflict may arise at a perceptual or response-related stage. In contrast, perceptual accounts predict that the simultaneous presentation of two kinds of linguistic input leads exclusively to perceptual conflict. Thus, both perceptual and motor accounts predict interference but diverge on where it is localized.

It is clear from the results that visible lip movements influence the pronunciation of either the corresponding or the noncorresponding syllable.

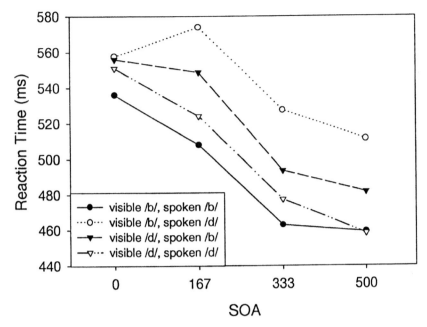

Figure 9.3. Mean response-time latencies are depicted as a function of visible gesture, spoken syllable and stimulus onset asynchrony. A robust compatibility effect can be observed.

RTs and PEs were lower (35 ms and 2.7 per cent, respectively) when visible speech gesture and spoken syllable compared, to when they did not correspond (see also Fig. 9.3). Because the response set shows dimensional overlap with both the relevant and the irrelevant stimulus sets that overlap themselves, the observed interference may either be at the stimulus side or between stimulus and response. If the interference effect was due to a stimulus conflict, perception of the visible gestures /bʌ/ or /dʌ/ interfered with perception of the printed "Ba" or "Da." In contrast, if the interference was due to SRC, the perception of the visible gesture interfered with the pronunciation of /bʌ/ or /dʌ/ . Therefore, this result is expected both from the perceptual and motor accounts of visual speech perception. Although no test of the predictions from the two conflicting accounts can be achieved at this point, the experiment is useful in establishing that reading responses may be influenced by a visible speech gesture. The influence of irrelevant information on reading responses is referred to as reversed Stroop effect, and it has been notoriously difficult to obtain (Glaser & Düngelhoff, 1984; Glaser & Glaser, 1982). For instance, in a Stroop experiment, reading color words suffers little from incongruent color information unless discrimination of the color word is decreased (Melara & Mounts, 1993). Therefore, the interference from mouth movements may result from privileged access to the response programming stage. This is what is predicted by the motor theory of speech perception; however, alternative explanations in terms of competing stimulus dimensions cannot be ruled out.

In subsequent experiments, we proceeded to determine the exact locus of interference. To exclude the possibility that the effect is located at the stimulus level only, we eliminated dimensional overlap between the relevant and irrelevant dimensions by using symbols unrelated to /b∧/ or /d∧/ as imperative stimuli. Thereby, only the irrelevant stimulus set, that is, the visible mouth movement, was similar to the response set. The relevant stimulus set, on the other hand, was dissimilar to both the irrelevant stimulus set and the response set. That is, now, the arbitrary symbols "&&" and "##" served as the imperative signal for the vocal responses. Consequently, any interference effects have to be attributed to stimulus-response interactions.

Consistent with a motor account of visual speech perception, responses were faster by 42 ms when irrelevant mouth movements and responses were congruent. Presumably, looking at the visual articulation of /b∧/ and /d∧/ caused an activation of the response codes associated with these consonant vocals (CV). That is exactly what is expected if speech perception relies on perceptuo-motor structures as claimed by the motor theory of speech perception: perception of speech stimuli should lead to activation of structures also used in speech production. In contrast, our findings are at odds with perceptual approaches to visual speech perception. If visible mouth movements are only processed up to a perceptual level, no Simon-like interference effect should be observed. Rather, interference should be restricted to the level of stimulus identification. Given that irrelevant and relevant stimulus dimension did not overlap in the present experiment, the RT-benefits and -costs could not arise at a perceptual level.

Nevertheless, the arbitrary symbols "&&" and "##" used in Experiment 2 may have acquired the meaning of /b∧/ and /d∧/ because the instruction tied them to these syllables. Therefore, in each trial the stimulus contained two perceptual signifiers for a CV syllable, allowing for perceptual conflict. To rule out perceptual interference between response relevant and irrelevant-stimulus dimensions, presentation of the response-relevant dimension preceded presentation of the irrelevant information.[3] Participants saw a response cue ("Ba" or "Da") indicating which response was to be performed at least 1 s before the irrelevant mouth movements were presented. Thus, they had enough time to complete identification of the response-relevant stimulus. Then, after a randomly determined interval, the mouth started moving pronouncing either /bʌ/ or /dʌ/ which indicated that the previously cued response should be emitted. Subjects were instructed to initiate the pre-specified response irrespective of what the mouth seemed to pronounce. Yet, the results were clear-cut in showing that interference from visual mouth movements persisted even if perceptual conflict was ruled out. Congruency of irrelevant speech gesture and spoken syllable resulted in a 17 ms reaction-time advantage.

In the last experiment we examined whether the interference from speech gestures could be accounted for by directional coding of the mouth movements. It is known that the McGurk effect obtains even if only isolated kinematic properties of visible speech are presented (Rosenblum & Saldaña, 1996). This leads to the question whether visible speech that is reduced to simple directional features suffices to produce the present SRC effect. Thus, the hypothesis may be entertained that the interference effect observed in Experiments 1–3 was due to an overlap of direction of displayed mouth movement (opening or closing) and response direction. That is, the influence of the visible speech gestures on verbal responses was accounted for by spatial compatibility and not by gestural compatibility. If the former alternative is accurate, then presentation of lines moving up and down in the same way as the speaker's mouth should have the same effects as presentation of the speaker's mouth. However, if the nature of the effect is not spatial but gestural, as a strong version of action-observation action-execution matching system would predict, no interference from line movements is expected. The results showed unambiguously that the observed SRC effect from mouth movements is not spatial. Lines mimicking the vertical opening–closing motion of the speaker's mouth producing /bʌ/ or /dʌ/ failed to interfere with the production of CV syllables.

To conclude, the experiments of Kerzel and Bekkering (2000) provide compelling evidence for the view that visible speech is processed up to a late, response-related processing stage. This is a finding in support of some of the assumptions underlying the motor theory of speech perception, since it shows perceptual-related visuo-motor effects. However, the more principal interpretation of the motor theory of speech in terms of analysis by synthesis is not directly addressed. Rather, the present findings are nicely in agreement with the mirror-system idea that the action observation and action execution are to some extent relying on the same neurocognitive processes.

Concluding remarks

Summary

The present chapter illuminated possible neurocognitive mechanisms underlying imitation. The main focus was on the relation between perception and action in imitation, or, to be more precise, on how the perception of a seen action affected the speed of the execution of a (non)similar action. Strong evidence for the view that a match between the action observed and the to-be-executed action takes place came from paradigms in which finger and mouth movements were explored. Interestingly, a recent fMRI study provided additional support for the notion of a direct neuronal substrate that matches finger-movement observation and execution.

Theoretical aspects of a direct matching system

Probably the most important theoretical aspect of such a matching system is that it clarifies to some extent a possible answer to two old, puzzling questions in action research: that of how we can perceive the intent of somebody else's action and that of how we can initiate the execution of our own actions. If a direct match takes place between actions observed and the actions represented in the observer's own action vocabulary, one might argue that we know the intention of the act seen by mapping it to the actions represented in our own brain. That is, a match takes place between the (premotor) activation caused by the action observed and that of an (imaginary) existing motor act, or, to put this idea in plain words, "aha, the model is doing this." Also, it might provide an answer to the question of how we have learned to initiate our own actions, that is we have learned our actions by imitating actions seen before.

Limitations of a direct matching system

Besides the theoretical problems as discussed before, it also needs to be pointed out that, so far, evidence for a matching system has only been observed in man and monkey for the finger/hand and mouth-movement systems. Typically, the neurophysiological correlate of this matching system has been reported to be Broca (F5 in monkey). The point that might be questioned, then, is if this is the case because Broca is known to have large receptive fields for mouth and hand movements? Alternatively, one might suggest that Broca's activity is related to a higher form of action interpretation (see also Rizzolatti & Arbib, 1998). In other words, it might be speculated that Broca is specialized in "coding" meaningful actions semantically, and since a lot of these actions are performed either by hand or mouth, Broca is activated. A lot more research from the whole field of cognitive neuroscience will be needed to answer this question. However, it can be easily argued that a system that matches actions observed with actions-to-be-executed at a semantic level is much more flexible than a system that matches acts at a motor level.

Notes

1 Of course, the same argument also works backwards. That is we are only able to perceive the intention of somebody else's act when it is part of the observer's action repertoire.

2 An exception to this is provided by a recent study by Stürmer (Stürmer, Aschersleben, & Prinz, 2000).

3 The logic behind this design was similar to the study of Brass, Bekkering, Wohlschläger, & Prinz (2000), in which subjects always had to make a pre-specified finger movement (e.g., lifting the finger upwards from a middle position) while watching congruent (lifting) or incongruent (tapping) digitized finger movements. Also here, a highly significant advantage was found in the congruent case compared to the incongruent case.

Acknowledgements

I would like to thank Marcel Brass, Merideth Gattis, Dirk Kerzel, Wolfgang Prinz, and Andreas Wohlschläger who collaborated with me on imitation projects over the last couple of years, and who co-developed many ideas about the underlying mechanisms presented here. In addition, I would like to thank Scott Jordan, Günther Knoblich, and Iring Koch for thoughtful discussions about action control in general. I also would like to thank Fiorello Banci, Henryk Milewsky, and Ursula Weber for technical assistance in many different projects on imitation.

References

Bekkering, H., & Prinz, W. (in press). Goal representations in imitative actions. In K. Dautenhahn & C. Nehaniv (Eds.), *Imitation in animals and artifacts*. Cambridge, MA: MIT Press.

Bekkering, H., Wohlschläger, A., & Gattis, M. (2000). Imitation of gestures in children is goal-directed. *Quarterly Journal of Experimental Psychology, 53A*, 153–164.

Brass, M., Bekkering, H., Prinz, W. (2001). Movement observation affects movement execution: Evidence from a simple response task paradigm. *Acta Psychologica, 106*, 3–22.

Brass, M., Bekkering, H., Wohlschläger, A., & Prinz, W. (2000). Compatibility between observed and executed finger movements: Comparing symbolic, spatial and imitative cues. *Brain & Cognition, 44*, 124–143.

Butterworth, G. (1990). On reconceptualizing sensori-motor coordination in dynamic system terms. In H. Bloch & B. I. Bertenthal (Eds.), *Sensory motor organizations and development in infancy and early childhood* (pp. 57–73). North-Holland: Kluwer Academic Press.

Craft, J. L., & Simon, J. R. (1970). Processing symbolic information from a visual display: Interference from an irrelevant directional cue. *Journal of Experimental Psychology, 83*, 415–420.

Davies, M., & Stone, T. (1995). *Folk psychology*. Oxford: Blackwell.

Fadiga, L., Fogassi, L., Pavesi, G., & Rizzolatti, G. (1995). Motor facilitation during action observation: A magnetic study. *Journal of Neurophysiology, 73*, 2608–2611.

Gallese, V., Fadiga, L., Fogassi, L., & Rizzolatti, G. (1996). Action recognition in the premotor cortex. *Brain, 119*, 593–609.

Gallese, V., & Goldman, A. (1998). Mirror neurons and the simulation theory of mind-reading. *Trends in Cognitive Science, 2*, 1262–1265.

Glaser, W. R., & Düngelhoff, F.-J. (1984). The time course of picture–word interference. *Journal of Experimental Psychology: Human Perception and Performance, 10 (5)*, 640–654.

Glaser, M. O., & Glaser, W. R. (1982). Time course analysis of the Stroop phenomenon. *Journal of Experimental Psychology: Human Perception and Performance, 8*, 875–894.

Gleissner, B., Meltzoff, A. M., & Bekkering, H. (2000). Children's coding of human action: Cognitive factors influencing imitation in 3-year-olds. *Developmental Science, 3*, 405–414.

Gray, J. T., Neisser, U., Shapiro B. A., & Kouns, S. (1991). Observational learning of ballet sequences: The role of kinematic information. *Ecological Psychology, 3*, 121–134.

Greenwald, A. G. (1970). Sensory feedback mechanisms in performance control: With special reference to the ideo-motor mechanism. *Psychological Review*, 73–99.

Hasbroucq, T., & Guiard, Y. (1991). Stimulus-response compatibility and the Simon effect. Toward a conceptual clarification. *Journal of Experimental Psychology: Human Perception and Performance, 17*, 246–266.

Hommel, B. (1998). Perceiving one's own action – and what it leads to. In J. S. Jordan (Ed.), *Systems theories and a priori aspects of perception* (pp. 143–179). North-Holland: Elsevier Science.

Iacoboni, M., Woods, R. P., Brass, M., Bekkering, H., Mazziotta, J. C., & Rizzolatti, G. (1999). Cortical mechanisms of human imitation. *Science, 286*, 2526–2528.

Kerzel, D., & Bekkering, H. (2000). Motor activation from visible speech: Evidence from stimulus-response compatibility. *Journal of Experimental Psychology: Human Perception and Performance, 26*, 634–647.

Kornblum, S., & Lee, J.-W. (1995). Stimulus-response compatibility with relevant and irrelevant stimulus dimensions that do and do not overlap with the response. *Journal of Experimental Psychology: Human Perception & Performance, 21 (4)*, 855–875.

Krams, M., Rushworth, M. F. S., Deiber, M.-P., Franckowiak, R. S. J., & Passingham, R. E. (1998). The preparation, execution and suppression of copied movements in the human brain. *Experimental Brain Research, 120*, 386–398.

Liberman, A. M., & Mattingly, I. G. (1985). The motor theory of speech perception revised. *Cognition, 21*, 1–36.

Lu, C.-H., & Proctor, R. W. (1995). The influence of irrelevant location information on performance: A review of the Simon and Stroop effects. *Psychonomic Bulletin & Review, 2*, 174–207.

MacDonald, J., & McGurk, H. (1978). Visual influences on speech perception processes. *Perception & Psychophysics, 24*, 253–257.

McGurk, H., & MacDonald, J. (1976). Hearing lips and seeing voices. *Nature, 264*, 746–748.

Melara, R. D., & Mounts, J. R. W. (1993). Selective attention to Stroop dimensions: Effects of baseline discriminability, response mode and practice. *Memory & Cognition, 21*, 627–645.

Meltzoff, A. N. (1993). The centrality of motor coordination and proprioception in social and cognitive development: From shared actions to shared mind. In G. J. P. Savelsbergh (Ed.), *The development of coordination in infancy* (pp. 463–496). Amsterdam: Free University Press.

Meltzoff, A. N., & Moore, K. M. (1977). Imitation of facial and manual gestures by human neonates. *Science, 198*, 75–78.

Pellegrino, G. di, Fadiga, L., Fogassi, L., Gallese, V., & Rizzolatti, G. (1992). Understanding motor events: A neurophysiological study. *Experimental Brain Research, 91*, 176–180.

Prinz, W. (1987). Ideomotor action. In H. Heuer & A. F. Sanders (Eds.), *Perspectives on perception and action* (pp. 47–76). Hillsdale, NY: Erlbaum.

(1990). A common coding approach to perception and action. In O. Neumann & W. Prinz (Eds.), *Relationships between perception and action* (pp. 167–201). Berlin: Springer.

(1992). Why don't we perceive our brain states? *European Journal of Cognitive Psychology, 4 (1)*, 1–20.

(1997). Perception and action planning. *European Journal of Cognitive Psychology, 9*, 129–154.

Rizzolatti, G., & Arbib, M. A. (1998). Language within our grasp. *Trends in Neuroscience, 21 (5)*, 188–194.

Rosenblum, L. D., & Saldaña, H. M. (1996). An audiovisual test of kinematic primitives for visual speech perception. *Journal of Experimental Psychology: Human Perception and Performance, 22 (2)*, 318–331.

Seymour, P. N. R. (1977). Conceptual encoding and locus of the Stroop effect. *Quarterly Journal of Experimental Psychology, 29*, 245–265.

Simon, J. R., & Rudell, A. P. (1967). Auditory S-R compatibility: The effect of an irrelevant cue on information processing. *Journal of Applied Psychology, 51*, 300–304.

Simon, J. R., & Small, A. M. (1969). Processing auditory information: Interference from an irrelevant cue. *Journal of Applied Psychology, 53*, 433–435.

Stuermer, B., Aschersleben, G., & Prinz, W. (2000). Correspondence effects with manual gestures and postures: A study of imitation. *Journal of Experimental Psychology: Human Perception and Performance, 26 (6)*, 1746–1759.

Vogt, S. (1995). On relations between perceiving, imagining and performing in the learning of cyclical movement sequences. *British Journal of Psychology, 86*, 191–216.

(1996). Imagery and perception-action mediation in imitative actions. *Cognitive Brain Research, 3*, 79–86.

10 Goal-directed imitation

Merideth Gattis, Harold Bekkering,
and Andreas Wohlschläger

"Stop copying me!" shrieks a friend's seven-year-old as she admires her bead-bedecked image in the mirror. "I not copying!" responds her three-year-old sister indignantly, while fingering rows of beaded necklaces around her own neck. Anyone who has observed a similar scene knows that a heated argument follows about "what counts" as copying, and whether playing with beads might be the result of the beckoning sparkle of beads or the desire to do whatever an older sibling does. What counts as copying, and similarly what counts as imitation, depends not only on arbitrary boundaries drawn by scientists and three-year-olds, but on the motivations and mechanisms involved. At least four mechanisms have been proposed to explain behaviors performed after seeing them performed by another animal. The likelihood of some behaviors is increased by stimulus enhancement when an object is manipulated by an animal subsequent to being handled or moved by another animal (Thorpe, 1956). The object itself is considered to trigger the behavior, perhaps through perceptual affordances, and the behavior of the first animal merely highlights the object, rather than providing an action model. Alternatively, some behaviors may be initiated by the observation of an action model, which triggers a specific and preorganized action pattern. Such innate releasing mechanisms (Lorenz & Tinbergen, 1938, as cited in Meltzoff & Moore, 1983) may explain exact copying of surprisingly complex behaviors observed in many nonhuman animals. Direct mapping between perceptual and motor neurons or brain systems, observed in both monkeys and humans (Fadiga, Fogassi, Pavesi, & Rizzolatti, 1995; Pellegrino *et al.*, 1992), has been proposed as a more sophisticated mechanism accounting for other copying behaviors, including neonate imitation of facial gestures (Meltzoff & Moore, 1983). None of these three mechanisms explains why "what counts" as imitation for most of us is rarely observed in the animal kingdom. Acquiring complex and skillful behaviors by observation, most researchers seem to agree, is a human-specific or primate-specific trait.

Why is imitation so rare? Recent work from developmental psychology, primatology, and motor learning seems to coalesce in a single proposal: some behaviors are generated from a goal-sensitive mapping between observed actions and performed actions. Observed behaviors are decomposed into constituent parts and recomposed as an action pattern, according to the perceived or inferred goals of the behavior. The purpose of this chapter is to review research concerning this fourth mechanism, goal-directed imitation.

Perceiving and inferring goals in imitation

Two sets of findings suggest that at least some forms of imitative behavior involve goals. First, enabling sequences of events are imitated more accurately than arbitrary sequences of events. Developmental psychologists using an elicited imitation paradigm to study event memory in very young children modeled action sequences for sixteen- to 24-month-old children and then encouraged the children to imitate the modeled actions (Bauer & Mandler, 1989; Bauer & Shore, 1987; Bauer & Travis, 1993). Novel-arbitrary sequences involved novel actions with simple objects, such as putting a sticker on a chalkboard, leaning the board against an easel, and drawing on the board with chalk. Novel-enabling sequences also involved novel actions with objects, with the difference that actions in a novel-enabling sequence enabled other actions in the sequence, and ultimately led to a salient novel event, such as a toy frog "jumping" in the air. The frog-jump sequence, for example, involved putting a wooden board on a wedge-shaped block to form a lever, placing a toy frog on one end of the board, and hitting the other end of the board, causing the toy frog to appear to jump in the air. Children of all ages performed the modeled actions in the modeled order more frequently for novel-enabling sequences than novel-arbitrary sequences. This result provides some evidence that the presence of an unambiguous, observable outcome leads to more accurate imitative behavior in young children. As Bauer (1992) has noted, however, enabling sequences must be performed in a particular order, whereas arbitrary sequences by definition do not impose this requirement.

Further research has demonstrated that an enabling sequence with a salient outcome is imitated more frequently than an enabling sequence without a salient outcome, and furthermore that the sequences themselves are reorganized by children during imitation. Travis (1997) demonstrated interleaved pairs of three-step action sequences to 24-month-old children. Children were shown either six actions (three actions for each pair), or only five actions, with the end-state for one sequence omitted. When shown two-end-state pairs, children imitated both action sequences equally. In contrast, when shown one-end-state pairs, children imitated more actions from the end-state-present sequence than from the end-state-absent sequence. Most important for our discussion here, however, is that children in both conditions performed actions leading to a particular end-state as a temporally contiguous sequence – despite the fact that end-state-related actions were not temporally contiguous in the modeled sequence, since they were interleaved with actions from another sequence. This temporal reorganization of actions during the imitation phase suggests that not only do goals motivate imitation, but they also play an important organizational role in imitative behavior.

We want to distinguish here between two senses in which the term "goal" has been used in describing imitative behavior. The end-states used by Bauer, Travis, and colleagues were salient outcomes involving movement, noise, or both. Many researchers have referred to salient outcomes as the goals of imitative acts (Byrne & Russon, 1998; Travis, 1997; Whiten & Ham, 1992), and appropriately so in that it is simple for an observer to conclude that the goal of the frog sequence is to make the frog jump. Strictly defined, however, a goal is "a mental state representing a desired state of affairs in the world" (Travis, 1997: 115), and is therefore not observable. Because goals are not observable, identifying the unobservable goal of an observable action always requires an inference. That inference is sometimes easy and sometimes difficult. Actions with highly salient outcomes simplify the task of inferring the mental states of others, and increase the likelihood that the goal inferred by an observer will be similar to the goal of the actor. Some behaviors have less salient or less observable consequences, however, or involve multiple goals, and can nonetheless be imitated, as for example when learning to dance the tango, to write an efficient computer program, to make new friends, or to cope with failure. An understanding of goal-directed imitation therefore is likely to benefit from an investigation of goals as mental and not merely physical states, and it is this aspect of goals to which we wish to direct attention in this chapter.

Appropriately then, the second set of experiments suggesting that goals play an important role in imitative behavior comes from developmental psychologists interested in children's understanding of the intentions of others (Carpenter, Akhtar, & Tomasello, 1998; Meltzoff, 1995). These experiments demonstrate that even very young children are capable of inferring goals from observed actions, and that inferred goals influence imitative behavior. Meltzoff (1995) compared eighteen-month-old children's re-enactments of an attempted but failed action, or an attempted and achieved action with five unique test objects. For example, an adult experimenter moved a rectangular wooden stick toward a rectangular recessed button on a box, and either inserted the stick in the hole, activating a buzzer, or touched an adjacent area on the box, missing the hole and not activating the buzzer. When given the opportunity to manipulate the objects immediately after the adult's demonstration, children shown an attempted but failed act were just as likely to perform the target act, for example inserting the stick in the hole and activating the buzzer, as children shown an attempted and achieved act. This result is especially surprising because children shown a failed attempt never actually saw the target act performed. Children in both groups performed the target act approximately four times as often as did children in control conditions. The finding that eighteen-month-olds imitated intended acts just as often as achieved acts suggests that even very young children infer the goals of others' behaviors, and imitate those inferred goals.

In a similar paradigm, Carpenter, Akhtar, and Tomasello (1998) compared fourteen- to eighteen-month-old children's reenactments of verbally marked intentional and nonintentional acts. An experimenter performed two unrelated actions on a unique test object, for instance lifting the top of a bird feeder, and pulling a ring on a string attached to the feeder. These actions were accompanied by vocal exclamations marking each action as either an intended act ("There!") or an accidental act ("Woops!"). After both actions had been performed (with some children seeing first an intentional and then an accidental act, and others seeing the opposite order), a salient event occurred, for instance a party favor attached to the bird feeder moved and made noise. Following two actions and the salient event, the experimenter offered the infant an opportunity, saying "Now you try. Can you make it work?" Irrespective of the order of the modeled actions, children reproduced the intentional acts approximately twice as often as nonintentional acts. Together these two sets of results suggest that when observing an adult's behavior, a child relies on observable information such as direction of movement and verbal exclamations to draw inferences about the nonobservable intentions of the adult, and that these inferences about goals or intentions influence subsequent imitative behavior.

Distinguishing goals from outcomes

The distinction between goals as outcomes and goals as mental states turns out to be crucial for understanding current debates about what counts as imitation and whether nonhuman primates do or do not imitate. Several investigations of imitative behavior in nonhuman primates suggest that while primates may reproduce the outcome of an observed event, the strategies employed in reproduction of that event do not reliably correspond to the actor's strategies. For example, Nagell, Olguin, and Tomasello (1993) reported two studies in which chimpanzees and 23- to 25-month-old children observed a human demonstrator use a tool resembling a rake to retrieve an out-of-reach reward (food or a toy, for chimpanzees and children respectively). The demonstrator began with a rake in one of two positions, either with the teeth down or with the crossbar down. When the rake began in a teeth-down position, the experimenter flipped the rake so that the cross bar was down, and then used the crossbar of the rake to drag the object within reach. When the rake began in a crossbar-down position, the experimenter simply dragged the object within reach, again using the crossbar of the rake. A similar rake was provided for human and chimpanzee observers, always resting in a teeth-down position. The question of interest was not simply whether children and chimpanzees used the rake to obtain the reward, but how they used it, and whether that use was influenced by the demonstrator's behavior. Children who observed the demonstrator flipping the rake to an edge-down position before beginning to pull were more likely to do the same and to use the edge-down rake to drag the object within reach compared to children who did not observe the flipping action. Children who observed the demonstrator pulling but not flipping used the rake in the found, teeth-down, position, and simply pulled. In contrast, chimpanzees flipped and pulled or pulled only with equal likelihood in both observer conditions. In other words, while both children and chimpanzees learned by observation to use the rake to obtain the reward, the demonstrator's behavior influenced the behavioral strategy employed by children but not the behavioral strategy employed by chimpanzees. Nagell, Olguin, and Tomasello (1993) concluded that chimpanzees attended to the end result of the task (obtaining a reward) and to the functional relations involved in the task (obtaining the reward using the rake) but failed to adopt the strategy used by the human model. Tomasello and colleagues name such behavior emulation learning (Tomasello, 1990, 1996; Tomasello & Call, 1997).

Most scientists seem to agree that the behaviors Tomasello and colleagues call emulation, such as the behaviors of chimpanzees above, do not count as imitation. Disagreement exists, however, about how to cognitively describe what animals are doing when they are emulating and not imitating. Several researchers have described emulation learning as the reproduction of goals to the exclusion of strategies, renaming the phenomenon goal emulation (Byrne & Russon, 1998; Whiten & Ham, 1992). The lesson learned from the results reported by Nagell, Olguin, and Tomasello and other similar studies (e.g., Call & Tomasello, 1995), however, is that while observable physical outcomes are frequently copied by nonhuman primates, goals are not (see Tomasello, 1998). The tendency of nonhuman primates to reproduce outcomes previously produced by a model has thus made the empirical distinction between imitation and emulation and other nonimitative actions difficult. This distinction has been further obscured by the use in empirical studies of enabling event sequences or sequences that involve observable functional relations.

One approach to clarifying the debate has been to use more elaborate event sequences (for instance, those described by Byrne & Russon, 1998; Call & Tomasello, 1995; Whiten, 1998). For the most part these elaborate event sequences involve multiple physical outcomes and/or multiple functional relations, all of which are observable (and in fact, whether researchers conclude that nonhuman primates are capable of imitation or not corresponds to whether the functional relations and outcomes used in their experiments are observable or not). It is important to note that such event sequences allow researchers to investigate whether nonhuman primates are capable of structuring multiple actions or outcomes during imitation, but not whether nonhuman primates infer the goals of others' actions, and whether those inferred goals then guide imitative behavior.

Both the numerosity and the unobservability of goals are characteristic of human behavior, and make life in a human colony interesting. Whenever two humans interact, each may expend considerable energy drawing inferences about the unspoken intentions of the other, and in most cases neither will know whether those inferences were correct. Such ambiguity is the very reason why many researchers of imitation have empirically defined goals as observable events, rather than mental states. In several recent studies (Bekkering, Wohlschläger, & Gattis, 2000; Wohlschläger, Gattis, & Bekkering, 2001), we chose instead to capitalize upon the ambiguity and multiplicity of goals as mental states. We used a task in which observable behaviors led to different imitative actions depending upon the goals inferred by observers, and their capacity to coordinate those goals.

Goal-directed gestural imitation

The hand-to-ear task

Whereas ethologists, comparative psychologists, and developmental psychologists have for the most part studied imitative learning of ecologically motivated behaviors, neurologists have often studied imitation of seemingly arbitrary behaviors such as gestures (for many examples, see

Berges & Lezine, 1965, and Goldenberg & Hermsdörfer, this volume). In one frequently studied gesture set, a model touches each ear with each hand, for a total of four different gestures, and asks an observer to copy each of the gestures. For these four gestures (and other similar hand-to-body-part gestures), researchers have observed a consistent error pattern in young children and aphasic adults: contralateral gestures, such as touching the right ear with the left hand, are imitated with ipsilateral gestures, such as touching the right ear with the right hand (Gordon, 1922; Head, 1920; Schofield, 1976a, 1976b). In cases of normal development, this pattern is strongest at about four years of age, decreases between ages four and six, and disappears by about age ten (Schofield, 1976b). The substitution of ipsilateral for contralateral movements during imitation has been attributed to brain lateralization and related difficulties of moving in contralateral hemispace. Developmental changes in the corpus callosum corresponding to the developmental decrease in substitution errors support this view (Salamy, 1976).

Schofield (1976a, 1976b) demonstrated, however, that substitution errors are not symmetric. In his experiments, contralateral movements were most frequent when the response involved a child's preferred hand, and least frequent when the response involved the nonpreferred hand. Schofield questioned whether immature callosal development could explain difficulties in crossing the body midline in one direction but not the other, and suggested that young children may not find contralateral movements more difficult than ipsilateral movements, but simply do not understand what is required in this particular imitation task. To rephrase and elaborate on Schofield's explanation, children seemed to be having difficulty inferring or processing the goals of the imitative task.

With this in mind, we used similar ipsilateral and contralateral gestures to investigate how inferring and processing goals influences imitative behavior in preschool-age children. Because this phenomenon had been previously demonstrated in three- to six-year-old children, we conducted these experiments with preschool children ranging from three to six years, with an average age of 4.5 years. Age was not used as a factor in the analyses described below.

In the first of these experiments, a model demonstrated six hand-to-ear movements and asked the children to mirror the movements (Bekkering, Wohlschläger, & Gattis, 2000). The six movements were the four gestures described above, plus two additional gestures: grasping both ears with both hands ipsilaterally (so that the arms are parallel) and grasping both ears with both hands contralaterally (so that the arms cross). We added the latter two movements to the gesture set to test the lateralization

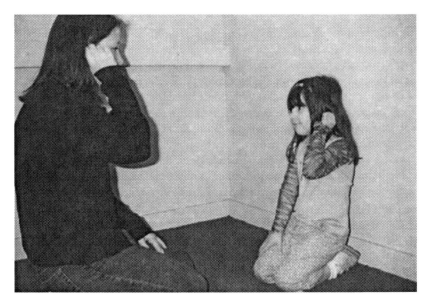

Figure 10.1. When the experimenter modeled an ipsilateral gesture, children responded appropriately with an ipsilateral gesture.

hypothesis against a goal-directed view. We reasoned that if substitution errors were due to immature callosal development, young children would make just as many substitution errors in imitating bimanual contralateral movements as in imitating unimanual contralateral movements. If, however, substitution errors were due to difficulties in inferring or processing the goals of the imitative task, the salience of crossed arms in the bimanual contralateral condition should result in fewer substitution errors compared to unimanual contralateral conditions. We expected that the salient feature of crossed arms could be encoded as a goal of the observed behavior, and therefore boost performance in the bimanual contralateral condition, relative to the unimanual contralateral condition. The results indicated that substitution errors cannot be due to immature callosal development alone. When imitating single-handed gestures, children accurately imitated ipsilateral gestures (see Fig. 10.1) but not contralateral gestures (see Fig. 10.2), substituting an ipsilateral movement for the modeled contralateral movement on 48 per cent of the trials. Significantly, however, this substitution error was dramatically decreased when the hand-to-ear movements involved both hands: children substituted an ipsilateral gesture for a contralateral gesture on only 10 per cent of bimanual trials (see Fig. 10.3).

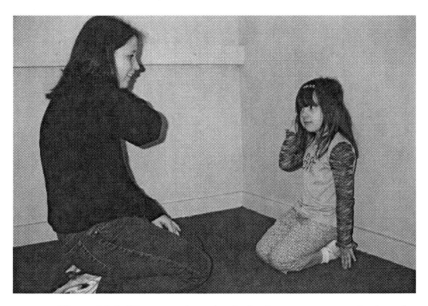

Figure 10.2. The contralateral substitution error occurred when the experimenter modeled a contralateral gesture, and children responded with an ipsilateral gesture.

The goal-directed view

To account for these results, we proposed that imitation entails representing an observed behavior as a set of goals, which subsequently drive the construction of an action pattern (Bekkering, Wohlschläger, & Gattis, 2000). Goals may represent the objects at which actions are directed (for instance, a particular ear), the agents that perform actions (a particular hand), movement paths (crossing the body or moving parallel to the body) or other salient features (crossing the arms). We also proposed that imitative goals are organized hierarchically with some goals dominating over others. When processing capacity is limited and multiple goals compete for capacity, goals higher in the hierarchy are reproduced at the expense of goals lower in the hierarchy. Because young children have difficulty processing multiple elements and relations, their failures to reproduce all the goals of a movement are more noticeable. Our results suggested that objects occupy the top of the goal hierarchy – children nearly always grasped the correct ear, but in cases of substitution errors used the wrong hand and the wrong movement path. This view of imitation predicts that children's imitation errors are malleable, and dependent on the number and type of goals identified in the task as a whole.

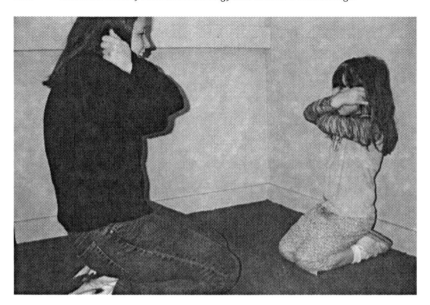

Figure 10.3. When the experimenter modeled a contralateral gesture involving both hands, children appropriately responded with a bimanual contralateral gesture.

Testing the goal-directed view

We tested this prediction in several additional experiments by reducing or increasing the number of goals identifiable in the imitative task as a whole. All of these experiments involved the same basic idea of a set of ipsilateral and contralateral gestures, and all involved the two gestures we were most interested in comparing: a unimanual ipsilateral gesture, and a unimanual contralateral gesture. What varied between the experiments is the context in which those two gestures occurred.

In one experiment, we limited the movements to only one ear, thereby eliminating the necessity for children to mentally specify the goal object (Bekkering, Wohlschläger, & Gattis, 2000). Children copied the movements of a model who always touched her right ear (first with one hand and then the other), or who always touched her left ear (again alternating hands). In this circumstance, children made virtually no errors, grasping the ear contralaterally whenever the model did so. Eliminating the necessity of specifying a particular ear as goal object thus enabled children to reproduce other goals in the imitative act, such as using the correct hand and the correct movement path.

In another experiment, we manipulated the number of identifiable goals by comparing the presence and absence of objects while keeping the total number of modeled gestures constant (Bekkering, Wohlschläger, & Gattis, 2000). Children sat at a desk across from the experimenter, who made four unimanual gestures similar to those described above, but directed at the desk rather than at her ears. Half of the children saw four dots on the table, two in front of the model and two in front of the child. The model touched her dots ipsilaterally and contralaterally, sometimes with her right hand and sometimes with her left hand. Children were encouraged to copy the model, and naturally directed their own actions at the two corresponding dots in front of them. For the other half of the children, the model directed her actions at the same locations on the table, with the crucial difference that no dots were on the table. Children in the dot condition produced the classic error pattern, substituting ipsilateral for contralateral gestures (see Fig. 10.4). In contrast, children

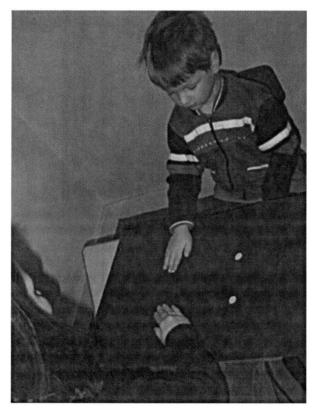

Figure 10.4. Children shown gestures directed at dots on a table produced the classic error pattern, substituting ipsilateral for contralateral gestures.

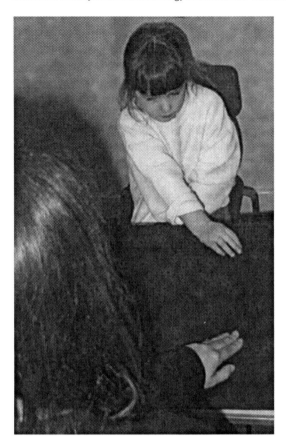

Figure 10.5. In contrast, children shown the identical gestures directed at locations on the table rather than dots imitated contralateral gestures more accurately.

in the no-dot condition who saw the identical movements directed at locations rather than dots produced significantly fewer contralateral errors (see Fig. 10.5). We concluded that manipulating the presence or absence of a physical object had effectively manipulated the necessity of specifying objects as goals. Despite the fact that the modeled movements were identical in both conditions, removing the dots from the table eliminated the object goal, and allowed children to reproduce other goals in the imitative act, such as the agent and the movement.

A third experiment attempted to reduce goal competition by segmenting the imitative task into two phases (Wohlschläger, Gattis, & Bekkering, 2001). In the first phase, the experimenter extended a hand, and waited for the child to extend a hand. Once the child had done so, the experimenter initiated the second phase by raising her extended hand to touch either the ipsilateral or contralateral ear. This two-phase procedure was used for all four unimanual gestures – touching the right ear with the right hand, the left ear with the left hand, the right ear with the left hand, and the left ear with the right hand. We reasoned that if goal competition causes imitative errors, segmenting the task into two phases, in which first a particular hand was chosen, and then a particular ear was chosen, would reduce competition and thereby reduce imitative errors. In this two-phase task, the substitution of contralateral for ipsilateral hand movements virtually vanished, once again supporting the claim that goal competition causes imitative errors. We should also note however, that somewhat contrary to our predictions, some unimanual contralateral movements were imitated with an unusual bimanual movement in which a child extended the left hand, and then touched the right ear with the right hand. This error can be interpreted as a subtle persistence of the substitution error, or perhaps as unexpected cleverness on the part of four-year-olds.

In a fourth experiment, we again tested the prediction that children's imitation errors are caused by competing goals but this time we did so by increasing, rather than reducing, the number of goals in the imitative task (Wohlschläger, Gattis, & Bekkering, 2001). For all trials of this experiment, the experimenter reached to the location in space near her left or right ear, using the left or right hand, so that once again half of the gestures were ipsilateral and half of the gestures were contralateral. Rather than touching her ear, however, the experimenter moved her hand to the space next to her ear, and either made a fist, or opened her hand, with the palm facing the child. We reasoned that the open-hand versus closed-hand introduced a new, salient gestural goal, and wanted to know whether a specific hand gesture, like the object goal, would displace other goals such as agents and movements. This was indeed the case. Children reproduced the open-hand or closed-hand of the experimenter nearly all the time, but frequently substituted a different hand (Fig. 10.6), and sometimes even performed the gesture on a different side of the head (Fig. 10.7). This result indicates that increasing the number of goals in the imitative task increases the number and type of imitative errors. More specifically, it also suggests that a specific hand gesture, much like objects, may take precedence in the goal hierarchy guiding imitative behavior.

Using a similar paradigm to the one described above, Gleissner, Meltzoff, and Bekkering (2000) manipulated whether gestures were directed at locations on the body, or locations near the body. A model performed ipsilateral and contralateral movements with her right or left hand or with both hands. The model either touched a body part (an ear

Figure 10.6. When the experimenter modeled open-hand and closed-hand gestures, children reproduced the correct hand movement but often substituted a different hand.

or a knee), or directed her movement at a location in space near the body part. In general, three-year-olds imitated more accurately when the model's actions were directed at locations near the body, than when her actions were directed at locations on the body. Error differences between the two conditions were generalized, however, and the classic substitution error was not significantly reduced in the near-a-body-part condition compared to the on-a-body-part condition (see Gleissner, 1998, for details). This result thus lends tentative support to the proposal that imitation is organized around goals, and that objects (such as an ear or a knee) tend to displace other goals in the imitative act, such as hand and movement path.

Testing alternative hypotheses

Several additional experiments investigated the hypothesis that children's difficulties in gestural imitation might be due to other cognitive constraints, such as limitations on perception or attention, rather

Figure 10.7. Children imitated open-hand and closed-hand gestures with the correct hand movement, but often substituted a different hand, and sometimes even performed the gesture on a different side of the body.

than limitations on goal-processing (Wohlschläger, Gattis, & Bekkering, 2001). In one experiment, children were shown the six gestures described above in a song-and-dance context. The song-and-dance context allowed for an investigation of spontaneous imitative behavior, without an explicit instruction to imitate, and for an investigation of practice effects. The experimenter taught children a song about a little man, and all the things that he can do. After every stanza of the song, the model performed the six gestures described in the first experiment above. The imitation task thus appeared within the song, as a continuation of movements the experimenter and children performed while singing. In this context, children spontaneously imitated the hand-to-ear movements without specific instruction to do so. The song had nine stanzas, thus the six gestures were repeated nine times each. Despite this extensive practice, and the motivating context in which it occurred, children made the same types of errors throughout the experiment, continuously substituting ipsilateral for contralateral gestures, and doing so for unimanual more than bimanual movements.

We further tested the hypothesis that limitations on attention or perception might be influencing children's gestural imitation by using a manipulation that called attention to the hands. Because children had in other experiments demonstrated a tendency on contralateral trials to touch the mirror-image ear but to do so with the inappropriate hand, we reasoned that focusing on the ear might simply have made it difficult for children to notice which hand the experimenter used. We explored this possibility by using black-and-white gloves to mark the mirror-image hands of experimenter and child. At the beginning of the experiment, the experimenter introduced two pairs of adult-sized gloves, one black pair and one white pair. The experimenter put a black glove on one hand and a white glove on the other, and assisted the child in putting the remaining gloves on the corresponding hands. For example if the experimenter wore a black glove on her right hand and a white glove on her left hand, she helped the child to put a black glove on his left hand and a white glove on his right hand. Once this was accomplished the experimenter modeled the six hand-to-ear movements as in the first experiment described above. Despite the salient cue of color-coded gloves, children made just as many errors in hand selection on contralateral trials as in the original experiment, once again substituting the ipsilateral hand (see Fig. 10.8).

Figure 10.8. Even when color-coded gloves called attention to the hands, children substituted the ipsilateral hand when imitating contralateral movements.

In another experiment, children were asked to match photographs of an adult performing each of the six gestures with photographs of a child performing the same gestures. We reasoned that if children's difficulties in imitating contralateral gestures were due to difficulties in perceiving the difference between the ipsilateral and contralateral gestures, their judgments of photographs would reveal the same error pattern. In this experiment, a child was first introduced to an imitative game in which the experimenter performed several actions, such as rubbing her head with her hand, and whenever the child performed the mirror action, the experimenter remarked, "Yes, that's right, you're playing the game right." After the child had demonstrated a sufficient understanding of the imitative game, the experimenter showed the child one photograph of an adult performing one of the six gestures described in the first experiment above. The experimenter then showed the child six photographs of a boy performing each of the six gestures, and asked the child, "Can you show me in which picture he is playing the game right?" This task was repeated for all six modeled gestures. In this nonimitative task, matching errors were equally distributed across all conditions: children did not match photographs of modeled contralateral gestures any less accurately than photographs of modeled ipsilateral gestures. From this result, we concluded that children's errors in gestural imitation are not due to difficulties in perceiving the difference between contralateral and ipsilateral actions.

The song-and-dance task, the black-and-white-gloves task, and the photograph-matching task repeatedly investigated whether children's difficulties in gestural imitation are due to a failure to perceive or notice the difference between different actions. The results of all three experiments indicate that this is not the case. Regardless of whether they were given a motivating context, lengthy practice, or a salient visual cue, children imitated unimanal ipsilateral gestures more accurately than unimanual contralateral gestures, usually substituting the former for the latter. In contrast, in a nonimitative task, children were able to match photographs of contralateral gestures just as well as photographs of ipsilateral gestures, suggesting that they were able to perceive the difference between gestures, but had difficulties imitating that difference.

Although we did not intend it as such, the results of the black-and-white-gloves task can also be seen as evidence against a feature-based account of imitative errors. According to that hypothesis, the difficulty of imitation depends on the number of features which have to be copied within one action, or in other words the informational load on copying. The feature-based hypothesis offers a plausible alternative explanation for substitution errors in some of the experiments described above, but does not fit with the result that a highly salient feature such as bulky, fuzzy, black-and-white gloves did not influence children's copying of hand movements.

A further experiment investigated another alternative hypothesis, whether children's imitation errors are due to more general difficulties with the organization of action. In this experiment the experimenter demonstrated two object-oriented actions: pointing and grasping. For all trials, the experimenter and child were seated at a table facing one another, and a pair of objects lay on the table in front of each person. The experimenter reached toward one of the objects in front of her with her right or left hand, or to both objects with both hands. As in the previous experiments, the experimenter varied whether she reached contralaterally or ipsilaterally and whether she reached with one hand or with both hands in a predetermined random order. For example, on one trial she reached contralaterally with her right hand to the object in front of her on the left, on the next trial she reached ipsilaterally toward both objects, with each hand extended to the object directly in front of it, and so on, until all six movements were modeled three times each. For half of the children the experimenter reached toward an object and pointed to it, and for half of the children the experimenter reached toward an object and grasped it. On pointing trials, imitation behavior was similar to that reported above for gestures aimed at the ears or at dots. Children always pointed at the correct object, but on contralateral trials they frequently pointed at that object with the ipsilateral hand. Interestingly, however, when the experimenter grasped rather than pointed at the objects, children had a tendency to imitate using their dominant right hand, sometimes even imitating an ipsilateral right-handed grasping movement with a contralateral right-handed movement. The strong influence of handedness errors on imitation of grasping but not pointing provides some indication that substitution errors in gestural imitation are not due to the influence of handedness alone. The difference between imitation of pointing and imitation of grasping also suggests that substitution errors are not due to general nonimitative difficulties with the organization of action.

Flexibility, goals, and imitation

The arguments of three-year-olds and research scientists have raised the question: "What's the difference between imitation and copying?" Some attempts to define this difference have focused on flexibility in imitative performance. Flexibility in imitation has been investigated by creating changes in the physical set-up of a task, such as demonstrating a tool-use task, rotating the apparatus 180°, and then offering children the opportunity to imitate (Want & Harris, 2001). When observers are able to successfully manipulate tools so as to obtain the demonstrated out-come despite changes in the specific physical arrangement of the task, their success goes beyond copying, and is taken as evidence that the observer has encoded a flexible representation of the modeled behav-ior (for more about flexible representation in imitation, see Byrne & Russon, 1998; Byrne, this volume; Whiten, this volume). The obser-vation that flexibility is important to scientists who are trying to define what really counts as imitation is one clue that imitation involves more than a direct mapping between perceptual input and motoric output. Definitionally and mechanistically, imitation seems to be far more than copying.

We have proposed a cognitive mechanism for imitation that allows for flexible representations and simultaneously accounts for consistent er-rors in the imitative behaviors of young children. In this view, imitation occurs through a goal-sensitive mapping between observed actions and performed actions. Observed behaviors are coded as constituent goals, and those goals are the units from which subsequent action patterns are composed. When multiple goals are identified within a task, goals com-pete for limited processing capacity, and some goals may be reproduced at the expense of other goals, leading to consistent and predictable errors in imitation.

Objects in imitation and action

We have suggested that three important goal-types are objects, agents, and movements, with other salient features also able to influence imita-tive behavior. We have also noted that of these three goal-types, objects appear to play an especially important role in generating imitative behav-ior. When imitative actions are directed at objects such as various body parts or at stickers on a table, children nearly always direct their actions at the appropriate target object, even at the cost of selecting the correct hand. In some ways this is not surprising, since objects are central to many aspects of human cognition, and play a particularly important role in early perception (Spelke & Hermer, 1996; Woodward, 1998). Body parts and stickers, however, lack many of the qualities normally consid-ered to characterize objects. In everyday life, children's imitative actions are surely directed at richer and more distinct objects, ranging from bot-tles and spoons to toy kangaroos. We find it interesting that body parts and stickers, despite their questionable status as true objects, can have such a significant influence on imitative behavior. Expanding future inves-tigations of goal-directed imitation to include a wider range of behavioral tasks is likely to add much to our understanding of the mental lexicon for describing and inferring goals, including object-goals.

Goal hierarchies and goal competition

We have proposed that goals are hierarchically organized, and that imitative errors result from the combination of limited processing capacity and hierarchical organization. In the studies reported here, we have focused on imitation in children, in part because we reasoned that developmental limitations on processing capacity make children especially likely to produce errors that can shed light on the hierarchical organization of goals. The goal-directed view predicts that the same processes should be revealed in adult imitative behavior. Some recent experiments (Wohlschläger & Bekkering, 1999) indicate that this is the case. When asked to imitate the standard hand-to-ear task, adults reproduce both ipsilateral and contralateral movements correctly. Initial movement tendency and response times indicate, however, that adults do show a preference for ipsilateral movements over contralateral movements. In addition, if the task is made more complex by adding features (such as multiple objects or multiple movement paths), adults, like children, make errors with respect to the movement but not with respect to the object.

Other investigators have called attention to the hierarchical organization of sequentially executed goals. Sequentially executed goals involve recursive loops executed to some criterion, and other similar chunked structures (Byrne & Russon, 1998). An interesting empirical question for future research is whether hierarchical organization of sequentially executed goals also leads to predictable imitative errors, or whether sequentially executed goals are not compromised by processing limitations.

Goals as mental states

Finally, we have also argued that unlike events or outcomes, goals are mental states, and are therefore not strictly observable but must be inferred. Together the proposals that goals are hierarchically organized and that the goals guiding imitation need to be inferred may provide some insight into debates about whether nonhuman primates can imitate. These proposals point to two specific accounts for differences between the imitative behavior of humans and that of other primates. One possibility is that goal-directed imitation is present in both humans and other primates, but that humans have expanded processing capacities compared to other primates. This account would predict in at least some imitative tasks, nonhuman primates would perform similarly to young children, reproducing one imitative goal at the expense of another, as when young children select the correct ear but not the correct hand in the hand-to-ear task. A second possibility is that goal-directed imitation is only present in animals capable of inferring the mental states of conspecifics. If it is true that humans are the only animals capable of inferring the mental states of others, this view would make the interesting prediction that nonhuman primates should make less contralateral errors in the hand-to-ear task than young children. Whereas most studies comparing imitation in humans and nonhuman primates make the prediction that if an animal is incapable of imitation, that animal should perform worse on the experimental task, this hypothesis makes the unusual prediction that if an animal is incapable of goal-directed imitation, that animal should perform better on the experimental task.

The theory of goal-directed imitation thus suggests several novel and highly interesting directions for future research in imitation. By positing that imitation entails representing an observed behavior as a set of goals, and that subsequent actions are generated from this goal description, we have been able not only to account for persistent errors in the imitative behavior of young children, but also to make predictions about the circumstances in which those errors are diminished. Expanding future investigations of goal-directed imitation to include a wider range of behavioral tasks, and imitators, is likely to add much to our understanding of imitation, and of action in general.

Acknowledgments

The authors thank Andy Meltzoff and two anonymous reviewers for helpful comments on an earlier draft. This research was supported by the Max Planck Society.

References

Bauer, P. (1992). Holding it all together: How enabling relations facilitate young children's event recall. *Cognitive Development, 7,* 1–28.

Bauer, P., & Mandler, J. (1989). One thing follows another: Effects of temporal structure on 1- to 2-year-olds recall of events. *Developmental Psychology, 25,* 197–206.

Bauer, P., & Shore, C. M. (1987). Making a memorable event: Effects of familiarity and organization on young children's recall of action sequences. *Cognitive Development, 2,* 327–338.

Bauer, P., & Travis, L. (1993). The fabric of an event: Different sources of temporal invariance differentially affect 24-month-olds recall. *Cognitive Development, 8,* 319–341.

Bekkering, H., Wohlschläger, A., & Gattis, M. (2000). Imitation of gestures in children is goal-directed. *Quarterly Journal of Experimental Psychology, 53A,* 153–164.

Berges, J., & Lezine, I. (1965). The imitation of gestures: A technique for studying the body schema and praxis of children three to six years of age. *Clinics in Developmental Medicine No. 18.* London: The Spastics Society Medical

Education and Information Unit in Association with William Heinemann Medical Books Ltd.

Byrne, R., & Russon, A. (1998). Learning by imitation: A hierarchical approach. *Behavioral and Brain Sciences, 21*, 667–684.

Call, J., & Tomasello, M. (1995). Use of social information in the problemsolving of orangutans (*Pongo pygmaeus*) and human children (*Homo sapiens*). *Journal of Comparative Psychology, 109*, 308–320.

Carpenter, M., Akhtar, N., & Tomasello, M. (1998). Fourteen- through 18-month-old infants differentially imitate intentional and accidental actions. *Infant Behavior & Development, 21*, 315–330.

Fadiga, L., Fogassi, L., Pavesi, G., & Rizzolatti, G. (1995). Motor facilitation during action observation: A magnetic study. *Journal of Neurophysiology, 73*, 2608–2611.

Gattis, M., Bekkering, H., & Wohlschläger, A. (1998). When actions are carved at the joints. *Behavioral Brain Science, 21*, 691–692.

Gleissner, B. (1998). Imitation of hand gestures to body parts is guided by goals rather than perceptual-motor mapping. Unpublished diploma thesis. Ludwig-Maximillians-University, Munich.

Gleissner, B., Meltzoff, A. N., & Bekkering, H. (2000). Children's coding of human action: Cognitive factors influencing imitation in 3-year-olds. *Developmental Science, 3*, 405–414.

Gordon, H. (1922). Hand and ear tests. *British Journal of Psychology, 13*, 283–300.

Head, H. (1920). Aphasia and kindred disorders of speech. *Brain, 43*, 87–165.

Meltzoff, A. N. (1995). Understanding the intentions of others: Re-enactment of intended acts by 18-month-old children. *Developmental Psychology, 31*, 838–850.

Meltzoff, A. N., & Moore, M. K. (1983). Newborn infants imitate adult facial gestures. *Child Development, 54*, 702–709.

Nagell, K., Olguin, R. S., & Tomasello, M. (1993). Processes of social learning in the tool use of chimpanzees (*Pan troglodytes*) and human children (*Homo sapiens*). *Journal of Comparative Psychology, 107*, 174–186.

Pellegrino, G. di, Fadiga, L., Fogassi, L., Gallese, V., & Rizzolatti, G. (1992). Understanding motor events: A neurophysiological study. *Experimental Brain Research, 91*, 176–180.

Salamy, A. (1976). Commissural transmission: Maturational changes in humans. *Science, 200*, 1409–1410.

Schofield, W. N. (1976a). Do children find movements which cross the body midline difficult? *Quarterly Journal of Experimental Psychology, 28*, 571–582.

(1976b). Hand movements which cross the body midline: Findings relating age differences to handedness. *Perceptual and Motor Skills, 42*, 643–646.

Spelke, E. S., & Hermer, L. (1996). Early cognitive development: Objects and space. In R. Gelman & T. K.-F. Au (Eds.), *Perceptual and cognitive development* (pp. 71–114). San Diego: Academic Press.

Thorpe, W. (1956). *Learning and instinct in animals*. London: Methuen.

Tomasello, M. (1990). Cultural transmission in the tool use and communicatory signaling of chimpanzees? In S. Parker & K. Gibson (Eds.), *Language and intelligence in monkeys and apes: Comparative developmental perspectives.* Cambridge: Cambridge University Press.

(1996). Do apes ape? In C. Heyes & B. Galef (Eds.), *Social learning in animals: The roots of culture* (pp. 319–345). New York: Academic Press.

(1998). Emulation learning and cultural learning. *Behavioral and Brain Sciences, 21,* 703–704.

Tomasello, M., & Call, J. (1997). *Primate cognition.* Oxford: Oxford University Press.

Travis, L. L. (1997). Goal-based organization of event memory in toddlers. In P. W. van den Broek, P. J. Bauer, & T. Bourg (Eds.), *Developmental spans in event comprehension and representation: Bridging fictional and actual events* (pp. 111–138). Mahwah, NJ: LEA.

Want, S. C., & Harris, P. L. (2001). Learning from other people's mistakes: Causal understanding in learning to use a tool. *Child Development, 72,* 431–443.

Whiten, A., & Ham, R. (1992). On the nature and evolution of imitation in the animal kingdom: reappraisal of a century of research. In P. J. B. Slater, J. S. Rosenblatt, C. Beer, & M. Milinski (Eds.), *Advances in the study of behavior* (pp. 239–283). San Diego: Academic Press.

Whiten, A. (1998). Imitation of the sequential structure of actions by chimpanzees (Pantroglodytes). *Journal of Comparative Psychology, 112,* 270–281.

Wohlschläger, A., & Bekkering, H. (1999). Goal-directed imitation in adults. Manuscript in preparation.

Wohlschläger, A., Gattis, M., & Bekkering, H. (2001). Action generation and action perception in imitation: An instantiation of the action effect principle. Submitted for publication.

Woodward, A. L. (1998). Infants selectively encode the goal object of an actor's reach. *Cognition, 69,* 1–34.

11   Visuomotor couplings in object-oriented and imitative actions

Stefan Vogt

Introduction

A central aim of imitation research is to identify how complex patterns of motor output are generated based on observing a similarly complex pattern of motion produced by a model. How is imitative action informed by perception? During the 1990s a number of findings, and most markedly the discovery of "mirror neurons" by Rizzolatti and coworkers, supported the idea that motor structures are already involved in action perception and not only when reproducing the observed action. On first sight, this idea appears to provide a clear answer to the issue of imitative perception-action mediation: a *motor* representation of the observed act is formed already during model observation, which should allow its reproduction with high fidelity, at least when the model's action is in the behavioral repertoire of the observer. Also, this idea seems to depart from earlier theorizing about imitation and observational learning, in which typically two temporally distinct stages were implied: the formation of a cognitive (e.g., verbal or iconic) representation during action observation, and the later "translation" of this cognitive representation into action (e.g., Carroll & Bandura, 1990; Keele, 1986; Meltzoff, 1988). These two stages could be a few seconds, or even days, apart. Accordingly, this view may be characterized as *late mediation* between perception and action, whereas mirror neurons indicate the possibility of *early mediation*. In this chapter, I investigate the consequences of early mediation accounts for functional theories of human imitative behavior.

The step from the involvement of motor cortical structures in visual processing, or *visuomotor couplings* for short, to assuming that the same motor structures are functional in imitative performance is by no means trivial. Before investigating the implications of this step in greater detail, it is useful to reflect briefly on late mediation accounts. As noted by Adams (1987), cognitive representations have been assigned a dual role in these models, namely (1) to guide the observer's imitative behavior, and (2) to serve as a standard of correctness for the detection of deviations between imitative performance and the represented model. Indeed, without assuming some form of memory of the observed act that is distinct from the preparatory and executive motor processes on the side of the imitator, it is difficult to explain self-correction in repeated imitative attempts (Meltzoff & Moore, 1997). Also the first role of cognitive representations, namely, to be causally involved in the concurrent guidance of performance, may be a viable characterization of certain imitation tasks. For example, one may be able to retain a dynamic visual image of an observed greeting gesture. When asked to imitate, this visual image may be reactivated and, possibly by virtue of its similarity to the sensory feedback received when having performed this gesture before, the related motor commands may be issued. In this chapter I neither seek to defend nor to reject such explanations. Moreover, I wish to show that early mediation accounts provide a more complete picture of imitative behaviors than late mediation accounts alone can.

Actions and parameters

At the outset, a caveat about early mediation accounts is appropriate. It is tempting to assume that visuomotor couplings, due to the involvement of motor representations, necessarily specify all degrees of freedom in imitative performance. However, at least for the mirror neurons found in the monkey's premotor area F5, Rizzolatti and colleagues (this volume) stress the insensitivity of these neurons to kinematic details of the observed action (e.g., movement direction or speed). Instead, they see the primary role of the monkey's mirror system in *understanding* or identifying the type of action seen (e.g., grasping, or manipulating objects). That is, a motor representation in area F5 is still a rather high-level description of an action and would require further specification (e.g., from environmental and intentional constraints) for motor execution. In this respect, mirror neurons could almost be seen as the neural correlate of Adam's cognitive representations, although typically, the latter refer to nonmotor (iconic or verbal) descriptions.

Early mediation accounts are certainly not confined to high-level action coding, however. It is well possible that other visuomotor couplings specify more fine-grained details than F5 mirror neurons. That is, not only a representation of the type of the observed action, but also of the way in which it is carried out may be formed during observation. Accordingly, Rizzolatti, Fadiga, Fogassi, and Gallese (this volume) suggest both high- and low-level "resonance mechanisms," which they assume to rely on different neural substrate. Thus, on the basis of the available neurophysiological evidence it would seem premature to abandon the idea that a motor representation that is sufficient for reproduction is formed during model observation. Particularly the enhanced capability for detailed behavioral copying in humans (e.g., Byrne, this volume) may rely on the combined operation of a number of visuomotor couplings, or resonance mechanisms.

In this chapter I will focus on two types of displays used in imitation research: displays that show one out of a number of familiar actions, and displays that show the same action, with different parameterizations of this action in subsequent trials. In the latter, subjects have advance knowledge about the action to be shown next (e.g., grasp object), and are only required to adjust certain aspects of their performance, such as reach direction or grip orientation. For imitating different actions vs. parameters of a single act, I use the terms *imitative action selection (IAS)* and *imitative parameter selection (IPS)*. IAS tasks may involve both high- and low-level resonance mechanisms, whereas IPS tasks should mainly rely on low-level mechanisms. The focus of the present chapter also means that two important aspects of imitation will be largely ignored, human observational learning (for reviews see, e.g., Vogt, 1995, 1996a), and the imitation of sequences of actions (see chapters in this volume by Byrne and Whiten). At least, visuomotor couplings that are involved in IAS tasks should also play a role in sequence coding, since sequences firstly need to be parsed for constituent units before their serial order can be reconstructed.

In the following, I elaborate the concept of visuomotor couplings in two steps. In the next section, recent work on *object-oriented actions* is discussed, such as reaching for a cup of tea. Object-oriented and imitative (or model-guided) actions are different in that the former achieve complementarity between the displayed object and action, whereas the latter achieve similarity between displayed and performed action. Nevertheless, the excursion to object-oriented actions is useful for the following reasons. Firstly, the concept of visuomotor couplings has originally been developed for object-oriented actions, so the reviewed work serves to illustrate the general concept. Secondly, the systematic behavioral investigation of object-oriented actions is further advanced than the investigation of human imitative behavior, so that a number of working hypotheses can be derived from the former. Thirdly, object and action displays activate adjacent and possibly interacting motor cortical areas. In the monkey, the parieto-frontal circuits that process object displays and those that process action displays both involve neurons located in area F5 ("canonical" and mirror neurons, respectively; e.g., Rizzolatti, Luppino, & Matelli, 1998). Similarly, neuroimaging studies have shown that adjacent sectors in the region of Broca's area, the likely equivalent of the mirror system in humans, are activated during action observation (see chapters by Decety and Rizzolatti, Fadiga, Fogassi, & Gallese) and during object manipulation (Binkofski et al., 1999). And finally, imitation often requires interaction with objects. It is therefore appropriate to consider model- and object-guided actions in a coherent framework.

In the fourth section, evidence for visuomotor couplings in action observation and imitation is discussed. Furthermore, a core issue for imitative parameter selection is addressed, whether action displays may effect a similar modular, fast and automatic motor activation as object displays. A recent experiment from our lab (Vogt, in prep.) confirms the main prediction of a fast visuomotor coupling in imitative performance. No support was found, however, for the notion that multiple display properties may inform imitative actions in a similar way as multiple object properties can for object-oriented actions. The latter finding indicates severe processing constraints in online imitation tasks.

From object-guided to model-guided actions

Let us consider first object-oriented actions, in which a rich body of evidence for visuomotor couplings has accumulated over the last two decades. The main purpose is to derive hypotheses about possible equivalent couplings in model-guided actions in a heuristic manner, and not to provide an exhaustive review.

As Tucker and Ellis (1998) remind us, when an actor sets out to reach for and manipulate an object, how he uses the available visual information about this object depends on the goal of the action. In addition to the action goal, a multiplicity of local contingencies needs to be taken into account for successful performance. For example, a reaching movement is normally directed towards the target object, its velocity profile is scaled to the distance of the object from the hand's start position, grip orientation is aligned to the orientation of the object, and grip aperture reflects object size well before contact with the object (Jeannerod, 1996, 1997). A central conclusion from both neurophysiological and behavioral studies is that certain motor degrees of freedom (e.g., concerning grip aperture) are informed by an appropriate visual object property (e.g., object diameter) rather independently from others, so that each such visual-motor circuit forms a separate *visuomotor channel* (Paulignan & Jeannerod, 1996; see also Arbib, 1997). That is, we find a modular, semi-autonomous organization not only at the level of the two major visual pathways (dorsal and ventral streams, Milner & Goodale, 1995), but also within each stream. Individual elementary object properties, not necessarily bound together to form a unitary object as available in introspection, inform individual aspects of an action in the dorsal pathway, which extends from parietal directly to premotor areas (Rizzolatti, Luppino, & Matelli, 1998).

A key behavioral methodology to demonstrate independent, parallel processing at both levels (major visual pathways; visuomotor channels within the dorsal pathway) is the selective perturbation of certain visual properties of the target object. In Goodale, Pélisson, and Prablanc's (1986) seminal study, subjects reached toward a target light that was shifted, in 50 per cent of the trials, a few centimeters away from the original target location. The shift was triggered by saccade peak velocity, which occurs about when the hand begins to move. Subjects responded to the visual perturbation almost instantaneously and without increase of overall movement time, which the authors interpreted as evidence for a positional updating mechanism that is in operation in perturbed and unperturbed trials. This is a good example for a fast and direct visuomotor coupling. Furthermore, subjects were not aware of the jumps of the target location or of their corrective movements, which indicated a dissociation between the pragmatic visuomotor processing and perceptual awareness. Subsequent studies confirmed the short visuomotor latency, which has been estimated between 110 and 275 ms, depending on the particular method used (see Brenner & Smeets, 1997). Although effects of perturbing a certain component of prehension on other components are not always absent, Paulignan and Jeannerod (1996) found the available data in good agreement with the concept of semi-independent visuomotor channels (or couplings). Also, the dissociation between visuomotor processing and awareness has been supported in later perturbation studies (Jeannerod, 1997, Ch. 3.5).

Even when subjects are not overtly performing a grasping action, visuomotor couplings may be activated by the mere visual presentation of a graspable object. In the study by Tucker and Ellis (1998), subjects were asked to indicate whether a displayed object was upright or inverted by pressing a key with the right or left hand. In addition to showing different vertical orientations, the objects were also presented in different horizontal orientations which afforded either a right- or left-hand grasp. Although horizontal orientation was irrelevant for the task, it affected response times in the sense that right-hand keypresses were faster when the displayed object afforded a right-hand grasp. The authors conclude that seen objects automatically "potentiate" components of the actions they afford, and suggest that action goals may operate on already existing (partial) motor representations of the possible actions in a visual scene. Similar object-based visuomotor priming effects have been reported by Craighero, Fadiga, Umiltà, and Rizzolatti (1996).

Many factors remain to be explored here, such as ways of gating the range of objects for which motor representations are activated in parallel, and the range of object properties that yield priming effects. Nevertheless, the general notion that internal selection processes may operate on existing motor representations is well in line with the neurophysiological model of Gallese and colleagues (see Rizzolatti, Fogassi, & Gallese, 1997). In this model, inferior parietal area AIP "provides multiple descriptions of a 3D object, thus 'proposing' several grasping possibilities to (premotor) area F5...(which) then selects the most appropriate type of grip on the basis of contextual information (e.g. purpose of the action, spatial relation with other objects, etc.)" (*ibid.*, 563). The studies by Craighero, Fadiga, Umiltà, & Rizzolatti (1996) and Tucker and Ellis (1998) suggest that even task-irrelevant object properties may, at least when the variations in the display are limited, be automatically linked to action, that is, may activate certain visuomotor couplings.

Is it possible that watching a right or left hand grasping a (neutral) object will result in a similar "potentiation" as watching an object that affords a right- or left-hand grasp? More generally, two empirical questions emerge from this work for imitative actions: (1) do similarly fast and automatic visuomotor couplings between individual properties of an observed *action* and the imitative performance exist? (2) If this is the case, is it further possible that the observed action activates a number of such visuomotor couplings *in parallel*, thereby specifying the relevant degrees of freedom of the imitative response in a modular and elementary manner just as in object-guided actions? Taken to the extreme, this elementary "steering" of an imitative response by individual properties of an observed action could produce a successful imitation without prior understanding of the meaning of the action.

The work by Rumiati and Humphreys (1998) supports this counter-intuitive possibility in the domain of object-guided actions. The authors found that in speeded gesturing actions to pictures of a variety of objects, the number of visual errors was higher as compared to naming the actions afforded by the objects, whereas semantic errors were lower in gesturing. In accordance with earlier neuropsychological work (e.g., Riddoch & Humphreys, 1987), the authors conclude that stored structural descriptions (visual representations) of objects are directly associated with stored action patterns, without requiring full access to semantic knowledge ("direct visual route" vs. "semantic route"). They also discuss the possibility that the processing of crucial parts of an object, without recognition of the whole object, may have been sufficient to select an appropriate action in their task. Both interpretations (full vs. partial descriptions) can explain their results. These interpretations also provide two hypotheses for imitative action selection, either that the elementary properties of an observed action specify the response in a piecemeal manner, as suggested above, or that a compound visual representation of a seen gesture activates an appropriate action.

A third option for imitative action selection is, of course, the semantic coding of the observed action's meaning, which is then used to assemble the elementary degrees of freedom of the imitative act, in a sense rather independent of the elementary degrees of freedom in the action display. A corresponding goal-directed approach to imitation has been suggested by Bekkering, Wohlschläger, and Gattis (2000, see also Gattis, Bekkering, & Wohlschläger, this volume). Such an approach is certainly viable and can explain deviations between model and reproduction, as well as self-corrections in repeated imitative attempts. However, we can now see that such a semantic mediation is very likely not the only pathway from perception to imitative action, particularly not in online imitation and interference paradigms (see below).

To summarize, the proposed pathways are related to the two forms of imitation distinguished above, action and parameter selection, in the following way. Extrapolating from object-oriented actions, three hypothetical mechanisms for *IAS* have been suggested:

• guidance by partial visual descriptions of observed actions,
• guidance by compound visual descriptions, and
• guidance by semantic descriptions.

Particularly the first two hypotheses deserve empirical testing (e.g., by extending Rumiati & Humphreys' (1998) methodology to imitative action selection), whereas the existence of a semantic route is possibly the most easily agreed upon. For *IPS*, two empirical issues have been posed: (1) the existence of fast and automatic visuomotor couplings, and (2) the possible operation of a number of such couplings in parallel (note that an extension of this possibility results in the "partial visual descriptions" hypothesis of IAS). Both issues have been addressed in a recent study in our lab, described below.

Visuomotor couplings in action perception and imitation

Detailed reviews of the evidence for the involvement of motor structures in action observation are provided in the chapters by Bekkering, Decety, and Rizzolatti *et al.* Thus, this section can be reduced to the essentials in the present context. Our extrapolations from object- to model-guided actions are in certain respects already well supported by available evidence, and in other respects they call for future experimental work.

Neurophysiology of action observation

Visuomotor couplings for object- and model-guided actions have been described by Rizzolatti, Luppino, and Matelli (1998). The monkey's VIP-F5 circuit has been identified as one amongst a number of circuits involved in object-oriented actions, whereas parietal-premotor circuit PF-F5c includes premotor neurons with "mirror" properties. These neurons tend to discharge when a monkey observes another individual performing an action, as well as when the monkey performs this or a related action himself. The discharge during action observation does not manifest itself in overt behavior, and, as indicated above, the primary function of these visuomotor couplings is thus likely to detect the meaning of the observed actions, by relating the action seen to the observer's own motor repertoire (see Gallese & Goldman, 1998). Also in humans, the mere observation of an action, without the intention to imitate, tends to activate certain parts of the motor system of the observing individual, as shown in experiments using transcranial magnetic stimulation, PET, and MEG. Interestingly, based on Perrett's work (this volume) that demonstrated the coding of a variety of meaningful, observed actions in the monkey's superior temporal sulcus, Rizzolatti (1994) suggested that "Perrett's neurons might represent an initial description of motor events that, via parietal or prefrontal lobe, is then transmitted to the inferior premotor areas". We further speculate that, while in some observation tasks, the dorsal stream reaches premotor areas directly (e.g., PF-F5c), in other tasks it may do so more indirectly, involving the ventral stream. Displays that only show parametric variations of a certain action are prime candidates for the direct, dorsal pathway. In contrast, for displays of different meaningful actions, ventral stream contributions appear more likely. Although direct comparisons of these two display types have not yet been made, the available brain imaging studies are in line with this proposal.

Neurophysiology of action imitation

While I would like to defend the hypothesis that similar pathways are used in action observation and action imitation (IPS: dorsal stream; IAS: dorsal and ventral stream), some words of caution are appropriate. Firstly, reproducing observed actions almost certainly places additional demands on visuomotor processing than action recognition. Imagine, for example, imitating a juggler. In addition to selecting this action (and possibly certain parameters) based on the model, the imitator must also process information about the current position of his objects. This makes it very clear that information from the model display is only one amongst a number of constraints for motor preparation and execution (Vogt & Carey, 1998).

Secondly, extrapolating straight from two visual systems theory, one might expect imitative behavior (IPS *and* IAS) to be mediated largely by the dorsal stream. In fact, the study by Grèzes, Costes, and Decety (1998) appears to confirm this view. From their finding of a primarily dorsal stream involvement in their observe-to-imitate-later conditions, they concluded that "the reproduction of action(s) that involves initial observation does not require the semantic integration or verbal labelling" (p. 575). However, the authors mention a number of factors (use of pantomimed actions, habituation effects) which may have biased their results, so it would be inappropriate to principally deny the possibility of semantic mediation in imitation tasks. Unfortunately, no single-cell recordings that contrast action observation and immediate imitation are available – Rizzolatti's monkeys simply didn't imitate. Also the available brain imaging studies with humans have rarely provided such a comparison. In the first study that included immediate imitation (Krams *et al.*, 1998), this condition did not involve premotor cortical activity to the same extent as motor imagery-related instructions. Also in Fadiga, Fogassi, Pavesi, and Rizzolatti's (1995) study, a (deferred) imitation condition did not produce a stronger motor facilitation than an observe-to-recognize condition.

To summarize, although we have some evidence that motor structures are involved not only in action observation *per se* but also in the observational stage of imitative behavior, more research is needed about potential differences between the two. For example, it could be that motor involvement during observe-to-imitate conditions merely subserves the formation of a cognitive representation, which is only subsequently used for motor preparation. Alternatively, this motor involvement may inform motor preparation more directly, as suggested here.

Neuropsychology of imitation

The proposal of multiple routes in IAS tasks that parallel those in object-guided action selection tasks (sensu Rumiati & Humphreys, 1998) is well supported by neuropsychological studies with apraxic and pantomime agnosic patients. Rothi, Mack, and Heilman (1986) reported patients who, despite being unable to comprehend or discriminate gestures (hence the term "pantomime agnosia"), could nevertheless imitate these gestures – possibly as if these were a series of meaningless movements. Rothi, Ochipa, and Heilman (1997) suggested that these patients bypassed an impaired lexical mediation route and instead used a nonlexical, possibly iconic route, that is normally only used for the imitation of meaningless gestures and may be spared in those patients with ideomotor apraxia who show improvements in imitation tasks. A similar argument for a direct, nonsemantic route from vision to motor control was made by Goldenberg and Hagmann (1997) and Goldenberg & Hermsdörfer (this volume) based on a selective deficit of imitation of meaningless gestures found in two apraxic patients (indicating a selective impairment of this route).

Behavioral evidence

Whereas neurophysiological and neuropsychological studies have tended to use displays of different actions, displays with only parametric variations of a given action have been predominantly used in behavioral work. Amongst the first studies that indicated the involvement of motor structures in action observation are the experiments by Vogt (1995). Subjects' fluency of motor performance was assessed before and after a period of repeated observation of a sequential movement pattern in which no overt movements were carried out. It was found that fluency of posttest performance increased to the same extent as in a group of subjects who had physically performed the movement in the practice period. An additional finding was that a motor imagery condition also produced increases in fluency comparable to physical practice, which supplemented earlier results (see Jeannerod, 1997: Ch. 4). The finding of fine-grained effects of observational practice on motor output clearly supports the idea that motor representations are already accessed during model observation. This conclusion was confirmed in a further study (Vogt, 1996b) where subjects reproduced timed movements either immediately or after engagement in motor or visual imagery. Neither form of imagery was found to improve reproduction accuracy, which suggests that visuomotor couplings were already in operation during action observation and that no subsequent translation to action was necessary.

The recent work presented in the chapters by Bekkering and Prinz in this volume also indicates the involvement of motor structures in action perception. For example, the interference experiments by Stürmer, Aschersleben, and Prinz (2000) can be seen as related to the experiments by Tucker and Ellis (1998), in that Stürmer, Aschersleben, and Prinz used direction of hand movement instead of object affordance as irrelevant display dimension. Apparently, action and object displays give rise to similar compatibility effects. Also the experiments by Brass, Bekkering, and Prinz (2001) nicely demonstrate that an irrelevant display property (lifting finger) can affect motor responses to a go signal (movement onset), even when the response is predefined. Their interpretation of imitation in terms of an automatic, involuntary response priming converges with the concept of visuomotor couplings, and also with Tucker and Ellis' notion of a "potentiation" of action components (i.e., parameters). Nevertheless, regarding the precise mechanism of this priming, two possibilities should be distinguished as follows.

In this chapter, I have proposed an extension of recent views on object-oriented actions to imitative actions which does not rely on visual similarity to be functional in concurrent perception-action mediation. In object-oriented actions, object properties prime complementary, but not "similar" parameters of action (see the second section). In imitative actions, display properties, such as the direction of a moving hand, prime parameters of action that produce a similar movement as the one seen. In both cases, complementarity or similarity result from the particular visuomotor couplings established (obviously, the issue why certain couplings are established and others are not needs to be addressed eventually, both for object- and model-guided actions). In contrast, when Brass, Bekkering, and Prinz (2001, see also the chapters by Bekkering and Prinz in this volume) refer to ideomotor compatibility sensu Greenwald to explain their data, they imply "a match between the event perceived and the representation of what one intends to do, that is, an anticipation of the sensory consequences of the planned action" (p. 20). It is an empirical question if such a similarity-based match, presumably at a relatively early, visual processing stage, is required for compatibility effects between observed and planned actions to occur, or if interference and facilitation take place at a later, motor preparatory stage, as suggested here. The available data do not favor one over the other alternative.

Whereas the latter work utilized interference paradigms, which allow only indirect conclusions about the mechanisms underlying imitation proper, we have recently developed an online imitation paradigm where subjects are asked to imitate, in near synchrony, the direction of a reaching movement displayed by a model facing the subject (Vogt, in prep.). The experiment utilized the perturbation methodology as described above. In 75 per cent of trials, the model reached for the middle of three dowels in front of him, and subjects reached for the middle of another set of three dowels, each positioned next to the model's dowels (: : :), when they saw the model starting to move. In the remaining, perturbed trials (25 per cent), the model also set out to reach for the middle dowel, but its illumination was shifted to the right or left dowel at movement onset, and the model had to reorient his reach for the new dowel. This was closely followed by the subject's reorientation of reach, who could only see the model's hand but not the illumination shift. Thus, model and subject always lifted adjacent dowels. This procedure provided a precisely timed perturbation onset, which allowed us to measure the visuomotor latencies in model-guided actions from the model's and subject's hand trajectories (using a 120 Hz / 3D optical tracking system). Whereas in the model-guided blocks, subjects were only guided by view of the model's hand, in other blocks their movements were guided by a shift of illumination of their dowel (object guidance) or by the color of the illumination (arbitrary cueing).

The main finding was that the visuomotor latencies in model-guided performance were similarly short as in object-guided performance (approximately 240 ms and 225 ms, respectively). In contrast, in the arbitrary cueing condition, latencies were significantly longer (approximately 380 ms). This confirmed our prediction that visuomotor couplings between parameters of an observed action and imitative performance can operate in a similarly fast and automatic manner as in object-oriented actions (Question 1 above). It is likely that these fast responses are mediated by the dorsal cortical stream. The result that color cueing produced longer latencies matches the finding by Pisella, Arzi, and Rossetti (1998), who explained this by the involvement of the slower, ventral stream. To summarize, directionally compatible, but not arbitrary visual cues have direct access to response selection, and the former include displays of human hands.

The second question addressed in the study by Vogt (in prep.) was if a number of motor parameters can be specified in parallel by a model display. We have tested a strong version of this hypothesis. In twelve of the unperturbed trials of each model-guided block, the model had performed modulations of speed, height of transport, or grip aperture (extra wide or narrow opening). If subjects' motor preparation was automatically coupled to all display properties, we should expect that their movements would reflect these modulations, even though they were not explicitly instructed to do so. Preliminary analyses indicate that subjects were largely "immune" against these task-irrelevant modulations. That is, although they fully attended to the model's hand and redirected their reach very quickly when the model did so, they did not mirror other aspects of the model's action. Thus, rather than letting each parameter of their performance be visually guided by the model, subjects reduced this guidance to the task-relevant dimension. If replicable, this finding is very important for imitation research, since it indicates a strong limitation of visuomotor coupling in online model-guided performance. In contrast to object-oriented actions, imitative actions may be more limited regarding the range of display dimensions that have instant access to motor output.

Concluding remarks

An underlying tenet of this contribution is that object- and model-guided behavior can be understood in a coherent framework, despite their different objectives (complementarity vs. similarity). The hypotheses for imitative action and parameter selection derived from object-oriented actions have already been confirmed in certain respects, and provide many possibilities for future experimental work. For IPS, the issue of multiparametric specification of imitative behavior requires further study, so do the three hypothetical pathways that were proposed for IAS (semantic, whole and partial visual descriptions of actions). Whereas the semantic route is likely to rely on ventral stream processing, it is possible that the more direct, visual routes rely mainly on the dorsal cortical stream, which should be dissociable in behavioral and neuroimaging experiments.

The focus of this chapter has been on visuomotor couplings during model observation, and these have proven to be well-suited to explain the effects obtained in a range of experimental tasks. Whereas the explanation for interference effects provided here is response competition, the available evidence is also in line with competition at earlier (visual) processing stages. It was made clear that the possible role of visuomotor couplings in imitative actions does not exclude the involvement of cognitive representations that are central in late mediation accounts. Rather, the demonstration that we can come quite some way without implicating such representations will hopefully motivate a better-grounded characterization of their possible role(s) than previously available.

Acknowledgments

I wish to thank Heiko Hecht, Graham Hitch, Brian Hopkins, Wolfgang Prinz, Mary Smyth, and Peter Walker for helpful discussions and for their comments on earlier drafts of this article. Geoff Rushforth provided skillful and friendly technical assistance.

References

Adams, J. A. (1987). Historical review and appraisal of research on the learning, retention, and transfer of human motor skills. *Psychological Bulletin, 101*, 41–74.

Arbib, M. A. (1997). Modeling visuomotor transformations. In F. Boller, J. Grafman (Series Eds.), & M. Jeannerod (Vol. Ed.), *Handbook of*

Neuropsychology, Vol. 11, Section 16: Action and cognition (pp. 65–90). Amsterdam: Elsevier.

Bekkering, H., Wohlschläger, A., & Gattis, M. (2000). Imitation of gestures in children is goal-directed. *Quarterly Journal of Experimental Psychology: Section A: Human Experimental Psychology, 53A*, 153–164.

Binkofski, F., Buccino, G., Stephan, K. M., Rizzolatti, G., Seitz, R. J., & Freund, H.-J. (1999). A parieto-premotor network for object manipulation: Evidence from neuroimaging. *Experimental Brain Research, 128*, 210–213.

Brass, M., Bekkering, H., & Prinz, W. (2001). Movement observation affects movement execution in a simple response task. *Acta Psychologica, 106*, 3–22.

Brenner, E., & Smeets, J. B. J. (1997). Fast responses of the human hand to changes in target position. *Journal of Motor Behavior, 29*, 297–310.

Carroll, W. R., & Bandura, A. (1990). Representational guidance of action production in observational learning: A causal analysis. *Journal of Motor Behavior, 22*, 85–97.

Craighero, L., Fadiga, L., Umiltà, C. A., & Rizzolatti, G. (1996). Evidence for a visuomotor priming effect. *NeuroReport, 8*, 347–349.

Fadiga, L., Fogassi, L., Pavesi, G., & Rizzolatti, G. (1995). Motor facilitation during action observation: A magnetic stimulation study. *Journal of Neurophysiology, 73*, 2608–2611.

Gallese, V., & Goldman, A. (1998). Mirror neurons and the simulation theory of mind-reading. *Trends in Cognitive Sciences, 2*, 493–501.

Goldenberg, G., & Hagmann, S. (1997). The meaning of meaningless gestures: A study of visuo-imitative apraxia. *Neuropsychologia, 35*, 333–341.

Goodale, M. A., Pélisson, D., & Prablanc, C. (1986). Large adjustments in visually guided reaching do not depend on vision of the hand or perception of target displacement. *Nature, 320*, 748–750.

Grèzes, J., Costes, N., & Decety, J. (1998). Top-down effect of strategy on the perception of human biological motion: A PET investigation. *Cognitive Neuropsychology, 15*, 553–582.

Jeannerod, M. (1996). Reaching and grasping: Parallel specification of visuomotor channels. In H. Heuer & S. W. Keele (Eds.), *Handbook of perception and action, Vol. 2: Motor skills* (pp. 405–459). London: Academic Press.
(1997). *The cognitive neuroscience of action.* Oxford: Blackwell.

Keele, S. W. (1986). Motor control. In K. R. Boff, L. Kaufman, & J. P. Thomas (Eds.), *Handbook of perception and human performance, Vol. 2: Motor control* (pp. 30: 1–60). Wiley: New York.

Krams, M., Rushworth, M. F. S., Deiber, M.-P., Frackowiak, R. S. J., & Passingham, R. E. (1998). The preparation, execution and suppression of copied movements. *Experimental Brain Research, 120*, 386–398.

Meltzoff, A. N. (1988). Infant imitation after a 1-week delay: Long-term memory for novel acts and multiple stimuli. *Developmental Psychology, 24*, 470–476.

Meltzoff, A. N., & Moore, M. K. (1997). Explaining facial imitation: A theoretical model. *Early Development and Parenting, 6*, 179–192.

Milner, A. D., & Goodale, M. A. (1995). *The visual brain in action.* Oxford: Oxford University Press.

Paulignan, Y., & Jeannerod, M. (1996). Prehension movements: The visuomotor channels hypothesis revisited. In A. Wing, P. Haggard, & J. R. Flanagan

(Eds.), *Hand and brain: The neurophysiology and psychology of hand movements* (pp. 265–282). San Diego: Academic Press.

Pisella, L., Arzi, M., & Rossetti, Y. (1998). The timing of color and location processing in the motor context. *Experimental Brain Research, 121*, 270–276.

Riddoch, M. J., & Humphreys, G. W. (1987). Visual object processing in a case of optic aphasia: A case of semantic access agnosia. *Cognitive Neuropsychology, 4*, 131–185.

Rizzolatti, G. (1994). Nonconscious motor images (Commentary on a target article by M. Jeannerod). *Behavioral and Brain Sciences, 17*, 220.

Rizzolatti, G., Fogassi, L., & Gallese, V. (1997). Parietal cortex: From sight to action. *Current Opinion in Neurobiology, 7*, 562–567.

Rizzolatti, G., Luppino, G., & Matelli, M. (1998). The organization of the motor cortical system: New concepts. *Electroencephalography and Clinical Neurophysiology, 106*, 283–296.

Rothi, L. J. G., Mack, L., & Heilman, K. M. (1986). Pantomime agnosia. *Journal of Neurology, Neurosurgery, and Psychiatry, 49*, 451–454.

Rothi, L. J. G., Ochipa, C., & Heilman, K. M. (1997). A cognitive neuropsychological model of limp praxis. In L. J. G. Rothi & K. M. Heilman (Eds.), *Apraxia: The neuropsychology of action* (pp. 29–49). Hove: Psychology Press [originally published 1991 in *Cognitive Neuropsychology, 8*, 443–458].

Rumiati, R. I., & Humphreys, G. W. (1998). Recognition by action: Dissociating visual and semantic routes to action in normal observers. *Journal of Experimental Psychology: Human Perception and Performance, 24*, 631–647.

Stürmer, B., Aschersleben, G., & Prinz, W. (2000). Correspondence effects with manual gestures and postures: A study of imitation. *Journal of Experimental Psychology: Human Perception and Performance, 26*, 1746–1759.

Tucker, M., & Ellis, R. (1998). On the relations between seen objects and components of potential actions. *Journal of Experimental Psychology: Human Perception and Performance, 24*, 830–846.

Vogt, S. (1995). On relations between perceiving, imagining and performing in the learning of cyclical movement sequences. *British Journal of Psychology, 86*, 191–216.

(1996a). The concept of event generation in movement imitation – neural and behavioral aspects. *Corpus, Psyche et Societas, 3*, 119–132.

(1996b). Imagery and perception-action mediation in imitative actions. *Cognitive Brain Research, 3*, 79–86.

(in prep.). *Chronometry of imitative prehensile actions: Effects of directional perturbation and modulation of reach and grasp components.* Manuscript in preparation.

Vogt, S., & Carey, D. (1998). Toward a microanalysis of imitative actions (Commentary on a target article by Byrne & Russon). *Behavioral and Brain Sciences, 21*, 705–706.

12   On bodies and events

Barbara Tversky, Julie Bauer Morrison, and Jeff Zacks

A category is a category is a category. The whole point of categorization
is to treat unlike things as if they were alike. After all, if we treated each
encounter with each object or event as the unique thing it is, we would
be unable to generalize, unable to learn, unable to remember, unable to
communicate. Ignoring differences underlies all of cognition. But which
differences to ignore? And are all categories alike, or do some, in particular
those associated with our bodies and their actions, have a special status?
First, we review the structure of categories, then the special features of
bodies and events, and finally relate them together and to the topic of this
book, imitation.

Structure of categories

Defining features or family resemblance?

What has been termed the "classical theory" has been trounced in recent
decades as a theory of how people decide on category membership or
draw inferences about category members (e.g., Medin, 1989; Miller &
Johnson-Laird, 1976; Rosch, 1978; Smith & Medin, 1981). At the core of
the classical view is the notion of defining features, features that are singly
necessary and jointly sufficient for category membership. Certainly some
legal and mathematical categories, such as citizenship and odd number,
have that character. But psychologists want to know how people think
about categories: do they think of categories in terms of necessary and
sufficient conditions? The evidence suggests otherwise. It suggests that
people think of categories in terms of central tendencies or frequent features or typical examples. For one thing, people find it difficult to provide
lists of features that are necessary or sufficient for category membership,
for even such familiar categories as tables and trees. They do find it easy
to generate examples of categories, to rate the examples on how good
or typical they are, and to produce features of categories, though not
necessarily necessary and sufficient ones.

Typicality

The features people produce for categories have a family resemblance structure (Wittgenstein, 1958). Not all the features are shared by all category members, but the more typical category members are more likely to have more of the shared features (Rosch & Mervis, 1975). A table, for example, does not have to have four legs and a horizontal top, though typical tables do. Graphic artists may have tables with slanted tops and cafe owners tables with a single leg. These are still tables, albeit atypical ones.

Basic level

Natural categories, those formed spontaneously and used frequently within a culture, have a preferred level of abstraction, called the basic level, the level of chair and dog rather than the level of furniture and animal or kitchen chair and Pekinese. The basic level also has a structural basis determined by category features (Rosch *et al.*, 1976). People produce few features shared by members of superordinate categories like furniture, vehicle, or animal. In contrast, people produce many features shared by chairs, cars, and dogs, but not appreciably more for kinds of chairs, cars, and dogs. Given that specific levels of categorization entail more category distinctions, the basic level maximizes the amount of information conveyed by a category relative to the number of contrast categories. These fundamental features of natural categories, typicality within a category and basic level across levels of abstraction, have been extended beyond artifacts and natural kinds to other categories, colors (Rosch, 1975), scenes, the settings for objects (Tversky & Hemenway, 1983), events (Morris & Murphy, 1990; Rifkin, 1985; Rosch, 1978), people (Cantor & Mischel, 1979), and emotions (e.g., Ekman, 1984; Izard, 1992; Plutchik, 1993).

Part structure and the basic level

The basic level differs qualitatively as well as quantitatively from more abstract and more specific levels of categorization. Examining the features produced for categories at the three levels of abstraction, Tversky and Hemenway observed that features for superordinate categories generally referred to functions, such as "used for fixing things" for tools (Tversky & Hemenway, 1984). Features at basic and subordinate levels, in contrast, referred to observable properties, such as "handle" and "blade" for knife or "peel," "pulp," "seeds," "sweet," for apple. One kind of feature in particular proliferated at the basic level, namely, parts.

Part names have an inherently ambiguous ontological status. They refer simultaneously to appearance and to function. A "leg" has a certain appearance – it is vertically elongated – but it also has a certain function – support. Metaphoric uses of part names reflect both senses. The "head" of a pencil is the top, but the head of a committee is the coordinator. Tversky and Hemenway argued that the dual status of parts promotes inferences from appearance to function essential to deeper understanding and coherent conceptions of categories. Arms are long things that suggest reaching. Seats are the right shape, size, and height to invite sitting. The legs of a deer enable mobility, and the peel of an apple protects its seeds. Parts, then, afford inferences from appearance to function.

Qualities of different kinds of categories

Despite similarity in typicality and basic-level structure, some classes of categories appear to differ qualitatively in revealing ways. The comparison of objects, both natural kinds and artifacts, to substances is enlightening. Objects normally have rigid shapes; indeed, shape is an excellent cue to the identity of an object. Substances, however, take the shape of their containers, and are characterized by texture, color, and material. Although the object/substance distinction is captured by the count/mass distinction in English, two-year-olds seem to grasp it prior to using or understanding the related syntactic terms (Soja, Carey, & Spelke, 1991). Consider further the contrast between natural kinds and artifacts. Children (and adults) are more likely to draw inferences, especially about unseen properties such as internal organs, for natural kinds than for artifacts; for artifacts, they are more likely to rely on perceptual similarity (e.g., Gelman, 1988; Keil, 1989; Keil & Batterman, 1984). Biological categories are regarded as having internal cores, perhaps genetic, that determine their appearance and behavior. Nonliving natural kinds, such as metals, are thought to have essences related to their molecular structures. Finally, artifacts are thought to have cores based on function or intended uses (see, e.g., Carey, 1986; Bloom, 1996; Gelman, 1988; Keil, 1989; Rips, 1989). Beliefs about essences govern the kinds of and bases for inferences from categories. Nevertheless, demonstrating that such theories or cores are consistently related to judgments of category membership or to knowledge about categories or to inferences from categories has proved difficult (e.g., Malt & Johnson, 1992). The moral here may be that just as it is difficult to demonstrate necessary and sufficient features for particular categories, tables, dogs, or sand, it is difficult to demonstrate necessary and sufficient conditions for kinds of categories, artifacts, biological kinds, or physical kinds, objects or substances.

Bodies and events

Bodies and events are candidates for privileged categories. We experience the world through our own bodies, frequently through the actions they perform. Prominent aspects of that experience involve the bodies and actions of others. Our bodies are integral to the events we perceive and participate in at every moment in time. Natural kinds and artifacts turn out to be crucial parts of events, acted upon by bodies. We have begun exploring the special characteristic qualities of bodies and events. Both bodies and events have salient part structures, the former in space, the latter in time. Let us turn first to bodies.

Bodies

In some ways, bodies are like other kinds of objects, especially those that move. But unlike other objects, which can only be experienced from the outside, bodies are experienced from the inside. We know what it feels like to move or be pushed, to have pleasure or pain, to feel cold or hot, to be sluggish or energetic. The privileged status of bodies may give them privileged cognition. Self-regulated imitation in neonates suggests that rudimentary understanding of others' bodies comes from actions performed by one's own body (Meltzoff & Moore, 1995). Other evidence comes from studies of Reed and Farah (1995; Reed, this volume). Observers judged whether pairs of photos of people in contorted postures were the same or different. Same pairs depicted the same postures from a different angle. Different pairs differed in positions of arms or legs. Reed and Farah then introduced an interesting complication. While making the judgment, observers moved in a series of self-selected patterns different from the one to be remembered. When moving their arms, observers identified arm differences more accurately, and conversely, when moving their legs, observers identified leg differences more accurately. Special cognition of bodies has also been seen in experiments comparing apparent motion of bodies and artifacts. For bodies but not for artifacts, at longer interstimulus intervals, the shortest path of motion is not reported if that would violate the biomechanics of body movement (Chatterjee, Freyd, & Shiffrar, 1996; Shiffrar & Freyd, 1993).

Body motion seems to underlie both these findings. Motion of body parts is intimately tied to function of body parts. Arm movements are critical to reaching, to crafting, to manipulating, to all the functions arms can do. Similarly, leg movements are critical to walking, kicking, and standing, some of the functions legs can do. Different sets of body motions are associated with different body functions. Legs and feet are involved in navigation, though they can also exert crude actions on objects, like kicking or trampling. Arms and hands are involved in manipulating objects and gesturing. Heads house the primary perceptual modes, and are involved in eating and communicating. The chest points forward, the primary direction of perception and motion. Body parts that perform more movements or functions are likely to be more significant body parts. Thus, a crude index of functional significance is the relative size on the sensorimotor map in the cortex, the popular homunculus with oversized hands and undersized back.

Certain body parts, typically head, arms, hand, legs, feet, backs, and fronts, are named in languages all over the world (Andersen, 1978; Brown, 1976). Notably, these are the parts children include in their early drawings of people, a large circle over a small one, with four sticks protruding, each with smaller protrusions (Goodnow, 1977; Kellogg, 1969). It stands to reason that the body parts more frequently named and drawn are more salient than others. Why are these parts more salient? Is it that they are larger? Or more distinctive from the contour of the body? Or more significant in our interactions with the world?

These alternatives – size, contour discontinuity, and significance – correspond to three theories of part recognition derived from theories of imagery or object recognition. The size theory derives from research on imagery. Participants were asked to image an animal, such as a tiger or a rabbit, and then asked to search the image to determine if it has a particular property, such as stripes (Kosslyn, 1980). Larger parts were verified faster than smaller ones, presumably because larger parts were detected faster. A theory derived from imagery would predict that larger parts, such as back or chest, are more salient than smaller ones, such as hand or foot. Some theories of object recognition maintain that objects are recognized by their parts, and that parts of objects are distinguished by discontinuities in their contours (e.g., Biederman, 1987; Hoffman & Richards, 1984). A discontinuity theory would predict that parts with greater contour discontinuity, such as head, hand, arm, leg, and foot, would be more salient than those with less contour discontinuity, such as chest and back. As part of their project on parts, Tversky and Hemenway (1984) collected norms on part goodness. Parts rated as good or significant tended to be both perceptually salient and functionally significant. For natural kinds and common objects, these were correlated, making it difficult to know which was critical. For example, the top of a table and the handle of a hammer are both perceptually salient and functionally significant. A theory based on part significance makes predictions similar to a theory based on part discontinuity; the exception for bodies is chest, which is relatively significant, but lacks discontinuity.

In our work on bodies, we asked a straightforward question (Morrison & Tversky, 1997). Which of these theories, size, discontinuity, or significance, best accounts for the time it takes to verify body parts? We selected those body parts commonly named across languages and sketched by young artists, head, arm, hand, chest (front), back, leg, and foot. There were two types of experiments: those that compared named body parts to body parts highlighted on a realistic rendering of a body and those that compared two bodies in different orientations, each with one part highlighted. Parts were highlighted with a white dot. Bodies were shown in profile in a variety of realistic postures and possible and impossible orientations. In both sets of studies, participants responded "same" when the named part was the same part as the highlighted part or when the two highlighted parts were the same, and responded "different" otherwise.

Body-part verification times

Image size failed as a theory in both kinds of experiments, the named part–body comparisons and the body–body comparisons, and in a third paradigm using disembodied parts. In fact, image size was negatively correlated with verification times, probably because it correlates negatively with both contour discontinuity and significance. Remember that the largest parts, "back" and "chest," are also the least discontinuous and low in significance.

The two remaining and correlated theories predicted verification times quite well. Intriguingly, for the body–body comparisons, contour discontinuity correlated better with part verification times but for the name–body comparisons, part significance correlated better. Qualitative aspects of the data support this. For the body–body comparisons, "chest," which lacks discontinuity but is relatively significant, was relatively slow, second-to-last; however, for the name–body comparisons, "chest" was relatively fast, second to head.

Why should significance predict body-part verification better when naming is entailed but discontinuity predict better when bodies are compared directly? When two bodies appear together on the screen, and the task is to say whether the white dot appears on the same or different parts, the bodies seem to be perceived just like any other object, as visual forms, shapes with part boundaries suggested by contour discontinuities. Searching for the dots and comparing across objects does not require any cognizance of what the objects or the parts are. When a named part appears to be compared with a highlighted part, the name itself must be comprehended and transformed into an expectation of a subshape bearing a constrained spatial relation to the whole. This comprehension and translation seems to activate functional features in addition to perceptual ones. For the name–body comparisons, then, part-verification speed seems to depend on mental representations of the body that reflect internal experience of the body.

Events

Let us now turn to categories encompassing some of the functions bodies fulfill: events. The world presents us with a continuous stream of activity which the mind parses into events. Like objects, they are bounded; they have beginnings, (middles,) and ends. Like objects, they are structured, composed of parts. However, in contrast to objects, events are structured in time. Uncovering the perceived structure of events was our first goal. We selected everyday, goal-directed events involving a single actor. While natural events like hurricanes happen independent of people, and human events may involve multiple actors with cooperative or conflicting goals, we took action by a single goal-directed agent as a reasonable prototype.

Perhaps because they are the stuff of life, events have attracted the interest of philosophers, statisticians, sociologists, and psychologists of all varieties, not to mention artists, writers, and poets. Cognitive scientists have studied top-down knowledge of events. Schank and Abelson (1977), Bower, Black, and Turner (1979) and others have observed that knowledge of events embedded in scripts allows inferences and understanding. Because we know that going to a restaurant includes being seated, ordering, and eating, we can understand why a hungry person heads for a restaurant, and why that person shouldn't be hungry afterwards. Script knowledge forms a partonomic hierarchy; each high-level activity of the restaurant script can be decomposed into parts. The driving force for the script view of events is a hierarchical goal structure. Going to a restaurant is a way to satisfy the goal of reducing hunger. Once the overall goal is chosen, the script entails subgoals, getting seated, ordering, and so on.

Social psychologists have developed a powerful set of techniques for studying bottom-up perception of events. They have asked not just how events are conceived, but how they are perceived as they unfold. In a typical task, observers segment continuous activity into either coarse or fine natural units, called breakpoints. Breakpoints are thought to be cued by perceived large changes in physical activity (Newtson, 1973). One issue is whether perception of events is hierarchical. If perceivers actively encode events in terms of hierarchically organized schemas, breakpoints at a coarse time scale should coincide with breakpoints at a fine time scale. Some maintain that this is the case (e.g., Newtson, 1973; Newtson, Hairfield, Bloomingdale, & Cutino, 1987); others maintain that event unit boundaries are flexible, altered by momentary schemas (e.g., Cohen & Ebbesen, 1979).

To study the cognitive structure of events, we first sought to determine whether mundane events are perceived hierarchically. We began with a principled way of choosing events and a principled way of evaluating hierarchical structure, based both on the breakpoint technique and the language of description (Zacks & Tversky, 1997; Zacks, Tversky, & Iyer, 2001). It is possible that coarse units will be distinguished by goals and fine units by changes in physical activity, so that the breakpoints of these may not coincide. To select events to study, we asked undergraduates to rate a large set of events taken from previous norms and other sources on frequency and familiarity. From them, we chose two familiar events, making a bed and doing the dishes, and two unfamiliar events, fertilizing a plant and assembling a saxophone, which could be easily filmed from a fixed camera.

By tapping a key to indicate breakpoints, observers segmented the filmed events twice, once into the coarsest units that made sense and once into the finest units that made sense (in counterbalanced order). Some observers described the activity of each segment as they segmented, and others only segmented. To determine if segmentation was hierarchical, the breakpoints of fine and coarse units were compared for each observer. Hierarchical segmentation is indicated by greater than chance coincidence of coarse unit boundaries to fine unit boundaries.

Indeed, the analysis of coincidences supported hierarchical segmentation of the events. Moreover, describing the segments while parsing led to a higher degree of hierarchical segmentation than silent parsing, despite the fact that segmenting and describing take more cognitive resources than simply segmenting. The greater perceived hierarchical structure is probably due to greater top-down conceptualization induced by describing. There was a smaller effect of event familiarity: parsing of familiar events yielded a greater degree of hierarchical structure.

The analysis of the descriptions of coarse and fine segments supported hierarchical perception of events. Consider, for example, one participant's transcript for making a bed. The coarse unit description began: "walking in," "taking apart the bed," "putting on the sheet," "putting on the other sheet," "putting on the blanket." The coarse unit "putting on the sheet" consisted of the following fine units: "putting on the top end of the sheet," "putting on the bottom," "unfolding sheet," "laying it down," "straightening it out." Note that each coarse unit entails interacting with a different object. By contrast, each fine unit involves interacting in a different way with the same object, usually indicated by a different verb. Statistical analyses supported these observations. In fine units, objects were referred to more vaguely than in coarse units, often by use of pronouns or omission, and actions more specifically. For both coarse and fine units, the descriptive language was intentional and goal-directed, consisting of actions on objects. The analysis of language illuminates why top-down and bottom-up segmentation of events correlate. Interacting with different objects is likely to entail both different goals and different physical activity. Similarly, changing the mode of interacting with the same object is likely to entail different subgoals as well as different actions. Thus breaks in activity are likely to correspond to breaks in goals and subgoals.

Implications for imitation

In imitation, one body perceives the actions of another and produces them. The path from perception to performance is complex and mysterious. The discoveries of automatic copying of action in certain apraxias (Goldenberg & Hermsdoerfer, this volume) and single neurons responsive to both perception and production of the same action (Rizzolatti, Fadiga, Fogassi, & Gallese, this volume) suggest that copying action sequences may be hard-wired. Yet what is imitated is not a sequence of actions. From the first hours of life, imitations seem to be modulated toward goals (Meltzoff & Moore, 1995). Intentional imitations by young children copy the effects on objects, the goals, though they may not copy the actions (Bekkering, Wohlschläger, & Gattis, 2000; Meltzoff, 1995). Much of the research reported in this volume suggests that humans and other animals represent activity in a format that supports both perception and action. Our work suggests that these representations capture structure at a fairly abstract level. Rather than representing sequences of actions, what seems to be represented are configural features of the body that reflect our experiences in bodies and configural features of events that reflect our experiences as goal-seeking creatures.

Interweaving categories: objects, bodies, events, and scenes

We began by considering the paradigmatic case of objects, then turned to qualitative features distinguishing kinds of categories, here, bodies and the events they partake in. Bodies and objects play critical roles in segmentation of events. Consistent with this view are Byrne's and Whiten's (this volume) results on objects in gorilla and child imitation, Goldenberg and Hagmann's (1998) observations of apraxics unable to infer tool use, and Jellema, Baker, Oram, and Perrett's and Rizzolatti, Fadiga,

Fogassi, and Gallese's (both this volume) discovery of neurons in monkeys responsive to actions on objects. For infants, too, actions on objects appear to be critical for inferring intentions and segmenting events (Baldwin & Baird, 1996; Meltzoff, 1995; Meltzoff & Moore, 1998; Sharon & Wynn, 1998; Woodward, 1998). These separate categories, bodies, events, and objects, are intimately intertwined, and further intertwined with categories of scenes, the settings for events. Body parts that are functional in actions are more salient; events – goal-directed sequences of actions – are segmented by objects and actions on objects; scenes are characterized by the objects they contain and the activities they support. Cognition of central categories is not just embodied, it is embedded.

Acknowledgments

Harold Bekkering, Cathy Reed, and Wolfgang Prinz provided extensive and illuminating comments on an earlier draft, for which we are grateful.

References

Andersen, E. S. (1978). Lexical universals of body-part terminology. In J. H. Greenberg (Ed.), *Universals of human language* (pp. 335–368). Stanford: Stanford University Press.

Baldwin, D., & Baird, J. A. (1996). Action analysis: A gateway to intentional inference. In P. Rochat (Ed.), *Early social cognition* (pp. 215–240). Hillsdale, NJ: Erlbaum.

Bekkering, H., Wohlschläger, A., & Gattis, M. (2000). Imitation of gestures in children is goal-directed. *Quarterly Journal of Experimental Psychology: Section A: Human Psychology, 53A,* 153–164.

Biederman, I. (1987). Recognition-by-components: A theory of human image understanding. *Psychological Review, 94,* 115–147.

Bloom, P. (1996). Intention, history, and artifact concepts. *Cognition, 60,* 1–29.

Bower, G. H., Black, J. B., & Turner, T. J. (1979). Scripts in memory for text. *Cognitive Psychology, 11,* 177–220.

Brown, C. H. (1976). General principles of human anatomical partonomy and speculations on the growth of partonomic nomenclature. *American Ethnologist, 3,* 400–424.

Cantor, N., & Mischel, W. (1979). Prototypes in person perception. In L. Berkowitz (Ed.), *Advances in experimental social psychology* (Vol. 12). New York: Academic Press.

Carey, S. (1986). *Conceptual change in childhood.* Cambridge, MA: MIT Press.

Chatterjee, S. H., Freyd, J. J., & Shiffrar, M. (1996). Configural processing in the perception of apparent biological motion. *Journal of Experimental Psychology: Human Perception and Performance, 22,* 916–929.

Cohen, C. E., & Ebbesen, E. B. (1979). Observational goals and schema activation: A theoretical framework for behavior perception. *Journal of Experimental Social Psychology, 15*, 305–329.

Ekman, P. (1984). Expression and nature of emotion. In K. Scherer & P. Ekman (Eds.), *Approaches to emotion* (pp. 319–343). Hillsdale, NJ: Erlbaum.

Gelman, S. A. (1988). The development of induction within natural kind and artifact categories. *Cognitive Psychology, 20*, 65–95.

Goldenberg, G., & Hagmann, S. (1998). Tool use and mechanical problem solving in apraxia. *Neuropsychologia, 36*, 581–589.

Goodnow, J. (1977). *Children's drawing.* London: Open Books. Sequence Convention.

Hoffman, D. D., & Richards, W. A. (1984). Parts of recognition. *Cognition, 18*, 65–96.

Izard, C. E. (1992). Basic emotions, relations among emotions, and emotion-cognition relations. *Psychological Review, 99*, 561–565.

Keil, F. C. (1989). *Concepts, kinds, and cognitive development.* Cambridge, MA: MIT Press.

Keil, F. C., & Batterman, N. (1984). A characteristic-to-defining shift in the development of word meaning. *Journal of Verbal Learning and Verbal Behavior, 23*, 221–236.

Kellogg, R. (1969). *Analyzing children's art.* Palo Alto, CA: National Press.

Kosslyn, S. M. (1980). *Image and mind.* Cambridge, MA: Harvard University Press.

Malt, B. C., & Johnson, E. C. (1992). Do artifact concepts have cores? *Journal of Memory and Language, 31*, 195–217.

Medin, D. L. (1989). Concepts and conceptual structure. *American Psychologist, 44*, 1469–1481.

Meltzoff, A. N. (1995). Understanding the intentions of others: Re-enactment of intended acts by 18-month-old children. *Developmental Psychology, 31*, 838–850.

Meltzoff, A. N., & Moore, M. K. (1995). Infant's understanding of people and things: From body imitation to folk psychology. In J. L. Bermúdez, A. Marcel, & N. Eilan (Eds.), *The body and the self* (pp. 43–69). Cambridge, MA: MIT Press.

(1998). Object representation, identity, and the paradox of early permanence: Steps toward a new framework. *Infant Behavior and Development, 21*, 201–235.

Miller, G. A., & Johnson-Laird, P. N. (1976). *Language and perception.* Cambridge, MA: Harvard University Press.

Morris, M. W., & Murphy, G. L. (1990). Converging operations on a basic level in event taxonomies. *Memory and Cognition, 18*, 407–418.

Morrison, J. B., & Tversky, B. (1997). Body schemas. *Proceedings of the Meetings of the Cognitive Science Society* (pp. 525–529). Mahwah, NJ: Erlbaum.

Newtson, D. (1973). Attribution and the unit of perception of ongoing behavior. *Journal of Personality and Social Psychology, 28*, 28–38.

Newtson, D., Hairfield, J., Bloomingdale, J., & Cutino, S. (1987). The structure of action and interaction. *Social Cognition, 5*, 191–237.

Plutchik, R. (1993). Emotions and their vicissitudes: Emotions and psychopathology. In M. Lewis & J. M. Haviland (Eds.), *Handbook of emotions* (pp. 53–65). New York: Guilford.

Reed, C. L., & Farah, M. J. (1995). The psychological reality of the body schema: A test with normal participants. *Journal of Experimental Psychology: Human Perception and Performance, 21,* 334–343.

Rifkin, A. (1985). Evidence for a basic level in event taxonomies. *Memory and Cognition, 13,* 538–556.

Rips, L. J. (1989). Similarity, typicality, and categorization. In S. Vosniadou & A. Ortony (Eds.), *Similarity and analogical reasoning* (pp. 21–59). Cambridge: Cambridge University Press.

Rosch, E. (1975). The nature of mental codes for color categories. *Journal of Experimental Psychology: Human Perception and Performance, 1,* 303–322. (1978). Principles of categorization. In E. Rosch & B. B. Lloyd (Eds.), *Cognition and categorization* (pp. 27–48). Hillsdale, NJ: Erlbaum.

Rosch, E., & Mervis, C. B. (1975). Family resemblance studies in the internal structure of categories. *Cognitive Psychology, 7,* 573–605.

Rosch, E., Mervis, C. B., Gray, W., Johnson, D., & Boyes-Braem, P. (1976). Basic objects in natural categories. *Cognitive Psychology, 8,* 382–439.

Schank, R., & Abelson, R. (1977). Scripts, plans, goals, and understanding. Hillsdale, NJ: Erlbaum.

Sharon, T., & Wynn, K. (1998). Individuation of actions from continuous motion. *Psychological Science, 9,* 357–362.

Shiffrar, M., & Freyd, J. J. (1993). Timing and apparent motion path choice with human body photographs. *Psychological Science, 4,* 379–384.

Smith, E. E., & Medin, D. L. (1981). *Categories and concepts.* Cambridge, MA: Harvard University Press.

Soja, N. N., Carey, S., & Spelke, E. S. (1991). Ontological categories guide young children's inductions of word meaning: Object terms and substance terms. *Cognition, 38,* 179–211.

Tversky, B., & Hemenway, K. (1983). Categories of scenes. *Cognitive Psychology, 15,* 121–149.

Tversky, B., & Hemenway, K. (1984). Objects, parts and categories. *Journal of Experimental Psychology: General, 113,* 169–193.

Wittgenstein, L. (1958). *Philosophical investigations.* Oxford: Basil Blackwell.

Woodward, A. L. (1998). Infants selectively encode the goal object of an actor's reach. *Cognition, 69,* 1–34.

Zacks, J., & Tversky, B. (1997). What's happening? The structure of event perception. In M. G. Shafto & P. Langley (Eds.), *Proceedings of the Nineteenth Annual Conference of the Cognitive Science Society* (p. 1095). Mahwah, NJ: Erlbaum.

Zacks, J., Tversky, B., & Iyer, G. (2001). Perceiving, remembering and communicating structure in events. *Journal of Experimental Psychology: General.*

13   What is the body schema?

Catherine L. Reed

What is the body schema?

All of us have a stable perception of our body. We know whether we are sitting or standing, whether our left hand covers our right, and whether our feet are currently higher than our knees. Our sense of body not only includes its current configuration, but also knowledge of the relative locations of its parts and what actions it can perform. Despite our intimate knowledge of bodies, neurological and psychological research present conflicting pictures regarding the properties of our body representations. The term "body schema" has been used to refer to both general body knowledge and immediate body perception. These two concepts are typically confounded in the literature, leading to much confusion over the nature of the body schema. This chapter emphasizes and elucidates the different characteristics of the body schema and body percept. The distinction between these two concepts helps clarify current uncertainty regarding the neural substrates of body representation, contributions from sensory inputs to body representations, and distinctions between body and object representations.

"Body schema" has been frequently used to refer to long-term, organized knowledge about the spatial characteristics of human bodies. Taken in this sense, it refers to a particular class of long-term representations and can be placed in juxtaposition to other object representations. In this chapter, body schema denotes this type of representation. The body schema includes the invariant properties of the human body. For example, it stores information about the spatial relations among body parts, the degrees of freedom for movement at joints, and knowledge of body function. It is also supramodal in that it exists independent of modality-specific processing. Since it contains information relevant to all bodies, the body schema is used to represent others as well as the self.

However, "body schema" has also been used to refer to an entirely different concept referring to the particular body position that is being perceived at a certain point in time. In this chapter, "body percept" refers to this instance of immediate body perception. Sensory inputs from multiple senses modify the body percept and update it to keep track of current body positions and current locations of sensation. The body percept is dynamic. More importantly, the body percept represents the self exclusively because it contains privileged information about present body status, sensory feedback, and motor intention for performing actions in the environment. In other words, the body percept is *"referenced for personal action."*

Neurological evidence for body-specific representations

Neurologists first introduced the concept of a separate mental representation for the human body to account for a variety of selective impairments in spatial body perception following brain damage, such as finger agnosia, autotopagnosia, hemispatial neglect, and ideomotor apraxia (Frederiks, 1985). However, the traditional concept of "body schema" does little to explain common mechanisms underlying the disrupted behaviors. Distinguishing between the body schema and body percept brings order to these diverse impairments.

Brain damage can produce a deficit in the identification of body parts. Finger agnosia is usually associated with left parietal damage, and specifically with the angular gyrus. It is characterized as an inability to recognize, identify, differentiate, name, select, and orient the fingers on the individual's own hands as well as on another person's hands (Gerstmann, 1957). This difficulty with fingers is disproportionate to the difficulty encountered with other complex stimuli.

In addition, brain damage can produce an inability to localize body parts. Autotopagnosia, or somatotopagnosia, is the inability to locate body parts on the body, despite relatively intact spatial ability. Although it is rare, it appears to be associated with left-hemisphere parietal lesions and tumors (De Renzi & Scotti, 1970; Ogden, 1985). Autotopagnosic patients know that they have bodies, know where garments are typically worn, and remember where small objects were once placed on their bodies. They can recognize body parts individually, demonstrating that the problem is not with knowledge about the parts themselves or their perception. They can name body parts when an experimenter points to them, showing that the problem is not linguistic. What these patients cannot do is locate a part in the context of a whole body – whether the body is theirs, an experimenter's, or a doll's. Several recent cases of autotopagnosia have also reported that the deficit is specific to the body and is not a more general impaired ability to locate parts of complex objects. Further, autotopagnosia is not limited to the visual modality. A patient described by

Ogden (1985) could not localize a particular body part when he looked for it or when he closed his eyes and felt for it. This implies that the body schema is supramodal in that it represents the locations of both seen and felt body parts.

Brain damage can produce a loss of awareness for parts of one's body. Spatial neglect typically involves a right parietal lesion and produces an inability to represent or attend to the side of space contralateral to the lesion. Patients with neglect may ignore half of external space. Patients with personal neglect only dress or groom the ipsilesional side of their bodies. Case and group studies have demonstrated a double dissociation: spatial neglect can occur for the human body and not for objects in the external environment, and vice versa (Guariglia & Antonucci, 1992; Halligan & Marshall, 1991; Bisiach, Perani, Vallar, & Berti, 1986). These data suggest that attention to the body can be selectively impaired. Nonetheless, patients with personal neglect have intact knowledge about the spatial relations among their body parts, as they can locate parts of their body on the non-neglected side.

Last, brain damage can impair topographic knowledge about the human body. Ideomotor apraxia is associated with left parietal damage. Patients with ideomotor apraxia are impaired on the imitation of meaningless gestures (see Goldenberg & Hermsdoerfer's chapter in the present volume). Goldenberg (1997) proposes that general topographic knowledge about the human body mediates the transition from visual perception to motor execution. This reduces the visually perceived details of the gesture to simple relationships between several relevant body parts. Apraxic patients have difficulty translating a meaningless gesture's visual appearance in terms of the human body and make errors creating correspondences between the demonstrated gesture and their own motor output.

For any of these body representation deficits, patients never lose the perception of their bodies completely. This suggests that there may be different underlying neural substrates or mechanisms producing these deficits. Distinguishing the body schema from the body percept helps separate them. Finger agnosia and autotopagnosia suggest an impairment of long-term knowledge about the spatial relations among body parts that can be selectively impaired. This body schema is supramodal, in that it can be impaired regardless of input modality and it is used to represent both the self and others. The parietal lobes, especially the left parietal lobe, appear to play a major role in the construction of the body schema. In contrast, neglect and ideomotor apraxia describe deficits in the current perception of spatial relationships among body parts, or the body percept. The concept of the body percept is consistent with one theory of neglect that postulates that patients lose their multisensory representation for which to perform motor actions (see Bradshaw & Mattingley, 1995).

Sensory contributions to body representations

One assumption underlying the traditional body schema is that it is constructed from previous and current visual, tactile, proprioceptive, and vestibular sensations (Frederiks, 1985). However, this assumption does not emphasize the importance of distinguishing between past and present sensory contributions. In the terminology used in this chapter, the body schema represents multimodal sensations from past experiences only. In contrast, the body percept is in the present and dynamic. It incorporates the information from the body schema with current multisensory input and feedback. Sensory inputs not only provide information about the actual position and configuration of one's body, but also are used to update the body percept as different body parts are moved. Visual input informs us of the relative position of our body parts and our actions. Proprioceptive input allows us to monitor changes in our body position. The perception of the spatial relationships among body parts depends on the interaction of activity in joint receptors, muscle afferent signals, and topographically organized cortical maps of somatosensation.

A good illustration of how current sensory information can influence the body percept comes from Lackner (1988). The experiments used vibration to induce illusory motion. Participants' perception of the length of different body parts was affected by the apparent position of other body parts. For example, if the participant held his nose and the tricept brachii were vibrated, the participant perceived a lengthening of the nose. It appears that the body percept is computed from the interaction of muscle movement and body-part position relative to other body parts. In this case, the only solution that met the biological constraints of the system was the lengthening of the nose. Thus, the current perceptual representation of the body, or the body percept, is highly labile. It is constructed from both the long-term body schema and immediate sensory input.

In contrast, the body schema helps explain how an organized representation of the body can exist independently of sensory input. The phantom limb phenomenon provides a paradigm example of the body schema. After amputation, many individuals experience sensations of movement, position, and pain, as if the limb still existed. Because there are no sensory receptors, any kinesthetic sensation that an amputee may associate with voluntary attempts to flex or extend a phantom joint must arise internally. The experience of a phantom limb also does not require a developmental history of sensory input. In a study of thirty cases of aplasia, the congenital absence of limbs, 17 per cent experienced a phantom limb (Weinstein & Sersen, 1961). The fact that a representation exists for limbs that the person has never experienced suggests that the body schema may be partly innate, in the sense that it is not completely shaped by sensory experience.

Nonetheless, we use both our body schema and body percept to perform everyday actions, such as reaching for an object. It is the dynamic interplay of invariant body knowledge and current sensory feedback that updates the appropriate control variables and permits an action goal to be achieved. Evidence for interactions between the body percept and body schema comes from the fact that sensory experience influences the body schema. The reported frequency of phantom limb occurrence is higher the older a person is when the amputation occurs. The phantom limb phenomenon is experienced by a majority of adult amputees, but it is rare in children who have limbs amputated before six years of age or in children with aplasia. This difference would suggest that, in spite of being partly innate, the body schema is enhanced by continuing experience with the intact body. Thus, sensory input is important to the body percept, but not necessary for the existence of the body schema. In sum, the perception of the body and its parts results from an interaction between the relatively stable body schema which is not dependent upon current sensory input, and the body percept that relies on more transient processes such as sensory inputs.

Are body representations different from other object representations?

The distinction between the body schema and the body percept also helps clarify differences between body and other object representations. If body percepts and body schemas were considered together, the dynamic, self-oriented, privileged nature of the body percept could lead one to the potentially erroneous conclusion that bodies are represented differently from other objects. By focusing on the body schema alone, we can make more accurate comparisons between two types of representations that encode invariant properties.

The human body shares many features with other types of objects. Like many objects, the body has a visual hierarchical structure that is articulated and has a canonical orientation. It can also be manipulated and perform a variety of functions. However, is the body schema treated differently from other object representations in the cognitive architecture? The mere fact that the body schema can be selectively impaired by brain damage suggests the existence of a representation of the body separate from other object representations. Nonetheless, there are other reasons to believe that the body schema is a distinct representation from other objects.

Morrison and Tversky (1997; see Tversky, Morrison, & Zacks, this volume) have proposed a framework as a means for evaluating the relevance of current object recognition theories for body representations. One way that people may represent objects is by their visual characteristics, such as the size of part or concavities in the form. Another way that people may represent objects is by their functional properties, either by the action they perform or the amount of cortical representation they demand. Morrison and Tversky investigated relationships between language and the structure of body representations. Subjects were presented visually with a word naming a body part followed by a picture of a human body with a highlighted body part. They determined whether the named body part was the same as the highlighted part. In general, subjects responded more quickly for parts that performed functional activities and that were visually distinct from other parts. Thus, body representations may be organized by both visual and functional properties.

In my lab we used a different paradigm to investigate whether the body was represented differently from other types of objects. Our goal was to examine body representations without the organizing contributions of language. Using canonical line drawings of a human body, an animate object (a bear), and an inanimate object (a bike), we divided the drawings into various part combinations permitting participants to choose any categorization strategy. Participants performed a sorting task in which they placed parts that were similar into the same category. Our results indicated that the body was treated differently from the other objects. The body was organized primarily by functional properties. Arm, leg, and head categories were most salient. The other types of objects were organized by both functional and visual properties. After the body, the bike had more functional categories than the bear. What seemed to differentiate performance among the objects was the extent of functional experience people had with the objects. The more experience, the greater the functional categorization. Thus, the body schema may differ from other object representations in terms of experience. The fact that we perform multiple actions every day using our bodies means we have more experience with bodies than with other objects.

In a different study, we demonstrated that body-specific interactions between vision and proprioception occurred only for body stimuli and not for complex objects (Reed & Farah, 1995). We used a dual-task paradigm that evoked the body schema and body percept together. Participants determined whether the body position of a human model had changed while they were making nonrepetitive arm or leg movements. The proprioceptive information participants received from moving their own body part relatively facilitated performance when they attended the same body part on another person as the one they moved. However, when the target stimuli were changed from human models to complex block objects, proprioceptive information had no effect on the visual perception of block configurations.

In sum, although the body schema shares many characteristics with other object representations, it is different from them along a number of dimensions. Part of this difference may be due to the contributions of the body percept to the body schema. We have extensive experience using our bodies that is unmatched by experience with other objects. Our body schema includes privileged information from past multisensory bodily experiences obtained through the body percept. We use this visual, vestibular, somatosensory, and proprioceptive information to process information about other bodies as well as our own bodies. Last, the body schema is likely to be partly innate, in the sense of not being completely determined by experience, whereas schemas for other objects are probably not.

Contributions of body representations to perception and behavior

Differences between body and object representations have implications for their use in a variety of behaviors. First, the body schema and body percept may be important for understanding and perceiving the motion of other human bodies and other events involving the body. Knowledge of body-part relations and movement constrains and influences our perception of events involving the body. The body schema is used to constrain perceptual inputs regarding other people's bodies and movement to permit further interpretive analysis. The use of the body schema to constrain the visual perception of apparent motion was found by Shiffrar and Freyd (1993). Pitting shortest-path solutions against anatomically plausible solutions, they found that people tended to report alterations in the body position of human and human-like forms as moving in anatomically plausible paths. This is in contrast to other objects that typically are perceived as following the shortest path of apparent motion. These results indicate that people tend to use knowledge about the movement of bodies to perform tasks involving the spatial transformation of human forms.

Similarly, the body schema may be used to interpret human actions from impoverished visual information (e.g., Cutting & Proffitt, 1981; Thornton, Pinto, & Shiffrar, 1998). In light-point walker displays, observers see only points of light located on the joints of a moving body. Provided with only moving light information, observers can recognize friends, differentiate gender, and identify various actions. The perception of biological motion is disrupted when displays are static, upside down, or have lights mounted off the joints. To achieve these complex perceptions of human bodies in action, the observer must bring to perception some representation of body-part relations and knowledge about how human joints and limbs constrain movement.

By postulating interactions between the body schema and the body percept, we can understand the current spatial relationships between the self and other's bodies. Parsons (1987) investigated imagined spatial transformations of body parts in a task that used both the body schema and the body percept. Subjects were visually presented with a rotated human figure and they determined whether the left or right arm was extended. Increases in response times for left-right judgments of body parts reflected the disparity between the stimulus orientation and the observer. They also reflected biologically constrained, but nonefficient, rotational paths through which the imagined bodies were spatially transformed. Participants spontaneously used biologically possible trajectories to mentally simulate the movement of a personal body part to match the stimulus target position.

Second, body representations may be important for learning new skills through imitation. Imitation unites the perception of another human's action with one's own production of that action. The body schema provides the basis for knowing that one's own body is like someone else's body and can perform the same actions (Meltzoff & Moore, 1994, 1997). An implication of Meltzoff's theory is that during imitation an interaction between body schema and body percept occurs, even for very young infants. Infants can successfully imitate gestures using correct body parts and can recognize that they are being imitated. These findings suggest infants have body representations. Moreover, the fact that infants can imitate after delays and the fact that they show improvement in successive imitation attempts demonstrate that infant body representations are more than currently activated representations from sensory input. Meltzoff and colleagues propose that successful imitation is accomplished by merging motor output from the infant's own body with the visual perception of another body. The body arena provides a representational space within which the cross-modal matching is processed. When successfully imitating another body position or movement, a correspondence between the self and another person is obtained and a goal is achieved. The inferred goals of the observed behaviors appear to be what is most important for the learning of new skills (see Meltzoff, and Gattis, Bekkering,

& Wohlschläger, in this volume). A connection between the action sequence to be performed and the salient outcome of that action promotes successful imitation and learning.

Third, the interaction between the body schema and body percept may provide the means for developing an understanding of commonalities between the self and others. The mechanisms creating this self–other correspondence are not only important for learning new skills, but also for transmitting social information. There is good ecological reason to be able to recognize like species and to distinguish threatening postures from others early in life. Imitative movement by newborns is hypothesized to influence the development of spatial abilities, communication, and self-awareness (Meltzoff & Moore, 1994). Newborns show development in understanding the social relevance of the relationship between themselves and others. Meltzoff and Moore (1997) argue that the basis of social cognition may be rooted in the initial cross-modal equivalence between the self and other found in newborns.

Imitation can be a discovery procedure for understanding the actions of people. As a result of experience with our own bodies, bodies are predictable in terms of how they move and what can be accomplished with them. This personal experience provides us with insight into the goals and intents of other bodies that we perceive. The ability to infer motor intent from the postures and actions of others provides additional social and survival benefits. Our knowledge of our own bodies allows us to know that others are "like me" (Meltzoff & Moore, 1997), thereby forming the basis for skill acquisition and social interaction.

Research with adults suggests that interactions between the body schema and body percept continue to help the formation of self–other correspondences throughout the life span. Reed and Farah (1995) investigated whether a common body schema was used to process body-relevant information in the self and others. They found that personal body positioning, relative to another's position, influenced memory for the other person's body position. To demonstrate that the same body schema was used for the self and others, they used a dual-task paradigm. The primary task was a memory task for a body configuration. While performing the memory task, participants performed a secondary task in which they posed either their own arms or their own legs into a series of nonrepetitive positions that could not match the memory pose at any time. Thus, a representation of the model's body position was necessary for the primary task and a representation of personal body position was required for the secondary task. Evidence that the same body schema was used for the self and others came from the fact that performance of the secondary task influenced performance on the primary task. This correspondence may arise from the internal spatial organization of the body schema as well as from the fact that together the body schema and body percept integrate visual information about another person's body position with the proprioceptive information one receives about the position of one's own body.

Conclusions

The "body schema" is not a unitary concept. By distinguishing between the body schema and body percept, we can account for various neurological disorders and better understand the representations underlying perceptions and events involving the body and its actions. The body schema interacts with body percepts to permit translations between external and internal senses and produce organized, meaningful perceptions of the self and of others (Gallagher & Meltzoff, 1996). Together they allow a history of body experiences to influence current perceptions of spatial body information and permit intentional motor actions. The separation of the body schema from the body percept not only provides insights into existing research, but it also defines issues for future research. For example, little is known about the specific conditions under which the body schema and the body percept are evoked and how the body schema is modified through interactions with the body percept. Thus, when we ask the question "what is the body schema?" we must also ask "what is the body percept?"

References

Bisiach, E., Perani, D., Vallar, G., & Berti, A. (1986). Unilateral neglect: Personal and extrapersonal. *Neuropsychologia, 24,* 759–767.

Bradshaw, J. L., & Mattingley, J. B. (1995). *Clinical neuropsychology: Behavioral and brain science.* New York: Academic Press.

Cutting, J. E., & Proffitt, D. (1981). Gait perception as an example of how we may perceive events. In R. Walk & H. Pick (Eds.), *Intersensory perception and sensory integration* (pp. 249–273). New York: Plenum.

De Renzi, E., & Scotti, G. (1970). Autotopagnosia: fiction or reality? Report of a case. *Archives of Neurology, 23,* 221–227.

Frederiks, J. A. M. (1985). Disorders of the body schema. In J. A. M. Frederiks, (Ed.), *Handbook of clinical neuropsychology: Vol. 1* (pp. 373–393). Amsterdam: Elsevier Science Publications.

Gallagher, S., & Meltzoff, A. N. (1996). The earliest sense of self and others: Merleau-Ponty and recent developmental studies. *Philosophical Psychology, 9,* 211–233.

Gerstmann, J. (1957). Some notes on the Gerstmann Syndrome. *Neurology, 7,* 866–869.

Goldenberg, G. (1997). Disorders of body perception. In T. E. Feinberg & M. J. Farah (Eds.), *Behavioral Neurology and Neuropsychology* (pp. 289–296). New York: McGraw-Hill.

Guariglia, C., & Antonucci, G. (1992). Personal and extrapersonal space: A case of neglect dissociation. *Neuropsychologia, 30,* 1001–1009.

Halligan, P. W., & Marshall, J. C. (1991). Left neglect for near but not far space in man. *Nature, 350,* 498–500.

Lackner, J. R. (1988). Some proprioceptive influences on the perceptual representation of body shape and orientation. *Brain, 111,* 281–297.

Meltzoff, A. N., & Moore, M. K. (1994). Imitation, memory, and the representation of persons. *Infant Behavior and Development, 17,* 83–99.

(1997). Explaining facial imitation: A theoretical model. *Early Development and Parenting, 6,* 179–192.

Morrison, J. B., & Tversky, B. (1997). Body schemas. *Proceedings of the Nineteenth Annual Conference of the Cognitive Science Society* (pp. 525–529). Hillsdale, NJ: Lawrence Erlbaum.

Ogden, J. A. (1985). Autotopagnosia: Occurrence in a patient with nominal aphasia and with an intact ability to point to parts of animals and objects. *Brain, 108,* 1009–1022.

Parsons, L. M. (1987). Imagined spatial transformation of one's body. *Journal of Experimental Psychology: General, 116,* 172–191.

Reed, C. L., & Farah, M. J. (1995). The psychological reality of the body schema: A test with normal participants. *Journal of Experimental Psychology: Human Perception and Performance, 21,* 334–343.

Shiffrar, M., & Freyd, J. J. (1993). Timing and apparent motion path choice with human body photographs. *Psychological Science, 4,* 379–384.

Thornton, I. M., Pinto, J., & Shiffrar, M. (1998). The visual perception of human locomotion. *Cognitive Neuropsychology, 15,* 535–552.

Weigstein, S., & Sersen, E. A. (1961). Phantoms in cases of congenital absence of limbs. *Neurology, 11,* 905–911.

Part III

Neuroscience underpinnings of imitation and apraxia

14   From mirror neurons to imitation: Facts and speculations

*Giacomo Rizzolatti, Luciano Fadiga, Leonardo Fogassi,
and Vittorio Gallese*

Introduction

This chapter is composed of two parts. In the first we review the functional properties of an intriguing class of premotor neurons that we discovered in the monkey premotor cortex: the "mirror neurons." These neurons discharge both when the monkey performs an action and when it observes another individual making a similar action. The second part is basically speculative. It is based on the hypothesis that there is a very general, evolutionary ancient mechanism, that we will name "resonance" mechanism, through which pictorial descriptions of motor behaviors are matched directly on the observer's motor "representations" of the same behaviors. We will posit that resonance mechanism is a fundamental mechanism at the basis of inter-individual relations including some behaviors commonly described under the heading of "imitation."

Functional properties of area F5

Motor properties

Area F5 forms the rostral part of inferior area 6 (Matelli *et al.*, 1985). Microstimulation and single-neuron studies showed that F5 contains a hand and a mouth movement representation (Gentilucci *et al.*, 1988; Hepp-Reymond, Husler, Maier, & Qi, 1994; Okano & Tanji, 1987; Rizzolatti *et al.*, 1981; Rizzolatti *et al.*, 1988). Particularly interesting results were obtained when F5 neurons were studied in a semi-naturalistic context (Rizzolatti *et al.*, 1988). Awake monkeys were seated on a primate chair and presented with various objects (geometrical solids, pieces of food of different size and shape). The stimuli were introduced in various spatial locations around the monkey, inside and outside its peripersonal space. After object presentation, the monkey was allowed to reach and grasp the objects.

The results confirmed that most neurons become active in relation to distal movements. In addition, they showed also that, typically, the neuron discharge correlates much better with an action or with fragments of an action (motor acts) rather than with the individual movements that form it. Thus, many neurons discharge when an action (e.g., grasping) is performed with effectors as different as the right hand, the left hand, or the mouth. Furthermore, in most cases, the same movements which are effective in triggering a neuron when executed during a specific type of grasping (i.e., precision grip), are not effective during grasping made with a different grip or during nongrasping movements.

These properties markedly differentiate F5 neurons from most neurons located in area F1 (area 4). Neurons in the latter area discharge in association with specific movements regardless of their aim and the context in which they are executed (see Porter & Lemon, 1993). Properties similar to those of F1 neurons appear to be present also in the posterior subdivision of areas F2 and in area F3 (see Wise, 1985; Wiesendanger et al., 1987; Tanji, 1994, 1996).

By using action as classification criterion, F5 neurons were subdivided into the following main categories: "grasping-with-the-hand-and-the-mouth" neurons, "grasping-with-the-hand" neurons, "holding" neurons, "tearing" neurons, "poking" neurons, and "manipulating" neurons. Grasping neurons were the neuron type most represented (Rizzolatti et al., 1988).

Grasping is a complex action characterized by an initial opening phase, during which fingers are shaped according to the object's physical properties (size, shape) and the wrist is adapted to object orientation, and a second, closure phase, where fingers are flexed around the object until they touch it (Jeannerod, 1984). The type of hand shape depends on the size and shape of the object to be grasped (see Arbib, 1981; Jeannerod, 1988).

There are three grip types that monkeys most frequently use. They are: "precision grip," i.e., opposition of the thumb to the index finger (used for grasping small objects); "finger prehension," i.e., opposition of the thumb to the other fingers (used to grasp middle-size objects or to retrieve them from a narrow container); "whole-hand (or power) prehension," i.e., opposition of the fingers to the palm (used to grasp large objects). Neurons were recorded while monkeys grasped objects using these three grip types. The results showed that the large majority (85 per cent) of grasping neurons are selective for one of the three main grip types. The most represented type is precision grip, the least represented is whole-hand prehension.

Visual properties

The motor properties of F5 that were just described are found in all F5 neurons studied so far. There is, however, a certain percentage of them that responds to visual stimuli (Murata *et al.*, 1997; Rizzolatti *et al.*, 1988). These visuomotor neurons fall into two separate categories. Neurons of the first category, besides discharging during active movements, discharge also when the monkey observes graspable objects ("canonical neurons," Rizzolatti & Fadiga, 1998). These neurons play a crucial role in object-to-hand movement transformations (see Jeannerod, Arbib, Rizzolatti, & Sakata, 1995). Note that canonical F5 neurons respond to the visual presentation of objects whether or not these objects are the target of a grasping action. This is particularly important, because it shows that the discharge of F5 canonical neurons is not necessarily dependent on action execution. What they code is the motor "representation" of an action suitable to successfully interact with a particular object. For a comprehensive review of the functional properties of these neurons, see Rizzolatti and Fadiga (1998).

Neurons forming the second category of F5 visuomotor neurons discharge when the monkey observes another individual making an action in front of it. We named them "mirror neurons" (Gallese, Fadiga, Fogassi, & Rizzolatti, 1996; Rizzolatti, Fadiga, Gallese, & Fogassi, 1996a).

In the present chapter we will discuss only the functional properties of mirror neurons.

Mirror neurons

Mirror neurons do not respond to conventional visual stimuli. Even three-dimensional objects including interesting stimuli such as food items, or sight of faces, are ineffective. Mirror neurons are visually activated when the monkey observes another individual (the experimenter or another monkey) making a goal-directed action either with the hand or, in some cases, with the mouth. The responses evoked by these stimuli are highly consistent and do not habituate. Actions made using tools, even when very similar to those made using hands, do not activate or activate very weakly the neurons. Also ineffective are gestures having emotional meaning.

The observed actions that most frequently activate mirror neurons are grasping, placing and manipulating objects. The majority of mirror neurons become active only during the observation of a single type of action. Some are activated by two or three of these types of actions.

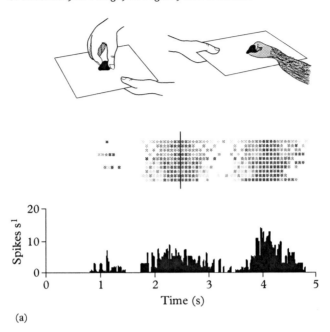

(a)

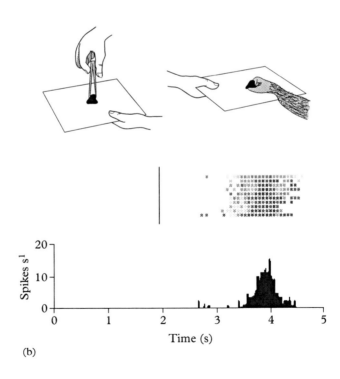

(b)

Figure 14.1 shows an example of a mirror neuron for grasping. Each trial started with stimulus presentation (a raisin placed on a tray). No discharge was present. In A, the stimulus was grasped by the experimenter. The neuron's discharge began during hand shaping and continued until the hand left the stimulus. No response was present during the phase subsequent to the grip when the tray with the food on it was moved toward the monkey. The neuron fired again when the monkey grasped the food. In B, the same stimulus was grasped using a tool. In this condition no discharge was elicited by action observation.

In most mirror neurons there is a clear relation between the visual action they respond to and the motor response they code. Using as classification criterion the congruence between the effective observed action and the effective executed action, we partitioned the mirror neurons into three broad classes: "strictly congruent," "broadly congruent," and "noncongruent" (Gallese, Fadiga, Fogassi, & Rizzolatti, 1996).

As strictly congruent we defined those mirror neurons in which the effective observed and executed actions correspond both in terms of general action (e.g., grasping) and in terms of the way in which that action was executed (e.g., precision grip). About 30 per cent of the neurons fell into this group. We defined neurons as broadly congruent, when there was a similarity, but not identity, between the effective observed and executed action. Neurons with this type of congruence represented about 60 per cent of the total of mirror neurons.

Finally, we defined as noncongruent those neurons (about 8 per cent) in which there was no clear-cut relationship between the effective observed action and the effective movement of the monkey.

Figure 14.1. Visual and motor responses of a mirror neuron. Testing conditions are schematically represented above the rasters. Response histograms represent the sum of ten consecutive trials (raster display). (a) A tray with a piece of food is presented to the monkey, the experimenter grasps the food, puts the food again on the tray and then moves the tray toward the monkey who grasps the food. The phases when the food is presented and when it is moved toward the monkey are characterized by the absence of neuronal discharge. In contrast, a strong activation is present during grasping movements of both the experimenter and the monkey. (b) As above, except that the experimenter grasps the food with pliers. In both (a) and (b), rasters and histograms are aligned with the moment at which the experimenter touches the food either with his hand or with the pliers (vertical line). Ordinates, spikes/bin; abscissae, time. Bin width, 20 ms. (Modified from Rizzolatti, Fadiga, Gallese, & Fogassi, 1996a.)

Resonance mechanisms

The motor system is hierarchically organized. It is composed of a chain of centers, the most peripheral of which contain neurons – alpha motoneurons – that innervate muscles. The probability to observe an overt movement is very high when neurons located in the peripheral centers are activated. In contrast, there is no obligatory relation between the discharge of neurons in the motor centers that are located higher in the chain and overt movements. The motor neurons of these higher centers discharge always in association with a particular movement (hence their definition as motor neurons), but they also discharge *in the absence* of any overt motor behavior, in response, for example, to a sensory stimulus. Their discharge, therefore, is not a "command" for action but an internal representation of the motor behavior they code. According to motivation and external contingencies the represented action will be executed or not.

Neurophysiological data indicate that in many motor centers, especially in the peripheral ones, neurons do not respond to visual stimuli. The visual stimuli to be effective in triggering these neurons must trigger also a movement. Neurons of other motor centers, however, do respond to visual stimuli, even in the absence of any movement. This behavior is observed in the areas forming the ventral premotor cortex – F4 (Gentilucci *et al.*, 1983, 1988; Fogassi *et al.*, 1996; Graziano, Hu, & Gross, 1997; see also for review Graziano & Gross, 1998), F5 (Rizzolatti *et al.*, 1988; Murata *et al.*, 1997) and, as recently shown, in sectors of the dorsal premotor cortex – peri-arcuate F2 of Matelli *et al.* (1998; Caminiti, Ferraina, & Johnson, 1996; Tanné, Boussaoud, Boyer-Zeller, & Rouiller, 1995; Fogassi *et al.*, 1999), F7 (di Pellegrino & Wise, 1991, see also Rizzolatti, Luppino, & Matelli, 1998). The characteristics of the visual stimuli that trigger the neurons of these motor areas may vary. In some cases they are objects of a particular size and shape (e.g., F5 canonical neurons), in others objects presented in specific egocentrically coded spatial locations (e.g., F4, and parietal areas VIP and V6a: Gentilucci *et al.*, 1983, 1988; Fogassi *et al.*, 1996; Graziano, Hu, & Gross, 1997; Graziano & Gross, 1998; Colby, Duhamel, & Goldberg, 1993; Galletti, Battaglini, & Fattor, 1993), in others biological actions (e.g., F5 mirror neurons, inferior parietal lobule: Gallese, Fadiga, Fogassi, & Rizzolatti, 1996; Rizzolatti, Fadiga, Gallese, & Fogassi, 1996a; Fogassi, Gallese, Fadiga, & Rizzolatti, 1998).

In motor areas (defined in a broad sense, see Rizzolatti, Luppino, & Matelli, 1998) that respond when the monkey observes biological actions, there are neurons that discharge both when the animal makes a specific action and when it observes another individual making a similar action. F5 mirror neurons are the best known example. Preliminary data suggest that the same is true also for the rostral part of the inferior parietal lobule, but with an important qualification (Fogassi, Gallese, Fadiga, & Rizzolatti, 1998, and our unpublished observations). In this area, in addition to neurons similar to F5 mirror neurons, there are neurons that do not require a specific goal-directed action to be triggered. They discharge when the monkey makes rather simple arm movements (e.g., arm flexion) regardless of the behavioral context in which these movements are executed. Most interestingly, these neurons discharge also when the monkey observes the experimenter making a similar arm movement. Unlike in F5, the congruence here is between the observed and executed movements and not between observed and executed actions.

A metaphor that describes well this correspondence between observed and executed biological motions is that of a physical "resonance." It is as if neurons in these motor areas start to "resonate" as soon as the appropriate visual input is presented. This "resonance" does not necessarily produce a movement or an action. It is an internal motor representation of the observed event which, subsequently, may be used for different functions, among which is imitation.

Imitation is a complex phenomenon the definition of which is highly debated. In common language imitation means "to do or to try to do after the manner of" (*Oxford English Dictionary*). However, if one examines imitation more closely, it becomes apparent that various types of phenomena are included under this term. Among them, Byrne (1995) distinguishes the following: "stimulus enhancement," "response facilitation," "emulation," and "true imitation."

Stimulus enhancement is a term that defines the probability that an individual approaches or contacts an object with which another individual of the same species is interacting (Spence, 1937). Because typically animals of the same species interact with identical objects in a rather similar way, "imitative" behavior is determined by a generic increase of the probability of acting on that object, rather than by the "true imitation" (see below) of the observed action. The neurophysiological mechanisms at the basis of stimulus enhancement should be related, therefore, to mechanisms that increase stimulus salience in the presence of physical or biological cues.

Response facilitation (Byrne, 1994) has been defined as a selective enhancement of motor responses: "Watching a conspecific performing an act (often one resulting in reward) increases the probability of an animal doing the same. Unlike imitation, only actions already in the repertoire can be facilitated."

The name emulation was used to define the behavior in which the observer duplicates the results of other individuals' behavior but not the specific way to achieve them (Wood, 1996; Tomasello, 1990).

Finally, several authors suggested employing the term imitation ("true imitation") only for those cases in which an animal learns a new behavior *and* precisely reproduces the movements that lead to that behavior goal (Tomasello, Kruger, & Rattner, 1993; Byrne & Tomasello, 1995).

In the next sections we will propose that resonance mechanisms may be at the basis of the three last behaviors. Furthermore, considering the organization of the motor system, we will submit that the resonance mechanism can be categorized according to the functional properties of the motor centers that do "resonate." By using this criterion we will distinguish resonance mechanisms which concern brain centers where *movements* are coded and resonance mechanisms which concern brain centers where *actions* are coded. We will refer to the former as "low-level resonance" mechanisms and to the latter as "high-level resonance" mechanisms, respectively. Our proposal is that the phenomena described under the heading of "response facilitation" can be accounted for by a low-level resonance mechanism, whereas emulation and "true imitation" require a high-level resonance mechanism.

Low-level resonance mechanism and response facilitation

A classical example of "response facilitation" is represented by the behavior of animals that reproduce, in particular occasions, movements made by a conspecific. This behavior has been extensively studied by classical ethology and explained in terms of releasing signals.

According to Tinbergen (1953) there are two fundamental types of releasing signals: *objects* of particular size, shape, and color and *movements* made by conspecifics. The presentation of these signals determines the automatic occurrence of stereotyped behaviors. Thus, movement observation represents, through response facilitation, a fundamental way in which the behavior of a group of animals acquires coherence. An example of this behavior is that displayed by shore birds when alarmed. Typically, in this condition one or few birds start wing flapping, then others repeat it and, eventually, the whole flock turns in flight (Thorpe, 1963). This behavior appears to be the consequence of a response facilitation of the observed movement (wing flapping) which, when repeated, entrains in the observer the complex movement synergies that eventually lead to flight. A low-level resonance mechanism would be a simple and very advantageous mechanism for reproducing the observed behavior.

Low-level resonance mechanism could explain also some behaviors present in humans. A well-known example of it is the capacity that newborn infants have of imitating oro-facial gestures and hand movements (Meltzoff & Moore, 1977; see also Meltzoff, this volume). A low-level resonance mechanism appears to be the most likely explanation of this behavior. Particularly so if one considers that the newborn infants that are able to imitate oro-facial gestures have never seen their own face.

There is, however, an important difference between the infant behavior and the "released" behavior of birds described above. As shown by Meltzoff and Moore (1977; see also Meltzoff & Moore, 1997), when the infant response is artificially delayed by using a pacifier, the behavior does not disappear as it should if it was simply a matter of response release, but is emitted subsequently when the response becomes possible. This difference is probably related to the presence in humans (as well as in species of animals with complex behavior) of mechanisms storing the externally evoked response and controlling its emission.

In adult humans the observation of an action does not usually determine the appearance in the observer's behavior of that action or of the individual movements that form it. Introspectively, however, the tendency to imitate the observed behaviors is very strong, especially in some occasions, as, for example, during the observation of sport events. A rather funny instance of this tendency, popularized by Hollywood movies, is that of people that cannot refrain, while watching a boxing match, from mimicking the arm movements of the boxers.

The validity of these introspective and anecdotal observations has been recently confirmed empirically by a series of studies in which transcranial magnetic stimulation (TMS), MEG/EEG recordings, and brain-imaging techniques were employed. These experiments, as described below, demonstrate that motor centers of adult humans do resonate during movement observation.

Fadiga, Fogassi, Pavesi, and Rizzolatti (1995) stimulated the left motor cortex of normal subjects using TMS while they were observing meaningless intransitive (nongoal directed) arm movements as well as hand-grasping movements performed by an experimenter. Motor-evoked potentials (MEPs) were recorded from various arm and hand muscles. As a control, the motor cortex was stimulated during the presentation of 3D objects and during an attentionally highly demanding dimming-detection task.

The rationale of the experiment was the following: if the mere observation of the hand and arm movements facilitates the motor system, this facilitation should determine an increase of MEPs recorded from hand and arm muscles. The results confirmed the hypothesis. A selective increase of motor-evoked potentials was found in those muscles that the subjects normally use for producing the observed movements. Note that the resonance phenomenon was present not only during the observation of goal-directed hand movements, but also during the observation of meaningless arm movements. These findings indicate that the presence of a goal in the observed action is not a necessary prerequisite for the motor system to resonate.

Further evidence that cortical motor areas are excited in humans during movement observation comes from MEG experiments. Hari *et al.* (1998) recorded neuromagnetic oscillatory activity of the human precentral cortex from healthy volunteers while (1) they were at rest, (2) they were rotating a small object kept in their right hand, and (3) they were observing another individual performing the same task. The cortical 15–25 Hz rhythmical activity was measured. In agreement with previous data (Salmelin & Hari, 1994), this activity was suppressed during movement execution. Most interestingly the rhythm was also significantly diminished during movement observation. Control experiments confirmed the specificity of the suppression effect. Because the recorded 15–25 Hz activity originates mostly in the anterior bank of the central sulcus, it appears that the human primary motor cortex desynchronizes (and therefore becomes more active) during movement observation in the absence of any active movement.

Similar results were also obtained by Cochin *et al.* (1998), who recorded EEG from subjects who observed video movies in which human movements were displayed. As a control, objects in movement, animal movements and still objects were also presented. The data showed that the observation of human movements, but not that of objects or animals, desynchronizes the EEG pattern of the precentral cortex.

Note that the EEG desynchronization of an area does not necessarily imply that that area "resonates" during movement observation. Monkey data indicate that neurons in the primary motor cortex do not respond to complex biological visual stimuli. It is likely therefore that the desynchronization of primary motor cortex is due to the arrival of action potentials originating from premotor areas, rather than to a direct visual input to the primary motor cortex describing the observed movements.

Further support for the notion that movement observation activates neural centers controlling movements comes from clinical studies. The classical example of this link between movement observation and movement production is the behavior named echopraxia (Dromard, 1905). Patients with echopraxia show an impulsive tendency to imitate other people's gestures. The imitation is performed immediately with the abruptness and speed of a reflex action. Imitation concerns gestures that are commonly executed as well as those that are rare and even bizarre for the observing patient.

Which are the brain areas that are involved in the low-level resonance mechanism? There are only few data on this issue. They come from PET studies carried out by the Lyon group (Decety *et al.*, 1997; Grèzes, Costes, & Decety, 1998). In those studies the authors instructed subjects to observe meaningful arm movements (movements with a goal) and meaningless arm movements. The main result of the condition in which subjects observed meaningless arm movements was an activation of the parietal lobe bilaterally. The activation included both inferior and superior parietal lobules, the intensity of the activation being stronger on the right side. Activation was found also in motor centers such as the left precentral gyrus and the cerebellum on the right side (Grèzes, Costes, & Decety, 1998). We will discuss the significance of these results in the next section after presenting experiments on meaningful actions.

High-level resonance mechanism, emulation, and "true imitation"

We defined as high-level resonance mechanism the resonance mechanism determined by sensory activation of neurons that code *actions*. The evidence in favor of the existence of this type of resonance mechanism came originally from the functional properties of monkey area F5 mirror neurons. This evidence can be summarized as follows.

When a monkey looks at an action, the firing of its F5 mirror neurons codes the motor representation of that action and not of the single movements forming it. In the case, for example, of "grasping" mirror neurons the response is present regardless of the direction along which the observed grasping is executed (toward or away from the monkey, from above the object or from below it). From a motor point of view all these movements are different, but in terms of meaning they all represent the same action, "grasping." Furthermore, in some neurons the observation of a given action is effective both when the monkey observes another individual making it with the hand or with the mouth. Neurons with these properties certainly do not code individual movements. Finally, as described above, the motor discharge of F5 neurons during active movements (mirror neurons included) correlates with specific actions and not with individual movements.

Because of these properties we have proposed that the activity of F5 mirror neurons mediates action understanding (Gallese, Fadiga, Fogassi, & Rizzolatti, 1996; Rizzolatti, Fadiga, Gallese, & Fogassi, 1996a). Our reasoning was the following: an individual that emits a movement usually "knows" (predicts) its consequences. This knowledge is acquired most likely during the first months of life and derives from an association between the representation of the motor action and the consequences of that action. The "resonance" mechanism in F5 mirror neurons does not determine the appearance of a motor response, but evokes a neural activity that corresponds to that which, when internally generated, represents a certain action. The meaning of an action can therefore be recognized because of the similarity between the two representations.

This interpretation implies that, unlike the low-level resonance mechanism, the purpose of the "resonance" in the F5 mirror neurons is to generate a representation of what another individual is doing. This understanding can be, subsequently, used to reproduce the observed behavior using either similar or different movements. It can also be followed by another action determined by the understanding of the observed one.

The similarity between the high-level resonance mechanism and emulation is evident. In emulation behavior the observation of a given action performed by a conspecific allows the observer to retrieve its most relevant information, the action goal. We propose that mirror neurons may constitute the first step, action-goal understanding, of the process that leads to emulation. How, however, the comprehension of the goal of an action made by another individual is then transformed into movements necessary to reach that same goal remains an open question.

A tentative explanation can be advanced, at least for the emulation of actions not implying complex sequences of movements. Let us imagine that a monkey observes another monkey while foraging with its hand. The observation of this action will activate several types of mirror neurons. Some of them will be strictly congruent with the observed action, not only in terms of goal ("grasp") but also in terms of the way to achieve that goal ("grasp with the thumb and the index finger"). Some others will be congruent only with respect to the goal ("grasp with the hand *or* with the mouth"). The activation of these different classes of neurons implies the activation of corresponding different motor representations of the same goal. The selection of the appropriate solution to goal achievement, and therefore the activation of the corresponding motor representation, will be guided by the environmental context (presence of other food, social rank of the observer, etc.) and by the internal drive of the observer.

An alternative explanation is of course that the mirror system provides the observer only with the meaning of the observed action, and then the emulated behavior derives from the activation of "decisional" centers, which subsequently determine the motor programs necessary for the achievement of the selected goal.

As far as humans are concerned, a series of brain-imaging experiments were made in order to assess which cortical area could be the homologue of the monkey F5 mirror system. Hand-grasping movements (Grafton, Arbib, Fadiga, & Rizzolatti, 1996; Rizzolatti et al., 1996b) as well as, more recently, more complex hand/arm movements were used as visual stimuli.

The results showed that during the observation of hand-grasping movements there was an activation of the left inferior frontal cortex, in correspondence of the Broca's region. In addition activations were found in the left superior temporal sulcus (STS), the rostral part of the left inferior parietal lobule (area 40), the left opercular parietal region and the rostral part of the supplementary motor area (SMA-proper) (Grafton, Arbib, Fadiga, & Rizzolatti, 1996; Rizzolatti et al., 1996b). The first three regions most likely correspond to the monkey cortical areas where there are neurons that discharge when the monkey observes biological actions, namely: area F5 (Gallese, Fadiga, Fogassi, & Rizzolatti, 1996), the STS region (Carey, Perrett, & Oram, 1997; Perrett et al., 1989), and the rostral part of the inferior parietal lobule (Fogassi, Gallese, Fadiga, & Rizzolatti, 1998). It is interesting to note that the hand/arm action recognition in humans is lateralized to the left hemisphere, that is to the hemisphere involved in the organization of hand/arm praxis.

Because a goal-directed action is formed by individual movements, the observation of such an action (e.g., grasping) should activate not only those mirror neurons that code it, but, at least in principle, also the system that mediates the low-level resonance mechanism. In PET experiments in which grasping observation was studied, the instructions given the subjects – "observe the action" – did not put any emphasis on the individual movements forming it. It is possible, therefore, that, because of this, the activation of regions mediating low-level resonance mechanism remained under the threshold of statistical significance, or was even absent.

An interesting attempt to find out whether the requirement of repeating movements would activate the same cortical areas as when the requirement is simply to observe the same movements was recently made by Grèzes, Costes, and Decety (1998). They presented subjects with two types of movements, that were similar in their visual form, but, in one condition, formed meaningful actions (e.g., cutting the bread), while in another condition they formed patterns of movement devoid of sense. Subjects were later required in separate blocks either to *observe* or to *reproduce* the presented movements. Observation of static hands served as the baseline condition. The results confirmed that the *observation* of meaningful hand actions activates the left inferior frontal gyrus (Broca's region), the left inferior parietal lobe plus various occipital and inferotemporal areas. An activation of the left precentral gyrus was also present. In contrast, in the condition in which subjects observed movements with the purpose of accurately *reproducing* them the activation was found mostly in the parietal lobe, regardless of whether the movements were meaningful or meaningless. Frontal activation was limited to the precentral gyrus (dorsal area 6) on both sides.

As mentioned above, Grèzes, Costes, and Decety (1998) also showed that in the condition in which subjects *observed* meaningless movements, there was no activation of Broca's region, and the pattern of activation resembled that of the conditions in which the subjects were required to reproduce the presented movements.

The most likely interpretation of these findings is that when subjects are required to replicate the observed actions, there is a recruitment of motor engrams for arm movements located in the parietal lobe. Single-neuron recording studies in the monkey clearly showed that neurons in the superior parietal lobule discharge in response to proprioceptive stimuli and in association with active movements (Sakata, Takaoka, Kawarasaki, & Shibutani, 1973; Mountcastle *et al.*, 1975; Kalaska, Cohen, Prud'homme, & Hyde 1990; Lacquaniti *et al.*, 1995). The similarity between the pattern of activated cortical areas in humans during *reproduction* of observed movements (meaningful or meaningless) and that occurring during the *observation* of meaningless movements suggests that in both cases a low-level resonance mechanism was responsible of the observed activations.

Summing up, the results of brain-imaging experiments suggest that the areas mediating low-level and high-level resonance mechanisms do not coincide. While the latter, which implies action understanding, involve the left inferior frontal gyrus (Broca's region), the former mostly involve the superior parietal lobule. Further experiments with more sensitive techniques like fMRI should better clarify the precise pattern of parietal activations and the relation between the activated parietal sites and the premotor areas with which they are anatomically strictly linked (see Rizzolatti, Luppino, & Matelli, 1998).

How do the results so far discussed relate to "true imitation"? As mentioned above, the use of the term imitation ("true imitation") should be restricted to those cases in which an animal learns a new behavior and is able to precisely reproduce the movements that lead to the goal of that behavior (Tomasello, Kruger, & Rattner, 1993; Byrne & Tomasello, 1995). As pointed out by Whiten and Custance (1996), it is very difficult to draw a sharp demarcation between emulation and true imitation. After all, as stressed by these authors, even consecutive performances of the same action by a single individual will never be identical. In spite of this difficulty, the concept of a motor similarity (even if not of a motor identity) between the observed and executed action appears to differentiate, at least logically, emulation from "true imitation."

Which can be the mechanisms at the basis of "true imitation"? Our interpretation is that "true imitation" results from the interplay of the two levels of resonance mechanism we discussed in the present chapter. The high-level resonance mechanism describes the *goal*[1] of the action. The attention is then focused on the *form* of the action, the repetition of which is mediated by the circuits involved in the low-level resonance mechanism.[2] The brain-imaging evidence discussed above suggests that the motor engrams for repeating the observed hand and arm movements are located in the superior parietal lobule plus the premotor cortex. How, however, the motor engrams activated by movement observation are then assembled in complex sequences is not known. It has been recently proposed on the basis of monkey studies (Tanji, 1994; Tanji, Shima, Mushiake, 1996; Hikosaka, Rand, Miyachi, & Miyashita, 1995; Hikosaka et al., 1998) that the mesial agranular cortical areas and basal ganglia could be involved in sequence learning. The presence of activation in pre-SMA/SMA and in the caudate nucleus found by Grèzes, Costes, and Decety (1998) during movement reproduction as contrasted with movement observation is in accord with this hypothesis and suggests that the same areas and centers that are involved in sequence learning are also involved in sequence learning by imitation.

Notes
Correspondence should be addressed to Giacomo Rizzolatti, Istituto di Fisiologia Umana, Via Volturno 39, I-43100, Parma, Italy. Fax: +39-0521-903900; e-mail: fisioum @ symbolic.pr.it

1 The term "goal" can be used in two different ways: (1) to indicate the aim of an action in which the effectors interact with the external world (transitive actions); (2) to indicate the capacity to make a *movement* identical to that shown by another individual. The term "goal" is always used as defined in (1).

2 The low-level resonance mechanism could be used also to disambiguate the goal of the action to be imitated when it is not completely clear to the observer. The attempts to simulate the witnessed movements may put the observer in a situation in which the goal can be better understood.

Acknowledgments

This work was supported by the Human Frontier Science Program and by the Ministero dell' Università e della Ricerca Scientifica e Tecnologica (MURST).

References

Arbib, M. A. (1981). Perceptual structures and distributed motor control. In V. B. Brooks (Ed.), *Handbook of physiology, section 1: The nervous system, vol. II: Motor control* (pp. 1449–1480). Baltimore: Williams and Wilkins.

Byrne, R. W. (1994). The evolution of intelligence. In P. J. B. Slater & T. R. Halliday (Eds.), *Behaviour and evolution* (pp. 223–265). Cambridge: Cambridge University Press.

—— (1995). *The thinking ape. Evolutionary origins of intelligence.* Oxford: Oxford University Press.

Byrne, R. W., & Tomasello, M. (1995). Do rats ape? *Animal Behavior, 50,* 1417–1420.

Caminiti, R., Ferraina, S., & Johnson, P. B. (1996). The sources of visual information to the primate frontal lobe: A novel role for the superior parietal lobule. *Cerebral Cortex, 6,* 319–328.

Carey, D. P., Perrett, D. I., & Oram, M. W. (1997). Recognizing, understanding and reproducing actions. In F. Boller & J. Grafman (Eds.), *Handbook of neuropsychology, vol. 11* (pp. 111–130). Amsterdam: Elsevier Science BV.

Cochin, S., Barthelemy, C., Lejeune, B., Roux, S., & Martineau, J. (1998). Perception of motion and qEEG activity in human adults. *Electroencephalography and Clinical Neurophysiology, 107,* 287–295.

Colby, C. L., Duhamel, J.-R., & Goldberg, M. E. (1993). Ventral intraparietal area of the macaque: Anatomic location and visual response properties. *Journal of Neurophysiology, 69,* 902–914.

Decety, J., Grèzes, J., Costes, N., Perani, D., Jeannerod, M., Procyk, E., Grassi, F., & Fazio, F. (1997). Brain activity during observation of actions. Influence of action content and subject's strategy. *Brain, 120,* 1763–1777.

Di Pellegrino, G., & Wise, S. P. (1991). A neurophysiological comparison of three distinct regions of the primate frontal brain. *Brain, 114,* 951–978.

Dromard, G. (1905). Etude psychologique et clinique sur l'échopraxie. *Journal of Psychology (Paris), 2,* 385–403.

Fadiga, L., Fogassi, L., Pavesi, G., & Rizzolatti, G. (1995). Motor facilitation during action observation: A magnetic stimulation study. *Journal of Neurophysiology, 73*, 2608–2611.

Fogassi, L., Gallese, V., Fadiga, L., Luppino, G., Matelli, M., & Rizzolatti, G. (1996). Coding of peripersonal space in inferior premotor cortex (area F4). *Journal of Neurophysiology, 76*, 141–157.

Fogassi, L., Gallese, V., Fadiga, L., & Rizzolatti, G. (1998). Neurons responding to the sight of goal-directed hand/arm actions in the parietal area PF (7b) of the macaque monkey. *Society for Neuroscience Abstracts, 24*, 257.5.

Fogassi, L., Raos, V., Franchi, G., Gallese, V., Luppino, G., & Matelli, M. (1999). Visual responses in the dorsal premotor area F2 of the macaque monkey. *Experimental Brain Research, 128*, 194–199.

Gallese, V., Fadiga, L., Fogassi, L., & Rizzolatti, G. (1996). Action recognition in the premotor cortex. *Brain, 119*, 593–609.

Galletti, C., Battaglini, P. P., & Fattori, P. (1993). Parietal neurons encoding spatial locations in craniotopic coordinates. *Experimental Brain Research, 96*, 221–229.

Gentilucci, M., Gentilucci, M., Scandolara, C., Pigarev, I. N., & Rizzolatti, G. (1983). Visual responses in the postarcuate cortex (area 6) of the monkey that are independent of eye position. *Experimental Brain Research, 50*, 464–468.

Gentilucci, M., Fogassi, L., Luppino, G., Matelli, M., Camarda, R., & Rizzolatti, G. (1988). Functional organization of inferior area 6 in the macaque monkey: I. Somatotopy and the control of proximal movements. *Experimental Brain Research, 71*, 475–490.

Grafton, S. T., Arbib, M. A., Fadiga, L., & Rizzolatti, G. (1996). Localization of grasp representations in humans by PET: 2. Observation compared with imagination. *Experimental Brain Research, 112*, 103–111.

Graziano, M. S. A., & Gross C. G. (1998). Spatial maps for the control of movement. *Current Opinion in Neurobiology, 8*, 195–201.

Graziano, M. S. A., Hu, X., & Gross C. G. (1997). Visuo-spatial properties of ventral premotor cortex. *Journal of Neurophysiology, 77*, 2268–2292.

Grèzes, J., Costes, N., & Decety, J. (1998). Top-down effect of strategy on the perception of human biological motion: A PET investigation. *Cognitive Neuropsychology, 15*, 553–582.

Hari, R., Forss, N., Avikainen, S., Kirveskari, S., Salenius, S., & Rizzolatti, G. (1998). Activation of human primary motor cortex during action observation: A neuromagnetic study. *Proceedings of the National Academy of Science USA, 95*, 15061–15065.

Hepp-Reymond, M.-C., Husler, E. J., Maier, M. A., & Qi, H.-X. (1994). Force-related neuronal activity in two regions of the primate ventral premotor cortex. *Canadian Journal of Physiology and Pharmacology, 72*, 571–579.

Hikosaka, O., Rand, M. K., Miyachi, S., & Miyashita, K. (1995). Learning of sequential movements in the monkey – process of learning and retention of memory. *Journal of Neurophysiology, 74*, 1652–1661.

Hikosaka, O., Miyashita, K., Miyachi, S., Sakai, K., & Lu, X. (1998). Differential roles of the frontal cortex, basal ganglia, and cerebellum in visuomotor sequence learning. *Neurobiology of Learning and Memory, 70,* 137–149.

Jeannerod, M. (1984). The timing of natural prehension movements. *Journal of Motor Behavior, 16,* 235–254.

——— (1988). *The neural and behavioural organization of goal-directed movements.* Oxford: Clarendon Press.

Jeannerod, M., Arbib, M. A., Rizzolatti, G., & Sakata, H. (1995). Grasping objects: The cortical mechanisms of visuomotor transformation. *Trends in Neuroscience, 18,* 314–320.

Kalaska, J. F., Cohen, D. A. D., Prud'homme, M., & Hyde, M. L. (1990). Parietal area 5 neuronal activity encodes movement kinematics, not movement dynamics. *Experimental Brain Research, 80,* 351–364.

Lacquaniti, F., Guigon, E., Bianchi, L., Ferraian, S., & Caminiti, R. (1995). Representing spatial information for limb movement: Role of area 5 in the monkey. *Cerebral Cortex, 5,* 391–409.

Matelli, M., Luppino, G., & Rizzolatti, G. (1985). Patterns of cytochrome oxidase activity in the frontal agranular cortex of the macaque monkey. *Behavioral Brain Research, 18,* 125–137.

Matelli, M., Govoni, P., Galletti, C., Kutz, D. F., & Luppino, G. (1998). Superior area 6 afferents from the superior parietal lobule in the macaque monkey. *Journal of Comparative Neurology, 402,* 327–352.

Meltzoff, A. N., & Moore, M. K. (1977). Imitation of facial and manual gestures by human neonates. *Science, 198,* 75–78.

——— (1997). Explaining facial imitation: A theoretical model. *Early Development and Parenting, 6,* 179–192.

Mountcastle, V. B., Lynch, J. C., Georgopoulos, A., Sakata, H., & Acuna, C. (1975). Posterior parietal association cortex of the monkey: Command functions for operations within extrapersonal space. *Journal of Neurophysiology, 38,* 871–908.

Murata, A., Fadiga, L., Fogassi, L., Gallese, V., Raos, V., & Rizzolatti, G. (1997). Object representation in the ventral premotor cortex (area F5) of the monkey. *Journal of Neurophysiology, 78,* 2226–2230.

Okano, K., & Tanji, J. (1987). Neuronal activities in the primate motor fields of the agranular frontal cortex preceding visually triggered and self-paced movement. *Experimental Brain Research, 66,* 155–166.

Perrett, D. I., Harries, M. H., Bevan, R., Thomas, S., Benson, P. J., Mistlin, A. J., Chitty, A. J., Hietanen, J. K., & Ortega, J. E. (1989). Frameworks of analysis for the neural representation of animate objects and actions. *Journal of Experimental Biology, 146,* 87–113.

Porter, R., & Lemon, R. (1993). *Corticospinal function and voluntary movement.* Oxford: Clarendon Press.

Rizzolatti, G., Camarda, R., Fogassi, L., Gentilucci, M., Luppino, G., & Matelli, M. (1988). Functional organization of inferior area 6 in the macaque monkey: II. Area F5 and the control of distal movements. *Experimental Brain Research, 71,* 491–507.

Rizzolatti, G., & Fadiga, L. (1998). Grasping objects and grasping action meanings: The dual role of monkey rostroventral premotor cortex (area F5). In G. R. Bock & J. A. Goode (Eds.), *Sensory guidance of movement* (pp. 81–103). Novartis Foundation Symposium 218. Chichester: John Wiley and Sons.

Rizzolatti, G., Fadiga, L., Gallese, V., & Fogassi, L. (1996a). Premotor cortex and the recognition of motor actions. *Cognitive Brain Research, 3*, 131–141.

Rizzolatti, G., Fadiga, L., Matelli, M., Bettinardi, V., Paulesu, E., Perani, D., & Fazio, G. (1996b). Localization of grasp representations in humans by PET: 1. Observation versus execution. *Experimental Brain Research, 111*, 246–252.

Rizzolatti, G., Luppino, G., & Matelli, M. (1998). The organization of the cortical motor system: New concepts. *Electroencephalography and Clinical Neurophysiology, 106*, 283–296.

Rizzolatti, G., Scandolara, C., Matelli, M., & Gentilucci, M. (1981). Afferent properties of periarcuate neurons in macaque monkeys. II. Visual responses. *Behavioral Brain Research, 2*, 147–163.

Sakata, H., Takaoka, Y., Kawarasaki, A., & Shibutani, H. (1973). Somatosensory properties of neurons in the superior parietal cortex (area 5) of the rhesus monkey. *Brain Research, 64*, 85–102.

Salmelin, R., & Hari, R. (1994). Spatiotemporal characteristics of rhythmic neuromagnetic activity related to thumb movement. *Neuroscience, 60*, 537–550.

Spence, K. W. (1937). Experimental studies of learning and higher mental processes in infra-human primates. *Psychological Bulletin, 34*, 806–850.

Tanji, J. (1994). The supplementary motor area in the cerebral cortex. *Neuroscience Research, 19*, 251–268.

(1996). New concepts of the supplementary motor area. *Current Opinion in Neurobiology, 6*, 782–787.

Tanji, J., Shima, K., & Mushiake, H. (1996). Multiple cortical motor areas and temporal sequencing of movements. *Cognitive Brain Research, 5*, 117–122.

Tanné, J., Boussaoud, D., Boyer-Zeller, N., & Rouiller, E. M. (1995). Direct visual pathways for reaching movements in the macaque monkey. *NeuroReport, 7*, 267–272.

Thorpe, W. H. (1963). *Learning and instinct in animals.* (2nd edition) London: Methuen and Co. Ltd.

Tinbergen, N. (1953). *Social behaviour in animals.* London: Methuen and Co.

Tomasello, M. (1990). Cultural transmission in the tool use and communicatory signaling of chimpanzees? In S. T. Parker & K. R. Gibson (Eds.), *Language and intelligence in monkeys and apes* (pp. 274–311). Cambridge: Cambridge University Press.

Tomasello, M., Kruger, A. C., & Rattner, H. H. (1993). Cultural learning. *Behavioral Brain Sciences, 16*, 495–511.

Whiten, A., & Custance, D. (1996). Studies of imitation in chimpanzees and children. In C. M. Hayes and B. G. Galef (Eds.), *Social learning in animals: The roots of culture.* New York: Academic Press.

Wiesendanger, M., Hummelsheim, H., Bianchetti, M., Chen, D. F., Hyland, B., Mayer, W., & Wiesendanger, R. (1987). Input and output organization of the supplementary motor area. In G. Bock, M. O'Connor, & J. Marsh

(Eds.), *Motor areas of the cerebral cortex.* Ciba Foundation Symposium 132 (pp. 40–62). Chichester: Wiley.

Wise, S. P. (1985). The primate premotor cortex: Past, present, and preparatory. *Annual Review of Neuroscience, 8,* 1–19.

Wood, D. (1996). Social interaction as tutoring. In M. H. Bornstein & J. S. Bruner (Eds.), *Interaction in Human Development* (pp. 59–80). Hillsdale, NJ: Lawrence Erlbaum Associates.

15 Cell populations in the banks of the superior temporal sulcus of the macaque and imitation

T. Jellema, C. I. Baker, M. W. Oram, and D. I. Perrett

Introduction

Imitation of a perceived, novel, action requires the action to be sufficiently "understood" in order to produce the appropriate sequence of motor commands resulting in the execution of a similar action. One way to "understand" a complex perceived motor action is to break it down into its elementary components. These components are the key: momentary positions, orientations, movements and directions, which, taken together, uniquely define the action. This seems to be the preferred way for the brain to process visual stimuli, not only in the primary visual cortex, but also in higher-level visual areas.

The literal characteristics of the observed action are not the only subject of imitation. The intentions of an agent performing an action, or the goals of the action, may also be imitated. When the intention or goal of an action is imitated, the precise movements of the imitator may differ from the model although the results of the imitated action may be the same.

The way in which a perceived action is defined depends on the perspective employed. In principle, an action can be defined from a viewer-centered, an object-centered or a goal-centered perspective (Perrett *et al.*, 1989). A viewer-centered description defines the object or action with respect to the observer (e.g., "that person's arm moved towards me"). For object-centered descriptions (Marr & Nishihara, 1978), the principal axis of the object is taken as the basis for the reference ("that person's arm moved to a position in front of the chest"). For goal-centered descriptions, the intention, aim or result of the action forms the defining characteristic ("that person directs his attention towards me"). To interact with objects (visuomotor behavior), viewer-centered descriptions seem most appropriate, but for object and scene recognition object-centered descriptions seem more suitable (Milner & Goodale, 1995; Baker, Keysers, Jellema, & Perrett, 2000).

Object-centered descriptions remain constant across different vantage points of the observer. Object-centered descriptions are therefore

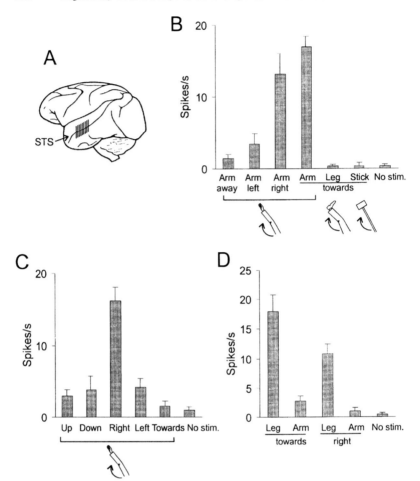

Figure 15.1. (A) View of the left side of the macaque brain, showing the location of the superior temporal sulcus (STS). The area where recordings were made was located in the upper and lower bank and the fundus of STSa, between 19 and 10 mm anterior to the inter-aural plane (indicated by vertical bars). (B–D) Selective responses to the sight of an arm or leg, moving in specific directions. The mean response ($+/-1$ SE) is illustrated for three cells to the sight of limb movements. (B) The cell responded to the sight of the experimenter extending his arm either towards the subject or towards the subject's right, but not towards the subject's left or away. Equivalent movements of the leg or a stick in the direction towards the subject produced lower response rates for this cell ($p < 0.0005$, Newman-Keuls posthoc test, for both leg and stick movements compared to arm

particularly important when the aim is to imitate the "form" of an observed action, because they are invariant across differences in posture, orientation and position between the imitated and imitator. One can thus envisage that the description of any perceived action will involve different types of descriptions for different purposes and that these descriptions coexist within the same brain system.

Cells in the temporal lobe of the macaque, and especially within the anterior part of the banks of the superior temporal sulcus (STSa, sometimes referred to as STPa, the anterior superior temporal polysensory region; Fig. 15.1a), have response properties which implicate them in the visual functions described above.

In the first section of this chapter, cell populations in STSa tuned to the analysis of actions are described, with emphasis on the coding of limb movements from a viewer-centered perspective. In the second section, detailed examples will be given of cells that code in an object-centered way for a particular action of a part, or the whole, of the body. We will argue that some of these STSa cells code for the direction of attention of another individual. In the third section, the possible construction of elaborate descriptions from "simpler" descriptions will be discussed. We will show that the category of goal-directed descriptions encompasses cell populations that code different aspects of the goal-directed action, and that therefore splitting this category into at least two subdivisions may be appropriate. One proposed subdivision involves cells coding specifically for the intention of an action (whether the goal is achieved is irrelevant), whereas another group of cells codes for the interaction between the agent and the object or goal of the action. The sight of just the intention of an action is not enough to drive this latter group of goal-directed cells; achievement of the goal is essential. Data will be presented in support

---

Fig. 15.1 (*cont.*)
movements towards). [ANOVA: $F(6, 38) = 34.5$, $p < 0.0005$; number of trials for each condition from left to right, $n = 5,5,5,10,5,5,10$.] (C) This cell responded selectively to an arm, reaching to the subject's right more than to other directions ($p < 0.0005$ in all comparisons). [ANOVA: $F(5, 24) = 19.5$, $p < 0.0005$, $n = 5$.] (D) A further cell which responded much more to a leg extension than to an equivalent arm extension, directed towards the subject ($p < 0.0005$) and to the subject's right ($p < 0.0005$). The cell was more responsive to the "Towards" direction than to the "Right" direction ($p < 0.005$). [ANOVA: $F(4, 20) = 26.7$, $p < 0.0005$, $n = 5$.] The "No stim" condition consisted of a static person, which did not produce a response in any of the three cells shown (B-D).

of this subdivision. The fourth section concludes the chapter with a discussion of how the perception of an action might be linked to the production of an action. This will include findings in other brain areas, most notably the premotor cortex.

Response properties of STSa cells tuned to the analysis of actions: examples of viewer-centered coding

In the macaque monkey and in humans there are two major cortical streams of visual information processing. One runs ventrally from the occipital cortex to the temporal cortex and is thought to be responsible for the perception of visual form. A second pathway runs dorsally from the occipital cortex towards the parietal cortex. This second pathway is thought to be responsible for the visual control of actions. Cellular systems in the parietal cortex analyze the size and orientation of objects such that grasping movements of the hand can be appropriately structured (Jeannerod, Arbib, Rizzolatti, & Sakata, 1995). We focus here, however, on the analysis of the visual form of actions rather than the visual form of objects which may be used to guide grasping movements of the hand.

The cortex of the superior temporal sulcus lies between these two pathways and appears to integrate information from both streams (Felleman & Van Essen, 1991; Young, 1992). In the macaque, motion information (dorsal stream) arrives at STSa cells coding body movements approximately 20 ms earlier than information about the static form (ventral stream) (Oram & Perrett, 1996).

In the early seventies, the first reports appeared of cells in the inferior temporal cortex of the monkey brain which responded specifically to the sight of animate objects such as a paw (Gross, Rocha-Miranda, & Bender, 1972). Since then this region of the brain, together with the adjacent superior temporal sulcus (Bruce, Desimone, & Gross, 1981; Perrett, Rolls, & Caan, 1982), has repeatedly been implicated in the visual analysis of animate objects and their actions (e.g., Hasselmo, Rolls, & Baylis, 1989; Perrett et al., 1989; Oram & Perrett, 1994, 1996; Perrett, 2000). Though highly sensitive to complex shapes, these cells often generalize this shape selectivity across changes in retinal position, the species (human or monkey), color and luminance (e.g., Perrett et al., 1984, 1989; Rolls & Baylis, 1986).

Some STSa cell populations are specifically activated by static images of animate objects and may, or may not, continue to respond when these images move. Other cells respond selectively to moving objects and remain inactive to static images of the same object (e.g., Perrett et al., 1989; Perrett, Hietanen, Oram, & Benson, 1992; Oram, Perrett, & Hietanen,

1993; Oram & Perrett, 1994, 1996; Jellema, Baker, Wicker, & Perrett, 2000). We will focus in this report on those cells responsive to the movements of animate objects.

Cells that respond to body movement combine information about the form of body components with information about the type of movement they are executing (Oram & Perrett 1994, 1996; Oram, Perrett, Wachsmuth, & Emery, 2000). Therefore, when describing the visual stimulus properties that activate and control these STSa cells, at least three main factors may be discriminated: (1) the *form* or *view* of the animate object, (2) the *type of movement* the object is making, and (3) the *direction* of these movements. We recently obtained preliminary evidence for a fourth factor, being the *spatial location* of the object (Baker *et al.,* 2000a, b) but this will not be treated in detail here. Cells can be found that respond selectively to just one of these factors, irrespective of the other factors, but often the cells show a sensitivity to a particular combination of two, three, or all factors.

1. *Form/view selectivity.* Some cells require only the movement of a specific part of the face or body, such as the mouth, eyes, head, torso, legs, arms, hands, and fingers to produce a response (Perrett *et al.,* 1985b, 1990a; Perrett, Mistlin, Harries, & Chitty, 1990b; Mistlin & Perrett, 1990; Jellema, Baker, Wicker, & Perrett, 2000), and thus show a high degree of form selectivity. Other cells can only be excited by the perception of movements of the whole body (Perrett *et al.,* 1985b, 1989; Perrett, Mistlin, Harries, & Chitty, 1990b; Oram & Perrett, 1996). The response selectivity of these latter cells probably results from combining the outputs of cells responsive to movements of individual components of the body. The majority of these cells are tuned to a particular view of the body (part), usually to one of six orthogonal views: front, back, right, left, top, or underneath. Only a minority of the cells responds to all possible views (see the second section of this chapter).

2. *Type of body movement.* Specific types of body movement that are processed include translation (linear displacement) and rotation (Perrett *et al.,* 1985b; Oram & Perrett, 1994). Some cells produce descriptions of coherent whole-body actions such as walking (Perrett *et al.,* 1985b, 1989; Perrett, Mistlin, Harries, & Chitty, 1990b; Oram & Perrett, 1996), crouching (Perrett *et al.,* 1984), climbing (Brothers & Ring, 1993) and turning (Oram & Perrett, 1994). When one part of the body, e.g., the head, is covered, the cell's responses can be maintained. A minority of the cells responds to just the type of movement, irrespective of the direction and view.

3. *Direction of body movement.* Often, optimal responses of motion sensitive cells are found for movements in only one direction of the three Cartesian axes (i.e., towards/away, left/right, up/down, with respect to the subject) (Oram & Perrett, 1996). Again, a minority of the cells responds to any direction of movement, irrespective of the type of movement or what it is that is moving. But for the majority of cells, the sensitivity to the direction of motion is tied in with the other factors.

Thus, seldom is an STSa cell responsive to just one of the three above factors, irrespective of the other stimulus properties. A combined *view–type of motion–direction of motion* sensitivity seems to be the rule (Oram & Perrett, 1996). This property uniquely defines the STSa cells as a distinct stage within the visual system. For example, an STSa cell may code for the right profile of the experimenter walking towards the right, but not for the left profile walking towards the right (i.e., backward walking), nor for the right profile walking towards the left (Perrett *et al.,* 1985b; Oram & Perrett, 1994, 1996).

Limb movements

We look here in more detail at cells that specifically code for limb movements. These cells constitute about 6 per cent of cells in STSa sensitive to body movements. Recently, we studied a population of 36 cells, of which fifteen cells responded selectively to arm movements and not to equivalent leg movements, sixteen responded selectively to leg movements and not to equivalent arm movements, while five cells responded equally strongly to both leg and arm movements (Jellema, Baker, Wicker, & Perrett, 2000). Figure 15.1 gives three examples of such cells. The cell in Figure 15.1B responded specifically to the sight of an arm movement when directed towards the subject or towards the subject's right, but not when directed away from the subject or to the left. Equivalent movements made with a leg or with a stick (directed to the same position, approximately 1.5 m above the ground and 1 m in front of the subject) failed to excite this cell. The cell thus showed both form and direction sensitivity. Most cells responsive to arm reaching were found to be optimally responsive to reaching directed towards the subject, but some cells responded selectively to reaching towards, for example, the subject's right, and remained silent to reaching in all other directions (including towards the subject) (Fig. 15.1C). One cell distinguished between movements of the left and right arm; it responded to movements of the left arm to the left, but did not respond to the right arm reaching in the same direction (to the left). Such cellular discrimination may underlie the explicit or implicit recognition of handedness (Gentilucci, Daprati, & Gangitano, 1998). In contrast, the cell shown in Figure 15.1D responded vigorously to the sight of a leg movement but much less to an equivalent arm movement. Again, the cell was directionally sensitive in that leg movements towards the subject were more effective than movements to the subject's right. Leg movements away from the subject also failed to produce a response (not shown). Remarkably, cells specifically responsive to arm or leg movements could be located very closely to one another. The two cells illustrated in Figures 15.1B and D were located only 60 μm apart on the same recording track.

There are several visual cues to the difference between arm and leg movement and we have yet to establish which of these are utilized by the STSa cells. Cells may use the form of the limb (including the position of attachment on the body) to differentiate between limbs. We have found that some cells responsive to an arm movement are less responsive if the torso is not simultaneously visible. Arm and leg movements also differ in the kinematics of articulation. This, however, did not account for cellular selectivity in some cases. For instance, cells responsive to leg movement often remained unresponsive to arm movements even when they were made to simulate the trajectory and articulation of the effective leg movements. Moreover, cells responsive to arm motion but not leg motion failed to respond to two sticks joined at one end made to articulate in the same manner as an arm.

Different cell populations within STSa thus appear equipped to "break down" a complex observed action into its basic components, i.e., the momentary postures, orientations and the type and directions of the movements of individual body parts, usually defined from a particular vantage point.

Examples of object-centered coding for actions

It is important to note that the cells responsive to limb movement described above all have in common the property that they use a viewer-centered coordinate system, in which the view and direction of motion of the object/action are defined relative to the observer. From the STSa cells that have been recorded in our lab during the last fifteen years, only a small number of cells coded explicitly in an object-centered way for an action or static body posture (e.g., Perrett *et al.*, 1985a, 1991; Oram & Perrett, 1996). By contrast, large numbers code in a viewer-centered way for similar actions and postures. Although we may have missed the presence of particular object-centered cells in the STSa, by any estimation object-centered coding is still relatively rare. This is probably the reason that such cells have received relatively little attention over the years compared to the viewer-centered cells.

Object-centered coding for the articulation of a part of the body

One example of a cell coding in an object-centered way for an articulation of a part of the body is illustrated in Figures 15.2–4. This cell responded vigorously to the sight of a backward articulation of the upper body (with respect to the main axis of the body), independently of the perspective of the observer. In this series of experiments, the experimenter sat on a rotating chair 1.5 m in front of the subject. Eye contact with the subject was avoided. Starting from the upright position, the experimenter bent the upper body either forwards or backwards through an angle of about 20°, remained static in that position for at least two seconds, and subsequently moved back to the upright position and again remained static for at least two seconds. He then moved on to perform the same actions from a different perspective of the observer by rotating the chair 90° or 180°, either clockwise or anti-clockwise. This produced four different perspectives: "front," the experimenter's front view was facing the subject, "back," the back view was facing the subject, and "left" and "right," the left or right profile was facing the subject. As a consequence of changing the view perspective, the direction of the movement changed with respect to the subject. Figure 15.2A shows that this cell responded selectively to backward bending of the upper body beyond the vertical when viewed from any of the four perspectives; forward bending failed to excite the cell from any view. Thus, the main factor determining these responses was the type of bending of the upper body (backward bending being much more effective than forward bending). The direction of motion did not contribute to the observed responses, while a just significant interaction between view and motion type probably reflected the reduced visibility (and hence discrimination of motion) of the back view.

It should be noted that the body movement also contained a small, but distinct, component along the vertical axis. Bending movements starting in the upright position will inevitably lower the head slightly while movements towards the upright position lift the head slightly. However, the downward movement by itself clearly did not cause the effect, since this movement was equally present in both types of bending.

Quite remarkably, the response turned out to be specific for backward articulation from the upright starting position. The same direction of articulation, which started with the body in bent forward position and ended with an upright posture, did not evoke a response when viewed from any of the perspectives (Fig. 15.2B). This stands in sharp contrast

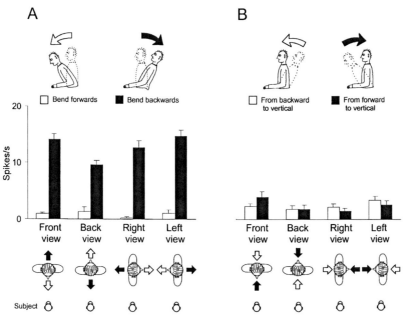

Figure 15.2. Object-centered coding for backward body articulation beyond the vertical. (A) The cell (T47_3375) responded to the sight of the experimenter bending his upper body backward (experimenter sitting on a chair). The cell responded vigorously to this action when viewed from any of four perspectives (front, back, right, and left profiles). Bending the upper body forward did not excite this cell for any of the perspectives. The type of bending movement (forward, backward) was a more important factor in determining responses than "direction of movement" (towards, away, to right, to left) or body "view" [Two-way ANOVA, overall effect of conditions, type of bending: $F(1,70) = 274.9$, $p < 0.0005$; direction of movement, $F(3,70) = 2.22$, $p = 0.09$; interaction, $F(3,70) = 2.77$, $p = 0.048$.] (B) Absence of responses for upward body articulation. The upper body was moved upwards, starting from either the bent-forward position or the bent-backward position, and ending in the upright position. These actions did not evoke a significant response in the cell (T47_3375) from any of the four perspectives tested. [Two-way ANOVA, overall effect for conditions, type of bending, $F(1,58) = 0.006$, $p = 0.94$; direction of movement, $F(3,58) = 0.47$, $p = 0.70$; interaction, $F(3,58) = 2.55$, $p = 0.06$.] The drawings at the top show the experimenter from the subject's view (only the left view is shown). The figure in interrupted outline represents the starting position; the solid outline figure represents the final position. The drawings at the bottom show a plan view of the subject and the experimenter. Note that the distance from subject to experimenter is not shown at scale (1.5 m). Black arrows indicate backward bending, white arrows indicate forward bending.

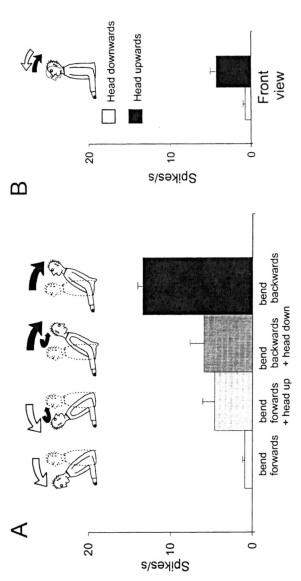

Figure 15.3. (A) Interaction of head and body articulation. The responses of the cell (T47.3375) to the motion of the upper body were modulated by simultaneous rotation of the head. Movements of the head during bending are indicated in the two middle drawings by small black arrows. The data shown represent the averaged responses over the four perspectives (front, back, right, left). The large response to the backward bending was significantly reduced when the head was simultaneously turned downwards ($p < 0.0002$, Newman–Keuls), whereas the small response to the forward bending of the torso was significantly increased when the head was simultaneously turned upwards ($p < 0.004$). [ANOVA, overall effect for type of bending, $F(3, 93) = 88.9$, $p < 0.0005$.] (B) Independent sensitivity to head movement. Rotation of the head backwards, starting from the upright position, produced more activity from the cell (T47.3375) than rotating the head forwards along the same trajectory and ending in the upright position [ANOVA, $F(1, 15) = 20.6$, $p < 0.0004$].

to the vigorous response observed when the articulation continued beyond the vertical plane (Fig. 15.2A). Similarly, movements that started with a backward bent posture and ended in the upright position also failed to evoke a response from any of the perspectives (Fig. 15.2B). This cell has all the hallmarks of object-centered coding. The action is defined not with respect to the observer, but with respect to a reference point located in the object (moving body) itself.

Three further observations on the same cell provided us with clues as to what the functional significance of such cell responses might be, apart from coding for the particular bending action *per se*.

The first observation was that the magnitude of the response to each bending movement (in any direction and from any perspective) could be modulated by changing the direction in which the head pointed during the movement (Fig. 15.3A). That is, the large response to backward bending was significantly reduced when, simultaneously with this movement, the head was turned downwards (compare the two right-most bars in Fig. 15.3A). Conversely, the extremely weak response to forward bending was significantly increased by simultaneously turning the head upwards (compare the two left-most bars in Fig. 15.3A). Similar results were obtained for each perspective.

The second observation was that moving only the head in the upward direction, starting from the normal horizontal posture (i.e., facing the horizon), also evoked a response, albeit a relatively small one, whereas movement in the opposite direction along the same trajectory evoked no response at all (Fig. 15.3B). Head movements downwards, starting from the horizontal position, or upwards along the same trajectory but starting from a head-lowered position and stopping at the horizontal position, also failed to evoke a response (data not shown).

A third and remarkable observation was that the response to backward bending extended into the subsequent static phase following the movement (during which phase the experimenter maintained the same posture; Fig. 15.4). This response was most pronounced for the front perspective and relatively small for the back perspective. In some cases, the static response would continue for up to 6 s provided the experimenter held the same posture.

We would argue that the above findings are compatible with a function of the cell in detecting an upward direction of attention in other individuals. The perception of the direction of attention of others may be based on the perception of their direction of gaze but can also be based on the orientation of the head, and body. Of course, attention can be oriented covertly without any overt movement but for the most part eye, head, and body movements can give important cues as to the likely focus of

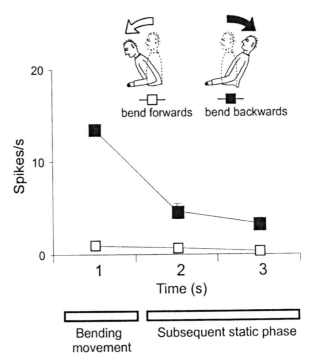

Figure 15.4. Persistence of the response to upper-body articulation. The response of the cell (T47_3375) to the backward bending of the upper body extended into the subsequent phase of testing, during which the experimenter remained static. Though reduced with respect to the response during the movement phase, the response in the static phase was sensitive to body posture. The responses (mean +/−1SE) illustrated represent the values averaged across the four perspective views (front, left, right, back). [ANOVA, overall effect for type of bending with time as a factor, $F(1,58) = 169.7$, $p < 0.0005$; backward posture > forward posture for the 1st, 2nd and 3rd s test epochs, $p < 0.0002$ each comparison; overall effect for time, $F(2,116) = 64.5$, $p < 0.0005$; interaction of stimulus and time, $F(2,116) = 54.9$, $p < 0.0005$.]

another individual's attention. The backward bending of the upper body results in the head pointing upwards towards the ceiling (or sky), from each perspective. Both the body and head posture signal an upward direction of attention. However, bending backwards while simultaneously turning the head downwards produces conflicting cues; one cue (upper body) suggests an upward direction, the other (head) suggests a downward direction, hence the much reduced response. Bending forwards and simultaneously turning the head upwards produces similarly conflicting cues, and results in an increase in the response magnitude compared to the situation where both head and body posture indicate attention directed downward. The finding that the cell only responded to those upward movements of the head which caused the head to point in a direction higher than horizon level, is also compatible with the notion of coding for upward directed attention.

Cells have been described in STSa that respond specifically to rotational movements of objects such as the limbs, in which one end of the object is fixed while the other end rotates about the fixed end (Perrett *et al.*, 1990a). Some of these cells respond to rotations over restricted trajectories, e.g., articulations above the horizontal and not below horizontal. The responses of the cell described in Figures 15.2–4 may be of this form, since the articulations of body parts such as the upper body and the head, which produced a response, shared this same restricted trajectory. Although to characterize the response fully it is necessary to consider both the type of articulation and the view of the body component moving, since only articulations raising the chest and face skyward provoke responses.

Object-centered coding for whole-body articulations

Cell populations have been described in STSa that code specifically for whole-body movements, such as walking (Oram & Perrett, 1994, 1996), instead of body-part articulations. Again, most of these cells are responsive to a particular combination of a view and a direction of movement, and thus code in a viewer-centered coordinate system. For example, they may respond to the experimenter walking forwards to the right, but not to the experimenter walking forwards to the left, nor to the experimenter walking backwards to the left or right. Object-centered coding for the perception of an individual walking is again much rarer. From a total of 161 cells that coded for the body view and the direction of motion of the experimenter walking in the lab, only four cells (3 per cent) did so in an object-centered manner: two cells coded for forward walking, two cells for backward walking. The other 157 cells (97 per cent) all responded in a viewer-centered manner (Oram & Perrett, 1996).

Figure 15.5 illustrates a cell which codes in an object-centered way for the sight of the experimenter walking forwards (following one's nose) in the lab, in any direction (towards, away, to the right, to the left of the subject), and thus when seen from any perspective. Backwards walking (i.e., the direction the body points in is opposite to the direction of the movement) along the same directions did not activate this cell at all. The

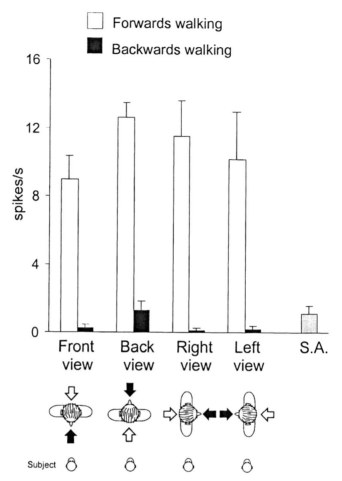

Figure 15.5. Object-centered coding of forward walking. This cell responds to the experimenter walking forwards (i.e., following the nose), independent of the perspective view of the experimenter (front, back, right, left). In contrast, walking backwards hardly produced a response. There was no effect of the direction of motion or the perspective view on responses. [Two-way ANOVA, overall effects of conditions, type of walking (forwards, backwards), $F(1,46) = 94.4$, $p < 0.0005$; direction of motion (towards, away, to the right, to the left), $F(3,46) = 0.39$, $p = 0.76$; interaction, $F(3,46) = 0.90$, $p = 0.45$; number of trials for each condition from left to right, n = 6,7,8,7,6,7,8,5,9.]

responses of this cell were almost completely determined by the mode of walking, i.e., forward walking, the factors "direction of motion" and "view" (front, back, right profile, left profile) produced no significant influence on the response.

The generalization in the visual coding of actions that has been described in this section is well suited to support the imitation of behavior. When an agent demonstrates a particular action of, e.g., the hand, the particular vantage point of the observer is arbitrary. To imitate the action, the same motor pattern must be triggered whatever the perspective view.

Goal-related coding for actions

Though the viewer-centered descriptions may serve purposes in their own right, at the same time they may also serve as the "building blocks" for other descriptions. Object-centered descriptions for an action could result from pooling the outputs of several viewer-centered cells, each of which codes for a particular perspective view of that action. In the same way goal-centered coding (e.g., reaching for a target) may arise from a combination of different view-centered cells sensitive to particular reaching movements from particular starting points, and other view-sensitive cells sensitive to the location and presence of the potential target object. Such cells have been described in STSa (Perrett *et al.*, 1989) and in the premotor cortex (Di Pellegrino *et al.*, 1992; Gallese, 1996; Gallese & Goldman, 1998).

The category of goal-centered descriptions, however, encompasses cell populations that code for different aspects of actions. Splitting up this category into at least two subdivisions seems therefore appropriate. One subdivision involves cells sensitive to the *intention* of an action. Whether or not the goal is achieved is irrelevant to the intention. The other subdivision involves cells specifically sensitive to the *interaction*, or *causality*, between the agent and the object or goal of the action. For these latter goal-directed cells, the perception of the intention is not enough to drive them; the result of the action needs to be perceived before the cell produces a response.

Several examples of STSa cells that are sensitive to the causal relationship between an action and the object or goal of that action have been reported (Perrett *et al.*, 1989). For instance, cells may respond to the sight of a hand manipulating an object, but not to the same manipulating action in the absence of the object, nor to movement of the objects as if manipulated but with the hand out of sight (Perrett *et al.*, 1989). Even when both hand and object are visible but the hand mimics the manipulating action just a few centimeters above the object, the cells do not respond. This sensitivity for the spatial relation between the agent and the object of the action puts the cells in a position to detect causal relations within actions. Distinct populations of cells are tuned to causal relations in different actions, such as holding, transporting, tearing apart or picking up an object (Perrett *et al.*, 1989; Perrett, Mistlin, Harries, & Chitty, 1990b).

Examples of cells coding specifically for the intention or goal of an action while that goal is not yet achieved include reaching for an object and walking towards a particular position (Perrett *et al.*, 1989, Perrett, Mistlin, Harries, & Chitty, 1990b). We are recently discovering more cell types that code the intentions or intentionality of actions.

One key to coding of intention in actions is sensitivity to information about the direction of attention of the individual performing the action. Usually an agent will attend to the goal of an action that is intended; by contrast the agent's attention may be elsewhere when an action is unattended. Cells in STSa (responsive to static postures) have been described whose response pattern can best be explained by assuming that they code for the direction of attention of the individual (Perrett, Hietanen, Oram, & Benson, 1992). The cell illustrated in Figures 15.2–4 shows that this also holds for cells sensitive to motion. Movements of different body parts may all indicate one and the same direction of attention ("upwards" in the case of the cell in Figs. 15.2–4).

We recently studied a population of STSa cells which seemed to combine information about the direction of attention of an agent with the action performed by that agent (Jellema, Baker, Wicker, & Perrett, 2000), and as such the cells appear sensitive to the intentionality of the action. These cells typically responded when an agent performing a reaching action with the arm focused attention onto the intended target-site of the reach. When the agent performed an identical reaching action but directed attention 90° away from the position in which the reaching was aimed the cells did not respond. These cells can be thought of as combining the outputs from cells specifically responsive to arm reaching with the outputs of cells specifically responsive to the direction of attention (as conveyed by the face, gaze, and body orientation). The presence of a specific object at the position the reaching was aimed for, e.g., a juice syringe located on a tray, did not affect the responses of these cells. The goal of the reaching in these cases appeared to be a position rather than an object.

Another example of coding that relates to the intention of an action is shown in Figure 15.6. This cell is typical of a recently discovered class of cells, which start to respond when an animate object moves out of sight and then continue to spike for three to eleven seconds while the object

A
In sight responses

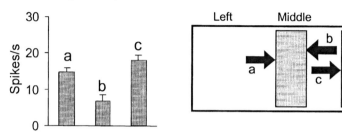

B   Out of sight responses

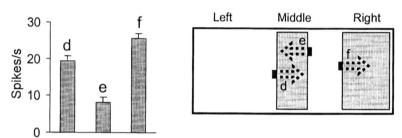

Figure 15.6. Responses (mean $+/-1$ SE) of one cell to the sight of the experimenter moving A in and B out of sight. The boxes on the right of the figure illustrate the monkey's view of the lab with two occluding screens (grey rectangles) located in the middle and on the right of the room at a distance of 4 m from the subject. Solid arrows indicate the position and direction of walking while the experimenter was visible (a-c). Dotted arrows indicate position of the experimenter when hidden from sight and the direction of movement prior to occlusion (d-f). [Two-way ANOVA, visibility of movement (in sight *vs.* out of sight), $F(1,24) = 15.7$, $p = 0.0006$; direction and position of movement (three levels; left position move right, right position move left, right position move right), $F(2,24) = 57.8$, $p < 0.0005$; interaction, $F(2,24) = 2.4$, $p = 0.12$; n = 5 for each condition. The response to condition f was greater than all other conditions a-e, $p < 0.004$, each comparison. A larger response was evoked when the experimenter walked towards the right screen (arrow c) than when he walked towards the middle screen (arrows a and b), c *vs.* b, $p < 0.0005$; c *vs.* a, $p < 0.05$, while walking towards the middle screen produced a larger response when starting from the left (arrow a) than when starting from the right (arrow b), a *vs.* b, $p < 0.002$.]

remains out of sight (Baker *et al.*, 2001). The cell illustrated responded significantly more in the three seconds following the disappearance from sight behind screens (Fig. 15.6B) than in the prior three seconds when the experimenter was visible and moving towards the screens (Fig. 15.6A). The direction and position of movement also significantly affected the cell's responses to movement.

For such cells which respond to hidden objects, the site where the animate object disappears from view is often crucial (Baker *et al.*, 2000b). The cell illustrated in Figure 15.6 responded maximally when the experimenter was hidden behind a screen located at the far-right side of the room (response to condition f is greater than all other conditions a-e). Hiding behind a neighboring screen located in the middle of the room at the same distance from the subject (arrows d and e) produced a smaller response. The cell's responses to the experimenter walking in-sight were consistent with the out-of-sight responses in that a larger response was evoked when the experimenter walked *towards* the right screen (arrow c) than when he walked *towards* the middle screen (arrows a and b). Additionally, walking towards the middle screen produced a larger response when starting from the left (arrow a) than when starting from the right (arrow b). Thus, the maximal out-of-sight response is obtained when the experimenter hides behind the right screen, and the maximal in-sight response is obtained when the direction of walking is towards the right screen and when the site of walking is closest to the right screen. These in- and out-of-sight responses are consistent with the idea that this cell codes not only for the presence of the experimenter behind the right screen, but also for the intention of the experimenter to go behind that screen. For this interpretation, we need only assume that walking towards the right screen reflects the intention to move behind that screen.

Cell sensitivity to the intentionality of actions might underlie the evolutionary beginning of "mind-reading" capabilities, which are thought to be fundamental to normal social functioning in humans (Baron-Cohen, 1994). We note that a mind-reading capacity in nonhuman primates remains controversial. Here we draw attention to simple visual cues that may enable intentions in the actions of others to be registered before the actions are completed. Awareness of these cues and their relation to the likely impending goals of actions would give a perceiver an advantage in predicting behavior in a competitive situation or in social interactions more generally. Predicting behavior allows for anticipatory responses.

In the case of imitation, attempts to reproduce the goal of actions of others can be more efficient than attempts to reproduce the precise movements that are witnessed. The agent modeling the action may fail to achieve the goal intended, but the observer who understands the intention or goal of the action can imitate the intended act and attain the intended goal (see Meltzoff, 1995, and also this volume).

From the perception of actions to the production of actions

Recently it has become apparent that visual information about motor acts is encoded in both the temporal and the premotor cortex. Rizzolatti and colleagues have found cells in areas F4 and F5 of the inferior area 6 of the premotor cortex, which respond to the sight of particular actions such as grasping, holding, tearing, and manipulating, executed by another monkey or by the experimenter (Di Pellegrino *et al.*, 1992; Gallese, 1996; Rizzolatti, Fadiga, Gallese, & Fogassi, 1996; Gallese & Goldman, 1998; and see Rizzolatti, this volume). These cells show striking similarities to the visual cells coding hand actions in STSa (Perrett *et al.*, 1989). Neurons in both areas show sensitivity to the interaction between the agent performing the action and the object or goal of the action. Moreover, there are indications that coding for the intentionality of visible and partially occluded actions, such as we described in STSa here, also occurs in the premotor cortex (L. Fogassi, personal communication; Rizzolatti, this volume). In contrast to the STSa cells, the premotor neurons also respond when the subject itself executes an identical action, in the light or dark. For example, a cell responding to the sight of the experimenter grasping an object but not to the sight of, e.g., picking up an object, also responds selectively during the execution of a grasping action. Such "mirror neurons," in the prefrontal cortex thus code both the motor components of the action (independent of vision) and the visual appearance of the action, and constitute an observation/execution matching system. They may, as such, enable the imitation of observed simple, familiar, behaviors (see Decety, this volume).

Gallese and Goldman (1998) suggested that the "action detecting" system in STSa could provide an initial "pictorial" description of the action that would then feed to the F5 motor vocabulary where it would acquire a meaning for the individual. We agree that it is quite possible that the results of the high-level visual analysis of animate actions in STSa are fed forward to the premotor cortex, where they activate circuits comprising mirror neurons, which can, in principle, reproduce the perceived action (Carey, Perrett, & Oram, 1997).

Thus, the premotor mirror neurons and subsets of STSa cells comprise two systems for the visual analysis of actions. A function of the mirror neurons might then be to complement the STSa description of the perceived action by adding information about the motor requirements

of the perceived action (how the same action would be executed if performed by the observer); these requirements could not *easily* be obtained
from purely visual features. In this view the mirror neurons in the premotor cortex are an integral part of the perceptual system for perceiving and understanding animate actions. (For alternative interpretations
of the premotor analysis of actions see chapters by Prinz and Bekkering,
this volume.) At a more speculative level, it has also been proposed that
the mirror neurons are involved in the ability to "read" others' minds.
The cells may allow an observer to "experience" and understand an action performed by another individual through the observer's ability to
"simulate" the same action (Gallese & Goldman, 1998).

Functional imaging studies in humans also suggest the involvement
of both the premotor and temporal cortex in the perception of actions.
Witnessing real hand movements activates the human brain in premotor
cortex and in left superior temporal sulcus: presumably in areas that
are homologous to those described in the brain of the macaque monkey
(Rizzolatti, Fadiga, Gallese, & Fogassi, 1996; Grafton, Arbib, Fadiga, &
Rizzolatti, 1996; see also chapters by Decety and Rizzolatti, this volume).

There are several reasons why the neural substrates for action production and action perception could be largely shared. For example, the
capacity to copy elaborate manual skills necessary for food processing
would seem to confer an advantage by obviating the need for learning
by trial and error in situations that may be painful (gorilla processing
stinging nettle leaves, Byrne & Byrne, 1991; Byrne, this volume) or dangerous (e.g., chimpanzees catching and eating scorpions). While it is clear
that great apes and even parrots do show evidence for the capacity to
imitate actions demonstrated visually by humans (Custance, Whiten, &
Bard, 1995; see Whiten, this volume), most reviews conclude that there
is little or no good behavioral evidence from observational studies or
laboratory experiments that monkeys imitate or comprehend the goals
of others (Galef, 1988; Visalberghi & Fragaszy, 1990; Whiten & Ham,
1992; Byrne, 1995; Gardner & Heyes, 1998, though see Bugnyar &
Huber, 1997; Whiten, this volume). Many instances of so-called
"imitative" behavior made by nonhuman animals may be instances of
"response facilitation" or "stimulus enhancement" with trial and error
learning (Byrne, this volume).

Nevertheless, the physiological recordings from frontal and temporal neocortex provide perhaps the most convincing evidence that there
are brain processes in monkey species that could provide a detailed
understanding of the actions of others, and that the sight of these actions
could be matched to the motor commands for the individual to reproduce

the actions that it sees. The properties of the visual cells that have been reviewed here demonstrate that visual representations of actions can generalize across different perspective views in which the observer may see an agent perform an action (Figs. 15.2-5). The visual representations also generalize across gaps in viewing while the agent is temporarily hidden from sight (Fig. 15.6). Perhaps of greatest interest is that the visual representation of actions includes sensitivity to intentionality. Each of these properties should facilitate an observer's attempts to reproduce the meaningful aspects of the behavior of another; in short, the visual coding of actions appears well suited to support understanding and imitation of others.

References

Baker, C. I., Keysers, C., Jellema, T., Wicker, B., & Perrett, D. I. (2000). Coding of spatial position in the superior temporal sulcus of the macaque. *Current Psychology Letters: Behaviour, Brain and Cognition, 1*, 71–87.

Baker, C. I., Keysers, C., Jellema, T., Wicker, B., & Perrett, D. I. (2001). Neuronal representation of disappearing and hidden objects in temporal cortex of the macaque. *Experimental Brain Research, 140*, 375–381.

Baron-Cohen, S. (1994). How to build a baby that reads minds: Cognitive mechanisms in mindreading. *Current Psychology of Cognition, 13*, 513–552.

Brothers, L., & Ring, B. (1993). Mesial temporal neurons in the macaque monkey with responses selective for aspects of social stimuli. *Behavioural Brain Research, 57*, 53–61.

Bruce, C., Desimone, R., & Gross, C. G. (1981). Visual properties of neurons in a polysensory area in superior temporal sulcus of the macaque. *Journal of Neurophysiology, 46*, 369–384.

Bugnyar, T., & Huber, L. (1997). Push or pull: An experimental study on imitation in marmosets. *Animal Behaviour, 54*, 817–831.

Byrne, R. W. (1995). *The thinking ape: Evolutionary origins of intelligence.* Oxford: Oxford University Press.

Byrne, R. W., & Byrne, J. M. E. (1991). Complex leaf-gathering skills of mountain gorillas (*Gorilla g. beringei*): Variability and standardization. *Cortex, 27*, 521–546.

Carey, D. P., Perrett, D. I., & Oram, M. W. (1997). Recognizing, understanding and reproducing action. In F. Boller & J. Grafman (Series Eds.), *Handbook of neuropsychology*, Vol. 11, *Action and Cognition* (M. Jeannerod, Vol. Ed.) (pp. 111–129). Amsterdam: Elsevier.

Custance, D. M., Whiten, A., & Bard, K. A. (1995). Can young chimpanzees (*Pan troglodytes*) imitate arbitrary actions? Hayes and Hayes (1952) revisited. *Behaviour, 132*, 837–859.

Di Pellegrino, G., Fadiga, L., Fogassi, L., Gallese, V., & Rizzolatti, G. (1992). Understanding motor events: A neurophysiological study. *Experimental Brain Research, 91*, 176–180.

Felleman, D. J., & Van Essen, D. C. (1991). Distributed hierarchical processing in the primate cerebral cortex. *Cerebral Cortex, 1,* 1–47.

Galef, B. G. (1988). Imitation in animals: Field and laboratory analysis. In T. Zentall & B. G. Galef (Eds.), *Social learning: Psychological and biological perspectives* (pp. 1–28). Hillsdale, NJ: Lawrence Erlbaum.

Gallese, V. (1996). Action recognition in the premotor cortex. *Brain, 119,* 593–609.

Gallese, V., & Goldman, A. (1998). Mirror neurons and the simulation theory of mind-reading. *Trends in Cognitive Sciences, 2,* 493–501.

Gardner, M., & Heyes, C. (1998). Splitting, lumping, and priming. *Behavioural and Brain Sciences, 21,* 690–697.

Gentilucci, M., Daprati, E., & Gangitano, M. (1998). Implicit visual analysis in handedness recognition. *Consciousness and Cognition, 7,* 478–493.

Grafton, S. T., Arbib, M. A., Fadiga, L., & Rizzolatti, G. (1996). Localization of grasp representations in humans by positron emission tomography. 2. Observation compared with imagination. *Experimental Brain Research, 112,* 103–111.

Gross, C. G., Rocha-Miranda, C. E., & Bender, D. B. (1972). Visual properties of neurons in inferotemporal cortex of the macaque. *Journal of Neurophysiology, 35,* 96–111.

Hasselmo, M. E., Rolls, E. T., & Baylis, G. C. (1989). The role of expression and identity in the face-selective responses of neurons in the temporal visual cortex of the monkey. *Behavioural Brain Research, 32,* 203–218.

Jeannerod, M., Arbib, M. A., Rizzolatti, G., & Sakata, H. (1995). Grasping objects: The cortical mechanisms of visuomotor transformation. *Trends in Neurosciences, 18,* 314–320.

Jellema, T., Baker, C. I., Wicker, B., & Perrett, D. I. (2000). Neural representation for the perception of the intentionality of hand actions. *Brain and Cognition, 44,* 280–302.

Marr, D., & Nishihara, H. K. (1978). Representation and recognition of the spatial organization from single two-dimensional images. *Proceedings of the Royal Society of London, B 200,* 269–294.

Meltzoff, A. N. (1995). Understanding the intentions of others: Re-enactment of intended acts by 18-month-old children. *Developmental Psychology, 31,* 838–850.

Milner, A. D., & Goodale, M. A. (1995). *The visual brain in action.* Oxford: Oxford University Press.

Mistlin, A. J., & Perrett, D. I. (1990). Visual and somatosensory processing in the macaque temporal cortex: the role of "expectation". *Experimental Brain Research, 82,* 437–450.

Oram, M. W., Perrett, D. I., & Hietanen, J. K. (1993). Directional tuning of motion-sensitive cells in the anterior superior temporal polysensory area of the macaque. *Experimental Brain Research, 97,* 274–294.

Oram, M. W., & Perrett D. I. (1994). Responses of anterior superior temporal polysensory (STPa) neurones to "biological motion" stimuli. *Journal of Cognitive Neuroscience, 6,* 99–116.

Oram, M. W., & Perrett, D. I. (1996). Integration of form and motion in the anterior superior temporal polysensory area (STPa) of the macaque monkey. *Journal of Neurophysiology, 76*, 109–129.

Perrett, D. I. (2000). A cellular basis for reading minds from faces and actions. In M. Hauser & M. Konishi (Eds.), *Behavioural and Neural Mechanisms of Communication*. MIT Press.

Perrett, D. I., Rolls, E. T., & Caan, W. (1982). Visual neurones responsive to faces in the monkey temporal cortex. *Experimental Brain Research, 47*, 329–342.

Perrett, D. I., Smith, P. A. J., Potter, D. D., Mistlin, A. J., Milner, A. D., & Jeeves, M. A. (1984). Neurones responsive to faces in the temporal cortex: Studies of functional organization, sensitivity to identity and relation to perception. *Human Neurobiology, 3*, 197–208.

Perrett, D. I., Smith, P. A. J., Potter, D. D., Mistlin, A. J., Head, A. S., Milner, A. D., & Jeeves, M. A. (1985a). Visual cells in the temporal cortex sensitive to face view and gaze direction. *Proceedings of the Royal Society, London, B., 223*, 293–317.

Perrett, D. I., Smith, P. A. J., Mistlin, A. J., Chitty, A. J., Head, A. S., Potter, D. D., Broenimann, R., Milner, A. D., & Jeeves, M. A. (1985b). Visual analysis of body movements by neurons in the temporal cortex of the macaque monkey: A preliminary report. *Behavioural Brain Research, 16*, 153–170.

Perrett, D. I., Harries, M. H., Bevan, R., Thomas, S., Benson, P. J., Mistlin, A. J., Chitty, A. J., Hietanen, J. K., & Ortega, J. E. (1989). Frameworks of analysis for the neural representation of animate objects and action. *Journal of Experimental Biology, 146*, 87–114.

Perrett, D. I., Harries, M. H., Benson, P. J., Chitty, A. J., & Mistlin, A. J. (1990a). Retrieval of structure from rigid and biological motion: An analysis of the visual response of neurons in the macaque temporal cortex. In T. Troscianko & A. Blake (Eds.), *AI and the eye* (pp. 181–201). Chichester: John Wiley & Sons.

Perrett, D. I., Mistlin, A. J., Harries, M. H., & Chitty, A. J. (1990b). Understanding the visual appearance and consequences of hand actions. In M. A. Goodale (Ed.), *Vision and action: The control of grasping* (pp. 163–180). Norwood, NJ: Ablex.

Perrett, D. I., Oram, M. W., Harries, M. H., Bevan, R., Hietanen, J. K., Benson, P. J., & Thomas, S. (1991). Viewer-centred and object-centred coding of heads in the macaque temporal cortex. *Experimental Brain Research, 86*, 159–173.

Perrett, D. I., Hietanen, J. K., Oram, M. W., & Benson, P. J. (1992). Organisation and functions of cells responsive to faces in the temporal cortex. *Philosophical Transactions of the Royal Society London, 335*, 23–30.

Rizzolatti, G., Fadiga, L., Gallese, V., & Fogassi, L. (1996). Premotor cortex and the recognition of motor actions. *Cognitive Brain Research, 3*, 131–141.

Rolls, E. T., & Baylis, C. G. (1986). Size and contrast have only small effects on the responses to faces of neurons in the cortex of the superior temporal sulcus of the macaque monkey. *Experimental Brain Research, 65*, 38–48.

Visalberghi, E., & Fragaszy, D. (1990). Do monkeys ape? In S. T. Parker & K. R. Gibson (Eds.), *'Language' and intelligence in monkeys and apes* (pp. 247–273). Cambridge: Cambridge University Press.

Whiten, A., & Ham, R. (1992). On the nature and evolution of imitation in the animal kingdom: Reappraisal of a century of Research. In P. J. B. Slater, J. S. Rosenblatt, C. Beer & M. Miliski (Eds.), *Advances in the study of behaviour* (Vol. 21, pp. 239–283). New York: Academic Press.

Young, M. P. (1992). Objective analysis of the topological organization of the primate cortical visual system. *Nature, 358,* 152–155.

16 Is there such a thing as functional equivalence between imagined, observed, and executed action?

Jean Decety

What do we mean by action?

In recent years, the domain of the physiology of action has been studied at many different levels, from single-cell recording in monkeys to functional imaging in healthy human volunteers. More importantly, the revival of interest in action may be seen as the consequence of the rapid growth of cognitive neuroscience, which is an interdisciplinary melding of studies of the brain, of behavior and cognition, and of computational systems. Not only each approach constrains the others, but rather each approach provides insights into different aspects of the same phenomena. In this heuristic perspective, information processing theory is not separated from or independent of the properties of the neural substrate.

An action may be described as the outcome of several information processing stages: intention, planning, preparing, and execution. According to the Causal Theory of Actions (e.g., Searle, 1983) what distinguishes actions from mere happenings is the nature of their causal antecedents. Indeed, a goal-directed action is often internally generated. This implies that the generation of action involves a representational stage which is synonymous with mental representation. However, it is clear that the concept of mental representation of action designates both the mental content related to the goal or the consequences of a given action and the covert neural operations that are supposed to occur before an action begins. There is no ontological reason to consider these two levels of description as separate and least of all independent from one another. Rather, contemporary approaches to this domain attempt to bridge with success both the cognitive description of representation of action and the neural circuitry subserving it (Fig. 16.1).

The idea that perception and action are intimately linked is not new. Indeed, Sperry proposed in 1952 that perception is basically an implicit preparation to respond, and even more, its function is to prepare the organism for adaptive action. Gibson (1979) stressed that not all organisms pick up the same information from the environment, but rather would

Functional equivalence

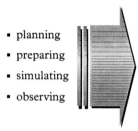

Same motor representations
Involving two main aspects:
1. a representation of the body in action as a generator of forces,
2. a representation of the goal of action encoded in a pragmatic mode.

- planning
- preparing
- simulating
- observing

Same neurophysiological substrate
As demonstrated by brain mapping techniques (PET and fMRI):
- premotor cortex, SMA, inferior parietal lobule, anterior cingulate, lateral cerebellum

Figure 16.1. A schematic representation of the functional equivalence working model. It postulates that the difference between the subcomponents that constitute an action is of degree and not of nature. The key idea of shared representations is also related to intersubjectivity and attribution of intentions to others.

resonate with information that is coordinated with their own potential for action. In fact, the study of perception and action is fundamentally the study of sensorimotor transformations. Sensory and motor data are generally in different formats and may refer to the same entities but in different coordinate systems.

There are several contemporary models that attempt to characterize the linkage between perception and action. For instance, Prinz (1997) has put forward the idea of a common coding model which postulates that perceived events and planned actions share a common representational domain. The model assumes: (1) that event codes and action codes should be considered the functional basis of percepts and action plans, respectively, and (2) that they share the same representational domain and are therefore commensurate. There is indeed supporting evidence from induction paradigms (i.e., how certain stimuli induce certain actions by virtue of similarity) and interference paradigms (i.e., mutual interference between the perception of ongoing events and the preparation and control of ongoing action) that are compatible with this model (see Prinz, 1992). Some researchers in the domain of imitation have offered similar theoretical models to account for the mechanism underlying early imitative behavior. For Meltzoff and Moore (1997) infant imitation depends on a process of active intermodal mapping.

Another approach has been developed in the field of computational motor control. A useful conceptualization was given by Jordan (1994) for whom there are two basic kinds of transformations that can be considered to manage the relationships between sensory variables and motor variables: sensory-to-motor transformations and motor-to-sensory transformations. The transformation from motor variables to sensory variables is accomplished by the environment and the musculoskeletal system; these physical systems transform efferent motor actions into reafferent sensory feedback. It is also possible to consider internal transformation, implemented by neural circuitry, that mimics the external motor-to-sensory transformation. Such internal transformations, or internal forward models, allow the motor control system to predict the consequences of particular choices of motor actions. We can also consider internal models that perform a transformation in the opposite direction, from sensory variables to motor variables. Such transformations are known as internal inverse models, and they allow the motor control system to transform desired sensory consequences into motor actions that yield these consequences. Internal inverse models are the basic module in open-loop control systems. Thus, the control of action requires predictive mechanisms (i.e., internal forward models) which in turn require a preselection of relevant sensory information.

The insights emerging from work on perception and action, at both cognitive and neural levels, are of major importance for the understanding of human mind. As a matter of fact, some philosophers of mind, such as Goldman (1992) and Currie and Ravenscroft (1997) have proposed the idea that we predict the actions of others by simulating their decision-making processes. This view, called "simulation theory," has generated considerable interest among cognitive scientists. Note that this view is close to the motor theories of perception, although not equivalent. Several authors have recently also argued, on the basis of experimental data, that our capacity to understand other people's behavior, to attribute intention of beliefs to others is rooted in a neural, most likely distributed, execution/observation mechanism (e.g., Gallese & Goldman, 1998; Corballis, 1998; Rizzolatti, this volume). Therefore, studies addressing perception of action and mental simulation of action (motor imagery), whether they are at the behavioral or at the neurophysiological levels (Decety, 1996), are of high relevance here and will thus be reviewed in this chapter.

Behavioral evidence for perception of actions

There is plenty of evidence that the human visual system is finely attuned to human movements. A number of early studies, based on the point-light technique, have revealed that the kinematic pattern of a movement is sufficient for the perception of people in action (Johansson, 1973). Using the same paradigm, Kozlowski and Cutting(1977) extended these findings by showing that observers can make very precise discriminations when watching point-light displays, such as the recognition of the gender of walkers. The fact that humans think in categories and that concepts influence the way of thinking and acting has lead Dittrich (1993) to investigate whether the ability to detect natural motions is in part determined by the content of independent categories of the information that physically characterize the event. In his study, locomotory (e.g., walking, going upstairs), instrumental (e.g., hammering, stirring), and social actions (e.g., greeting, boxing) were presented with the point-light display technique in a normal situation (light attached to joints), inter-joint (light attached between joints), and upside-down. Subjects' verbal responses and recognition times showed that locomotory actions were recognized much better and faster than social and instrumental actions. Furthermore, biological motions were recognized much better and faster when the light-spot displays were presented in the normal orientation rather than upside-down. Finally, the recognition rate was only slightly impaired under the inter-joint condition. The author argued that coding of dynamic phase relations and semantic coding take place at very early stages of the processing of biological motion. It may thus be hypothesized that the recognition of biological motion is that perception and recognition processes are mediated by the implicit knowledge of production (motor) rules.

Shiffrar and Freyd (1990, 1993) have performed a series of elegant studies by using the apparent motion paradigm (i.e., the impression of visual motion resulting from the sequential presentation of static objects in different spatial locations) with body pictures. They have challenged the fundamental important characteristic of classical apparent motion studies, namely that object identity does not influence the motion perceived since objects appear to move along the shortest or most direct path. Indeed, while static objects appear to move across 2D and 3D space, and over a wide range of stimulus presentation rates, apparent motion perception of human figures tends to respect the biomechanical constraints of normal human movement (see the next section for neurophysiological evidence of this effect). Difference in handedness may affect perception of action just as it affects motor performance. For instance, De'Sperati and Stucchi (1997) presented subjects with a rotating screwdriver on a computer screen and asked them whether it was screwing or unscrewing. Clear differences emerged in the response time between right- and left-handers.

Neurophysiological evidence for perception of actions

It is generally accepted that the monkey visual cortex is organized along two major anatomical and functional streams (Ungerleider & Mishkin, 1982). The ventral stream projecting from V1 through areas V2 and V4 to the inferior temporal cortex and to the anterior section of superior temporal sulcus is considered to be primarily concerned with the recognition of objects. The dorsal stream, projecting from V1 through areas V2 and V3 to the middle temporal area (V5/MT) and thence to the superior temporal and parietal cortex, is concerned with the perception of spatial information and with the visual guidance of actions towards objects (Milner & Goodale, 1995). The two pathways are not completely separate since a polysensory area in the superior temporal cortex (STPa) receives inputs both from the ventral and dorsal pathways (Boussaoud, Ungerleider, & Desimone, 1990).

In the monkey, Perrett et al. (1989) have found that there are neurons in the superior temporal sulcus (STS) sensitive to the sight of static and dynamic information about the body. The majority were selective for one perspective and are considered to provide viewer-centered descriptions which can be used in guiding behavior. For some cells in the lower bank of STS (area Tea) the responses to body movements were related to the object or to the goal of the movements. The same group has also used the point-light technique for presenting human biological motion to monkeys while recording cells in STPa (Oram & Perrett, 1994). One-third of the cells selective for the form and motion of a walking body showed sensitivity to the moving-light display.

Numerous electrophysiological recordings, performed by the Parma group, in the rostral part of the monkey inferior premotor cortex (area F5) have indicated that there are neurons that discharge during execution of hand and mouth movements (e.g., Rizzolatti et al., 1988). Some years later, the same authors have discovered that most of these neurons discharge not only when the monkey performed an action, but also when the monkey observed the experimenter making a similar action (e.g., Gallese, Fadiga, Pavesi, & Rizzolatti, 1996). Neurons that exhibited such properties were therefore called "mirror neurons." Thus, the physiological results from STS and F5 neurons indicate that there are brain processes in monkeys which could support the understanding of others' actions, and that the sight of these actions could be matched to the motor commands in order to imitate or reproduce actions that the monkey sees (Rizzolatti & Arbib, 1998).

Another brain region involved in the visual analysis and control of action lies in the parietal cortex. Recent neurophysiological studies in alert monkeys have revealed that the parietal association cortex plays a crucial role in depth perception and in visually guided hand movement. Sakata *et al.* (1997) suggested that neural representation of 3D objects with real physical dimensions and their egocentric positions seems to occur in the parietal association cortex. The major purpose of the 3D representation is the visual guidance of goal-directed action. Early indications are that parietal cells in area Tpa (homologous with the rostral part of the inferior parietal cortex in human?) code the sight of action (see Rizzolatti, this volume). Thus from electrophysiological recordings in nonhuman primates, three key regions (namely in the superior temporal, parietal, and inferior frontal cortices) have been identified that are specifically responsive to the visual perception of action.

In human subjects, Fadiga, Fogassi, Pavesi, and Rizzolatti (1995) have demonstrated with magnetic transcranial stimulation an increase in excitability of the motor system (MEP) during the perception of actions performed by another individual. This enhancement of MEP is selective since it occurred in the muscles that the subjects would use for producing the action observed. Converging evidence has been reported by Cochin *et al.* (1998) in a study that used EEG cartography during the perception of different sorts of video movies consisting of objects in movement, animals in motion, gymnastic movements executed by a person and still shots. Significant decreases in the alpha 1, beta 1 and beta 2 power values of the EEG over the centro-parietal regions, in both hemispheres, were shown during the perception of human motion sequences. Their results suggest the specific participation of the sensorimotor cortex during the observation of human motion. Magnetoencephalographic recordings have come to the same conclusion (Hari *et al.*, 1998).

There have been a number of brain-imaging studies that have addressed the question of the neural substrate involved in the perception of movement and action. Howard *et al.* (1996) have performed a functional magnetic resonance imaging (fMRI) study in which they contrasted different motion displays including biological motion. They found that each of the motion stimuli (i.e., coherent, optic flow, and biological motion) activated specific parts of the V5/MT complex. The biological motion stimulus produced an area of activation that overlapped with the other two and was located along the superior border of V5. Both optical flow and biological motion stimuli produced small areas of activation within both dorsal and ventral V3, but neither produced any differential activation of area V1. This study demonstrates that there is a specialization for visual motion within the V5 complex and may help to account for some odd clinical observations of patients unable to perceive objects in motion while they can correctly identify biological motion (e.g., Vaina *et al.*, 1990; Marcar, Zihl, & Cowey, 1997). It should be emphasized that

V5 responds to motion imagery, visual apparent motion (Goebel *et al.*, 1998). The generation of words denoting actions associated with visually presented objects activates an area anterior to V5 which extends to the left posterior temporal gyrus (Martin *et al.*, 1995).

Recently, on the basis of the findings by Shiffrar and Freyd (1990, 1993), we have adapted the apparent motion paradigm to present subjects with conditions of possible and impossible bodily motion (Stevens, Fonlupt, Shiffrar, & Decety, 2000). The V5 complex was found to be activated in both conditions. However several other cortical areas were selectively activated by each condition. When subjects perceived possible paths of apparent human movement the most significant bilateral rCBF increase was found in the left precentral gyrus. Significant bilateral activations were also found in the superior parietal gyrus, superior frontal gyrus, superior temporal gyrus and in the left inferior parietal lobule (Fig. 16.2). By contrast, perception of impossible apparent

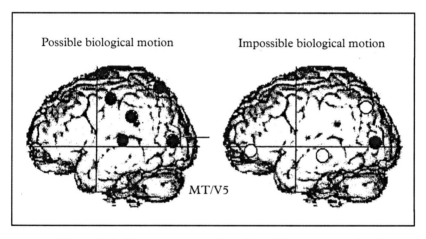

Figure 16.2. The apparent motion of possible movements involves an explicit motor representation as demonstrated here. Motor executive regions and the inferior parietal cortex are selectively activated to process actions which conform to the capabilities of the observer. The apparent motion paradigm was adapted to a PET experiment in which apparent motion perception of human possible movements versus impossible movements were visually presented to ten healthy subjects. This figure shows the significant rCBF increases selective to the perception of possible movements displayed on a left hemisphere in the Talairach coordinates. Note the activation in the precentral gyrus which was predominant on the left side. The MT/V5 complex (dark circle) was bilaterally activated and its coordinates correspond to those found by Watson *et al.* (1993).

human motion lead to strong rCBF increases bilaterally in the medial orbitofrontal cortex. These results demonstrate that visual perception of apparent human movement selectively activates motor executive regions of the brain, just as explicitly perceived, imagined, and executed actions do. The selective activation of the orbital frontal cortex during the perception of impossible human movements likely reflects subjects' detection of deviations from normal motor action paths. Significant activation in this region has been found during perception of violations in visual tasks outcomes (Nobre, Coull, Frith, & Mesulam, 1999) and when subjects plan for but then subsequently inhibit themselves from completing physical action (Krams *et al.*, 1998).

Additional evidence on the neurophysiological substrate underlying the perception of action in humans is provided by several PET experiments. Rizzolatti *et al.* (1996) scanned subjects under three experimental conditions: observation of an actor grasping common physical objects, grasping the same objects themselves and as a control, passive object observation. The results of subtracting object observation from observation of an actor grasping the object resulted in rCBF activations in the middle temporal gyrus including that of the adjacent superior temporal sulcus, in the caudal part of the inferior frontal gyrus, as well as activations in the precuneus and in the medial frontal gyrus. All activations were located in the left hemisphere. Their data show that there is a good correspondence between humans and monkeys in the cortical areas devoted to hand-action recognition. The activation in the left temporal lobe would correspond to the STS in monkeys (Perrett *et al.*, 1989; Perrett, 1990; Oram & Perrett, 1994) and the activation in the inferior frontal gyrus might be similar to F5 (e.g., Gallese, Fadiga, Fogassi, & Rizzolatti, 1996). These results have recently been confirmed and extended by Decety *et al.* (1997) in a PET experiment that contrasted the visual perception of meaningful and meaningless pantomimes. Subjects were instructed to watch the actions with two aims: either to recognize or to imitate them later. It was found that the meaning of the action, irrespective of the strategy used during observation, led to different patterns of brain activity and clear left/right asymmetries. Meaningful actions strongly engaged the left hemisphere in frontal and temporal regions while meaningless actions involved mainly the right occipito-parietal pathway. Observing with the intent to recognize activated memory-encoding structures. By contrast, observation with the intent to imitate was associated with activation in the regions involved in the planning and in the generation of actions. Thus, the pattern of brain activation during observation of actions is dependent, both on the nature of the required executive processing and the type of the extrinsic properties of the action presented. Another PET study, conducted by

Grèzes, Costes, and Decety (1998) used a similar paradigm. Perception of meaningful and of meaningless hand actions without any purpose was contrasted with the perception of the same kind of stimuli with the goal to imitate them later. A condition which consisted in the perception of stationary hands served as a baseline level. Perception of meaningful actions and meaningless actions without any aim was associated with activation of a common set of cortical regions. In both hemispheres, the occipito-temporal junction and the superior occipital gyrus were involved. In the left hemisphere, the middle temporal gyrus and the inferior parietal lobe were found to be activated. These regions are interpreted as related to the analysis of hand movements. The precentral gyrus, within the area of hand representation, was activated in the left hemisphere. In addition to this common network, meaningful and meaningless movements engaged specific networks, respectively: meaningful actions were associated with activations mainly located in the left hemisphere in the inferior frontal gyrus (Ba 44/45) and the fusiform gyrus, whereas meaningless actions involved the dorsal pathway bilaterally and the right cerebellum. In contrast, meaningful and meaningless actions shared almost the same network when the aim of the perception was to imitate. Activations were located in the right cerebellum and bilaterally in the dorsal pathway reaching the premotor cortex. Additional bilateral activations were located in the SMA and in the orbitofrontal cortex during observation of meaningful actions. Thus, when perception has no goal, the pattern of brain activation is dependent on the nature of the movements presented. But when perception has a goal, namely to imitate, the subject's strategy has a top-down effect on the information processing which seems to give priority to the dorsal pathway involved in perception for action (Goodale, 1997).

Behavioral evidence for mental simulation of actions

The involvement of common mechanisms in motor imagery and motor behavior is supported by a growing body of evidence since the paper by Decety and Ingvar (1990). In this paper we suggested that mental simulation of action requires the construction of a dynamic motor representation in working memory which makes use of spatial and kinesthetic components retrieved from long-term memory, as well as the activation of serial plans of action.

Several experiments using the mental chronometry paradigm clearly support the hypothesis that mental simulation of action is assigned to the same motor representation system as preparation and execution. Parsons (1987) has shown that, when a photograph of a hand was presented at a given orientation and the subjects required to judge whether it is a right or a left hand, the time taken to respond closely mimics the actual time of the real movement. In subjects requested either to imagine or actually walk towards targets placed at different distances, Decety, Prablanc, and Jeannerod (1989) reported that the duration of simulation was similar and related to the distance covered. Other evidence for the implementation of motor production rules during mental simulation has been demonstrated with the use of Fitts' law paradigm (i.e., the tradeoff between speed and accuracy). For instance, Decety and Jeannerod (1996) designed an experiment to verify whether Fitts' law holds in mental simulation. Subjects, immersed in a virtual reality system, were instructed to walk mentally along a path and through gates of different widths positioned at different distances. In accordance with Fitts' law, the time needed to imagine walking through a given gate was found to be affected both by its relative distance and by its relative width, namely the duration of the simulation increased linearly as a function of task difficulty. Difference in handedness performance also affects mental simulation as it does in motor performance (e.g., De'Sperati & Stucchi, 1997). In a recent experiment, Johnson (1998) exploited the well-known contralateral organization of the visual and motor systems with a divided-visual-field task that required subjects to determine whether they would use an underhand or overhand grip if they were to reach for a dowel-shaped object, briefly presented to either visual field. Although no actual reaching movements were performed, a significant advantage in grip-selection time was found when the information was presented to the cerebral hemisphere contralateral to the designated response hand.

There is confirmatory evidence from studies of neurological patients which demonstrate that deficit in motor performance is reflected in motor imagery. Dominey *et al.* (1995) examined hemi-Parkinson patients in both visual and motor imagery tasks involving either side of the body. They reported a selective deficit in motor imagery on the affected side but not in visual imagery that closely matched the deficit in actual motor performance. A correlation between actual and mental movement times was found in a patient with motor cortex damage in the right hemisphere (Sirigu *et al.*, 1995). The left arm was slower in executing motor tasks with the fingers and elbow, but not with the shoulder. The same difference was observed for mentally simulated movements. Sirigu *et al.* (1996) also reported that patients with lesions restricted to the parietal cortex were found to be selectively impaired at predicting, through mental imagery tasks, the time necessary to perform finger movements, in comparison to normal subjects and to the previously described patient with damage to the primary motor area. A similar observation has been reported in a single case study of a patient with severe ideomotor apraxia who was selectively impaired in motor imagery while his capacity in visual imagery of objects was spared (Ochipa *et al.*, 1997).

Neurophysiological evidence for mental simulation of actions

Studies of cerebral metabolic activity have shown overlapping patterns of rCBF variations during motor imagery, motor preparation, and actual motor performance. In a group of normal subjects requested to imagine grasping objects relative to the visual inspection of the same objects, the prefrontal cortex, the anterior cingulate, the premotor cortex, the inferior parietal lobule, the cerebellum, the ventrolateral thalamus, and the caudate nucleus were found to be activated mainly in the left hemisphere (Decety *et al.*, 1994). Lang *et al.* (1994) reported bilateral activations in the SMA, in the precentral gyrus, and in the anterior cingulate gyrus during the simulation of saccadic eye movements. Another PET activation study during an internally guided motor imagery of a joy-stick movement reported activations in the medial and lateral premotor areas, including the SMA as well as the superior and inferior parietal areas bilaterally (Stephan *et al.*, 1995). Until recently, there was agreement that the early stages of the process of action generation, such as planning or programming, involved the premotor cortex and the SMA, while MI was considered to be responsible for proper execution only. This view now has been challenged by the use of functional magnetic resonance imaging (fMRI), whose temporal and spatial resolution is much better than PET. For example, Roth *et al.* (1996) measured hemodynamic changes with fMRI in normal right-handed subjects during actual and mental execution of a finger-to-thumb opposition task with either the right or the left hand. The data show no significant differences between the two hands with either execution or simulation. A significant involvement of the contralateral motor cortex (30 per cent of the activity found during execution) was detected. The premotor cortex and the rostral part of the posterior SMA were activated bilaterally during motor imagery.

Few neuroimaging studies have examined the neural correlates of motor preparation in humans. Decety, Kawashima, Gulyas, and Roland (1992) instructed subjects to prepare for pointing towards visual targets previously displayed on a screen and found bilateral activations in the prefrontal cortex, SMA, left parietal lobe and supramarginal gyrus, the ventrolateral thalamus and the cerebellum. Recently, Krams *et al.* (1998) measured movement set-related changes when subjects were asked to copy hand movements during four conditions: prepare and execute, immediate execution, preparation only, and a baseline condition. They demonstrated that regions involved in motor preparation were a subset of the areas involved in the preparation and execution condition. However, the finding that the ventrolateral prefrontal cortex and the anterior cingulate were significantly more active during preparation than in a coupled preparation/execution condition was interpreted as reflecting an inhibitory mechanism. The activation of representations for actions by motor imagery is not limited to increased metabolism in brain areas. It also includes autonomic mechanisms which represent an interesting case since they are normally not submitted to voluntary control. Indeed several papers have reported cardiorespiratory changes during motor imagery, namely increases in heart rate, respiratory rate, ventilation, and blood pressure (e.g., Decety, Jeannerod, Durozard, & Baverel, 1993; Wang & Morgan, 1992). The same phenomenon has been observed during motor preparation (see Requin, Brener, & Ring, 1991).

Discussion

An action may be described as the outcome of several information processing stages: intention, planning, preparing, and execution. It is widely accepted that an internal model underlies these mechanisms. Several cognitive models have been put forward to account for the capacity to generate an action but also to understand, predict actions performed by others and even distinguish our own actions from events caused by external agents (e.g., Frith, 1992; Jeannerod, 1997). This is not restricted to motor actions but can be generalized to the expression and recognition of emotions. Indeed there is considerable evidence that we tend to imitate (not consciously) facial expressions to which we are exposed, via feedback mechanisms we realize that our own imitated facial expression is associated with an emotion, and then attribute this emotion to the person confronting us (e.g., Wallbott, 1991). An attractive hypothesis is that a similar neural system operates for action production and action recognition (e.g., Rizzolatti & Arbib, 1998; Gallese & Goldman, 1998). Such a system is likely to be distributed among different brain areas. Indeed, a common network seems to be consistently recruited during several action modalities, namely the inferior parietal lobule, the prefrontal and premotor cortex and perhaps the primary motor cortex, although there is no strict overlap between each modality (see Rizzolatti, this volume).

Yet the respective role of each of these components that make this system work is not clearly understood in humans. Even if it is true that we do gain clues from the detailed comparison of the human brain with that of the macaque monkey, those homologies have to be carefully employed since less is known in the chimpanzee brain, our nearest relative according to genetic and comparative psychology studies (see Passingham, 1998).

For instance, if area F5, in which mirror neurons are recorded in monkeys, has evolved into Broca's area in man as suggested by MacNeilage (1998), then one should hypothesize that lesion of the left inferior frontal gyrus would lead to deficits in gesture recognition and in gesture imitation. Several clinical observations since the time of Jackson in the nineteenth century have indeed reported oral apraxia to be associated with Broca's aphasia but not with Wernicke's aphasia (e.g., De Renzi, Pieczuro, & Vignolo, 1966). Mateer and Kimura (1977) tested nonfluent aphasics as well as fluent aphasics in the imitation of nonverbal oral movement tasks. They found that, while the former were impaired in imitating single oral movements, the latter showed impairments in the imitation of complex oral movements. An interesting question is whether such impairment is specific to oral movements *per se* or can be extended to hand gestures. Very few systematic studies have addressed this issue. Bell (1994) has presented a pantomime recognition test (involving a combination of limb, hand, and facial actions) to a group of aphasic patients (regardless of various forms of aphasia, i.e., Broca's, conduction, Wernicke's, anomic, global, nonfluent) and compared their results to a group of control subjects. Patients performed significantly poorer than the controls. However, when one looks carefully at the data reported in the article, only ten patients out of 23 scored incorrectly on the recognition test. We have recently examined the ability to recognize and to imitate meaningful and meaningless pantomimes in a group of neurological patients sorted by the location of the vascular lesion, as opposed to a group of control subjects (Genouilhac, 1998). While all patients' performance in the recognition of meaningless and meaningful action tasks was comparable to that of normals regardless of the laterality of the lesion, only one case (left paramesial protuberance lesion) was impaired. We have since examined three Broca's patients in various systematic recognition and imitation tasks involving object-directed movements, meaningful and meaningless pantomimes. None of the patients exhibited impairment in any of these tasks. Patients with left hemisphere infarct involving Broca's area and surrounding regions were not impaired in ordering groups of words to form a logical sequence of action (Sirigu et al., 1998). The test used consisted of a set of cards with an action written on each one. Hence the patients had first to recognize the action before ordering it into a sequence. Thus there is clearly a need for more studies of patients to assess the role of the inferior frontal gyrus in action recognition.

The middle temporal gyrus (Brodmann area 21) is another region of interest for the perception of action. Here again, the homologies between monkey and human should be taken with caution. While in macaque areas 21 and 22 act as visual association cortex, in humans, area 21 is engaged in language tasks (e.g., Demonet et al., 1992; Martin et al., 1995) and in the perception of hand and body movements in its posterior portion (e.g., Grafton, Arbib, Fadiga, & Rizzolatti, 1996; Decety *et al.*, 1997; Grèzes, Costes, & Decety, 1998). This region is distinct from V5 and is found predominantly activated in the right hemisphere. Puce *et al.* (1998) have also reported that a region in the posterior part of the temporal lobe, in the STS, was activated when subjects view a face in which the eye or mouth is moving. These activations were not attributable to movement *per se* but to the fact that the movement was biological. Thus, there is no doubt that an area preferentially responsive to biological movements is present in human STS.

Conclusion

We know from evolutionary psychology that there is a continuity between nonhuman and human primates. It is thus plausible that our ability to recognize and attribute intentions to ourselves as well as to others has evolved from the capacity to perceive and identify movements performed by other living organisms. This system exploits the same motor representations for both reading others' actions (in a wide sense, e.g., gaze direction, emotion) and for producing them.

It is acknowledged that newborns are wired for perceptual-motor coupling as it is attested by the studies on immediate imitation (see Meltzoff & Moore, 1999 for a recent review). Imitative interaction sequences play a constitutive role in intersubjectivity as well as in the learning of social rules (see Nadel & Butterworth, 1999). The prefrontal cortex which appears to exert its functions mostly through inhibition is not fully mature immediately after birth. While cytoarchitecture reaches full development before birth in humans, the myelination of prefrontal connective fibers extends long after birth, until adolescence (Fuster, 1997). This lack of inhibition, or mild inhibition, at the beginning of childhood confers developmental benefits through imitation. Then, inhibitory mechanisms progressively develop, in parallel to cognitive abilities for which inhibition is a requisite. Substantial evidence for the inhibitory role of the lower half of the prefrontal cortex has been reported in brain-damaged individuals (Lhermitte, Pillon, & Serdaru, 1986) who exhibit unsuppressed imitation or utilization behavior. The orbitofrontal region was consistently found to be activated when healthy subjects watched actions for later imitation (Decety *et al.*, 1997; Grèzes, Costes, & Decety, 1998) and not when subjects observed for later recognition. Furthermore this activation was detected only for those actions that were in the motor repertoire of the subjects, e.g., meaningful actions, but not for meaningless actions. However, it was recently demonstrated that when meaningless actions were learned by subjects a few days before the PET exam and thus became familiar, the orbitofrontal cortex was then engaged during observation with the intent to imitate. It was not the case for unfamiliar meaningless actions although the difference between the two sets of movements was very small (Grèzes & Decety, 1999).

The lines of evidence presented in this chapter are largely compatible with the idea that neural and cognitive representations involved in the generation of actions are also recruited by observation and by mental simulation. Thus perception and action are not separate phenomena. Rather there is a common neural substrate that directly translates sensory experience into action or schemas of actions (see Rizzolatti, this volume). Whether the overlap between the cortical regions is true not only at a macro-anatomical but chiefly at a micro-anatomical level remains to be elucidated (Grèzes & Decety, 2001).

Finally, if one accepts the idea of shared representations for recognition, imitation, or self-production, then how do we distinguish our own actions from the actions from the environment? Several researchers have proposed that knowledge of our intentions or motor commands is used to distinguish the sensory consequences of our own actions from externally produced sensory stimuli (Frith, 1992; Wolpert, Ghahramani, & Jordan, 1995). Frith has argued for a central monitoring system, which can be considered as a cognitive model similar to the forward model but with an extension of the functional properties of the efference copy concept into covert actions such as thinking. This model captures the forward or causal relationship between actions, as signaled by the efference copy and the predicted sensory outcome. By comparing this prediction with the actual sensory feedback it is possible to distinguish the sensory consequences of our movements from sensory signals due to changes in the outside world. Different cortical areas for expected stimuli and sensory consequences of self-generated actions have been discovered by Blakemore, Rees, and Frith (1998). They have observed an interaction between the predictability of the stimuli and self-generated actions in the medial posterior cingulate cortex, the left insula, the dorsomedial thalamus and the right inferior temporal cortex. In a recent fMRI study, Blakemore, Wolpert, and Frith (1999) examined neural responses when subjects experienced a tactile stimulus that was either self-produced or externally produced. More activity was detected in the somatosensory cortex when the stimulus was externally produced and a reduction of activity was seen for self-produced action. There was less activity in the cerebellum when a movement generated a tactile stimulus than with a movement that did not. This difference suggests that the cerebellum is involved in predicting the specific sensory consequences of movements, providing the signal that is used to cancel the sensory response to self-generated stimulation. Such selective activity for the externally generated signal is also evident at the single-cell level (see Perrett, this volume). An alternative for distinguishing self-generated actions from actions produced by others may be based on the partial overlap between the activated network and/or the level (intensity of the signal) of neural activation within each subregion which composes the network.

References

Bell, B. D. (1994). Pantomime recognition impairment in aphasia: An analysis of error types. *Brain and Language, 47,* 269–278.

Blakemore, S. J., Rees, G., & Frith, C. D. (1998). How do we predict the consequences of our actions? A functional imaging study. *Neuropsychologia, 36,* 521–529.

Blakemore, S. J., Wolpert, D. L., & Frith, C. D. (1999). Central cancellation of self-produced tickle sensation. *Nature Neuroscience, 1,* 635–640.

Boussaoud, D., Ungerleider, L. G., & Desimone, R. (1990). Pathways for motion analysis: Cortical connections of the medial superior temporal and fundus of the superior temporal visual areas in the macaque. *Journal of Comparative Neurology, 296,* 462–495.

Cochin, S., Barthelemy, C., Lejeune, B., Roux, S., & Martineau, J. (1998). Perception of motion and qEEG activity in human adults. *Electroencephalography and Clinical Neurophysiology, 107,* 287–295.

Corballis, M. C. (1998). Evolution of the human mind. In M. Sabourin, F. Craik, & M. Robert (Eds.), *Advances in psychological science, Volume 2: Biological and cognitive aspects* (pp. 31–62). Hove: Psychology Press.

Currie, G., & Ravenscroft, I. (1997). Mental simulation and motor imagery. *Philosophy of Science, 64,* 161–180.

De'Sperati, C., & Stucchi, N. (1997). Recognizing the motion of graspable object is guided by handedness. *Neuroreport, 8,* 2761–2765.

Decety, J. (1996). Do imagined and executed actions share the same neural substrate? *Cognitive Brain Research, 3,* 87–93.

Decety, J., Grèzes, J., Costes, N., Perani, D., Jeannerod, M., Procyk, E., Grassi, F., & Fazio, F. (1997). Brain activity during observation of actions: Influence of action content and subject's strategy. *Brain, 120,* 1763–1777.

Decety, J., & Ingvar, D. H. (1990). Brain structures participating in mental simulation of motor behavior: A neuropsychological interpretation. *Acta Psychologica, 73,* 13–34.

Decety, J., & Jeannerod, M. (1996). Mentally simulated movements in virtual reality: Does Fitts's law hold in motor imagery? *Behavioural Brain Research, 72,* 127–134.

Decety, J., Jeannerod, M., Durozard, D., & Baverel, G. (1993). Central activation of autonomic effectors during mental simulation of motor actions in man. *Journal of Physiology, 461,* 549–563.

Decety, J., Kawashima, R., Gulyas, B., & Roland, P. (1992). Preparation for reaching: A PET study of the participating structures in the human brain. *NeuroReport, 3*, 761–764.

Decety, J., Perani, D., Jeannerod, M., Bettinardi, V., Tadary, B., Woods, R., Mazziotta, J. C., & Fazio, F. (1994). Mapping motor representations with positron emission tomography. *Nature, 371*, 600–602.

Decety, J., Prablanc, C., & Jeannerod, M. (1989). The timing of mentally represented actions. *Behavioral Brain Research, 34*, 35–42.

Demonet, J. F., Chollet, J. F., Ramsay, S., Cardebat, D., Nespoulous, J. L., & Wise, R. (1992). The anatomy of phonological processing in normal subjects. *Brain, 115*, 1753–1768.

De Renzi, E., Pieczuro, A., & Vignolo, L. A. (1966). Oral apraxia and aphasia. *Cortex, 2*, 50–73.

Dittrich, W. H. (1993). Action categories and the perception of biological motion. *Perception, 22*, 15–22.

Dominey, P., Decety, J., Broussolle, E., Chazot, G., & Jeannerod, M. (1995). Motor imagery of a lateralized sequential task is asymmetrically slowed in hemi-Parkinson patients. *Neuropsychologia, 33*, 727–741.

Fadiga, L., Fogassi, L., Pavesi, G., & Rizzolatti, G. (1995). Motor facilitation during action observation: A magnetic stimulation study. *Journal of Neurophysiology, 73*, 2608–2611.

Frith, C. D. (1992). *The cognitive neuropsychology of schizophrenia.* Hillsdale, NJ: Lawrence Erlbaum Associates.

Fuster, J. M. (1997). *The prefrontal cortex.* Philadelphia: Lippincott, Raven.

Gallese, V., Fadiga, L., Fogassi, L., & Rizzolatti, G. (1996). Action recognition in the premotor cortex. *Brain, 119*, 593–609.

Gallese, V., & Goldman, A. (1998). Mirror neurons and the simulation theory of mind-reading. *Trends in Cognitive Sciences, 2*, 493–501.

Genouilhac, V. (1998). La perception des actions chez des patients cérébrolésés. *Master Thesis.* Institute of Psychology, University Lumière, Lyon 2.

Gibson, J. J. (1979). *The ecological approach to visual perception.* Hillsdale, NJ: Lawrence Erlbaum Associates.

Goebel, R., Khorram-Sefat, D., Muckli, L., Hacker, H., & Singer, W. (1998). The constructive nature of vision: Direct evidence from functional magnetic resonance imaging studies of apparent motion and motion imagery. *European Journal of Neuroscience, 10*, 1563–1573.

Goldman, A. I. (1992). In defense of the simulation theory. *Mind and Language, 7*, 104–119.

Goodale, M. A. (1997). Visual routes to perception and action in the cerebral cortex. In F. Boller & J. Grafman (Eds.), *Handbook of neuropsychology* (Vol. 11, pp. 91–109). Amsterdam: Elsevier.

Grafton, S. T., Arbib, M. A., Fadiga, L., & Rizzolatti, G. (1996). Localization of grasp representations in humans by positron emission tomography. *Experimental Brain Research, 112*, 103–111.

Grèzes, J., & Decety, J. (2001). Functional anatomy of execution, mental simulation, observation, and verb generation of actions: A meta-analysis. *Human Brain Mapping, 12*, 1–19.

Grèzes, J., Costes, N., & Decety, J. (1998). Top-down effect of the strategy on the perception of biological motion: A PET investigation. *Cognitive Neuropsychology, 15*, 553–582.

———— (1999). The effect of learning on the neural networks engaged by the perception of meaningless actions. *Brain, 122*, 1875–1887.

Hari, R., Forss, N., Avikainen, S., Kirveskari, E., Salenius, S., & Rizzolatti, G. (1998). Activation of human primary motor cortex during action observation: A neuromagnetic study. *Proceedings National Academy of Science USA, 95*, 15061–15065.

Howard, R. J., Brammer, M., Wright, I., Woodruff, P. W., Bullmore, E. T., & Zeki, S. (1996). A direct demonstration of functional specialization within motion-related visual and auditory cortex of the human brain. *Current Biology, 6*, 1015–1019.

Jeannerod, M. (1997). *The cognitive neuroscience of action.* Oxford: Blackwell.

Johansson, G. (1973). Visual perception of biological motion and a model for its analysis. *Perception and Psychophysics, 14*, 201–211.

Johnson, S. H. (1998). Cerebral organization of motor imagery: Contralateral control of grip selection in mentally represented prehension. *Psychological Science, 9*, 219–222.

Jordan, M. I. (1994). Computational motor control. In M. Gazzaniga (Ed.), *Cognitive neuroscience* (pp. 597–699). Cambridge, MA: MIT Press.

Kozlowski, L. T., & Cutting, J. E. (1977). Recognizing the sex of a walker from point-lights display. *Perception and Psychophysics, 21*, 575–580.

Krams, M., Rushworth, M. F. S., Deiber, M.-P., Frackowiak, R. S. J., & Passingham, R. E. (1998). The preparation, execution and suppression of copied movements in the human brain. *Experimental Brain Research, 120*, 386–398.

Lang, W., Petit, L., Höllinger, P., Pietrzyk, U., Tzourio, N., Mazoyer, B., & Berthoz, A. (1994). A positron emission tomography study of oculomotor imagery. *NeuroReport, 5*, 921–924.

Lhermitte, F., Pillon, B., & Serdaru, M. (1986). Human autonomy and the frontal lobes. Part I: Imitation and utilization behavior: A neuropsychological study of 75 patients. *Annals of Neurology, 19*, 326–334.

MacNeilage, P. F. (1998). The frame/content theory of evolution of speech production. *Behavioral and Brain Sciences, 21*, 499–546.

Marcar, V. L., Zihl, J., & Cowey, A. (1997). Comparing the visual deficits of a motion blind patient with the visual deficits of monkeys with area MT removed. *Neuropsychologia, 35*, 1459–1465.

Martin, A., Haxby, J. V., Lalonde, F. M., Wiggs, C. L., & Ungerleider, L. G. (1995). Discrete cortical regions associated with knowledge of color and knowledge of action. *Science, 270*, 102–105.

Mateer, C., & Kimura, D. (1977). Impairment of non-verbal oral movements in aphasia. *Brain and Language, 4*, 262–267.

Meltzoff, A. N., & Moore, M. K. (1997). Explaining facial imitation: A theoretical model. *Early Development and Parenting, 6*, 179–192.

———— (1999). Persons and representation: Why infant imitation is important for theories of human development. In J. Nadel & G. Butterworth (Eds.), *Imitation in infancy* (pp. 9–35). Cambridge: Cambridge University Press.

Milner, A. D., & Goodale, M. A. (1995). *The visual brain in action.* Oxford: Oxford University Press.

Nadel, J., & Butterworth, G. (1999). *Imitation in infancy.* Cambridge: Cambridge University Press.

Nobre, A. C., Coull, J. T., Frith, C. D., & Mesulam, M. M. (1999). Orbitofrontal cortex is activated during breaches of expectation in tasks of visual attention. *Nature Neuroscience, 2,* 11–12.

Ochipa, C., Rapesak, S. Z., Maher, L. M., Rothi, L. J. G., Bowers, D., & Heilman, K. M. (1997). Selective deficit of praxis imagery in ideomotor apraxia. *Neurology, 49,* 474–480.

Oram, M. W., & Perrett, D. I. (1994). Responses of anterior superior temporal polysensory (STPa) neurons to biological motion stimuli. *Journal of Cognitive Neuroscience, 6,* 99–116.

Parsons, L. M. (1987). Imagined spatial transformations of one's hands and feet. *Cognitive Psychology, 19,* 178–241.

Passingham, R. E. (1998). The specializations of the human neocortex. In A. D. Milner (Ed.), *Comparative neuropsychology* (pp. 271–298). Oxford: Oxford University Press.

Perrett, D. I. (1990). Understanding the visual appearance and consequence of actions. In M. A. Goodale (Ed.), *Vision and action* (pp. 163–180). Norwood, NJ: Ablex Publishing Corporation.

Perrett, D. I., Harries, M. H., Bevan, R., Thomas, S., Benson, P. J., Mistlin, A. J., Chitty, A. J., Hietanen, J. K., & Ortega, J. E. (1989). Frameworks of analysis for the neural representation of animate objects and actions. *Journal of Experimental Biology, 146,* 87–114.

Prinz, W. (1992). Why don't we perceive our brain states? *European Journal of Cognitive Psychology, 4,* 1–20.

    (1997). Perception and action planning. *European Journal of Cognitive Psychology, 9,* 129–154.

Puce, A., Allison, T., Bentin, S., Gore, J. C., & McCarthy, G. (1998). Temporal cortex activation in humans viewing eye and mouth movements. *The Journal of Neuroscience, 18,* 2188–2199.

Requin, J., Brener, J., & Ring, C. (1991). Preparation for action. In J. R. Jennings & M. G. H. Coles (Eds.), *Handbook of cognitive psychophysiology: Central and autonomic nervous system approaches* (pp. 357–458). New York: John Wiley & Sons.

Rizzolatti, G., & Arbib, M. A. (1998). Language within our grasp. *Trends in Neurosciences, 21,* 188–194.

Rizzolatti, G., Camarda, R., Fogassi, L., Gentilucci, M., Luppino, G., & Matelli, M. (1988). Functional organization of inferior area 6 in the macaque monkey. II. Area F5 and the control of distal movements. *Experimental Brain Research, 71,* 491–507.

Rizzolatti, G., Fadiga, L., Matelli, M., Bettinardi, V., Perani, D., & Fazio, F. (1996). Localization of grasp representations in humans by PET: 1 Observation versus execution. *Experimental Brain Research, 111,* 246–252.

Roth, M., Decety, J., Raybaudi, M., Massarelli, R., Delon-Martin, C., Segebarth, C., Gemignani, A., Decorps, M., & Jeannerod, M. (1996). Possible involvement of primary motor cortex in mentally simulated movement: A functional magnetic resonance imaging study. *NeuroReport, 7*, 1280–1284.

Sakata, H., Taira, M., Kusunoki, M., Murata, A., & Tanaka, Y. (1997). The parietal association cortex on depth perception and visual control of hand action. *Trends in Neurosciences, 20*, 350–357.

Searle, J. (1983). *Intentionality*. Cambridge: Cambridge University Press.

Shiffrar, M., & Freyd, J. J. (1990). Apparent motion of the human body. *Psychological Science, 1*, 257–264.

(1993). Timing and apparent motion path choice with human body photographs. *Psychological Science, 4*, 379–384.

Sirigu, A., Cohen, L., Duhamel, J. R., Pillon, B., Dubois, B., Agid, Y., & Pierrot-Deseilligny, C. (1995). Congruent unilateral impairments for real and imagined hand movements. *NeuroReport, 6*, 997–1001.

Sirigu, A., Cohen, L., Zalla, T., Pradat-Diehl, P., Van Eechout, P., Grafman, J., & Agid, Y. (1998). Distinct frontal regions for processing sentence syntax and story grammar. *Cortex, 34*, 771–778.

Sirigu, A., Duhamel, J. R., Cohen, L., Pillon, B., Dubois, B., & Agid, Y. (1996). The mental representation of hand movements after parietal cortex damage. *Science, 273*, 1564–1868.

Sperry, R. W. (1952). Neurology and the mind-brain problem. *American Scientist, 40*, 291–312.

Stephan, K. M., Fink, G. R., Passingham, R. E., Silbersweig, D., Ceballos-Baumann, A. O., Frith, C. D., & Frackowiak, R. S. J. (1995). Functional anatomy of the mental representation of upper extremity movements in healthy subjects. *Journal of Neurophysiology, 73*, 373–386.

Stevens, J. A., Fonlupt, P., Shiffrar, M., & Decety, J. (2000). New aspects of motion perception: Selective neural encoding of apparent human movements. *NeuroReport, 11*, 109–115.

Ungerleider, L. G., & Mishkin, M. (1982). Two visual systems. In D. J. Ingle, M. A. Goodale, & R. J. W. Mansfield (Eds.), *Analysis of visual behavior* (pp. 549–586). Cambridge, MA: MIT Press.

Vaina, L. M., LeMay, M., Bienfang, D. C., Choi, A. Y., & Nakayama, K. (1990). Intact biological motion and structure from motion perception in a patient with impaired motion mechanisms: A case study. *Visual Neuroscience, 5*, 353–369.

Wallbott, H. G. (1991). Recognition of emotion from facial expression via imitation? Some indirect evidence for an old theory. *British Journal of Social Psychology, 30*, 207–219.

Wang, Y., & Morgan, W. P. (1992). The effects of imagery perspectives on the physiological responses to imagined exercise. *Behavioural Brain Research, 52*, 167–174.

Watson, J. D., Myers, R., Frackowiak, R. S. J., Hajnal, J. V., Woods, R. P., Mazziotta, J. C., Shipp, S., & Zeki, S. (1993). Area V5 of the human brain: evidence from a combined study using positron emission tomography and magnetic resonance imaging. *Cerebral Cortex, 3*, 79–94.

Wolpert, D. M., Ghahramani, Z., & Jordan, M. I. (1995). An internal model for sensorimotor integration. *Science, 269*, 1880–1882.

17 The role of imitation in body ownership and mental growth

Marcel Kinsbourne

Imitating, copying what someone else does, is only one of the many things humans can do. Yet while most vertebrates are sensitive to the timing of conspecifics' behavior, only a few nonhuman species learn by imitating. Songbirds, parrots (Pepperberg, 2000), and cetaceans (Janik & Slater, 1997) exhibit vocal imitation and to some extent nonhuman primates imitate nonvocally (Whiten, this volume). The species that imitate do tend to be comparatively advanced cognitively (e.g., Pepperberg, 2000). These facts make imitation a prime suspect for being a precursor of much that is uniquely human in human cognition, including its enrichment by sociocultural influences (see also Donald, 1991). In the neurodevelopmental context, I shall present imitation as a foundational building block of cognitive development, and specifically as a source of body awareness and of interpersonal affiliation.

I propose the following: attention is preparatory for action. Percepts are encoded enactively, that is, in terms of the response possibilities that they afford. Mature individuals hold the actual, overt, response in abeyance until the situation calls for it. They accomplish this not by mere inaction but by active restraint, exerted through prefrontal inhibition. Prefrontally injured patients exhibit excessive, unwanted imitation. Infants are also prefrontally inadequate, because the requisite relatively late-occurring neural maturation has not yet taken place. Infants' imitation may be uninhibited enactive perception. Applying this line of reasoning to *bodily awareness*, I suggest that the child's overt imitation of its own or someone else's movement affords him/her a further percept, the imitated movement, which again is enactively encoded, a cycle that gives rise to Meltzoff's body babbling, Piaget's circular reaction. Functionally these movement patterns shape the innately available ability to attend in the somatosensory modalities into body awareness, the ability to attend to specified body parts at will. Applying the same reasoning to *social interaction*, I suggest that repetitive imitation, that gives rise to familiarity with one's own body, also facilitates bonding with a caretaker and, later in development, affiliation with a group.

Attention

Schilder (1935:15) remarked: "There are no perceptions without actions. Every impression carries with it efferent impulses." That attention is preparatory for action has been argued by Jeannerod (1979) and Allport (1987), among others, and Prinz (1990) has suggested "common coding" for perception and action. Vogt (1995) has demonstrated the close relationship between perception and imitative action. Jeannerod and Decety (1995) and Decety (1996, this volume) found shared neural substrates between imagined and executed movements. Di Pellegrino, Fadiga, Fogassi, and Rizzolatti (1992) and Fadiga, Fogassi, Pavesi, and Rizzolatti (1995) observed increased motor cortex activation while monkeys and humans, respectively, observe movements. Rizzolatti, Fadiga, Gallese, and Fogassi (1996) identified "mirror neurons" that respond both during a personal movement and the same movement when someone else is seen to perform it (Rizzolatti *et al.*, this volume). Iacoboni *et al.* (1999) found enhanced brain activity on fMRI in left area 44 (Broca's area) when subjects imitated a model. This area is homologous with monkey area F5, the site of the mirror neurons. One way of interpreting the role of mirror neurons is that they embody the priming of personal movements by the movements of others (or even, perhaps, by imaging them from memory oneself they mediate imitation or remembering).

I consider attention to be selection: the network's self-organized amplifications of the firing of particular neuronal assemblies. Correspondingly, in the connected network, perturbation of the circuitry by attended input activates motor output areas. Saron, Foxe, Simpson, and Vaughan (in press) showed that a lateralized flash stimulus, beyond activating local visual cortex, within less than 80 ms, generates activation in motor cortex, even when no motor response is called for or attempted. Attending involves covert responding. It may be because of their enactive nature ("common coding") that attended inputs are consciously perceived (Prinz, 1992). The enactive nature of representations lends them a causal potential, over and above their much-discussed logical interrelationships. I shall discuss the biological significance of imitation in the context of this enactive characteristic of the brain's response to stimulation.

Neuropsychology of imitation

In certain extreme situations, normal people act in ways that are more often used by people with neuropathology. What is anticipated in the imagination becomes overt when, in an impending traffic emergency, the front-seat passenger performs a vigorous braking movement (see Prinz, this volume, on "intentional induction"). The urgency of the passenger's anticipatory image, of the driver applying the brakes, overcomes the usual inhibitory barrier between adult thought and action. When inhibition is not yet well developed, in the young child, or is compromised by brain dysfunction, such overflow occurs more often.

Brain lesions can make imitation more frequent, or they can impair it. Though it falls short when applied to normal cognition, the traditional stimulus-response psychology better characterizes people without the benefit of prefrontal cortical function. These are brain-damaged people, or infants. Bilateral prefrontal cortex lesions can release "echopraxia" (Stengel, 1947; Luria, 1973), which is unintended, automatic imitation. Lhermitte, Pillon, and Seradou (1986) have described pseudo-voluntary imitation, which the frontal patient attempts to rationalize if questioned. Frontal lesions characteristically make it difficult for the patient to restrain himself from imitating what the examiner does (Luria, 1973). For instance, the frontal patient has particular difficulty with the no-go instruction in a go/no-go reaction paradigm. With the instruction systematically to move when the examiner moves, but in a contrasting way, the patient inadvertently breaks into the imitative mode. We learn that the underlying response predisposition is to imitate. It takes an act of inhibition to hold this primitive response in check. So the primitive response is imitative. Frontal control helps restrain it.

Transcortical aphasics repeat verbatim, though they do not understand what they are repeating. Their echolalia is an automatic disinhibited verbal imitation. Echolalia appears in some normally developing children, but it is much more prevalent and persistent in infantile autism – a condition in which prefrontal dysfunction has been implicated (Minshew *et al.*, 1991). It is probably in states of high arousal (frequent in autists) that echolalia is apt to occur. Overarousal is thought to constrain attention of the most salient of available cues (Easterbrook, 1959), and foster high-frequency repetitive responses, adaptive to the internal state rather than the environment (Kinsbourne, 1980).

When a processor is damaged rather than disinhibited, imitative response may become degraded and global, conserving the domain but not the specifics of the model. Such imperfect imitation is seen in facial and limb apraxia (Goldenberg, this volume). In conduction aphasia, imitation aborts for lack of motor activation (Kinsbourne, 1972). Two patients with conduction aphasia, although not able to repeat more than one digit name at a time, could match two spoken four-digit sequences for sameness or difference by one digit. There may be inertia in the transition from the listening to the speaking mode. During listening, speaking is inhibited. When it is time to speak, impaired reciprocal relations between the posterior listening (Wernicke) and the anterior speaking (Broca) areas inhibits the imitative speech output. The link between percept and response, though intimate, is not indissoluble, as it would be if the same circuitry performs both. That link can be severed by a brain lesion.

Self-imitation

More subtle is a form of repetition that can be understood as self-imitation. The patient (usually schizophrenic) has a mental image, perhaps of an utterance that he intensely anticipates, perceives his own mental image enactively, and generates the corresponding response, which he then perceives. He has hallucinated (Kinsbourne, 1990). Self-imitation is more overt in the clinical phenomenon of perseveration, commonly with widespread brain damage, especially frontal. A previous response is repeated, though it is not relevant to the current situation. The patient failed to inhibit it and change response set as dictated by the task.

When one action is being programmed, a secondary concurrent act, though intended to be different, readily conforms to the first. This happens when people are unable to sustain a difficult dual-task requirement, such as playing unrelated melodies simultaneously on the piano (Kinsbourne & Hicks, 1978). The two hands lapse into a single melody, that had been played by one of the hands. Spread of activation to mirror-image motor facilities, resulting in the unintended mirror movements of young children, can also be characterized as gratuitous self-imitation. The implication is that if a paired body part undertakes an action pattern, it requires intervening inhibition for its opposite number not to do the same. The younger the child, the less the inhibition, and the more is the mirror overflow. In the absence of contralateral inhibition, or orthogonal engagement of the untrained hand, transfer of training from the trained to the untrained hand results (Hicks, Frank, & Kinsbourne, 1982), even in adults, in whom overt overflow movement is not apparent. Imitation is inherent in the organization of the central nervous system and may have to be restrained for nonimitative responses to occur. Whereas in intact individuals, inhibitory barriers preclude the overt imitative act, in the developing infant these barriers are yet to be erected.

Development

The cardinal behavioral attributes of the immature nervous system are lack of differentiation and lack of inhibitory control (reviewed by Kinsbourne, 1993).

How does the preverbal infant come to know what things mean? Without meanings innately flagged in his brain, and uninstructed by others, whose speech he cannot yet understand, and whose ambiguous activities lend themselves to multiple interpretations, the infant nonetheless arrives at a rudimentary understanding of objects and actions. He understands them sufficiently so as then to bootstrap further knowledge gained when he acquires useful language and is specifically instructed. Given the ambiguity of appearances, left open by the poverty of the stimulus, how can these primitive meanings be acquired?

Action coding of percepts

When a preverbal child perceives an object, how is she able to represent more than its physical characteristics? Early meaning seems to be registered in terms of the potential individualized responses, based on the "affordances" for action (Gibson, 1979) that it offers (Piaget, 1954). "Also, actions performed by the child while interacting with animate and inanimate objects may subsequently be internalized to form the child's primitive notions of objects and events" (Lempert & Kinsbourne, 1979:282). Action is the infant's vehicle toward discovery. It is true that the response repertoire of the human species is immeasurably less diverse than its potential for arriving at distinctions about stimuli. Perception and action are in a many-to-few correspondence. Many stimuli come, but few are chosen to control the moment's behavior, whereas a simple act, turning right or left, opens up a panorama of new input. Correspondingly, most of the vast cortical surface is specialized for perception, rather little for action control. Therefore there cannot be an individualized response for every perceptual distinction. Conceivably the infant parses the world into crude categories by means of differential response, crude but sufficient for the massive bootstrapping that follows in the course of maturation. On this view, not only is there common coding between stimulus and response, but responses to percepts are crucial in percepts' acquisition of meaning, at least in infants.

Another hallmark of infancy is imperfect ability to inhibit, which corresponds to immature prefrontal lobes that lack control over behavior (Thatcher, Krause, & Hrybyk, 1986). Responses can be overt or covert. Overt, observable responding is simpler, and becomes available sooner to the developing child than programming a contemplated behavior covertly without releasing it. Maintaining responses covert and private is thinking. To the extent that there is motor overflow from thought to action, thought becomes public. Body movement is online thought. The very young child's thought is altogether public, an open book, with rather few pages. No inhibition intervenes. To know what an infant thinks, observe what she does. I shall take this point very seriously when I consider infant imitation.

Lacking inhibitory capability, infants can implement only a limited range of settings on behavioral dimensions. Whereas the older child and adult can graduate their actions, babies assume extreme positions along these dimensions. A simple example is applying manual pressure to a balloon. The adult can compress the balloon to whatever extent is required, in a graduated fashion. The toddler either squeezes it to the limit, or completely relaxes his grip (Luria, 1932). Moving along a behavioral dimension is not simply adjusting a reading. Rather, the setting is implemented by a control mechanism that consists of a prime mover (agonist) opposed by an antagonist. This coupled system yields the precise settings of skilled action. The infant cannot inhibit, so that whatever agent becomes the prime mover, will fully and obligatorily exert its full effect.

If perception is indeed enactive, then ongoing perceptual ability should be made manifest by observable actions that capture some aspect of what is being perceived. If what is being perceived is an action of which the child is capable, then the act of perception would appear to the onlooker to be an act of imitation.

Infant imitation

Meltzoff and colleagues (e.g., Meltzoff & Moore, 1995, 1997; Meltzoff, this volume) have observed an unexpectedly rich repertoire of imitation by young infants. These include imitation of another's tongue movements, including tilting of the head if necessary (Meltzoff & Moore, 1994, 1995), delayed if the mouth is occupied by a nipple, recurrent if the agent is again encountered on another day (Meltzoff, 1988). Meltzoff and colleagues contend convincingly that these imitations are not reflex, or "fixed action patterns" (Kaitz, Meschulach-Sarfaty, & Auerbach, 1988); they must involve some element of reflection or at least intention. I suggest a further development of these concepts: infant imitation *is* infant perception captured on the fly.

Imitation as uninhibited perception

I suggest that infant imitation is neither deliberate nor reflex. It is the infant perceiving (enactively) the other's facial gesture. The act of perception activates the infant's own innate corresponding movement patterns. The delayed and the recurrent imitations are the infant remembering the expression; remembering is re-experiencing, that is, again enactively perceiving (an internal image, this time). When successive imitations increasingly faithfully replicate the model (Meltzoff & Moore, 1994), this would reflect perceptual learning; the child progressively accommodates, in Piaget's sense, to the appearance. The same applies when the infant is observed while imitating a vocalization; she is perceiving the utterance (an overt precursor of speech perception as postulated by the motor theory of Liberman & Mattingly, 1985). In particular, imitation as perception is consistent with the ability of infants to imitate static gestures, accomplished by movements which the infants did not observe (Field, Goldstein, Vaga-Lahr, & Porter, 1986; Meltzoff & Moore, 1992). Under these conditions the infant cannot be mapping the model's movements. An early instance of a response that incorporates attributes of the stimulus is the young child's tendency to exert a degree of pressure on a response key that parallels the intensity of the stimulus (Luria, 1932). The "infectiousness" of smiling and laughing are further examples; in each case the child is actually perceiving – although to the onlooker he is imitating the vocalization or reciprocating the affect. When an infant sucks nonnutritively, is he thinking milk? Sometimes the infant initiates an expression, which is then reciprocated by the caretaker. Is the infant really imitating from memory, or merely remembering the previous exchange? Sometimes the infant initiates the imitation interaction. Is she actually anticipating, in imagery, the adult's facial expression? Provocative findings in imitation by parrots also lend themselves to reinterpretation along the above lines. Pepperberg, Brese, and Harris' (1991) parrot, observed talking to himself: "Six; not six, three. What color" etc., may not have been practicing, but merely remembering. Interestingly, parrots are considered to be at the peak of birds' cognitive development, rather like primates are at the peak among mammals.

When imitating, the very young infant uses action sequences that are already in her spontaneous repertoire. The child will spontaneously smile, laugh, babble, move her tongue in several directions. When the child perceives someone else make these movements, she becomes able to calibrate her own movements, which reinforces those movements that are perceived. What she imitates is not the perceived movements, but the accomplished end state, that is, the action effect (see discussion by Bekkering, this volume). The same applies to vocalizations (Kuhl & Meltzoff, 1996). Vocalizations that are not perceived, because they are not featured in the language spoken in the child's presence, gradually drop out (Werker, 1986). The deaf infant's babbling ultimately ceases after a time, without being replaced by speech. Early imitations, particularly facial, decrease in frequency in the first few months. Perhaps inhibition is gradually being established, or perhaps the child has habituated to what are now familiar percepts and attends elsewhere. Imitation becomes voluntary; that is, it can be restrained. Braitenberg and Schutz (1992) likened the babbling infant to a random phoneme generator. The repeated associations between a heard and a produced phoneme train the brain to produce phonemes at will. My suggestion bridges the gap between hearing and willing. The act of active selective listening to a particular self-generated phoneme generates, by its enactive components, the self-imitated speech sound.

Much of what the infant perceives he cannot imitate, in detail or at all, if only because no movement is involved. An enactive response is still possible. Even orienting to a stimulus does capture one of its response characteristics – the direction in which to approach it. As the infant grows older, the orienting is attended by directional arm flapping, then reaching, then pointing. These gestures are motor enactments of the percept. Pointing as pointing out to another person emerges about two months later (Lempert & Kinsbourne, 1985). At first superimposed on pointing, speech also has a central orienting function. Internal speech orients the self, and interactive speech orients someone else, to a topic or domain of interest. The other enters into, or imitates, the speaker's train of thought. Joint regard, entraining with another's point of view, is a precursor of the orienting function of speech.

Although all perception may have an enactive component, even newborns do not imitate all that they see. It appears that the action becomes overt when attention is intense and effortful, to a novel stimulus. An instance is a beginning or inexpert reader, perusing a text. Although articulation is irrelevant to understanding the passage, the reader is visibly forming speech sounds. Electromyography reveals that subarticulations are common when the text is difficult. The enactive coding breaks through. Infants' attention is particularly compelled by the skilled caretaker, who thereby elicits information. According to this interpretation, the reason why infants do not imitate mechanical devices set up to perform acts that infants do imitate when they are done by people (Meltzoff, 1995), is because they do not attend to mechanical objects as intensely. Autists who lack interpersonal interest do not imitate (Smith & Bryson, 1998). They may become fascinated with words, however, and repeat jingles and other catch phrases. Animals in the wild generally do not imitate what they observe. If they did, they would betray their intentions and fail, both as predators and as prey.

I now apply the above concepts to the manner in which infants acquire a sense of owning their bodies.

Body ownership

I begin by examining what can be learned about how the body is represented in the brain from the effects of lesions that compromise awareness of the body or its parts. Relying upon studies of the acquisition and dissolution of self/body knowledge, I shall argue for a dynamic view of the body image, as derived from the focusing of attention (for action) on body parts.

The body image has been conceived as a static supramodal neural representation of the body parts in their natural articulation (Bonnier, 1905; Critchley, 1953; Denes, 1989). This representation is conceived as separate from the cerebral projection areas for the somatic senses, and is available to awareness for reference as needed. It is distinct from the body schema, which is a compendium term for the systematic way in which postural rearrangements of the body are unconsciously organized (Head & Holmes, 1911–1912; Gallagher, 1986). Different again is the information that we accumulate about our own bodies. This "body archive" is an achievement of construct formation, which enriches our semantic repertoire. Neither schema nor archive is the subject of this discussion. Our ability to refer to body parts that we own, online, in their trajectory from posture to posture, is quite a different skill. It could be based on the availability of a dedicated map (representation in the brain) of the body to which to refer. Alternatively, it relies on the ability to attend on the fly, via its sensorimotor representation, to any one of the most body parts as needed, regardless of its actual spatial position at the time. Attending may in turn rely upon activating one of the body part's response potentialities, knowledge of which has been accumulated across many trials. Since we (i.e., we brains) are nested within bodies, body sensation is always available for ready reference. So, having a stored data base in the form of a body image is not a logical necessity. Whether the body image exists separate from the representations of the body parts in sensorimotor cortex cannot be resolved by observing the normal mature individual. It requires the assistance of findings gleaned from individuals whose brains have suffered selective demolition by injury.

Brain injury can cause a mental representation to become:

> *Dedifferentiated*, leading to a coarser representation that incorporates fewer than the normally available set of distinctions.

> *Misarticulated*, leading to a sense of unnatural conjunctions between parts.
>
> *Depleted*, leading to selective loss of the sense of ownership of the full set of parts.

Have focal lesions been reported to coarsen body sensation, scramble it, or selectively deplete it (across cases)? Brain damage has been reported to implicate the body image as a whole or in part. The former syndrome, total asomatognosia (Ogden, 1985; Semenza, 1988; Sirigu, Grafman, Bressler, & Sunderland, 1991), and its reverse, selective sparing of body-part knowledge (Shelton, Fouch, & Caramazza, 1998) as reported does not reveal the correct choice between models. It could reflect loss of a dedicated body scheme. But it could also result from inactivation of a system of somatosensory attention. But the construct of partial asomatognosia offers a more effective critique of the existence of a static dedicated body image.

I have characterized as a "nonexistence proof," the observation that a particular manifestation (sign, symptom, syndrome) has not been documented, although the opportunities to observe it if it occurs have been plentiful over a long period of time (Kinsbourne, 1998). A nonexistence proof takes the form of the null hypothesis, and could be disconfirmed by future observations. But as a working hypothesis, it can help the theorist choose between competing models, if one but not the other predicts the "nonexisting" manifestation.

A body image, even if it is distributed like Melzack's (1990) neuromatrix, must, like every other part of the brain, be vulnerable to focal partial injury, which should deplete it of some component or constituent detail. Reports should be available of partial asomatognosias for most if not all the body's parts, gleaned through a century and a half of investigative effort. Indeed, a collage of these cases should add up to the total body image. In fact, the yield of partial asomatognosias is limited to one syndrome, unilateral neglect (which, I maintain below, can be otherwise explained). The yield of reports of scrambled body image is zero. Abandoning the body-image concept, I turn to attention as an explanatory construct. Perhaps one accesses body-part information by activating an attentional system that highlights a corresponding area of somatosensory cortex. If such an attentional system is injured, it should suffer bias and restriction of range, but not a lacuna, in its sweep across its substrate. This would be analogous to vision, which features scotomas, like somesthesis features numbness, but does not feature visual attention deficits that obscure the various parts of a scene, independent of their retinotopic location.

Unilateral neglect

Organic impairment of bodily awareness is confined to the lateral coordinate of the body, and biased around it. One may be, and act, unaware of one side of the body, to a greater (hemisomatognosia) or lesser (neglect of left arm and hand) extent. Unawareness that is explicit on questioning goes along with disuse of the affected body part (usually left-sided, consequent upon extensive right posterior parietal lesions). This neglect is not specific to a demarcated body territory (a hand, a limb, etc.), but represents a gradient of unawareness/disuse that varies from case to case, and from time to time in the individual patient (Kinsbourne, 1994). It is referable to an imbalance in the activation levels of the two sides of the brain, that biases the interaction of laterally disposed opponent processors (Kinsbourne, 1987). The vertebrate nervous system, laterally duplicated, harbors multiple mirror-image facilities that program opposite and incompatible behaviors (turn right vs. turn left, etc.). These processors are in feedback interaction, such that balance between them is continually reset, to permit action to either side as called for by circumstances. The resetting is implemented by a gain in activation on one side, resulting in more inhibition of the other, but with inbuilt stabilizing feedback. This feedback ensures that the direction of behavior does not obligatorily swing from one extreme to the other, but stabilizes so that the vector resultant of the coupled system is appropriately directed. The outcome is all or nothing for incompatible actions, such as turning right vs. turning left, but it is graduated when the direction of attention or action shifts along the lateral plane (Kinsbourne, 1974).

A lesion that diminishes activation of one half-brain renders the opponent processors on that side unable to hold their contralateral partners in check. Attention and planned action swing toward the opposite side of personal and extrapersonal space. If the lesion is severe, attention cannot be fully deployed in the contralesional direction, and the person remains oblivious of the environment or of his body parts on that side. In humans, though apparently not in other mammals, the coupled system has a rightward bias, such that right lesions occasion a rightward overshoot of lateral orienting, whereas left lesions generate only a mild contralateral bias of behavior (Kinsbourne, 1987). Although spatial and personal neglect can dissociate (Bisiach, Perani, Vallar, & Berti, 1986), they both usually result from right-sided lesions. The most contralateral body part is the one that is most deprived of attention, manifesting as disregard, disuse and denial of ownership. In somatic sensation, the term contralateral does not apply to a spatial dimension; the body can of course assume a great variety of positions in space. Rather, the hands appear to be at the

extreme of an innately specified right–left attentional gradient that conforms to the articulation of body parts (Kinsbourne, 1995). The forearm
may also be ignored and disavowed, but only if the hand is. The upper
arm may also be denied, but only if the forearm and hands are. And in
each case the severity of the neglect deepens as the distal part of the limb
is approached. Neglect rarely affects the trunk as well as the extremities,
and if it does, it does so mildly. There is no sharp demarcation between a
neglected body-half, or part, and an attended one. So unilateral neglect
is not a partial asomatognosia, but an imbalance in lateral somatosensory
attention. (For a similar point about the nonexistence of an inner model
of the visual world, see O'Regan, 1992.) Our brains do not construct
static models for inspection by an inner observer, but dynamic trajectories through brain activation state space for self-regulated action.

While performing routine caloric testing, Silberpfennig (1941) observed that stimulating the inner ear opposite the cerebral lesion by ir-
rigating the external ear canal with lukewarm water, can abolish neglect
symptomatology for the period of the irrigation and a while afterwards.
Neglect relapses as the effects of the irrigation wear off. This maneuver,
which is effective for unilateral neglect of the body as well as of space
(Bisiach, Rusconi, & Vallar, 1991) appears to redress a lateral imbalance
in brain activation due to the lesion, by activating the crossed ascending
projection of the vestibular system to the posterior parietal lobe, perhaps
via the intralaminar nuclei of the thalamus (Schiff & Pulver, 1999).

Attending to a body part makes it "figure" against the "ground" supplied by the rest of the body. Being ground, the rest of the body is rather
undifferentiated in perception. I suggest that the body as ground is the
basis of the feeling of unity or personhood, undifferentiated into parts
(Kinsbourne, 1995). Constructs of the self are cognitive elaborations
on this undifferentiated somatic ground. Since no lesions can strip the
ground from a figure, the sense of self as a unit survives the most drastic
limitations in the amount of body sensation, or sense of ownership of its
parts (Cole & Paillard, 1995).

Distortions of body sensation

Case reports of distorted body sensations fit poorly with the static body-
scheme concept. Parts of the body may feel swollen, misshapen, abnor-
mally heavy or light, displaced from the rest of the body, positioned in an
anatomically impossible manner, or reduplicated (e.g., Critchley, 1953).
The following observations bear on the brain basis of body sensation.
Observations (i), (ii), and (iii) are based on Brugger, Regard & Landis
(1997).

(i)   There is no one brain territory, abnormality of which gives rise to all distortions of body sensations. This weakens the case for a localized body image.

(ii) The distortion is always in one modality only, depending on where the lesion is. A body image would be expected to be multimodal.

(iii) Distortions within a modality are not accompanied by adjustments in other modalities, as would occur normally. A limb feels swollen and twisted, but it does not hurt. Position sense misleads, but kinesthesis does not follow suit. Again, an integrated body image would make cross-modality adjustments.

(iv) The affected part may be experienced as detached from the body, or so disposed as to violate the way the limbs are articulated. Sensed body positions that are physically impossible can even be induced in normal subjects. For instance, applying vibration to the biceps of an arm held with the hand resting on the scalp made the hand feel deeply embedded in the inside of the head (Lackner & DeZio, 1984). It appears that when attention is focused on each body part, it is experienced in isolation, and that the articulation of the other body parts is not correspondingly adjusted.

(v)   There are no reports of body parts seemingly hooked up unnaturally.

Abnormal signals may obtrude a body part on attention. They do so in a fractionated, not integrated, way, so that conflicting information emanates from different modalities. They do not act like distortions of a centralized body image, but like localized modality specific signals that misinform.

Abnormal perceptions abound in body dysmorphic disorder, among the symptoms of dissociation and in states of extreme elation. To cite Nietzsche, speaking through his alter ego, Zarathustra: "Now I am light, now I fly" – "now I see myself under myself, now a god dances through me. . . " (Nietzsche, 1980, IV:50). It is clearly possible to represent, in imagery, impossible bodily states that could not have been learned through experience. Rather, selective attention rearranges body parts. During periods in which the calibration of kinesthetic or spatial input relative to body parts and postures is distorted, a rich variety of aberrant perceptions of the body occurs.

Emerging sense of body ownership

As they emerge into functionality, neural networks are tuned by their interaction with the environment (both within and outside the body). Infants' nascent sense of their own bodies may arise from innate movement patterns that become calibrated against the infants' perceptions of their own movements by self-imitation.

The concept of perception as in part a motor act can be applied to the special case of the infant's sense of ownership of the parts of his own body. I have already suggested that the mature sense of body ownership is based on the background of body sensation against which attention highlights the body part that is relevant for the purpose of the moment. The infant discovers a preprogrammed ability to attend to body parts, which, because of the lack of inhibitory capability, involves moving them. The differentiation into parts of the infant's body image would arise from individual acts of attention for action to body parts. I suggest that the child moves to a body part and perceives the kinesthetic feedback from the movement enactively (by repeating the act). As discussed, the act of perception has a motor component, which in the neonate is overt, because it is not inhibited. The child moves the body part again. The moving part is perceived, and in being perceived, again moves, setting up a chain reaction. I conceptualize Piaget's circular reaction, and Meltzoff and Moore's (1997) body babbling as driven by successive acts of perception. The reciprocally engaged body part feels "owned." What the observer sees is simply a baby kicking its legs. Correlated inputs from the body-surface indicate subareas of the same body part, whereas imperfectly correlated inputs indicate separate body parts (as Clark, Allard, Jenkins, & Merzenich, 1988, demonstrated for the owl monkey's fingers, and as modeled by Montague, Gally, & Edelman, 1991). This sequence continues, until it finally habituates, as some other salient stimulus captures the child's attention. Positive affect associated with this type of sequence may be why infants' actions are so frequently repetitive, and also why infants so much relish being moved repetitively (rocked, etc.). Engaging in a circular reaction with another may define the self–nonself distinction, depending on whether feedback is present or not. By her own actions, the other provokes movements of selected body parts (Meltzoff & Moore, 1997). Engaging reciprocally with another, as in imitation or joint regard, may also incorporate some of the positive valence of reciprocal engagement with one's own body parts, particularly if the engagement is rhythmically reciprocal.

Rhythms and social behavior

Why do infants strive to interact rhythmically with caretakers? Interactional synchrony (Condon & Sander, 1974) or coordinated interpersonal timing (Beebe *et al.*, 1985) exists between infant and caretaker. A rhythmic interaction with another would then resemble, in form, the infant's interaction with her own body. (This does not necessitate the extreme view that the infant is confusing self and others (Piaget, 1973:153).) The other appears to the infant to affiliate with the infant's own body sense, which, presumably positively valanced, may be the rudiment of social affiliation or bonding on the part of the child. Imitation fosters a pleasurable sense of kinship between parent and child (Meltzoff & Gopnik, 1993). Indeed, infants become upset when, after imitating them, an adult does something different (Meltzoff & Moore, 1997).

The power of imitation reverberates into the social domain. The effect of rhythmic input in inducing rhythmic behavior is not a biological primitive, general across species, but is a specific adaptation found in humans (Prinz, 1993). Perceived behavior gives a leg up to more of the same in the observer, who becomes a participant (Bargh & Chartrand, 1999). Yawning and laughter are contagious, fashions are slavishly obeyed, catch phrases permeate everyday speech, and the mob drags along its unthinking but strangely comforted individual mobsters. The rhythm of the drum drowns out independent judgment and induces a reversion to the primordial state. To cite Freeman (1995:153) "to dance is to engage in rhythmic movements that invite corresponding movements from others." Dancers synchronize, reciprocate, or alternate – all of which are forms of entrainment open to the infant. Entraining with others into a shared rhythm – marching, chanting, dancing – may trigger a primitive sense of irrational and beguiling belonging, and a shared mindset. Music elaborates this effect, and by virtue of its diverse complexity, averts habituation. Even rhythmic activity confined to oneself – rocking, spinning, finger tapping, leg shaking – may dearouse and confer a pleasing sense of calm (Kinsbourne, 1980).

Concluding remarks

I have mustered evidence for the view that the brain takes advantage of its privileged nesting within its prime data sources – its body and its ambient space. It stores information externally to the extent feasible, and neither needs nor uses internal models of the actual world and body (as opposed to constructs about them). The information from these sources is encoded enactively by prepared circuitry. The means for an infant's self-discovery are prefigured in the neural network. This self-discovery is self-organized, using the body and the world as substrate. To a degree it incorporates other individuals as well, and the means by which it does so are not reasoned or consequential, but a feature of the way the organization of the neural network has evolved under selection pressures. Subjective feelings, reasons and rationalizations are glosses and commentaries after the fact.

Imitation is the newborn infant in the act of perceiving or remembering. It becomes the source of most of one's social knowledge base. Imitation is the route of spread of Dawkins' (1976) memes, culturally generated concepts and predispositions that feed back powerfully upon the genomes of the individuals that generate them. Innate predispositions are calibrated through the social context, and social learning imitates at times a model individual, at times a group. No doubt a rational creature would deliberately take advantage of the accumulated wisdom of the species. But imitation begins far too early in development to have originated as a deliberate and reasoned choice. Also, its role is far-reaching, beyond adaptation to the social norm. It is a prime mover in mental development, and, I suggest, it underlies affiliation both to individuals and to the group. If so, affiliation has a neurobiological rudiment, mediated by imitation.

References

Allport, A. (1987). Selection for action: Some behavioral and neurophysiological considerations of attention and action. In H. Heuer & A. F. Sanders (Eds.), *Perspectives on perception and action* (pp. 395–419). Hillsdale, NJ: Erlbaum.

Bargh, J. A., & Chartrand, T. L. (1999). The unbearable automaticity of being. *American Psychologist, 54*, 462–479.

Beebe, B., Feldstein, S., Jaffe, J., Mays, K., & Alson, D. (1985). Interpersonal timing: The application of an adult dialogue model to mother–infant vocal and kinesic interactions. In T. Field & N. Fox (Eds.), *Social perception in infants* (pp. 217–248). Norwood, NJ: Ablex.

Bisiach, E., Perani, D., Vallar, G., & Berti, A. (1986). Unilateral neglect: Personal and extrapersonal. *Neuropsychologia, 24*, 759–767.

Bisiach, E., Rusconi, M. L., & Vallar, G. (1991). Remission of somatoparaphrenic delusion through vestibular stimulation. *Neuropsychologia, 29*, 1029–1031.

Bonnier, P. (1905). L'Aschematie. *Revue Neurologique, 13*, 604–609.

Braitenberg, V., & Schutz, A. (1992). Basic features of cortical connectivity and some consideration of language. In B. H. Bichakjian, A. Nocentini, & B. Chiarelli (Eds.), *Language origin: A multidisciplinary approach* (pp. 89–102). Dordrecht: Kluwer.

Brugger, P., Regard, M., & Landis, T. (1997). Illusory reduplication of one's own body: Phenomenology and classification of autoscopic phenomena. *Cognitive Neuropsychiatry, 2*, 19–38.

Clark, S. A., Allard, T., Jenkins, W. M., & Merzenich, M. M. (1988). Receptive fields in the body-surface map in adult cortex defined by temporally correlated inputs. *Nature, 332*, 444–445.

Cole, J., & Paillard, J. (1995). Living without touch and peripheral information about body position and movement: Studies with deafferented subjects. In J. L. Bermudez, A. Marcel, & N. Eilan (Eds.), *The body and the self* (pp. 245–266). Cambridge, MA: MIT Press.

Condon, W. S., & Sander, L. W. (1974). Neonate movement is synchronized with adult speech: International participation and language acquisition. *Science, 183,* 98–101.

Critchley, M. (1953). *The parietal lobes.* New York: Hafner.

Dawkins, R. (1976). *The selfish gene.* Oxford: Oxford University Press.

Decety, J. (1996). Do imagined and executed actions share the same neural substrate? *Cognitive Brain Research, 3,* 87–93.

Denes, G. (1989). Disorders of body awareness and body knowledge. In F. Boller & J. Grafman (Eds.), *Handbook of neuropsychology* (Vol. 2, pp. 207–228). Amsterdam: Elsevier.

Di Pellegrino, G., Fadiga, L., Fogassi, L., & Rizzolatti, G. (1992). Understanding motor events: A neurophysiological study. *Experimental Brain Research, 901,* 176–180.

Donald, M. (1991). *Origins of the modern mind.* Cambridge, MA: Harvard University Press.

Easterbrook, J. (1959). The effect of emotion on cue utilization and the organization of behavior. *Psychological Review, 66,* 183–201.

Fadiga, L., Fogassi, L., Pavesi, G., & Rizzolatti, G. (1995). Motor facilitation during action observation: A magnetic stimulation study. *Journal of Neurophysiology, 73,* 2608–2611.

Field, T. M., Goldstein, S., Vaga-Lahr, N., & Porter, K. (1986). Changes in imitative behavior in early infancy. *Infant Behavior and Development, 9,* 415–421.

Freeman, W. J. (1995). *Societies of brains.* Hillsdale, NJ: Erlbaum.

Gallagher, S. (1986). Body image and body schema: A conceptual clarification. *Journal of Mind and Behavior, 7,* 541–554.

Gibson, J. J. (1979). *The ecological approach to visual perception.* Boston: Houghton Mifflin.

Head, H., & Holmes, G. (1911–1912). Sensory disturbances from cerebral lesions. *Brain, 34,* 102–254.

Hicks, R. E., Frank, J. M., & Kinsbourne, M. (1982). The locus of bimanual skill transfer. *Journal of General Psychology, 107,* 277–281.

Iacoboni, M., Woods, R. P., Brass, M., Bekkering, H., Mazziotta, J. C., & Rizzolatti, G. (1999). Cortical mechanisms of human imitation. *Science, 286,* 2526–2528.

Janik, V. M., & Slater, P. J. B. (1997). Vocal learning in mammals. *Advances in the Study of Behavior, 26,* 59–99.

Jeannerod, M. (1979) *The cognitive neuroscience of action.* Oxford: Blackwell.

Jeannerod, M., & Decety, J. (1995). Mental motor imagery: A window into the representational stages of action. *Current Opinion in Neurobiology, 5,* 727–732.

Kaitz, M., Meschulach-Sarfaty, O., & Auerbach, J. (1988). A reexamination of newborns' ability to imitate facial expressions. *Developmental Psychology, 24,* 3–7.

Kinsbourne, M. (1972). Behavioral analysis of the repetition deficit in conduction aphasia. *Neurology, 22,* 1126–1132.

   (1974). Lateral interactions in the brain. In M. Kinsbourne & W. L. Smith (Eds.), *Hemispheric disconnection and cerebral function* (pp. 239–259). Springfield, IL: Thomas.

(1980). Do repetitive movement patterns in children and animals serve a de-arousing function? *Journal of Developmental and Behavioral Pediatrics, 1,* 39–42.

(1987). Mechanisms of unilateral neglect. In M. Jeannerod (Ed.), *Neurophysiological and neuropsychological aspects of neglect* (pp. 69–86). North-Holland: Elsevier.

(1990). Voiced images, imagined voices. *Biological Psychiatry, 27,* 811–812.

(1993). Development of attention and metacognition. In I. Rapin & S. Segalowitz (Eds.), *Handbook of neurology* (Vol. VII, pp. 261–278). Amsterdam: Elsevier.

(1994). Orientational bias model of unilateral neglect: Evidence from attentional gradients within hemispace. In I. H. Robertson & J. C. Marshall (Eds.), *Unilateral neglect: Clinical and experimental studies* (pp. 63–86). New York: Erlbaum.

(1995). Awareness of one's own body. In J. Bermudez, A. J. Marcel, & N. Eilan (Eds.), *The body and the self* (pp. 205–223). Cambridge, MA: MIT Press.

(1998). Unity and diversity in the human brain: Evidence from injury. *Daedalus, 127,* 233–256.

Kinsbourne, M., & Hicks, R. E. (1978). Functional cerebral space: A model for overflow, transfer and interference effects in human performance: A tutorial review. In J. Requin (Ed.), *Attention and performance VII* (pp. 345–362). Hillsdale, NJ: Erlbaum.

Kuhl, P. K., & Meltzoff, A. M. (1996). Infant vocalization in response to speech: Vocal imitation and developmental change. *Journal of the Acoustical Society of America, 100,* 2425–2438.

Lackner, J. R., & DeZio, P. (1984). Some efferent and somatosensory influences on body orientation and oculomotor control. In L. Spillman & B. R. Wooten (Eds.), *Sensory experience, adaptation and perception* (pp. 281–301). Hillsdale, NJ: Erlbaum.

Lempert, H., & Kinsbourne, M. (1979). Action as a substrate for early syntax. In P. L. French (Ed.), *The development of meaning* (pp. 282–299). Hiroshima: Bunka, Hyoron.

(1985). Possible origin of speech in selective orienting. *Psychological Bulletin, 97,* 62–73.

Lhermitte, F., Pillon, B., & Seradou, M. (1986). Human autonomy and the frontal lobes, Part 1: Imitation and utilization behavior: A neuropsychological study of 75 patients. *Annals of Neurology, 19,* 326–334.

Liberman, A. M., & Mattingly, I. G. (1985). The motor theory of speech perception revised. *Cognition, 21,* 1–36.

Luria, A. R. (1932). *The nature of human conflicts.* New York: Liveright.

(1973). *The working brain.* New York: Penguin.

Meltzoff, A. N. (1988). Infant imitation and memory: Nine-month-olds in immediate and deferred tests. *Child Development, 59,* 217–255.

(1995). Understanding the intentions of others: Re-enactment of intended acts by 18-month-old children. *Developmental Psychology, 31,* 838–850.

Meltzoff, A. N., & Gopnik, A. (1993). The role of imitation in understanding persons and developing a theory of mind. In S. Baron-Cohen,

H. Tager-Flusberg, & D. J. Cohen (Eds.), *Understanding other minds: Perspectives from autism* (pp. 335–366). New York: Oxford University Press.

Meltzoff, A. N., & Moore, M. K. (1992). Early imitation within a functional framework: The importance of person identity, movement and development. *Infant Behavior and Development, 15,* 479–505.

(1994). Imitation, memory and the representations of persons. *Infant Behavior and Development, 17,* 83–99.

(1995). Infants' understanding of people and things: From body imitation to folk psychology. In J. L. Bermúdez, A. Marcel, & N. Eilan (Eds.), *The body and the self* (pp. 43–70). Cambridge, MA: MIT Press.

(1997). Explaining facial imitation: A theoretical model. *Early Development and Parenting, 6,* 179–192.

Melzack, R. (1990). Phantom limbs and the concept of a neuromatrix. *Trends in Neurosciences, 13,* 88–92.

Minshew, N. J., Pettegrew, J. W., Goldstein, G., Phillips, N. E., & Wendy, S. R. (1991). Correlations between in vivo brain phospholipid and high energy phosphate metabolism and cognitive functioning in autism. *Biological Psychiatry, 29,* 48A.

Montague, P. R., Gally, J. A., & Edelman, G. M. (1991). Spatial signalling in the development and function of neural connections. *Cerebral Cortex, 1,* 199–220.

Nietzsche, F. (1980). *Nietzsche: Kritische Studienausgabe.* G. Colli & M. Montinari (Eds.). Berlin: de Gruyter.

Ogden, J. A. (1985). Autotopagnosia. Occurrence in a patient without nominal aphasia and an intact ability to point to parts of animals and objects. *Brain, 108,* 1009–1022.

O'Regan, J. K. (1992). Solving the "real" mysteries of visual perception: The world as outside memory. *Canadian Journal of Psychology, 46,* 461–488.

Pepperberg, I. M. (2000). *The Alex studies: The cognitive and communicative abilities of Grey parrots.* Cambridge, MA: Harvard University Press.

Pepperberg, I. M., Brese, K. J., & Harris, B. J. (1991). Solitary sound play during acquisition of English by an African Gray parrot (Psittacus erithacus): Possible parallels with children's monologue speech. *Applied Psycholinguistics, 12,* 151–177.

Piaget, J. (1954). *The construction of reality in the child.* New York: Basic Books.

(1973). *The child's conception of the world.* St. Albans: Paladin.

Prinz, W. (1990). A common-coding approach to perception and action. In O. Neumann & W. Prinz (Eds.), *Relations between perception and action: Current approaches* (pp. 167–201). Berlin: Springer.

(1992). Why don't we perceive our brain states? *European Journal of Cognitive Psychology, 4,* 1–20.

(1993). *Handlungen als Ereignisse: Kognitive Grundlagen der Handlungssteuerung* (Actions as events: The cognitive basis of action control.). Paper 2/1993. Munich: Max-Planck-Institute for Psychological Research.

Rizzolatti, G., Fadiga, L., Gallese, V., & Fogassi, L. (1996). Premotor cortex and the recognition of motor actions. *Cognitive Brain Research, 3,* 131–141.

Saron, C., Foxe, J. J., Simpson, G. V., & Vaughan, H. G. (in press). Electrophysiological indices of intra and interhemispheric visuomotor interaction.

In M. Iacoboni & E. Zaidel (Eds.), *The parallel brain.* Cambridge, MA: MIT Press.

Schiff, N. D., & Pulver, M. (1999). Does vestibular stimulation activate thalamocortical mechanisms that reintegrate impaired cortical regions? *Proceedings of the Royal Society of London, B. 266*, 421–423.

Schilder, P. (1935). *The image and appearance of the human body.* London: Kegan, Paul, Trench, Taubner.

Semenza, C. (1988). Impairment of localization of body parts following brain damage. *Cortex, 24*, 443–449.

Shelton, J. R., Fouch, E., & Caramazza, A. (1998). Selective sparing of body part knowledge: A case study. *Neurocase, 4*, 339–351.

Silberpfennig, J. (1941). Contribution to the problem of eye movements. III. Disturbances of ocular movements with pseudo-hemianopia in frontal lobe tumors. *Confinia Neurologica, 4*, 1–13.

Sirigu, A., Grafman, J., Bressler, K., & Sunderland, T. (1991). Multiple representations contribute to body knowledge processing. *Brain, 114*, 629–642.

Smith, I. M., & Bryson, S. E. (1998). Imitation in autism. *Cognitive Neuropsychology, 15*, 747–771.

Stengel, E. (1947). A clinical and psychological study of echo-reactions. *Journal of Mental Science, 93*, 518–612.

Thatcher, R. W., Krause, P. J., & Hrybyk, M. (1986). Cortico-cortical associations and EEG coherence: A two-compartmental model. *Electroencephalogr. Clin. Neurophysiol., 64*, 123–143.

Vogt, S. (1995). Imagery and perception-action mediation in imitative actions. *Cognitive Brain Research, 3*, 79–86.

Werker, J. F. (1986). The effect of multilingualism on phonetic perceptual flexibility. *Applied Psycholinguistics, 7*, 141–156.

18   Imitation, apraxia, and hemisphere dominance

Georg Goldenberg and Joachim Hermsdörfer

Introduction

Neuropsychological research on imitation has a history of nearly a hundred years. Liepmann (1908) investigated performance of meaningful gestures on command, like giving a military salute or showing how to turn a key, in patients with damage to the right or left hemisphere and normal controls. He found that only patients with left-brain damage (LBD) committed errors even when they performed the gestures with the nonparetic left hand. As most LBD patients were aphasic they might have had difficulties understanding the verbal instructions. However, they also committed errors when imitating the same gestures. Liepmann ascribed defective gesturing in LBD patients to "apraxia." He emphasized that, in contrast to other motor sequels of unilateral brain damage, apraxia affects not only the contralesional but also the ipsilesional limbs, and concluded that it interferes with motor actions at a level beyond "elementary" motor control. He conceived of two possibilities for a higher level of disturbances of motor control: apraxia might stem from an inability to conjure up a mental representation of the required action, or from an inability to convert the mental representation into appropriate motor commands. Errors on imitation testified to Liepmann that "there is not only an inexactness of the spatial-temporal image of the movement, but a difficulty or inability to direct the leftsided members according to certain spatial conceptions" (Liepmann, 1908). As he observed errors on imitation only in LBD patients, he concluded that the conversion of mental representations of actions into motor actions depends on integrity of the left hemisphere and proposed that the left hemisphere is dominant for the deliberate control of motor actions.

The reliability of Liepmann's finding that imitation of gestures is disturbed in apraxia following LBD has been firmly established by numerous replications (e.g., Heilman, 1979; Lehmkuhl, Poeck, & Willmes, 1983), and most researchers accept Liepmann's proposal that impaired imitation indicates an inability to translate a given concept of the gesture into appropriate motor commands. (Heilman, 1979; De Renzi, Motti, & Nichelli, 1980; Poeck, 1982; Roy, & Hall, 1992).

In the first part of this chapter we will present converging evidence from kinematic analyses of motor execution in apraxic patients and from clinical single case studies demonstrating that faulty imitation in apraxia is not due to defective motor execution of correctly intended actions. Then, we consider the alternative proposal that apraxia interrupts a direct route from perception to motor control. We pursue the idea that imitation of gestures by this direct route requires mediation by knowledge about the human body, and that access to this knowledge is defective in LBD patients with apraxia. Finally, we ask whether the human body is just one instance of a multipart mechanical device, and the inability to code gestures in terms of general knowledge about the human body one instance of a general inability to comprehend functional relationships between significant parts of complex mechanical devices.

Apraxia and motor execution

Kinematic analysis of imitation

Kinematic features of skilled hand movements are constant across a wide variety of movements. For example, when reaching for a target, the velocity of the hand follows a bell-shaped profile with one single peak which scales linearly with movement amplitude (Hogan, 1984; Morasso, 1999). Pathological or unskilled movements often lack this feature (Jeannerod, 1986; Trombly, 1993). Demonstration of kinematic abnormalities in apraxic imitation would endorse the idea that motor execution is deficient.

Previous studies of kinematics of apraxic patients' movements have revealed kinematic abnormalities for pantomime of object use, actual object use, and the reproduction of a pre-learned arm movement (Clark *et al.*, 1994; Poizner *et al.*, 1990; Poizner *et al.*, 1995; Platz & Mauritz, 1995). They did not, however, examine imitation. We (Hermsdörfer *et al.*, 1996) investigated the kinematics of imitation of gestures in a representative sample of normal controls and patients with unilateral right- or left-brain damage.

--→

Figure 18.1. Target gesture, movement paths, and velocity profiles of a healthy control subject during the imitation of meaningless gestures with the left arm are illustrated. The three-dimensional positions of the wrist (solid line) and of the base of the index finger (broken line) were continuously recorded with an ultrasound measurement system (CMS70, Zebris, Isny). Movement paths are shown in a frontal plane. The tangential velocity is displayed for the wrist movement.

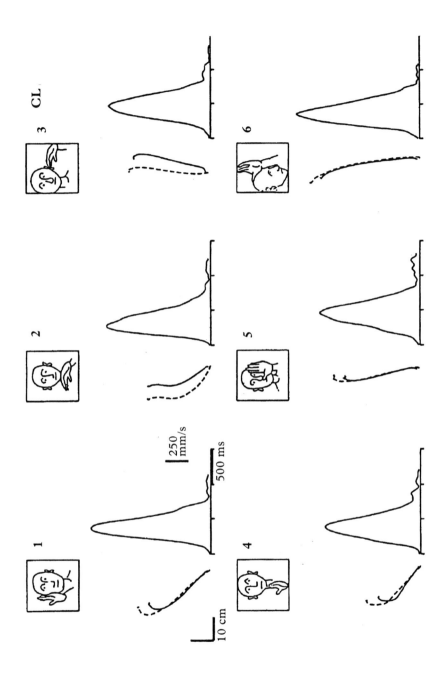

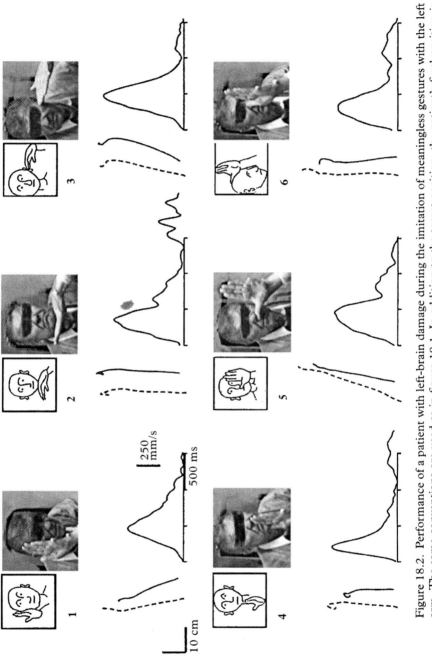

Figure 18.2. Performance of a patient with left-brain damage during the imitation of meaningless gestures with the left arm. The same conventions are used as in figure 18.1. In addition to the target position, the patient's final position is illustrated.

All subjects were asked to imitate six meaningless hand positions three times. Patients performed imitation with the hand ipsilateral to the lesion; half of the controls used their right hand and half the left. The movement kinematics were registered from ultrasonic markers attached to the hand. The spatial end-position of the hand was classified as being spatially correct or not, and incorrect end-positions were scored as apraxic errors. For statistical evaluation of kinematics, we distinguished two phases of the movement: an initial transport component, which brought the hand to the head, and an optional subsequent adjustment phase which led to the final position. For the transport phase, we evaluated whether it had a single peak or not. For the adjustment phase the length of the path traveled by the hand was determined.

Figure 18.1 shows performance of a healthy subject during the first run of imitating the six gestures. Although the gestures were unfamiliar to the subject, the final positions were always correct, and the movement kinematics exhibited the features of skilled goal-directed movements: the movement paths were smooth and approximately straight. The velocity profiles had a single peak, the magnitude of maximum velocity correlated positively with path length, and there were only minimal adjustment phases.

The ability of healthy subjects to implement routine kinematics in the imitation of novel and meaningless movements was confirmed by statistical analysis. Regardless of whether imitation was performed by the left or right hand, nearly all movements yielded a single-peaked transport component and negligible adjustment paths. Apraxic errors were virtually absent.

Patients with right-brain damage showed only a very mild augmentation of the frequencies of apraxic errors and kinematic abnormalities.

Figure 18.2 shows the kinematics of one LBD patient who committed many apraxic errors. Movement paths were frequently irregular, maximum velocity was reduced, the movement time was prolonged, and the velocity profiles were irregular. In one gesture (middle of upper row) a late corrective movement occurred.

LBD patients committed many apraxic errors and their movements showed many kinematic abnormalities. Thirteen out of twenty LBD patients committed more apraxic errors than any control or RBD patients. Kinematic abnormalities were registered in fourteen LBD patients.

There was virtually no correlation between end position and kinematic course of individual movements (r = 0.15). Movements leading to correct final positions were with abnormal kinematics as frequently as with normal kinematics (35.9 per cent abnormal, 32.2 per cent normal). In 9.8 per cent of all gestures apraxic errors were reached by kinematically perfect movements. Only in 22.0 per cent of gestures were apraxic errors associated with abnormal kinematics.

The lack of a correlation between apraxic errors and kinematic abnormalities and particularly the observation that apraxic errors can result from kinematically normal movements contradict the assumption that defective motor execution is the cause of apraxic errors. Nevertheless, both apraxic errors and kinematic abnormalities occurred nearly exclusively in patients with left-brain damage. There are two possible ways to explain this coincidence. One possibility is that spatial errors and kinematic abnormalities are independent sequels of left-hemisphere lesions which can occur in variable combinations in different patients. Alternatively, the coincidence may result from an interaction between one common basic deficit and strategies to cope with this deficit. The basic deficit may concern the mental representation of the target position. LBD patients may react to the lack of an appropriate representation of the target by switching to a strategy of slowed, online controlled movements followed by prolonged adjustments for finding the required final position. The combination of a correct final position with abnormal kinematics may indicate successful application of such a strategy. If patients do not recognize, or care about, defective representation of the target, they may move the hand smoothly and with normal speed to an insufficiently specified location, thus producing the combination of apraxic errors with normal kinematics.

Kinematics of prehension movements in LBD and RBD

If kinematic abnormalities are an independent sequel of LBD which bears no functional relationship to the imitation disorder, they should manifest themselves in motor tasks other than imitation. Indeed, several studies documented impaired performance of the ipsilesional hand of both LBD and RBD patients on tasks requiring fast, repetitive, skilled movement, like placing small pegs into holes or rapid tapping (Haaland & Delaney, 1981; Winstein & Pohl, 1995; Goodale, 1988). We (Hermsdörfer et al., 1999) found abnormal kinematics of prehension movements of the ipsilesional hand in patients with left- and with right-brain damage. The nature of kinematic abnormalities varied with the laterality of the lesion. In RBD patients the final phase of the movement was prolonged. In LBD patients the whole movement was slowed down. However, the velocity profiles of LBD patients' prehension movements were always single-peaked and their adjustment phases were of normal length. They thus differed from the kinematic abnormalities observed during the imitation of meaningless gestures. This discrepancy suggests a different origin of kinematic abnormalities of imitative movements and target oriented elementary motor activities. It supports the contention that the kinematic abnormalities of imitative movements are a reaction to insufficient mental representation of the target position.

Visuo-imitative apraxia

Further evidence against defective motor execution being the cause of defective imitation in LBD comes from dissociations between defective imitation of meaningless gestures and other manifestations of apraxia. Disturbed imitation of gestures in apraxia can affect meaningful and familiar gestures as well as meaningless and novel ones. Other manifestations of apraxia are disturbed performance of meaningful gestures retrieved from memory (e.g., pantomime of object use after verbal indication of the object) and disturbed use of actual tools and objects. There is ample evidence that the different aspects of apraxia may be present in different severity or even dissociate completely (for example Poeck, 1982; Barbieri & De Renzi, 1988; Goldenberg & Hagmann, 1997).

The hypothesis that defective imitation is indicative of a disturbance in motor execution of gestures makes testable predictions concerning associations and dissociations between different manifestations of apraxia (Roy, Square-Storer, Hogg, & Adams, 1991). First, patients who commit errors when imitating gestures should also commit errors when gestures are evoked from long-term memory. Secondly, defective imitation should affect meaningful and meaningless movements equally. Both of these predictions follow from the assumption that imitation tests the execution stage through which each gesture must pass on its way to motor commands.

Both predictions are contradicted by the observation of patients with visuo-imitative apraxia (Mehler, 1987; Goldenberg & Hagmann, 1997). These patients have left-parietal lesions. They commit errors when imitating meaningless gestures but not when imitating meaningful gestures or performing them on verbal command.

Figure 18.3 demonstrates errors on the imitation of hand postures by a patient with visuo-imitative apraxia (Goldenberg & Hagmann, 1997). The patient was able to carry out very similar gestures when they were presented to him by their meaning, as, for example, when he was verbally asked to demonstrate a military salute or how to brush his teeth with a toothbrush. When meaningful gestures were demonstrated without a verbal label and he was asked to imitate, he could do this too. However, it was clear from his comments that he recognized the symbolic significance of the gestures and hence reproduced them from their meaning rather than imitating their shape.

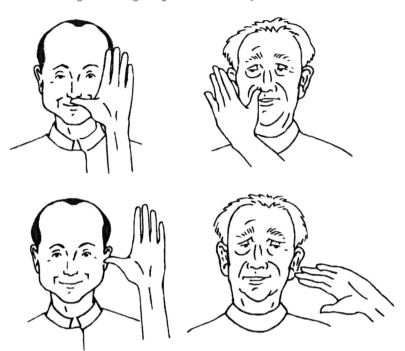

Figure 18.3. Errors on the imitation of hand postures by a patient with visuo-imitative apraxia (Goldenberg & Hagmann, 1997). The left column shows the demonstrated posture and the right column shows its imitation.

A direct route for imitation

Having collected evidence that defective imitation in LBD cannot be explained by an inability to convert mental representations of gestures into appropriate motor commands we have to look for alternative explanations. An attractive hypothesis is interruption of a direct route from visual perception to motor action.

Rothi, Ochipa, and Heilman (1991) postulate two routes mediating between perception and motor execution in imitation of gestures. One route passes via long-term memory representations of the shapes of familiar gestures. This route cannot be used for imitation of meaningless gestures as meaningless gestures are generally novel and do not have representations in long-term memory. The other route provides a direct link from perception to motor control. This route can be used for both meaningful and meaningless gestures. If there is interruption of only the second route, imitation of meaningful gestures could still be achieved by the first route. This would bring forward the dissociation between impaired imitation of meaningless gestures and preserved imitation of meaningful gestures in visuo-imitative apraxia. As interruption of the direct route from vision to motor control would not interfere with performance of gestures evoked from long-term memory, it would give rise to the additional dissociation between impaired imitation of meaningless gestures and preserved performance of meaningful gestures to verbal command.

The idea that perception of motor action can directly be linked to their imitation receives support from studies of imitation in primates and in normal human subjects. In the monkey, Rizzolatti and coworkers (Di Pellegrino *et al.*, 1992; Gallese, Fadiga, Fogassi, & Rizzolatti, 1996) demonstrated premotor neurons which are active when specific actions are performed by the monkey as well as when the monkey observes another monkey or a human perform the action. Activity in these "mirror neurons" thus indicates recognition of actions independently of who is performing them. The equivalence of actions across subjects holds for actions performed by oneself and by someone else. Recognition of equivalence of actions performed by oneself and other subjects seems to be an essential prerequisite for their imitation.

Meltzoff and Moore (1994) demonstrated that human neonates spontaneously imitate simple facial and manual gestures. Fadiga, Fogassi, Pavesi, and Rizzolatti (1995) applied transcranial magnetic stimulation to subjects who were watching movements without consciously intending to imitate them. Observation of the movements facilitated stimulation of the same muscles that would have been active if the subjects had actually performed the same movement. These findings demonstrated that imitation is deeply rooted in human biology. Although they do not directly speak to the mechanisms by which imitation is accomplished, they make it very plausible that the human brain provides a dedicated route for the imitation of gestures which links the perception of actions directly to their production.

Imitation and conceptual knowledge about the human body

The conclusion that the route for imitation bypasses knowledge about the meaning and conventional shape of gestures, leaves open the possibility that other kinds of cognitive mediation intervene between the perception and execution of gestures. The translation of the visually perceived shape of a gesture into appropriate motor commands is far from trivial (Prinz, 1987; Meltzoff & Moore, 1997). It becomes particularly tricky for gestures performed without an external object. Such gestures have no external reference or anchor point. They are defined as a particular configuration of the body itself. The target of the motor action is a configuration of one's own body, but the model is provided by the configuration of another person's body. Imitation affords not only a mapping from visual to motor modality, but also a mapping from another person's body to one's own body. This mapping has to abstract from the different spatial position of one's own and another's body as well as from differences in the size and shape of the bodies.

A feasible way to achieve these translations would be to code the features of the gesture with reference to a general concept of the human body which provides a classification of significant body parts and specifies the boundaries that define them (Sirigu, Grafman, Bressler, & Sunderland, 1991). Its application reduces the multiple visual features of the demonstrated gesture to simple relationships between a limited number of significant body parts. Presumably these relationships can easily be mapped onto motor programs. Furthermore, translating the gesture's visual appearance into the categories of a generally valid body schema produces an equivalence between demonstration and imitation which is independent of the particular angle of view under which the demonstration is perceived and of accidental minor differences in the exact shapes of demonstrated and imitated gestures.

According to this interpretation, the route for imitation includes three stages: at the perceptual stage the visuo-spatial features of the gesture are analyzed. At the conceptual stage, they are coded in terms of conceptual knowledge about the structure of the human body. At the motor stage, this code is implemented in motor actions.

Imitation of hand and finger postures

The requirements for conceptual mediation of the demonstrated gesture may be different for hand and finger postures as shown in Figure 18.4. Hand postures are determined by relationships between a considerable number of different body parts, like lips, nose, ear, chin, cheek, back of hand, or palm of hand. Knowledge about the classification and boundaries of all of these parts is needed for conceptual mediation of hand postures. By contrast, finger postures concern only a uniform set of five body parts, and the conceptual distinction between them is largely exhausted by an appreciation of their serial position. Conceptual mediation of hand postures may therefore be more difficult and demand more knowledge about the structure of the human body than conceptual mediation of finger postures.

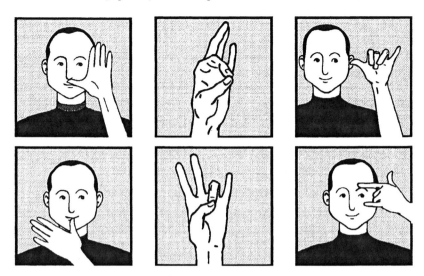

Figure 18.4. Examples of hand postures (left column), finger configurations (middle column) and combined gestures (right column) (Goldenberg, 1996).

The reverse order of difficulties may apply to the perceptual analysis of the demonstrated gesture. Hand positions are determined by relationships between perceptually salient and body parts with very different shapes. Fingers are perceptually similar, and their identity is mainly determined by their spatial position with respect to other fingers. A distinction between, for example, the index and the middle finger is likely to put higher demands on visuo-spatial exploration than a distinction between the mouth and the chin. Thus, perceptual analysis is probably more difficult for finger than for hand postures.

Goldenberg (1996) examined patients with LBD and aphasia, patients with RBD, and controls for imitation of three types of meaningless gestures: hand positions, finger configurations and combined gestures which required a defined hand position as well as a defined configuration of the fingers (see Fig. 18.4). Regardless of whether imitation of hand positions and finger configurations were tested each on their own or together, they proved to show differential susceptibility to right- and left-brain damage. Whereas imitation of finger configurations was about equally impaired in right- and left-brain damage, defective imitation of hand positions occurred almost exclusively in LBD patients, and whereas controls as well as RBD patients committed fewer errors with hand positions than with finger configurations, the reverse was the case in LBD patients.

This result confirms previous studies that have demonstrated that some impairment of imitation can be found not only in left- but also in right-brain-damaged patients (e.g., De Renzi, Motti, & Nichelli, 1980; Roy, Square-Storer, Hogg, & Adams, 1991). It would be compatible with the hypothesis that patients with right-brain damage have problems with the visuo-spatial analysis of the perceived gestures, whereas left-brain damage affects conceptual mediation based on general knowledge about the human body. There is no need to assume additional damage to motor execution in any of the brain-damaged patients.

Matching and imitation of hand and finger postures

In a further study Goldenberg (1999) tested more directly the contributions of perceptual and conceptual disturbances to defective imitation of meaningless hand and finger postures. Reproduction of meaningless postures of either the hand or the fingers was examined in two conditions. First, a match to a photograph of the target gesture had to be selected from an array of four photographs showing gestures performed by different persons and seen under different angles of view. Second, the examiner demonstrated the gestures and the patient imitated them. LBD patients had more difficulties with imitation than with matching, while RBD patients had more difficulties with matching than with imitation. Regardless of whether imitation or matching was tested, LBD patients made more errors with hand than with finger postures whereas RBD patients made more errors with finger than with hand postures. This constellation of results is compatible with the assumption that imitation errors are caused by faulty visuo-perceptual processing in RBD, and by defective conceptual mediation in LBD. Again, there is no need to assume additional damage to motor execution in any of the groups. The observation that LBD patients have generally more difficulties with imitation than with matching can be accounted for by a greater importance of conceptual mediation for motor imitation than for perceptual matching. For imitating, the shape of the gesture must be translated from an externally observed body to one's own body. The perceptual difference between another person's and one's own body is greater than that between different views of other persons. Presumably, the need for conceptual mediation by a generally valid classification of body parts increases with decreasing perceptual similarity. Moreover, conceptual classification of gestures provides a common code for visual perception and motor execution of gestures that is needed for imitation but not for matching of gestures. For both of these reasons demands on conceptual mediation will be higher for imitation than for matching of gestures.

The human body as a mechanical device

In the final part of this chapter we want to dare some speculation as to the nature of knowledge about the structure of the human body. The evidence reviewed so far strongly suggests that access to this knowledge depends on integrity of the left hemisphere. It does not tell, however, whether we have to conceive of it as a distinct category of knowledge or as one instance of a wider class of knowledge. Certainly, the human body is special, because it houses the human mind. The mind experiences its body from "within" and employs it for acting upon the external world. There is, however, another peculiarity: the human body is a very complicated, multipart mechanical device, and for most persons it is the most complex mechanical device they use in daily life. This raises the possibility that the inability to exploit general knowledge about the structure of the human body for imitating gestures is only a special case of an inability to analyze the functionally significant details of multipart devices and to comprehend mechanical relationships.

We have argued that imitation of gestures may differ from, and be more difficult than, imitation of actions on external objects, because the target of the action is constituted by a particular configuration of one's own body, and because one's own body is experienced in a fundamentally different way than another person's body. We now suggest that the distinction between actions on external objects and gestures without object may be only apparent. The object of body-related gestures is that complex mechanical object which every human being has at their disposal, the human body.

The fragility of the distinction between the human body and mechanical objects is illustrated by a study which assessed imitation of hand postures on a manikin rather than on the patients' own bodies (Goldenberg, 1995). Patients with left-brain damage who had difficulties with the imitation of hand postures committed errors also when asked to replicate these same postures on a manikin. This is, of course, further evidence that their difficulties reside at the level of conceptual mediation rather than at the level of motor execution, because the demands on motor execution are fundamentally different between imitation of gestures and manipulating a manikin. Beyond this confirmation the study illustrates the similarity between man and manikin, or, respectively, between the human body and mechanical devices. One might wonder whether these patients would not encounter very similar difficulties when trying to replicate configurations of multipart objects that do not resemble a human body. Conversely, one may ask whether their difficulties with imitation of gestures are just one manifestation of a general inability to comprehend and manipulate mechanical multipart objects that is tested by asking them to manipulate the multipart objects which are their own bodies.

One cannot, however, reduce the apraxic patients' difficulties with the comprehension of mechanical multipart objects to being part of a general visuo-constructional disorder. Patients with RBD mastered the imitation of hand postures on their own body and on the manikin as well as controls and hence much better than apraxic patients, but they were significantly worse than apraxic patients on a visuo-constructional test, the WAIS block design (Goldenberg, 1995).

Conclusion

Theories of apraxia have considered disorders of imitation as being a manifestation of defective motor execution. We have provided evidence that this account is insufficient. Rather than being a convenient way of testing the integrity of motor execution, imitation of gestures is a task which poses difficulties at the perceptual and conceptual level. If apraxic disturbances of imitation are analyzed from this angle of view, they disclose a prominent role of conceptual knowledge about the human body for imitation. They leave open the possibility that this knowledge is just one instance of the ability to appreciate functionally significant parts of multipart objects, and that imitation of meaningless gestures is difficult because it requires comprehension of changing relationships between multiple parts of the complex mechanical device which is the human body.

References

Barbieri, C., & De Renzi, E. (1988). The executive and ideational components of apraxia. *Cortex, 24*, 535–544.

Clark, M., Merians, A. S., Kothari, A., Poizner, H., Macauley, B., Rothi, L. J. G., & Heilman, K. M. (1994). Spatial planning deficits in limb apraxia. *Brain, 117*, 1093–1106.

De Renzi, E., Motti, F., & Nichelli, P. (1980). Imitating gestures – A quantitative approach to ideomotor apraxia. *Archives of Neurology, 37*, 6–10.

Di Pellegrino, G., Fadiga, L., Fogassi, L., Gallese, V., & Rizzolatti, G. (1992). Understanding motor events: A neurophysiological study. *Exp. Brain, Res., 91*, 176–180.

Fadiga, L., Fogassi, L., Pavesi, G., & Rizzolatti, G. (1995). Motor facilitation during action observation: A magnetic stimulation study. *Journal of Neurophysiology, 73*, 2608–2611.

Gallese, V., Fadiga, L., Fogassi, L., & Rizzolatti, G. (1996). Action recognition in the premotor cortex. *Brain, 119*, 593–609.

Goldenberg, G. (1995). Imitating gestures and manipulating a manikin – The representation of the human body in ideomotor apraxia. *Neuropsychologia, 33*, 63–72.

(1996). Defective imitation of gestures in patients with damage in the left or right hemisphere. *Journal of Neurology, Neurosurgery, and Psychiatry, 61,* 176–180.

(1999). Matching and imitation of hand and finger postures in patients with damage in the left or right hemisphere. *Neuropsychologia, 37,* 559–566.

Goldenberg, G., & Hagmann, S. (1997). The meaning of meaningless gestures: A study of visuo-imitative apraxia. *Neuropsychologia, 35,* 333–341.

Goodale, M. A. (1988). Hemispheric differences in motor control. *Behavioural Brain Research, 30,* 202–214.

Haaland, K. Y., & Delaney, H. D. (1981). Motor deficits after left or right hemisphere damage due to stroke or tumor. *Neuropsychologia, 19,* 17–27.

Heilman, K. M. (1979). Apraxia. In K. M. Heilman & E. Valenstein (Eds.), *Clinical neuropsychology* (pp. 159–185). New York, Oxford: Oxford University Press.

Hermsdörfer, J., Mai, N., Spatt, J., Marquardt, C., Veltkamp, R., & Goldenberg, G. (1996). Kinematic analysis of movement imitation in apraxia. *Brain, 119,* 1575–1586.

Hermsdörfer, J., Ulrich, S., Marquardt, C., Goldenberg, G., & Mai, N. (1999). Prehension with the ipsilesional hand after unilateral brain damage. *Cortex, 35,* 139–162.

Hogan, N. (1984). An organizing principle for a class of voluntary movements. *Journal of Neuroscience, 4,* 2745–2754.

Jeannerod, M. (1986). The formation of finger grip during prehension. A cortically mediated visuomotor pattern. *Beh. Brain Res., 19,* 99–116.

Lehmkuhl, G., Poeck, K., & Willmes, K. (1983). Ideomotor apraxia and aphasia: An examination of types and manifestations of apraxic symptoms. *Neuropsychologia, 21,* 199–212.

Liepmann, H. (1908). *Drei Aufsätze aus dem Apraxiegebiet.* Berlin: Karger.

Mehler, M. F. (1987). Visuo-imitative apraxia. *Neurology, 37, Suppl. 1.*

Meltzoff, A. N., & Moore, M. K. (1994). Imitation, memory, and the representation of persons. *Infant Behavior and Development, 17,* 83–99.

(1997). Explaining facial imitation: A theoretical model. *Early Development and Parenting, 6,* 179–192.

Morasso, P. (1999). Spatial control of arm movements. *Exp. Brain Res., 42,* 223–227.

Platz, T., & Mauritz, K. H. (1995). Human motor planning, motor programming, and use of new task – Relevant information with different apraxic syndromes. *European Journal of Neuroscience, 7,* 1536–1547.

Poeck, K. (1982). The two types of motor apraxia. *Archives Italiennes de Biologie, 120,* 361–369.

Poizner, H., Clark, M., Merians, A. S., Macauley, B., Rothi, L. J. G., & Heilman, K. M. (1995). Joint coordination deficits in limb apraxia. *Brain, 118,* 227–242.

Poizner, H., Mack, L., Verfaellie, M., Rothi, L. J. G., & Heilman, K. M. (1990). Three-dimensional computergraphic analysis of apraxia. *Brain, 113,* 85–101.

Prinz, W. (1987). Ideo-motor action. In H. Heuer & A. F. Sanders (Eds.), *Perspectives on perception and action* (pp. 47–76). Hillsdale NJ: Lawrence Erlbaum Associates.

Rothi, L. J. G., Ochipa, C., & Heilman, K. M. (1991). A cognitive neuropsycho-logical model of limb praxis. *Cognitive Neuropsychology, 8,* 443–458.

Roy, E. A., & Hall, C. (1992). Limb apraxia: A process approach. In L. Proteau & D. Elliott (Eds.), *Vision and motor control* (pp. 261–282). Amsterdam: Elsevier.

Roy, E. A., Square-Storer, P., Hogg, S., & Adams, S. (1991). Analysis of task demands in apraxia. *International Journal of Neuroscience, 56,* 177–186.

Sirigu, A., Grafman, J., Bressler, K., & Sunderland, T. (1991). Multiple repre-sentations contribute to body knowledge processing. *Brain, 114,* 629–642.

Trombly, C. A. (1993). Observations of improvement of reaching in five subjects with left hemiparesis. *Journal of Neurology, Neurosurgery, and Psychiatry, 56,* 40–45.

Winstein, C. J., & Pohl, P. S. (1995). Effects of unilateral brain damage on the control of goal-directed hand movements. *Exp. Brain Res., 105,* 163–174.

Index

Printed in the United Kingdom
by Lightning Source UK Ltd.
133359UK00001B/145-147/A